Microsoft Visual C++ Windows Applications by Example

Code and Explanation for Real-World MFC
C++ Applications

Stefan Björnander

PUBLISHING

BIRMINGHAM - MUMBAI

Microsoft Visual C++ Windows Applications by Example

First published: June 2008

Production Reference: 1170608

Published by Packt Publishing Ltd.
32 Lincoln Road
Olton
Birmingham, B27 6PA, UK.

ISBN 978-1-847195-56-2

www.packtpub.com

Cover Image by karl.moore (karl.moore@ukonline.co.uk)

Credits

Author

Stefan Björnander

Reviewer

S. G. Ganesh

Senior Acquisition Editor

David Barnes

Development Editor

Swapna V. Verlekar

Technical Editor

Bhupali Khule

Editorial Team Leader

Akshara Aware

Project Manager

Abhijeet Deobhakta

Project Coordinator

Brinell Catherine Lewis

Indexer

Monica Ajmera

Proofreader

Angie Butcher

Production Coordinator

Shantanu Zagade

Cover Work

Shantanu Zagade

About the Author

Stefan Björnander is a Ph.D. candidate at Mälardalen University, Sweden. He has worked as a software developer and has taught as a senior lecturer at Umeå University, Sweden. He holds a master's degree in computer science and his research interests include compiler construction, mission-critical systems, and model-driven engineering. You can reach him at `stefan.bjornander@mdh.se`.

I dedicate this book to my parents
Ralf and Gunilla, my sister Catharina, her husband Magnus,
and their son Emil

About the Reviewer

S. G. Ganesh is currently working as a research engineer in Siemens Corporate Technology, Bangalore. He works in the area of Code Quality Management (CQM). He has good experience in system software development having worked for around five years in Hewlett-Packard's C++ compiler team in Bangalore. He also represented the ANSI/ISO C++ standardization committee (JTC1/SC22/WG21) from 2005 to 2007. He has authored several books. The latest one is *60 Tips for Object Oriented Programming* (Tata-McGraw Hill/ISBN-13 978-0-07-065670-3). He has a master's degree in computer science. His research interests include programming languages, compiler design and design patterns. If you're a student or a novice developer, you might find his website www.joyofprogramming.com to be interesting. You can reach him at sgganesh@gmail.com.

Table of Contents

Preface

This is a book about Windows application development in C++. It addresses some rather difficult problems that occur during the development of advanced applications. Most books in this genre have many short code examples. This one has only four main code examples, but rather extensive ones. They are presented in increasing complexity order. The simplest one is the *Tetris* application, which deals with graphics, timing, and message handling. The *Draw* application adds a generic coordinate system and introduces more complex applications states. The *Calc* application deals with formula interpretation and graph searching. Finally, in the *Word* application every character is allowed to hold its own font and size, resulting in a rather complex size and position calculation.

The book starts with an introduction to object-oriented programming in C++, followed by an overview of the Visual Studio environment with the *Ring* demonstration application as well as a presentation of some basic generic classes. Then the main applications are presented in one chapter each.

What This Book Covers

Chapter1. Introduction to C++ – C++ is a language built on C. It is strongly typed; it has types for storing single as well as compound values. It supports dynamic memory management with pointers. It has a large set of operators to perform arithmetic, logical, and bitwise operations. The code can be organized into functions, and there is a pre-processor available, which can be used to define macros.

Chapter 2. Object-oriented Programming in C++ – C++ is an object-oriented language that fully supports the object-oriented model. The main feature of the language is the *class*, which can be instantiated into *objects*. A class can *inherit* another class. The inheritance can be *virtual*, which provides *dynamic binding*. A class can contain an object or have a *pointer* to another object. We can *overload operators* and we can throw *exceptions*. We can create generic classes by using *templates* and we can organize our classes into *namespaces*.

Chapter 3. Windows Development—The development environment of this book is Microsoft Visual Studio, which holds several *Wizards* that generate skeleton code. With their help, we create a framework which we can add our own application specific code to. Microsoft Foundation Classes (MFC) is a powerful C++ class library built upon the Windows 32 bits Application Interface (Win32 API). It holds many classes to build and modify graphical Windows applications.

When an event occurs in Windows, a *message* is sent to the application in focus. When we want to paint or write in a window, we need a *device context*, which can be thought of both as painting toolbox and a connection to the painting canvas. When we develop an application such as a spreadsheet program, we want the users to be able to save their work. It can easily be obtained by *serialization*.

Chapter 4. Ring: A Demonstration Example—As an introduction to the main applications of this book, we go through the step-by-step development process of a simple application that draws rings on the painting area of a window. The rings can be painted in different colors. We increase the painting area by using *scroll bars*. We increase the user-friendliness by introducing *menus*, *toolbars*, and *accelerators*. The RGB (Red, Green, Blue) standard can theoretically handle more than sixteen million colors. We use the *Color Dialog* to allow the user to handle them. Finally, we add serialization to our application.

Chapter 5. Utility Classes—There are several generic classes available in MFC, we look into classes for handling points, sizes, and rectangles. However, some generic classes we have to write ourselves. We create classes to handle fonts, colors, and the caret. We also inherit MFC classes to handle lists and sets. Finally, we look into some appropriate error handling.

Chapter 6. The Tetris Application—Tetris is a classic game. We have seven figures of different shapes and colors falling down. The player's task is to move and rotate them into appropriate positions in order to fill as many rows as possible. When a row is filled it disappears and the player gets credit. The game is over when it is not possible to add any more figures.

Chapter 7. The Draw Application—In the Draw application, the users can draw lines, arrows, rectangles, and ellipses. They can move, resize, and change the color of the figures. They can cut and paste one or more figures, can fill the rectangles and ellipses, and can load and save a drawing. They can also write and modify text in different fonts.

Chapter 8. The Calc Application – The Calc application is a spreadsheet program. The users can input text to the cells and they can change the text's font as well as its horizontal and vertical alignment. They can also load and save a spreadsheet and can cut and paste a block of cells. Furthermore, the user can input a formula into a cell. They can build expressions with the four arithmetic operators as well as parentheses.

Chapter 9. The Word Application – The Word application is a word processor program. The users can write and modify text in different fonts and with different horizontal alignment. The program has paragraph handling and a print preview function. The users can cut and paste blocks of text, they can also load and save a document.

What You Need for This Book

In order to execute the code you need Visual C++ 2008, which is included in Visual Studio 2008.

Who is This Book for

The book is ideal for programmers who have worked with C++ or other Windows-based programming languages. It provides developers with everything they need to build complex desktop applications using C++.

If you have already learned the C++ language, and want to take your programming to the next level, then this book is ideal for you.

Conventions

In this book, you will find a number of styles of text that distinguish between different kinds of information. Here are some examples of these styles, and an explanation of their meaning.

There are three styles for code. Code words in text are shown as follows: "The predefined constant NULL (defined in the header file cstdlib) holds the pointer equivalence of the zero value"

A block of code will be set as follows:

```
int i = 123;
double x = 1.23;
int j = (int) x;
double y = (double) i;
```

When we wish to draw your attention to a particular part of a code block, the relevant lines or items will be made bold:

```
// Standard print setup command
  ON_COMMAND(ID_FILE_PRINT_SETUP, CWinApp::OnFilePrintSetup)
  ON_COMMAND(ID_APP_EXIT, OnAppExit)
END_MESSAGE_MAP()
```

New terms and **important words** are introduced in a bold-type font. Words that you see on the screen, in menus or dialog boxes for example, appear in our text like this: "Let us start by selecting **New Project** in the **File** menu and choosing **Visual C++ Projects** and **MFC Application** with the name **Ring** and a suitable place on the hard drive".

Reader Feedback

Feedback from our readers is always welcome. Let us know what you think about this book, what you liked or may have disliked. Reader feedback is important for us to develop titles that you really get the most out of.

To send us general feedback, simply drop an email to `feedback@packtpub.com`, making sure to mention the book title in the subject of your message.

If there is a book that you need and would like to see us publish, please send us a note in the **SUGGEST A TITLE** form on `www.packtpub.com` or email `suggest@packtpub.com`.

If there is a topic that you have expertise in and you are interested in either writing or contributing to a book, see our author guide on `www.packtpub.com/authors`.

Customer Support

Now that you are the proud owner of a Packt book, we have a number of things to help you to get the most from your purchase.

Downloading the Example Code for the Book

Visit `http://www.packtpub.com/files/code/5562_Code.zip` to directly download the example code.

The downloadable files contain instructions on how to use them.

Errata

Although we have taken every care to ensure the accuracy of our contents, mistakes do happen. If you find a mistake in one of our books—maybe a mistake in text or code—we would be grateful if you would report this to us. By doing this you can save other readers from frustration, and help to improve subsequent versions of this book. If you find any errata, report them by visiting http://www.packtpub.com/support, selecting your book, clicking on the **Submit Errata** link, and entering the details of your errata. Once your errata are verified, your submission will be accepted and the errata are added to the list of existing errata. The existing errata can be viewed by selecting your title from http://www.packtpub.com/support.

Questions

You can contact us at questions@packtpub.com if you are having a problem with some aspect of the book, and we will do our best to address it.

1

Introduction to C++

C++ is a large object-oriented language that supports many modern features. As the name implies, it is a further development of the language C. In this chapter, you will learn the basics of the language. The next chapter deals with the object-oriented parts of C++. This chapter covers:

- An introduction to the langue, how the compiler and linker works, the overal structure of a program, and comments.

- C++ is a **typed** language, which means that every value stored in the computer memory is well defined. The type can be an integer, a real value, a logical value, or a character.

- An array is a sequence of values of the same type. Pointers and references hold the address of a value.

- In C++ there are possibilities to calculate values by using the four fundamental rules of arithmetic. We can also compare values as well as perform logical and bitwise operations.

- The flow of a program can be directed with **statements**. We can choose between two or more choices, repeat until a certain condition is fulfilled, and we can also jump to another location in the code.

- A **function** is a part of the code designed to perform a specific task. It is called by the main program or by another function. It may take input, which is called **parameters**, and may also return a value.

- The preprocessor is a tool that performs textual substitution by the means with **macros**. It is also possible to include text from other files and to include or exclude code.

The Compiler and the Linker

The text of a program is called its **source code**. The compiler is the program that translates the source code into **target** code, and the linker puts several compiled files into an **executable** file.

Let us say we have a C++ program in the source code file Prog.cpp and a routine used by the program in Routine.cpp. Furthermore, the program calls a function in the standard library. In this case, the compiler translates the source code into object code and the linker joins the code into the executable file Prog.exe.

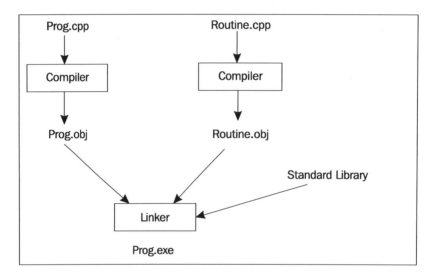

If the compiler reports an error, we refer to it as compile-time error. In the same way, if an error occurs during the execution of the program, we call it a run-time error.

The First Program

The execution of a program always starts with the function main. Below is a program that prints the text Hello, World! on the screen.

```cpp
#include <iostream>
using namespace std;

void main()
{
   cout << "Hello, World!" << endl;
}
```

Comments

In C++, it is possible to insert comments to describe and clarify the meaning of the program. The comments are ignored by the compiler (every comment is replaced by a single space character). There are two types of comments: line comments and block comments. Line comments start with two slashes and end at the end of the line.

```cpp
cout << "Hello, World!" << endl; // Prints "Hello, World!".
```

Block comments begin with a slash and an asterisk and end with an asterisk and a slash. A block comment may range over several lines.

```cpp
/* This is an example of a C++ program.
   It prints the text "Hello, World!"
   on the screen. */
#include <iostream>
using namespace std;
void main()
{
  cout << "Hello, World!" << endl; // Prints "Hello, World!".
}
```

Block comments cannot be nested. The following example will result in a compile-time error.

```cpp
/* A block comment cannot be /* nested */ inside another
   one. */
```

A piece of advice is that you use the line comments for regular comments, and save the block comments for situations when you need to comment a whole block of code for debugging purposes.

Types and Variables

There are several types in C++. They can be divided into two groups: simple and compounded. The simple types can be further classified into *integral*, *floating*, and *logical* types. The compounded types are *arrays*, *pointers*, and *references*. They are all (directly or indirectly) constituted by simple types. We can also define a type with our own values, called the *enumeration* type.

Simple Types

There are five simple types intended for storing integers: *char*, *wchar_t*, *short int*, *int*, and *long int*. They are called the *integral types*. The types *short int* and *long int* may be abbreviated to *short* and *long*, respectively. As the names imply, they are designed for storing characters, small integers, normal integers, and large integers, respectively. The exact limits of the values possible to store varies between different compilers.

Furthermore, the integral types may be *signed* or *unsigned*. An unsigned type must not have negative values. If the word signed or unsigned is left out, a *short int*, *int*, and *long int* will be signed. Whether a *char* will be signed or unsigned is not defined in the standard, but rather depends on the compiler and the underlying operational systems. We say that it is **implementation-dependent**.

However, a character of the type *char* is always one byte long, which means that it always holds a single character, regardless of whether it is unsigned or not. The type *wchar_t* is designed to hold a character of a more complex sort; therefore, it usually has a length of at least two bytes.

The *char* type is often based on the **American Standard Code for Information Exchange (ASCII)** table. Each character has a specific number ranging from 0 to 127 in the table. For instance, 'a' has the number 97. With the help of the ASCII table, we can convert between integers and characters. See the last section of this chapter for the complete ASCII table.

```
int i = (int) 'a'; // 97
char c = (char) 97; // 'a'
```

The next category of simple types is the *floating types*. They are used to store real values; that is, numbers with decimal fractions. The types are *float*, *double*, and *long double*, where *float* stores the smallest value and *long double* the largest one. The value size that each type can store depends on the compiler. A floating type cannot be unsigned.

The final simple type is *bool*. It is used to store logical values: *true* or *false*.

Variables

A variable can be viewed as a box in memory. In almost every case, we do not need to know the exact memory address the variable is stored on. A variable always has a name, a type, and a value. We define a variable by simply writing its type and name. If we want to, we can initialize the variable; that is, assign it a value. If we do not, the variable's value will be undefined (it is given the value that happens to be on its memory location).

```
int i = 123, j;
double d = 3.14;
char c = 'a';
bool b = true;
```

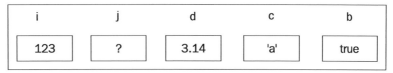

As a *char* is a small integer type, it is intended to store exactly one character. A *string* stores a (possibly empty) sequence of characters. There is no built-in type for describing a string; however, there is a library class *string* with some basic operations. Note that characters are enclosed by single quotations while strings are enclosed by double quotations. In order to use strings, we have to include the header file *string* and use the namespace std. Header files, classes, and namespaces are described in the next chapter.

```
#include <string>
using namespace std;
char c = 'a';
string s = "Hello, World!";
```

We can transform values between the types by stating the new type within parentheses. The process of transforming a value from one type to another is called **casting** or **type conversions**.

```
int i = 123;
double x = 1.23;
int j = (int) x;
double y = (double) i;
```

Constants

As the name implies, a constant is a variable whose value cannot be altered once it has been initialized. Unlike variables, constants must always be initialized. Constants are often written in capital letters.

```
const double PI = 3.14;
```

Input and Output

In order to write to the standard output (normally a text window) and read from standard input (normally the keyboard), we use **streams**. A stream can be thought of as a connection between our program and a device such as the screen or keyboard. There are predefined objects `cin` and `cout` that are used for input and output. We use the stream operators `>>` and `<<` to write to and read from a device. Similarily to the strings above, we have to include the header file `iostream` and use the namespace `std`.

We can write and read values of all the types we have gone through so far, even though the logical values true and false are read and written as one and zero. The predefined object `endl` represents a new line.

```cpp
#include <iostream>
#include <string>
using namespace std;
void main()
{
  int i;
  double x;
  bool b;
  string s;
  cin >> i >> x >> b >> s;
  cout << "You wrote i: " << i << ", x: " << x << ", b: " << b
       << ", s: " << s << endl;
}
```

Enumerations

An enumeration is a way to create our own integral type. We can define which values a variable of the type can store. In practice, however, enumerations are essentially an easy way to define constants.

```cpp
enum Cars {FORD, VOLVO, TOYOTA, VOLKSWAGEN};
```

Unless we state otherwise, the constants are assigned to zero, one, two, and so on. In the example above, FORD is an integer constant with the value zero, VOLVO has the value one, TOYOTA three, and VOLKSWAGEN four.

We do not have to name the enumeration type. In the example above, `Cars` can be omitted. We can also assign an integer value to some (or all) of the constants. In the example below, TOYOTA is assigned the value 10. The constants without assigned values will be given the value of the preceding constant before, plus one. This implies that VOLKSWAGEN will be assigned the value 11.

```cpp
enum {FORD, VOLVO, TOYOTA = 10, VOLKSWAGEN};
```

Arrays

An array is a variable compiled by several values of the same type. The values are stored on consecutive locations in memory. An array may be initialized or uninitiated. An uninitiated array must always be given a size. In the following example, *b* is given the size 2 and *c* is given the size 4, even though only its first two values are defined, which may cause the compiler to emit a warning.

```
int a[3] = {11, 12, 13};
double b[2] = {1.2, 3.4};
char c[4] = {'a', 'b'}, d[3];
```

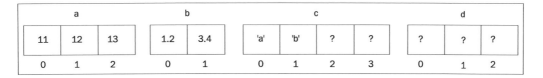

A value of an array can be accessed by index notation.

```
int i = a[2];
double x = b[0];
char t = c[1];
```

Pointers and References

A pointer is a variable containing the address of value. Let us say that the integer *i* has the value 999 which is stored at the memory address 10,000. If *p* is a pointer to *i*, it holds the value 10,000.

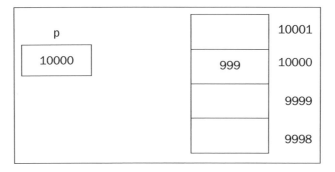

A clearer way to illustrate the same thing is to draw an arrow from the pointer to the value.

In almost all cases, we do not really need to know the address of the value. The following code gives rise to the diagram above, where the ampersand (&) denotes the address of the variable.

```
int i = 999;
int *p = &i;
```

If we want to access the value pointed at, we use the asterisk (*), which derefers the pointer, "following the arrow". The address (&) and the dereferring (*) operator can be regarded as each others reverses. Note that the asterisk is used on two occasions, when we define a pointer variable and when we derefer a pointer. The asterisk is in fact used on a third occasion, when multiplying two values.

```
int i = 999;
int *p = &i;
int j = *p; // 999
```

A reference is a simplified version of a pointer; it can be regarded as a constant form of a pointer. A reference variable must be initialized to refer to a value and cannot be changed later on. A reference is also automatically dereferred when we access its value. Neither do we need to state the address of the value the reference variable is initialized to refer to. The address-of (&) and dereferring (*) operators are only applicable to pointers, not to references. Note that the ampersand has two different meanings. It used as a reference marker as well as to find the address of an expression. In fact, it is also used as the bitwise *and* operator. A reference is usually drawn with a dashed line in order to distinguish it from a pointer.

```
int i = 999;
int &r = i;
int j = r; // 999
```

Pointers and Dynamic Memory

Pointers (but not references) can also be used to allocate **dynamic** memory. There is a section of the memory called the **heap** that is used for dynamically allocated memory blocks. The operators `new` and `delete` are used to allocate and deallocate the memory. Memory not dynamically allocated is referred to as **static** memory.

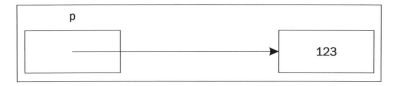

```
int *p = new int;
*p = 123;
delete p;
```

We can also allocate memory for a whole array. Even though *p* is a pointer in the example below, we can use the array index notation to access a value of the array in the allocated memory block. When we deallocate the array, we have to add a pair of brackets for the whole memory block of the array to be deallocated. Otherwise, only the memory of the first value of the array would be deallocated.

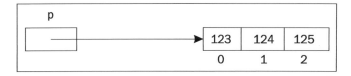

```
int *p = new int[3];
p[0] = 123;
p[1] = 124;
p[2] = 125;
delete [] p;
```

The predefined constant NULL (defined in the header file `cstdlib`) holds the pointer equivalence of the zero value. We say that the pointer is set to null. In the diagram, we simply write NULL.

```
#include <cstdlib>
// ...
int *p = NULL;
```

Sometimes, the electric ground symbol is used to symbolize a null pointer. For this reason, a null pointer is said to be a *grounded* pointer.

There is a special type `void`. It is not really a type, it is rather used to indicate the absence of a type. We can define a pointer to `void`. We can, however, not derefer the pointer. It is only useful in low-level applications where we want to examine a specific location in memory.

```
void* pVoid = (void*) 10000;
```

The void type is also useful to mark that a function does not return a value, see the function section later in this chapter.

In the example below, the memory block has been deallocated, but *p* has not been set to null. It has become a *dangling pointer*; it is not null and does not really point at anything. In spite of that, we try to access the value *p* points at. That is a dangerous operation and would most likely result in a run-time error.

```
int *p = new int;
*p = 1;
delete p;
*p = 2
```

In the example below, we allocate memory for two pointers, *p* and *q*. Then we assign *p* to *q*, by doing so we have created a *memory leak*. There is no way we can access or deallocate the memory block that was pointed at by *p*. In fact, we deallocate the same memory block twice as both pointers by then point at the same memory block. This dangerous operation will most likely also result in a run-time error.

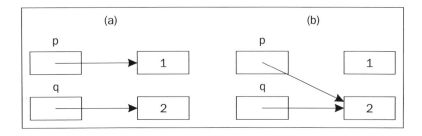

```
int *p = new int; // (a)
int *q = new int;
*p = 1;
*q = 2;
p = q; // (b)
delete p; // Deallocates the same memory block twice, as p
delete q; // and q point at the same memory block.
```

As a reference variable must be initialized to refer to a value and it cannot be changed, it is not possible to handle dynamic memory with references. Nor can a reference take the value null.

If we continue to allocate dynamic memory from the heap, it will eventually run out of memory. There are two ways to handle that problem. The simplest one is to mark the new call with nothrow (defined in namespace std). In that case, new will simply return a null pointer when it is out of memory.

```
const int BLOCK_SIZE = 0x7FFFFFFF;
void* pBlock = new (nothrow) char[BLOCK_SIZE];

if (pBlock != NULL)
{
  cout << "Ok.";
  // ...
  delete [] pBlock;
}
else
{
  cout << "Out of memory.";
}
```

The other way is to omit the `nothrow` marker. In that case, the `new` call will throw the exception `bad_alloc` in case of memory shortage. We can catch it with a *try-catch* block.

```cpp
using namespace std;
const int BLOCK_SIZE = 0x7FFFFFFF;
try
{
  void* pBlock = new char[BLOCK_SIZE];
  cout << "Ok.";
  // ...
  delete [] pBlock;
}
catch (bad_alloc)
{
  cout << "Out of memory.";
}
```

See the next chapter for more information on exceptions and namespaces.

Defining Our Own Types

It is possible to define our own type with `typedef`, which is a great tool for increasing the readability of the code. However, too many defined types tend to make the code less readable. Therefore, I advise you to use `typedef` with care.

```cpp
int i = 1;
typedef unsigned int unsigned_int;
unsigned_int u = 2;
typedef int* int_ptr;
int_ptr ip = &i;
typedef unsigned_int* uint_ptr;
uint_ptr up = &u;
```

The Size and Limits of Types

The operator `sizeof` gives us the size of a type (the size in bytes of a value of the type) either by taking the type surrounded by parentheses or by taking a value of the type. The size of a character is always one byte and the signed and unsigned forms of each integral type always have the same size. Otherwise, the sizes are implementation-dependent. Therefore, there are predefined constants holding the minimum and maximum values of the integral and floating types. The operator returns a value of the predefined type `size_t`. Its exact definition is implementation-dependent. However, it is often an unsigned integer.

```cpp
#include <iostream>
using namespace std;

#include <climits> // The integral type limit constants.
#include <cfloat>  // The floating type limit constants.
void main()
{
  int iIntSize1 = sizeof (int);
  int iIntSize2 = sizeof iIntSize1;
  cout << "integer size: " << iIntSize1 << " " << iIntSize2
       << endl;

  int* pSize = &iIntSize1;
  int iPtrSize = sizeof pSize;
  cout << "pointer size: " << iPtrSize << endl;

  int array[3] = {1, 2, 3};
  int iArraySize = sizeof array;
  cout << "array size: " << iArraySize << endl << endl;

  cout << "Minimum signed char: " << SCHAR_MIN << endl;
  cout << "Maximum signed char: " << SCHAR_MAX << endl;
  cout << "Minimum signed short int: " << SHRT_MIN << endl;
  cout << "Maximum signed short int: " << SHRT_MAX << endl;
  cout << "Minimum signed int: " << INT_MIN << endl;
  cout << "Maximum signed int: " << INT_MAX << endl;
  cout << "Minimum signed long int: " << LONG_MIN << endl;
  cout << "Maximum signed long int: " << LONG_MAX << endl
       << endl;

  // The minimum value of an unsigned integral type is always
  // zero.
  cout << "Maximum unsigned char: " << UCHAR_MAX << endl;
  cout << "Maximum unsigned short int: " << USHRT_MAX << endl;
  cout << "Maximum unsigned int: " << UINT_MAX << endl;
  cout << "Maximum unsigned long int: " << ULONG_MAX << endl
       << endl;

  // There are no constants for long double.
  cout << "Minimum float: " << FLT_MIN << endl;
  cout << "Maximum float: " << FLT_MAX << endl;
  cout << "Minimum double: " << DBL_MIN << endl;
  cout << "Maximum double: " << DBL_MAX << endl;
}
```

Hungarian Notation

In order to identify a variable's type and thereby increase the readability of the code, naming them in accordance with the Hungarian Notation is a good idea. The name of a variable has one or two initial small letters representing its type. The notation is named after Microsoft programmer Charles Simonyi, who was born in Budapest, Hungary.

Letter(s)	Type	Example
i	int	int iNum;
d	double	double dValue;
c	char	char cInput;
u	UINT (unsigned integer)	UINT uFlags;
x	int, the variable is a position in the x direction.	int xPos;
y	int, the variable is a position in the y direction.	int yPos;
cx	int, the variable is a size in the x direction.	int cxSize;
cy	int, the variable is a size in the y direction.	int cySize;
st	string	string stName;
cr	COLORREF	COLORREF crText;
lf	LOGFONT	LOGFONT lfCurrFont;

Objects of some common classes have in the same manner two initial small letters representing the class. Note that the C++ class *string* and the MFC class *CString* have the same initial letters. However, the C++ string class will not be used in the MFC applications of this book.

Letters	Class	Example
st	CString	CString stBuffer;
pt	CPoint	CPoint ptMouse;
sz	CSize	CSize szText;
rc	CRect	CRect rcClip;

A pointer to an object has the initial *p*.

```
SyntaxTree* pTree;
```

Expressions and Operators

The operations of C++ are divided into the *arithmetic*, *relational*, *logical*, and *bitwise* operators as well as simple and compound *assignment*. Moreover, there is the *conditional* operator.

In the figure below, + is an operator, a and b are operands, and the whole term is an expression.

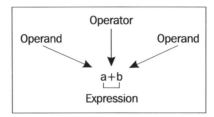

Arithmetic Operators

The arithmetic operators are addition (+), subtraction (-), multiplication (*), division (/), and modulo (%). The first four operators are equivalent to the four fundamental rules of arithmetic. The operators can take operands of integral and floating types. The last operator—modulo—gives the remainder of integer division. If we mix integral and floating types in the expression, the result will have floating type. The modulo operator, however, can only have integral operands. The last assignment in the following code may give rise to a compiler warning as the result of the division is a double and is converted into an int.

```
int a = 10, b = 3, c;
c = a + b; // 13
c = a - b; // 7
c = a * b; // 30
c = a / b; // 3, integer division
c = a % 3; // 1, remainder
double d = 3.0;
c = a / d; // 3.333, floating type
```

Pointer Arithmetic

The addition and subtraction operators are also applicable to pointers. It is called *pointer arithmetic*. An integral value can be added to or subtracted from a pointer. The value of the pointer is then changed by the integral value times the *size* of the type the pointer points at. As the *void* type is not really a type, but rather the absence of a type, it has no size. Therefore, we cannot perform pointer arithmetic on pointers to void.

In the code below, let us assume that iNumber is stored at memory location 10,000 and that the integer type has the size of four bytes. Then the pointer pNumber will assume the values 10,000, 10,004, 10,008, and 10,012, *not* the values 10,000, 10,002, 10,003, and 10,013, as pointer arithmetic always take the size of the type into consideration.

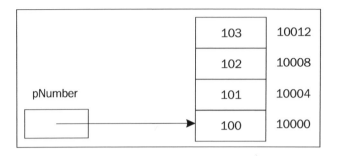

```
int iNumber = 100;
int* pNumber = &iNumber;

pNumber = pNumber + 1;
*pNumber = iNumber + 1;

pNumber = pNumber + 1;
*pNumber = iNumber + 2;

pNumber = pNumber + 1;
*pNumber = iNumber + 3;
```

It is also possible to subtract two pointers pointing at the same type. The result will be the difference in bytes between their two memory locations divided by the size of the type.

```
int array[] = {1, 2, 3};
int* p1 = &array[0];
int* p2 = &array[2];
int iDiff = p2 - p1; // 2
```

The index notation for arrays is equivalent to the dereferring of pointers together with pointer arithmetic. The second and third lines of the following code are by definition interchangeable.

```
int array[] = {1, 2, 3};
array[1] = array[2] + 1;
*(array + 1) = *(array + 2) + 1;
```

Increment and Decrement

There are two special operators: increment (++) and decrement (--). They add one to or subtract one from its operand. The operator can be placed before (prefix) or after (postfix) its operand.

```
int a = 1, b = 1;
++a; // 2, prefix increment
b++; // 2, postfix increment
```

However, there is a difference between prefix and postfix increment/decrement. In the prefix case, the subtraction occurs first and the new value is returned; in the postfix case, the original value is returned after the subtraction.

```
int a = 1, b = 1, c, d;
c = --a; // c = 0, prefix decrement
d = b--; // d = 1, postfix decrement
```

Relational Operators

There are six relational operators: *equal to* (==), *not equal to* (!=), *less than* (<), *less than or equal to* (<=), *greater than* (>), and *greater than or equal to* (>=). Note that the *equal to* operator is constituted by two equals signs rather than one (one equals sign represents the assignment operator). The operators give a logical value, true or false. The operands shall be of integral or floating type.

```
int i = 3;
double x = 1.2;
bool b = i > 0; // true
bool c = x == 2; // false
```

Logical Operators

There are three logical operators: *not* (!), *or* (||), and *and* (&&). They take and return logical values of the boolean type.

```
int i = 3;
bool b, c, d, e;
b = (i == 3); // true
c = !b; // false
d = b || c; // true
e = b && c; // false
```

C++ applies lazy (also called short-circuit) evaluation, which means that it will not evaluate more parts of the expression than is necessary to evaluate its value. In the following example, the evaluation of the expression is completed when the left expression (i != 0) is evaluated to false. If the left expression is false, the whole expression must also be false because it needs both the left and right expressions to be true for the whole expression to be true. This shows that the right expression (1 / i == 1) will never be evaluated and the division with zero will never occur.

```
int i = 0;
bool b = (i != 0) && (1 / i == 1); // false;
```

Bitwise Operators

An integer value can be viewed as a bit pattern. Our familiar decimal system has the base ten; it can be marked with an index 10.

$$234_{10} \Rightarrow 2.100+3.10+4.1=2.10^2+3.10^1+4.10^0$$

An integer value can also be viewed with the binary system, it has the base two. A single digit viewed with the base two is called a *bit*, and the integer value is called a *bit pattern*. A bit may only take the values one and zero.

$$1010_2 \Rightarrow 1.2^3+0.2^2+1.2^1+0.2^0=1.8+0.4+1.2+0.1=8+2=0$$

There are four bitwise operations in C++: *inverse* (~), *and* (&), *or* (|), and *exclusive or* (^). *Exclusive or* means that the result is one if one of its operand bits (but not both) is one. They all operate on integral values on bit level; that is, they examine each individual bit of an integer value.

```
    10101010₂        10101010₂        10101010₂
 & 10010110₂      | 10010110₂      ^ 10010110₂        ~ 10010110₂
 -----------      -----------      -----------        -----------
 = 10000010₂      = 10111110₂      = 00111100₂        = 01101001₂
```

```
int a = 170; // 10101010₂
int b = 150; // 10010110₂
int c = a & b; // 10000010₂ = 130₁₀
int d = a | b; // 10111110₂ = 190₁₀
int e = a ^ b; // 00111100₂ = 60₁₀
int f = ~b;    // 01101001₂ = 105₁₀
```

An integer value can also be shifted to the left (<<) or to the right (>>). Do not confuse these operators with the stream operators; they are different operators that happen to be represented by the same symbols. Each left shift is equivalent to doubling the value, and each right shift is equivalent to (integer) dividing the value by two. Overflowing bits are dropped for unsigned values; the behavior of signed values is implementation-dependent.

```
unsigned char a = 172;    // 10101100, base 2
unsigned char b = a << 2; // 10110000, base 2 = 160, base 10

unsigned char c = 166;    // 10100110, base 2
unsigned char d = c >> 2; // 00101001, base 2 = 41, base 10

cout << (int) a << " " << (int) b << " " << (int) c << " "
     << (int) d << endl;
```

Assignment

There are two kinds of assignment operators: *simple* and *compound*. The simple variant is quite trivial, one or more variables are assigned the value of an expression. In the example below, *a*, *b*, and *c* are all assigned the value 123.

```
int a, b, c, d = 123;
a = d;
b = c = d;
```

The compound variant is more complicated. Let us start with the additional assignment operator. In the example below, a's value is increased by the value of b; that is, a is given the value 4.

```
int a = 2, b = 4, c = 2;
a += c; // 4, equivalent to a = a + c.
b -= c; // 2, equivalent to a = a - c.
```

In a similar manner, there are operations -=, *=, /=, %=, |=, &=, and ^= as well as |=, &=, ^=, <<=, and >>=.

The Condition Operator

The *condition* operator resembles the `if-else` statement of the next section. It is the only C++ operator that takes three operands. The first expression is evaluated. If it is true, the second expression is evaluated and its value is returned. If the first expression instead is false, the third expression is evaluated and its value is returned.

```
int a = 1, b = 2, max;
max = (a > b) ? a : b; // The maximal value of a and b.
```

Too frequent use of this operator tends to make the code compact and hard to read. A piece of advice is that to restrict your use of the operator to the trivial cases.

Precedence and Associativity

Given the expression 1 + 2 * 5, what is its value? It is 11 because we first multiply two with five and then add one. We say that multiplication has a higher *precedence* than addition.

What if we limit ourselves to one operator, let us pick subtraction. What is the value of the expression 8 – 4 – 2? As we first subtract four from eight and then subtract two, the result is two. As we evaluate the value from left to right, we say that subtraction is *left associative*.

Below follows a table showing the priorities and associativities of the operator of C++. The first operator in the table has the highest priority.

Group	Operators	Associatively
Brackets and fields	() [] -> .	Left to Right
Unary operator	! ~ ++ -- + - (type) sizeof	Right to Left
Arithmetic operators	* / %	Left to Right
	+ -	Left to Right
Shift- and streamoperators	<< >>	Left to Right
Relation operators	< <= > >=	Left to Right
	== !=	
Bitwise operators	&	Left to Right
	^	
	|	
Logical operators	&&	Left to Right
	||	
Conditional operator	?:	Right to Left
Assignment operators	= += -= */ /= %= &= ^= |= <<= >>=	Right to Left
Comma operator	,	Left to Right

Note that unary +, -, and * have higher priority than their binary forms. Also note that we can always change the evaluation order of an expression by inserting brackets at appropriate positition. The expression (1 + 2) * 5 has the value 15.

Statements

There are four kinds of statements in C++ : selection, iteration, jump, and expression.

Group	Statements
Selection	if, if-else, switch
Iteration	for, while, do-while
Jump	break, continue, goto, return
Expression	expression ;

Selection Statements

The `if` statement needs, in its simplest form, a logical expression to decide whether to execute the statement following the if statement or not. The example below means that the text will be output if `i` is greater than zero.

```
if (i > 0)
{
  cout << "i is greater then 0";
}
```

We can also attach an `else` part, which is executed if the expression is false.

```
if (i > 0)
{
  cout << "i is greater then zero";
}
else
{
  cout << "i is not greater than zero";
}
```

Between the `if` and `else` part we can insert one or more `else if` part.

```
if (i > 0)
{
  cout << "i is greater then zero";
}
else if (i == 0)
{
  cout << "i is equal to zero";
}
else
{
  cout << "i is less than zero";
}
```

In the examples above, it is not strictly necessary to surround the output statements with brackets. However, it would be necessary in the case of several statements. In this book, brackets are always used. The brackets and the code in between is called a *block*.

```cpp
if (i > 0)
{
  int j = i + 1;
  cout << "j is " << j;
}
```

A warning may be in order. In an `if` statement, it is perfectly legal to use one equals sign instead of two when comparing two values. As one equals sign is used for assignment, not comparison, the variable `i` in the following code will be assigned the value one, and the expression will always be true.

```cpp
if (i = 1) // Always true.
{
  // ...
}
```

One way to avoid the mistake is to swap the variable and the value. As a value can be compared but not assigned, the compiler will issue an error message if you by mistake enter one equals sign instead of two signs.

```cpp
if (1 = i) // Compile-time error.
{
  // ...
}
```

The `switch` statement is simpler than the `if` statement, and not as powerful. It evaluates the `switch` value and jumps to a `case` statement with the same value. If no value matches, it jumps to the `default` statement, if present. It is important to remember the `break` statement. Otherwise, the execution would simply continue with the code attached to the next `case` statement. The `break` statement is used to jump out of a `switch` or iteration statement. The `switch` expression must have an integral or pointer type and two `case` statements cannot have the same value. The `default` statement can be omitted, and we can only have one `default` alternative. However, it must not be placed at the end of the `switch` statement, even though it is considered good practice to do so.

```cpp
switch (i)
{
  case 1:
    cout << "i is equal to 1" << endl;
    break;
```

```
  case 2:
    cout << "i is equal to 2" << endl;
    break;
  case 3:
    cout << "i is equal to 3" << endl;
    int j = i + 1;
    cout << "j = " << j;
    break;
  default:
    cout << "i is not equal to 1, 2, or 3." << endl;
    break;
}
```

In the code above, there will be a warning for the introduction of the variable j. As a variable is valid only in its closest surrounding scope, the following code below will work without the warning.

```
switch (i)
{
  // ...
  case 3:
    cout << "i is equal to 3" << endl;
    {
      int j = i + 1;
      cout << "j = " << j;
    }
    break;
  // ...
}
```

We can use the fact that an omitted break statement makes the execution continue with the next statement to group several case statements together.

```
switch (i)
{
  case 1:
  case 2:
  case 3:
    cout << "i is equal to 1, 2, or 3" << endl;
    break;
  // ...
}
```

Iteration Statements

Iteration statements iterate one statement (or several statements inside a block) as long as certain condition is true. The simplest iteration statement is the `while` statement. It repeats the statement as long as the given expression is true. The example below writes the numbers 1 to 10.

```
int i = 1;
while (i <= 10)
{
  cout << i;
  ++i;
}
```

The same thing can be done with a `do-while` statement.

```
int i = 1;
do
{
  cout << i;
  ++i;
}
while (i <= 10);
```

The `do-while` statement is less powerful. If the expression is false at the beginning, the `while` statement just skips the repetitions altogether, but the `do-while` statement must always execute the repetition statement at least once in order to reach the continuation condition.

We can also use the `for` statement, which is a more compact variant of the while statement. It takes three expressions, separated by semicolons. In the code below, the first expression initializes the variable, the repetition continues as long as the second expression is true, and the third expression is executed at the end of each repetition.

```
for (int i = 1; i <= 10; ++i)
{
  cout << i;
}
```

Similar to the `switch` statement, the iteration statements can be interrupted by the `break` statement.

```
int i = 1;
while (true)
{
  cout << i;
  ++i;
```

```
    if (i > 10)
    {
      break;
    }
}
```

Another way to construct an eternal loop is to omit the second expression of a for statement.

```
for (int i = 1;  ;  ++i)
{
  cout << i;
  if (i > 10)
  {
    break;
  }
}
```

An iteration statement can also include a continue statement. It skips the rest of the current repetition. The following example writes the numbers 1 to 10 with the exception of 5.

```
for (int i = 1; i <= 10; ++i)
{
  if (i == 5)
  {
    continue;
  }
  cout << i;
}
```

The following example, however, will not work. Because the continue statement will skip the rest of the while block, i will never be updated, and we will be stuck in an infinite loop. Therefore, I suggest you use the continue statement with care.

```
int i = 1;
while (i <= 10)
{
  if (i == 5)
  {
    continue;
  }
  cout << i;
  ++i;
}
```

Jump Statements

We can jump from one location to another inside the same function block by marking the latter location with a `label` inside the block with the `goto` statement.

```cpp
int i = 1;
label: cout << i;

++ i;
if (i <= 10)
{
  goto label;
}
```

The `goto` statement is, however, considered to give rise to unstructured code, so called "spaghetti code". I strongly recommend that you avoid the `goto` statement altogether.

Expression Statements

An expression can form a statement.

```cpp
a = b + 1; // Assignment operator.
cout << "Hello, World!"; // Stream operator.
WriteNumber(5); // Function call.
```

In the above examples, we are only interested in the side effects; that `a` is assigned a new value or that a text or a number is written. We are allowed to write expression statements without side effects; even though it has no meaning and it will probably be erased by the compiler.

```cpp
a + b * c;
```

Functions

A function can be compared to a black box. We send in information (input) and we receive information (output). In C++, the input values are called *parameters* and the output value is called a *return value*. The parameters can hold every type, and the return value can hold every type except the array.

To start with, let us try the function `Square`. This function takes an integer and returns its square.

```cpp
int Square(int n)
{
  return n * n;
}

void main()
{
  int i = Square(3); // Square returns 9.
}
```

In the example above, the parameter n in `Square` is called a *formal* parameter, and the value 3 in `Square` called in `main` is called an *actual* parameter.

Let us try a more complicated function, `SquareRoot` takes a value of double type and returns its square root. The idea is that the function iterates and calculates increasingly better root values by taking the mean value of the original value divided with the current root value and the previous root value. The process continues until the difference between two consecutive root values has reached an acceptable tolerance. Just like `main`, a function can have local variables. `dRoot` and `dPrevRoot` hold the current and previous value of the root, respectively.

```cpp
#include <iostream>
using namespace std;
double SquareRoot(double dValue)
{
  const double EPSILON = 1e-12;
  double dRoot = dValue, dOldRoot = dValue;
  while (true)
  {
    dRoot = ((dValue / dRoot) + dRoot) / 2;
    cout << dRoot << endl;
    if ((dOldRoot - dRoot) <= EPSILON)
    {
      return dRoot;
    }
    dOldRoot = dRoot;
  }
}
```

```
void main()
{
  double dInput = 16;
  cout << "SquareRoot of " << dInput << ": "
       << SquareRoot(dInput) << endl;
}
```

Void Functions

A function does not have to return a value. If it does not, we set void as the return type. As mentioned above, void is used to state the absence of a type rather than a type. We can return from a void function by just stating return without a value.

```
void PrintSign(int iValue)
{
  if (iValue < 0)
  {
    cout << "Negative.";
    return;
  }

  if (iValue > 0)
  {
    cout << "Positive.";
    return;
  }

  cout << "Zero";
}
```

There is no problem if the execution of a void function reaches the end of the code, it just jumps back to the calling function. However, a non-void function shall always return a value before reaching the end of the code. The compiler will give a warning if it is possible to reach the end of a non-void function.

Local and Global Variables

There are four kinds of variables. Two of them are *local* and *global* variables, which we consider in this section. The other two kinds of variables are *class fields* and *exceptions*, which will be dealt with in the class and exception sections of the next chapter.

A global variable is defined outside a function and a local variable is defined inside a function.

```
int iGlobal = 1;

void main()
{
  int iLocal = 2;
  cout << "Global variable: " << iGlobal // 1
       << ", Local variable: " << iLocal // 2
       << endl;
}
```

A global and a local variable can have the same name. In that case, the name in the function refers to the local variable. We can access the global variable by using two colons (::).

```
int iNumber = 1;

void main()
{
  int iNumber = 2;
  cout << "Global variable: " << ::iNumber // 1
       << ", Local variable: " << iNumber; // 2
}
```

A variable can also be defined in an inner block. As a block may contain another block, there may be many variables with the same name in the same scope. Unfortunately, we can only access the global and the most local variable. In the inner block of the following code, there is no way to access iNumber with value 2.

```
int iNumber = 1;

void main()
{
  int iNumber = 2;
  {
    int iNumber = 3;
    cout << "Global variable: " << ::iNumber // 1
         << ", Local variable: " << iNumber; // 3
  }
}
```

Global variables are often preceded by g_ in order to distinguish them from local variables.

```
int g_iNumber = 1;

void main()
{
  int iNumber = 2;
  cout << "Global variable: " << g_iNumber // 1
       << ", Local variable: " << iNumber; // 3
}
```

Call-by-Value and Call-by-Reference

Say that we want to write a function for switching the values of two variables.

```
#include <iostream>
using namespace std;

void Swap(int iNumber1, int iNumber2)
{
  int iTemp = iNumber1; // (a)
  iNumber1 = iNumber2;  // (b)
  iNumber2 = iTemp;     // (c)
}

void main()
{
  int iNum1 = 1, iNum2 = 2;
  cout << "Before: " << iNum1 << ", " << iNum2 << endl;
  Swap(iNum1, iNum2);
  cout << "After: " << iNum1 << ", " << iNum2 << endl;
}
```

Unfortunately, this will not work; the variables will keep their values. The explanation is that the values of *iFirstNum* and *iSecondNum* in *main* are copied into iNum1 and iNum2 in Swap. Then iNum1 and iNum2 exchange values with the help if iTemp. However, their values are not copied back into *iFirstNum* and *iSecondNum* in main.

	iFirstNum		(a) iNum1	(b) iNum1	(c) iNum1
Main:	1	Swap:	1	2	2
	iSecondNum		iNum2	iNum2	iNum2
	2		2	2	1
			iTemp	iTemp	iTemp
			1	1	1

The problem can be solved with *reference calls.* Instead of sending the values of the actual parameters, we send their addresses by adding an ampersand (&) to the type. As you can see in the code, the Swap call in main is identical to the previous one without references. However, the call will be different.

```cpp
#include <iostream>
using namespace std;

void Swap(int& iNum1, int& iNum2)
{
  int iTemp = iNum1; // (a)
  iNum1 = iNum2;     // (b)
  iNum2 = iTemp;     // (c)
}

void main()
{
  int iFirstNum = 1, iSecondNum = 2;
  cout << "Before: " << iFirstNum << ", " << iSecondNum
       << endl;

  Swap(iFirstNum, iSecondNum);
  cout << "After: " << iFirstNum << ", " << iSecondNum
       << endl;
}
```

In this case, we do not send the values of iFirstNum and iSecondNum, but rather their addresses. Therefore, iNum1 and iNum2 in Swap does in fact contain the addresses of iFirstNum and iSecondNum of main. As in the reference section above, we illustrate this with dashed arrows. Therefore, when iNum1 and iNum2 exchange values, in fact the values of iFirstNum and iSecondNum are exchanged.

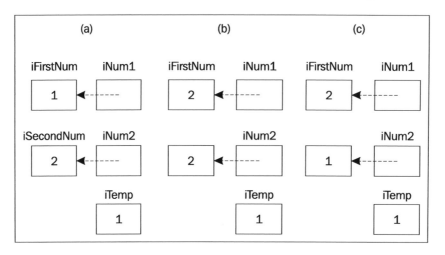

A similar effect can be obtained with pointers instead of references. In that case, however, both the definition of the function as well as the call from main are different.

```cpp
#include <iostream>
using namespace std;
void Swap(int* pNum1, int* pNum2)
{
  int iTemp = *pNum1; // (a)
  *pNum1 = *pNum2;    // (b)
  *pNum2 = iTemp;     // (c)
}
void main()
{
  int iFirstNum = 1, iSecondNum = 2;
  cout << "Before: " << iFirstNum << ", " << iSecondNum
       << endl;
  Swap(&iFirstNum, &iSecondNum);
  cout << "After: " << iFirstNum << ", " << iSecondNum
       << endl;
}
```

In this case, pNum1 and pNum2 are pointers, and therefore drawn with continuous lines. Apart from that, the effect is the same.

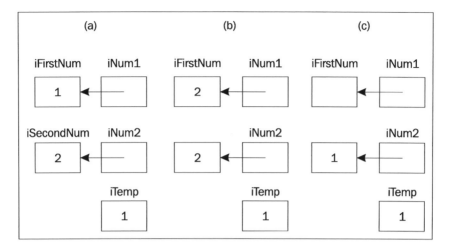

Default Parameters

A default parameter is a parameter that will be given a specific value if the call does not include its value. In the example below, all three calls are legitimate. In the first call, iNum2 and iNum3 will be given the values 9 and 99, respectively; in the second call, iNum3 will be given the value 99. Default values can only occur from the right in the parameter list; when a parameter is given a default value, all the following parameters must also be given default values.

```
#include <iostream>
using namespace std;

int Add(int iNum1, int iNum2 = 9, int iNum3 = 99)
{
   return iNum1 + iNum2 + iNum3;
}

void main()
{
   cout << Add(1) << endl;       // 1 + 9 + 99 = 109
   cout << Add(1, 2) << endl;    // 1 + 2 + 99 = 102
   cout << Add(1, 2 ,3) << endl; // 1 + 2 + 3 = 6
}
```

Overloading

Several different functions may be *overloaded*, which means that they may have the same name as long as they do not share exactly the same parameter list. C++ supports *context-free* overloading, the parameter lists must differ, it is not enough to let the return types differ. The languages **Ada** and **Lisp** support *context-dependent* overloading, two functions may have the same name and parameter list as long as they have different return types.

```cpp
#include <iostream>
using namespace std;
int Add(int iNum1)
{
   return iNum1;
}
int Add(int iNum1, int iNum2)
{
   return iNum1 + iNum2;
}
int Add(int iNum1, int iNum2, int iNum3)
{
   return iNum1 + iNum2 + iNum3;
}
void main()
{
   cout << Add(1) << endl;        // 1
   cout << Add(1, 2) << endl;     // 1 + 2 = 3
   cout << Add(1, 2 ,3) << endl; // 1 + 2 + 3 = 6
}
```

Static Variables

In the function below, iCount is a static local variable, which means that it is initialized when the execution of the program starts. It is not initialized when the function is called.

```cpp
void KeepCount()
{
   static int iCount = 0;
   ++iCount;
   cout << "This function has been called " << iCount
        << "times." << endl;
}
```

If `iCount` was a regular local variable (without the keyword `static`), the function would at every call write that the function has been called once as `iCount` would be initialized to zero at every call.

The keyword `static` can, however, also be used to define functions and global variables invisible to the linker and other object files.

Recursion

A function may call itself; it is called *recursion*. In the following example, the mathematical function factorial (*n*!) is implemented. It can be defined in two ways. The first definition is rather straightforward. The result of the function applied to a positive integer *n* is the product of all positive integers up to and including *n*.

n!=1.2.3....n

```
int Factorial(int iNumber)
{
  int iProduct = 1;
  for (int iCount = 1; iCount <= iNumber; ++iCount)
  {
    iProduct *= iCount;
  }
  return iProduct;
}
```

An equivalent definition involves a recursive call that is easier to implement.

$$n! = \begin{cases} 1, n=1 \\ (n-1), n>1 \end{cases}$$

```
int Factorial(int iNumber)
{
  if (iNumber == 1)
  {
    return 1;
  }
  else
  {
    return iNumber * Factorial(iNumber - 1);
  }
}
```

Definition and Declaration

It's important to distinguish between the terms *definition* and *declaration*. For a function, its definition generates code while the declaration is merely an item of information to the compiler. A function declaration is also called a *prototype*.

When it comes to mutual recursion (two functions calling each other), at least the second of them must have a prototype to avoid compiler warnings. I recommend that you put prototypes for all functions at the beginning of the file. In the following example, we use two functions to decide whether a given non-negative integer is even or odd according to the following definitions.

$$Even(n) = \begin{cases} true, & n=0 \\ Odd(n\text{-}1) & n>0 \end{cases}$$

$$Odd(n) = \begin{cases} false, & n=0 \\ Even(n\text{-}1) & n>0 \end{cases}$$

```cpp
bool Even(int iNum);
bool Odd(int iNum);
bool Even(int iNum)
{
  if (iNum == 0)
  {
    return true;
  }
  else
  {
    return Odd(iNum - 1);
  }
}
bool Odd(int iNum)
{
  if (iNum == 0)
  {
    return false;
  }
  else
  {
    return Even(iNum - 1);
  }
}
```

If we use prototypes together with default parameters, we can only indicate the default value in the prototype, not in the definition.

```cpp
#include <iostream>
using namespace std;
int Add(int iNum1, int iNum2 = 9, int iNum3 = 99);
void main()
{
  cout << Add(1) << endl; // 1 + 9 + 99 = 109
}
int Add(int iNum1, int iNum2 /* = 9 */, int iNum3 /* = 99 */)
{
  return iNum1 + iNum2 + iNum3;
}
```

Higher Order Functions

A function that takes another function as a parameter is called a *higher order function*. Technically, C++ does not take the function itself as a parameter, but rather a pointer to the function. However, the pointer mark (*) may be omitted. The following example takes an array of the given size and applies the given function to each integer in the array.

```cpp
#include <iostream>
using namespace std;
void ApplyArray(int intArray[], int iSize, int Apply(int))
{
  for (int iIndex = 0; iIndex < iSize; ++iIndex)
  {
    intArray[iIndex] = Apply(intArray[iIndex]);
  }
}
int Double(int iNumber)
{
  return 2 * iNumber;
}
int Square(int iNumber)
{
  return iNumber * iNumber;
}
void PrintArray(int intArray[], int iSize)
{
  for (int iIndex = 0; iIndex < iSize; ++iIndex)
  {
    cout << intArray[iIndex] << " ";
  }
```

```
      cout << endl;
}
void main()
{
   int numberArray[] = {1, 2, 3, 4, 5};
   int iArraySize = sizeof numberArray / sizeof numberArray[0];
   PrintArray(numberArray, iArraySize);
   // Doubles every value in the array.
   ApplyArray(numberArray, iArraySize, Double);//2,4,6,8,10
   PrintArray(numberArray, iArraySize);
   // Squares every value in the array.
   ApplyArray(numberArray, iArraySize, Square);//4,16,36,64,100
   PrintArray(numberArray, iArraySize);
}
```

One extra point in the example above is the method of finding the size of an array; we divide the size of the array with the size of its first value. This method only works on static arrays, not on dynamically allocated arrays or arrays given as parameters to functions. A parameter array is in fact converted to a pointer to the type of the array. The following two function definitions are by definition equivalent.

```
void PrintArray(int intArray[], int iSize)
{
   // ...
}
void PrintArray(int* intArray, int iSize)
{
   // ...
}
```

The main() Function

The main program is in fact a function; the only special thing about it is that it is the start point of the program execution. Just like a regular function it can have formal parameters and return a value. However, the parameter list must have a special format. The first parameter iArgCount is an integer indicating the number of arguments given by the system. The second parameter vpValues (*vp* stands for vector of pointers) holds the arguments. It is an array of pointers to characters, which can be interpreted as an array of strings, holding the system arguments. However, the first value of the array always holds the path name of the program. In some tutorials, the traditional parameter names argc and argv are used instead iArgCount and vpValues. The program below writes its path name and its arguments.

```
#include <iostream>
using namespace std;
int main(int iArgCount, char* vpValues[])
{
```

```
    cout << "Path name: " << vpValues[0] << endl;
    cout << "Parameters: ";
    for (int iIndex = 1; iIndex < iArgCount; ++iIndex)
    {
      cout << vpValues[iIndex] << " ";
    }
}
```

The arguments can be input from the command prompt.

The return value of the main function can (besides void) only be signed or unsigned int. The return value is often used to return an error code to the operating system; usually, zero indicates ok and a negative value indicates an error. The program below tries to allocate a large chunk of memory. It returns zero if it turns out well, minus one otherwise.

```
#include <cstdlib>
int main()
{
  const int BLOCK_SIZE = 7FFFFFFF;
  void* pBlock = new (nothrow) char[BLOCK_SIZE];
  if (pBlock != NULL)
  {
    // ...
    delete [] pBlock;
    return 0;
  }
  return -1;
}
```

The Preprocessor

The *preprocessor* is a tool that precedes the compiler in interpreting the code. The #include directive is one of its parts. It opens the file and includes its text. So far, we have only included system header files, whose names are surrounded by arrow brackets (< and >). Later on, we will include our own header files. Then we will use parentheses instead of arrow brackets. The difference is that the preprocessor looks for the system header files in a special system file directory while it looks for our header files in the local file directory.

Another part of the preprocessor is the *macros*. There are two kinds: with or without parameters. A macro without parameters works like a constant.

```
#define ARRAY_SIZE 256
int arr[ARRAY_SIZE];
```

The predefined macros __DATE__, __TIME__, __FILE__ , and __LINE__ holds today's date, the current time, the current line number, and the name of the file, respectively.

Macros with parameters act like functions with the difference being that they do not perform any type checking, they just replace the text. A macro is introduced with the #define directive and is often written with capitals.

```
#define ADD(a, b) ((a) + (b))
cout << ADD(1 + 2, 3 * 4) << endl; // 15
```

One useful macro is assert, it is defined in the header file cassert. It takes a logical parameter and exits the program execution with an appropriate message if the parameter is false. exit is a standard function that aborts the execution of the program and returns an integer value to the operating system. When a macro definition stretches over several lines, each line except the last one must end with a backslash.

```
#define assert(test)                                       \
{                                                          \
  if (!(test))                                             \
  {                                                        \
    cout << "Assertion: \"" << #test << "\" on line "    \
         << __LINE__ << " in file " << __FILE__ << "."; \
    ::exit(-1);                                            \
  }                                                        \
}
```

In the error handling section of the next chapter, we will define an error checking macro displaying the error message in a message box.

It is also possible to perform *conditional programming* by checking the value of macros. In the following example, we define a system integer according to the underlying operating system.

```
#ifdef WINDOWS
  #define SYSINT int
#endif

#ifdef LINUX
  #define SYSINT unsigned int
#endif
```

```
#ifdef MACHINTOCH
  #define SYSINT long int
#endif
SYSINT iOpData = 0;
```

The ASCII Table

0	*nul* \0	26	*sub*	52	4	78	N	104	h
1	*soh*	27	*esc*	53	5	79	O	105	i
2	*stx*	28	*fs*	54	6	80	P	106	j
3	*etx*	29	*gs*	55	7	81	Q	107	k
4	*eot*	30	*rs*	56	8	82	R	108	l
5	*enq*	31	*us*	57	9	83	S	109	m
6	*ack*	32	*blank*	58	:	84	T	110	n
7	*bel* \a	33	!	59	;	85	U	111	o
8	*bs* \b	34	"	60	<	86	V	112	p
9	*ht* \t	35	#	61	=	87	W	113	q
10	*lf* \n	36	$	62	>	88	X	114	r
11	*vt* \vt	37	%	63	?	89	Y	115	s
12	*ff* \f	38	&	64	@ É	90	Z	116	t
13	*cr* \r	39	'	65	A	91	[Ä	117	u
14	*soh*	40	(	66	B	92	\ Ö	118	v
15	*si*	41	)	67	C	93	] Å	119	w
16	*dle*	42	*	68	D	94	^ Ü	120	x
17	*dc1*	43	+	69	E	95	_	121	y
18	*dc2*	44	,	70	F	96	` é	122	z
19	*dc3*	45	-	71	G	97	a	123	{ ä
20	*dc4*	46	.	72	H	98	b	124		ö
21	*nak*	47	/	73	I	99	c	125	} å
22	*syn*	48	0	74	J	100	d	126	~ ü
23	*etb*	49	1	75	K	101	e	127	*delete*
24	*can*	50	2	76	L	102	f		
25	*em*	51	3	77	M	103	g		

Summary

Let's revise the points quickly in brief as discussed in this chapter:

- The text of a program is called its *source code*. It is translated into *target code* by the *compiler*. The target code is then *linked* to target code of other programs, finally resulting in *executable* code.

- The basic types of C++ can be divided into the integral types *char*, *short int*, *int*, and *long int*, and the floating types *float*, *double*, and *long double*. The integral types can also be *signed* or *unsigned*.

- Values of a type can be organized into an *array*, which is indexed by an integer. The first index is always zero. An *enum* value is an enumeration of named values. It is also possible to define new types with *typedef*, though that feature should be used carefully.

- A *pointer* holds the memory address of another value. There are operators to obtain the value pointed at and to obtain the address of a value. A reference is a simpler version of a pointer. A reference always holds the address of a specific value while a pointer may point at different values. A pointer can also be used to allocate memory dynamically; that is, during the program execution.

- The operators can be divided into the arithmetic operators *addition*, *subraction*, *multiplication*, *division*, and *modulo*; the relational operators *equal to*, *not equal to*, *less than*, *less than or equal to*, *greater than*, and *greater than or equal to*; the logical operators *not*, *and*, and *or*; the bitwise operators *inverse*, *and*, *or*, and *xor*; the assignment operators, and the condition operator. There is also the operator *sizeof*, which gives the size in bytes of values of a certain type.

- The statments of C++ can divided into the selection statements *if* and *switch*, the iteration statements *while* and *for*, and the jump statements *break*, *continue*, and *goto*, even thought goto should be avoided.

- A function may take one or more *formal parameters* as input. When it is called, a matching list of *actual parameters* must be provided. A function may also return a value of arbitrary type, with the exception of array. Two functions may be *overloaded*, which means they have the same name, as long as they differ in their parameter lists. A function may call itself, directly or indirectly; this is called *recursion*. A function can also have default parameters, which means that if the caller does not provide enough parameters, the missing parameters will be given the default values.

- A *macro* is a textual substitution performed by the *preprocessor* before the compilation of the program. Similar to functions, they may take parameters. We can also include the text of other files into our program. Finally, we can include and exclude certain parts of the code by *conditional programming*.

2

Object-Oriented Programming in C++

As C++ is an object-oriented language, it fully supports the object-oriented model. Even though it is possible to write working programs in C++ only by means of the techniques presented in the previous chapter, I strongly suggest that you learn the techniques of this chapter. They are what makes C++ a modern and powerful language. This chapter covers the following topics:

- First, we look into the theoretical foundation of the object-oriented model. It consists of the three *cornerstones* and the five *relations*.

- The basic feature of the object-oriented model is the *class*. A class can be *instanced* into an *object*. A class consists of members, which are functions or variables. When located inside a class, they are called *methods* and *fields*.

- A class can *inherit* another class with its members. A method of the baseclass can be *virtual*, resulting in *dynamic binding*. This means that the methods connected to an object is bound during the execution of the program rather than its compilation.

- As mentioned in the previous chapter, an array consists of a sequence of values. However, it can also consist of a sequence of objects. In that case, there are some restrictions on the class in order to ensure that all objects are properly initialized.

- Also in the previous chapter, we looked at pointers. A pointer can very well point at an object. The object may hold a pointer of its own that points at another object of the same class. This will result in a *linked list*, a very useful structure.

- C++ holds a number of operations that operate on values of basic types. We can also extend our classes so that objects of the classes are allowed as operands. It is called *operator overloading*.

- When an error occurs, an elegant solution is to throw an *exception* with information about the error to be caught and processed in another part of the program.

- Say that we want a class to hold a list of integers or real values. Do we need to write two different classes? Not at all. Instead, we write a *template* class. Instead of integer or real, we use a generic type, which we replace with a suitable type when we create an instance of the class.

- In the previous chapter, we organized our code in functions. In this chapter, we organize functions into classes. On top of that, we can place classes and freestanding functions into *namespaces*.

- Finally, we look into file processing with *streams*.

The Object-Oriented Model

The object-oriented model is very powerful. An object-oriented application consists of objects. An object exists in memory during the execution of the application. In C++, an object is defined by its *class*. A class can be considered a blueprint for one or more objects with the same features. A class is defined by *methods* and *fields*. A method is a function enclosed in a class. A field is a variable common to the whole class. The methods and fields of a class are together referred to as its *members*.

The foundation of the object-oriented theory rests on three cornerstones: part of class can be *encapsulated*, classes can *inherit* each other, and objects can be bound *dynamically*.

There are five relations in the object-oriented model. A class is defined in the source code, and one or more object of that class is created during the execution, the objects are *instances* of the class. A method of one class *calls* a method of the same class or another class. A class can *inherit* one or more other classes to reuse its functionality (a class cannot inherit itself, neither directly or indirectly). The inheriting class is called the *subclass* and the inherited class is called the *baseclass*. A class may have a member that is an object of another class; this is called *aggregation*. A class may also have a member pointing or referencing to an object of its own class or of another class, this is called *connection*.

A member of a class (field or method) may be encapsulated. There are three levels of encapsulation; public — the member is completely accessible, protected — the member is accessible by subclasses, and private — the member is only accessible by the class itself. If we omit the encapsulation indicator, the member will be private. A struct is a construction very similar to a class. The only difference is that if we omit the encapsulation indicator, the members will be public.

Similar to a local variable, a member can also be static. A static method cannot call a non-static method or access a non-static field. A static field is common to all objects of the class, as opposed to a regular field where each object has its own version of the field. Static members are not part of the object-oriented model, a static method resembles a freestanding function and a static field resembles a global variable. They are, however, directly accessible without creating any objects.

There is also single and multiple inheritance. Multiple inheritance means that a subclass can have more than one baseclass. The inheritance can also be public, protected, and private, which means that the members of the baseclass are public, protected, and private, respectively, regardless of their own encapsulation indicators. However, a member cannot become more public by a protected or public inheritance. We can say the inheritance indicator lowers (straightens) the encapsulation of the member. Private and protected inheritances are not part of the object-oriented model, and I recommend that you always use public inheritance. I also recommend that you use multiple inheritance restrictedly.

A function or a method with a pointer defined to point at an object of a class can in fact point at an object of any of its subclasses. If it calls a method that is defined in both the subclass and the baseclass and if the method of the baseclass is marked as *virtual*, the method of the subclass will be called. This is called *dynamic binding*. The methods must have the same name and parameter lists. We say the method of the baseclass is *overridden* by the method of the subclass. Do not confuse this with *overloaded* methods of the same class or of freestanding functions.

A method can also be declared as *pure virtual*. In that case, the class is abstract, which means that it cannot be instantiated, only inherited. The baseclass that declare's the pure virtual methods do not define them and its subclasses must either define all of its baseclasses' pure virtual methods or become abstract themselves. It is not possible to mark a class as abstract without introducing at least one pure virtual method. In fact, a class becomes abstract if it has at least one pure virtual method.

Classes

A class is *defined* and *implemented*. The definition of the class sets the fields and the prototypes of the methods, and the implementation defines the individual methods.

The methods can be divided into four categories: *constructors*, *destructors*, *modifiers*, and *inspectors*. One of the constructors is called when the object is created and the destructor is called when it is destroyed. A constructor without parameters is called a *default* constructor. A class is not required to have a constructor; in fact, it does not have to have any members at all. However, I strongly recommend that you include at least one constructor to your classes. If there is at least one constructor, one of them has to be called when the object is created, which means that unless the default constructor is called, parameters have to be passed to the constructor when the object is created. Methods may be overloaded the same way as freestanding functions and a class may have several constructors as long as they have different parameter lists. However, the class can only have one destructor because it cannot have parameters and can therefore not be overloaded. As the names imply, modifiers modify the fields of the class and inspectors inspect them.

The First Example

Let us start with a simple example. How about a car? What can we do with a car? Well, we can increase and decrease the speed, we can turn left and right, and we can read the speed and the direction of the car (let us assume we have a compass as well as a speedometer in the car).

Let us define two constructors, one with and one without parameters (default constructer). Every constructor has the name of the class without a return type (not even void). The destructor does also have the name of the class preceded by a tilde (~). In this class, we really do not need a destructor, but let us throw one in anyway.

A field in a class is often preceded by m_, identifying it as a field ('m' stands for *member*) in order to distinguish them from local and global variables.

We have two fields for speed and direction: m_iSpeed and m_iDirection. We want to increase and decrease the speed as well as turn left and right. This gives us four modifiers: IncreaseSpeed, DecreaseSpeed, TurnLeft, and TurnRight. We also want to read the speed and direction, which gives us two inspectors: GetSpeed and GetDirection.

The code is often divided into several files: one *header* file, often named after the class with extension .h, containing the class definition, and one *implementation* file, with extension .cpp, containing the method definitions. The main function is often placed in a third file. In this example, the files are named Car.h, Car.cpp, and Main.cpp.

Car.h

```
class Car
{
  public:
    Car();
    Car(int iSpeed, int iDirection);
    ~Car();
    void IncreaseSpeed(int iSpeed);
    void DecreaseSpeed(int iSpeed);
```

```
      void TurnLeft(int iAngle);
      void TurnRight(int iAngle);

      int GetSpeed();
      int GetDirection();
   private:
      int m_iSpeed, m_iDirection;
};
```

In every class implementation file, we have to include the header file. Then we define the methods, every method must be marked with its class name followed by two colons (`Car::` in this case) in order to distinguish between class methods and freestanding functions.

In the first constructor, we initialize the fields value to zero with *colon notation*. The colon notation can only be used in constructors and is used to initialize the values of the fields. We have to do that in the constructor. Otherwise, the fields would be uninitialized, meaning they would be given arbitrary values. The second constructor initializes the fields with the given parameters. The destructor is usually used to free dynamically allocated memory or to close opened files. We have nothing of that kind in this program, so we just leave the destructor empty.

The modifiers take each parameter and update the values of the fields. The inspectors return the value of one field each.

Car.cpp

```
#include "Car.h"
Car::Car()
 :m_iSpeed(0),
  m_iDirection(0)
{
    // Empty.
}
Car::Car(int iSpeed, int iDirection)
 :m_iSpeed(iSpeed),
  m_iDirection(iDirection)
{
  // Empty.
}
Car::~Car()
{
  // Empty.
}
```

```
void Car::IncreaseSpeed(int iSpeed)
{
  m_iSpeed += iSpeed;
}
void Car::DecreaseSpeed(int iSpeed)
{
  m_iSpeed -= iSpeed;
}
void Car::TurnLeft(int iAngle)
{
  m_iDirection -= iAngle;
}
void Car::TurnRight(int iAngle)
{
  m_iDirection += iAngle;
}
int Car::GetSpeed()
{
  return m_iSpeed;
}
int Car::GetDirection()
{
  return m_iDirection;
}
```

The `main` function file must also include the header file. We create an object by writing the class name followed by the object name. If there is at least one constructor in the class, we have to call it by sending a list of matching actual parameters (or no parameters at all in the case of a default constructor). In this case, we can choose between two integers (speed and direction) or no parameters at all.

One important issue to notice is that if we do not send parameters, we will also omit the parentheses. If we do add parentheses, it would be interpreted as a function declaration (prototype). The following line would interpret `car3` as a freestanding function that returns an object of the class `Car` and take no parameters. As the function is not defined, it would result in a linking error.

```
Car car3();
```

Notice that the fields of the class are private. That means that attempting to the field `m_iSpeed` at the last line would result in a compile-time error. We do not have to set fields to `private`; however, it is a good practice to do so.

Main.cpp

```cpp
#include <iostream>
using namespace std;

#include "Car.h"

void main()
{
  Car car1(100, 90);
  cout << "Car1: " << car1.GetSpeed()         // 100
      << " degrees, " << car1.GetDirection() // 90
      << " miles per hour" << endl;
  Car car2(150, 0);
  car2.TurnRight(180);
  cout << "Car2: " << car2.GetSpeed()         // 150
      << " degrees, " << car2.GetDirection() // 180
      << " miles per hour" << endl;

  Car car3;
  car3.IncreaseSpeed(200);
  car3.TurnRight(270);
  cout << "Car3: " << car3.GetSpeed()        // 200
     << " degrees, " << car3.GetDirection() // 270
     << " miles per hour" << endl;
// Causes a compiler error as m_iSpeed is a private member.
// cout << "Speed: " << car3.m_iSpeed << endl;
}
```

The Second Example

Let us go on to the next example, this time we model a bank account. There are a few new items. As mentioned in the first chapter, we can define a constant inside a function. We can also define a constant field in a class. It can only be initialized by the constructors; thereafter, it cannot be modified. In this example, the account number is a constant. It is written in capital letters, which is an established style.

We can also define methods to be constant. Only inspectors can be constant, as a constant method cannot modify the value of a field. In this example, the inspectors GetNumber and GetSaldo are constant. We cannot mark any other methods as constant, and neither constructors nor the destructor can be constant.

In addition, objects can be constant. A constant object can only call constant methods; that is inspectors marked as constant. In this way, we assure that the values of the fields are not altered since the object was created.

We also add a *copy constructor* to the class, which takes a (possible constant) reference to another object of the same class. As the name implies, it is used to create a copy of an object. The new object can be initialized with the parentheses or the assignment operator. The second and third of the following lines are completely interchangeable.

```
BankAccount accountOriginal(123);
BankAccount accountCopy1(accountOriginal);
BankAccount accountCopy2 = accountOriginal;
```

In the same way as a freestanding function, a method may have default parameters. However, just as is the case of freestanding functions, we can indicate the default values only in the method declarations. I recommend that you state the value in the method's declaration in the header file, and surround the values by block comments in the definition. In this example, the first constructor has a default parameter.

A method (including the constructors and the destructor) can also be inline. That means that it is defined (not just declared) in the class definition of the header file. There is a good rule of thumb to limit the inline methods to short ones, preferably methods whose whole code goes into one row. In this example, the modifiers `Deposit` and `Withdraw` as well as the inspectors `GetNumber` and `GetSaldo` are inline.

BankAccount.h

```
class BankAccount
{
  public:
    BankAccount(int iNumber, double dSaldo = 0);
    BankAccount(const BankAccount& bankAccount);

    void Deposit(double dAmount)   {m_dSaldo += dAmount;}
    void Withdraw(double dAmount)  {m_dSaldo -= dAmount;}

    int GetNumber()    const {return m_iNUMBER;}
    double GetSaldo() const {return m_dSaldo; }
  private:
    const int m_iNUMBER;
    double m_dSaldo;
};
```

The implementation file is short; it only contains the definitions of the constructors. Note the comments around the default value in the constructor's parameter list. It would result in a compile-time error if we indicated the value in the implementation file.

BankAccount.cpp

```cpp
#include "BankAccount.h"

BankAccount::BankAccount(int iNumber, double dSaldo /* = 0 */)
 :m_iNUMBER(iNumber),
  m_dSaldo(dSaldo)
{
  // Empty.
}

BankAccount::BankAccount(const BankAccount& bankAccount)
 :m_iNUMBER(bankAccount.m_iNUMBER),
  m_dSaldo(bankAccount.m_dSaldo)
{
  // Empty.
}
```

The `main` function creates two objects of the `BankAccount` class. The second one is constant, which means that the call of the non-constant method `Withdraw` at the last line would result in an error.

Main.cpp

```cpp
#include <iostream>
using namespace std;

#include "BankAccount.h"

void main()
{
  BankAccount account1(123);
  account1.Deposit(100);
  cout << "Account1: number " << account1.GetNumber() // 123
       << ", $" << account1.GetSaldo() << endl;        // 100
  account1.Withdraw(50);
  cout << "Account1: number " << account1.GetNumber() // 123
       << ", $" << account1.GetSaldo() << endl;        // 50
  BankAccount copyAccount(account1);
  cout << "Copy Account: number " << copyAccount.GetNumber()
       << ", $" << copyAccount.GetSaldo() << endl;  // 50, 123
  const BankAccount account2(124, 200);
  cout << "Account2: number " << account2.GetNumber() // 124
       << ", $" << account2.GetSaldo() << endl;        // 200
// Would cause a compiler error.
// account2.Withdraw(50);
}
```

Inheritance

So far, we have only dealt with freestanding classes, let us now put three classes together in a *class hierarchy*. We start with the baseclass `Person`, which has a constructor that initializes the field `m_stName`, and a method `Print` that writes the name. `Print` is marked as virtual; this means that dynamic binding will come into effect when we, in the `main` function, define a pointer to an object of this class. We do not have to mark the methods as virtual in the subclasses, it is sufficient to do so in the baseclass. The constructors of a class cannot be virtual. However, every other member, including the destructor, can be virtual and I advise you to always mark them as virtual in your baseclass. Non-virtual methods are not a part of the object-oriented model and were added to C++ for performance reasons only.

Person.h

```
class Person
{
  public:
    Person(string stName);
    virtual void Print() const;
  private:
    string m_stName;
};
```

Person.cpp

```
#include <iostream>
#include <string>
using namespace std;
#include "Person.h"
Person::Person(string stName)
 :m_stName(stName)
{
  // Empty.
}
void Person::Print() const
{
  cout << "Name: " << m_stName << endl;
}
```

`Student` and `Employee` are subclasses to `Person`, which means that they inherit all public members of `Person`. Generally, they also inherit all protected members, even though we do not have any of those in the baseclass in this case. They define their own versions of `Print` with the same parameter list (in this case no parameters at all). It is called *overriding*. This is not to be confused with *overloading*, which was refs to freestanding functions or methods of the same class. For overriding to come into effect, the methods must have the same name and parameters list and the method of the baseclass must be virtual. As constructors cannot be virtual, they cannot be overridden. Two overridden methods cannot have different return types.

Student.h

```
class Student : public Person
{
  public:
    Student(string stName, string stUniversity);
    void Print() const;

  private:
    string m_stUniversity;
};
```

Student.cpp

```
#include <iostream>
#include <string>
using namespace std;

#include "Person.h"
#include "Student.h"

Student::Student(string stName, string stUniversity)
 :Person(stName),
  m_stUniversity(stUniversity)
{
  // Empty.
}
void Student::Print() const
{
  Person::Print();
  cout << "University: " << m_stUniversity << endl;
}
```

Employee.h

```
class Employee : public Person
{
  public:
    Employee(string stName, string stEmployer);
    void Print() const;

  private:
    string m_stEmployer;
};
```

Employee.cpp

```cpp
#include <iostream>
#include <string>
using namespace std;

#include "Person.h"
#include "Employee.h"

Employee::Employee(string stName, string stEmployer)
  :Person(stName),
   m_stEmployer(stEmployer)
{
  // Empty.
}

void Employee::Print() const
{
  Person::Print();
  cout << "Company: " << m_stEmployer << endl;
}
```

Dynamic Binding

In the example above, it really is no problem to create static objects of the classes. When we call `Print` on each object, the corresponding version of `Print` will be called. It becomes a bit more complicated when we introduce a pointer to a `Person` object and let it point at an object of one of the subclasses. As `Print` in `Person` is virtual, dynamic-binding comes into force. This means that the version of `Print` in the object the pointer actually points at during the execution will be called. Had it not been virtual, `Print` in `Person` would always have been called. To access a member of an object given a pointer to the object, we could use the dot notation together with the dereferring operator. However, the situation is so common that an arrow notation equivalent to those operations has been introduced. The following two lines are by definition interchangeable:

```cpp
pPerson->Print();
(*pPerson).Print();
```

Main.cpp

```cpp
#include <iostream>
using namespace std;

#include "Person.h"
#include "Student.h"
#include "Employee.h"
```

```
void main()
{
  Person person("John Smith");
  person.Print();
  cout << endl;

  Student student("Mark Jones", "MIT");
  student.Print();
  cout << endl;

  Employee employee("Adam Brown", "Microsoft");
  employee.Print();
  cout << endl;

  Person* pPerson = &person;
  pPerson->Print(); // Calls Print in Person.
  cout << endl;

  pPerson = &student;
  pPerson->Print(); // Calls Print in Student.
  cout << endl;

  pPerson = &employee;
  pPerson->Print(); // Calls Print in Employee.
}
```

Had we omitted the word `virtual` in the class `Person` above, we would not have dynamic-binding, but rather static-binding. In that case, `Print` in `Person` would always be called. As mentioned above, static-binding is present for performance reasons only and I suggest that you always mark every method of the baseclass in the class hierarchy as virtual.

Let us take the next logical step and continue with abstract baseclasses and pure virtual methods. An abstract baseclass cannot be instantiated into an object, but can be used as a baseclass in a class hierarchy. In the example above, we became acquainted with virtual methods. In this section, we look into pure virtual methods.

A pure virtual method does not have a definition, just a prototype. A class becomes abstract if it has at least one pure virtual method, which implies that a class cannot be abstract without a pure virtual method. A subclass to an abstract class can choose between defining all pure virtual methods of all its baseclasses, or become abstract itself. In this manner, it is guaranteed that a concrete (not abstract) subclass always has definitions of all its methods.

The next example is a slightly different version of the hierarchy of the previous section. This time, `Person` is an abstract baseclass because it has the pure virtual method `Print`. Its prototype is virtual and succeeded with `= 0`.

The field m_stName is now `protected`, which means that it is accessible by methods in subclasses, but not by methods of other classes or by freestanding functions. Another difference in these classes is the use of constant references in the constructor. Instead of sending the object itself as an actual parameter, which might be time and memory consuming, we can send a reference to the object. To make sure that the fields of the object are not changed by the method, we mark the reference as constant. Compare the constructor of `Person` in this case with the previous case. The change does not really affect the program, it is just a way to make the program execute faster and use less memory.

Person.h

```
class Person
{
  public:
    Person(const string& stName);
    virtual void Print() const = 0;
  protected:
    string m_stName;
};
```

Person.cpp

```
#include <string>
using namespace std;

#include "Person.h"

Person::Person(const string& stName)
 :m_stName(stName)
{
  // Empty.
}
```

As `Person` is an abstract class, `Student` must define `Print` in order not to become abstract itself.

Student.h

```
class Student : public Person
{
  public:
    Student(const string& stName, const string& stUniversity);
    void Print() const;
  private:
    string m_stUniversity;
};
```

In the `Student` class of the previous example, `Print` called `Print` in `Person`. This time, `Person` does not have a definition of `Print`, so there is no method to call. Instead, we access the `Person` field `m_stName` directly; this is allowed because in this version it is protected in `Person`.

Student.cpp

```
#include <string>
#include <iostream>
using namespace std;

#include "Person.h"
#include "Student.h"

Student::Student(const string& stName, const string& stUniversity)
    :Person(stName),
     m_stUniversity(stUniversity)
{
  // Empty.
}

void Student::Print() const
{
  cout << "Name: " << m_stName << endl;
  cout << "University: " << m_stUniversity << endl;
}
```

`Employee` works in the same way as `Student`.

Employee.h

```
class Employee : public Person
{
  public:
    Employee(const string& stName, const string& stEmployer);
    void Print() const;
  private:
    string m_stEmployer;
};
```

Employee.cpp

```
#include <string>
#include <iostream>
using namespace std;

#include "Person.h"
#include "Employee.h"
```

```
Employee::Employee(const string& stName,
                   const string& stEmployer)
 :Person(stName),
  m_stEmployer(stEmployer)
{
  // Empty.
}
void Employee::Print() const
{
  cout << "Name: " << m_stName << endl;
  cout << "Company: " << m_stEmployer << endl;
}
```

In the `main` function, we cannot create an object of the `Person` class as it is an abstract class. Neither can we let the pointer `pPerson` point at such an object. However, we can let it point at an object of the class `Student` or `Employee`. The condition for `Student` and `Employee` being concrete classes was that they defined every pure virtual method, so we can be sure that there always exists a definition of `Print` to call.

Main.cpp

```
#include <string>
#include <iostream>
using namespace std;

#include "Person.h"
#include "Student.h"
#include "Employee.h"

void main()
{
// Does not work as Person is an abstract class.
// Person person("John Smith");
// person.Print();
// cout << endl;

  Student student("Mark Jones", "Berkeley");
  student.Print();
  cout << endl;

  Employee employee("Adam Brown", "Microsoft");
  employee.Print();
  cout << endl;
// In this version, there is no object person to point at.
// Person* pPerson = &person;
// pPerson->Print();
// cout << endl;
```

```
    Person* pPerson = &student;
    pPerson->Print(); // Calls Print in Student.
    cout << endl;

    pPerson = &employee;
    pPerson->Print();// Calls Print in Employee.
}
```

Arrays of Objects

An array of objects is not really so much different from an array of values. However, one issue to consider is that there is no way to call the constructor of each object individually. Therefore, the class must have a default constructor or no constructor at all. Remember that if a class has one or more constructors, one of them must be called every time an object of the class is created.

```
    // The default constructor is called for each car object.
    Car carArray[3];
    carArray[2].IncreaseSpeed(100);
    // The default constructor is called for each car object.
    Car *pDynamicArray = new Car[5];
    pDynamicArray[4].IncreaseSpeed(100);
    delete [] pDynamicArray;
```

Just as for values, we can also initialize an object array with a list. In that case, we can call constructors other than the default constructor. Note that when we introduce a new object in an array initialization list and call the default constructor, we have to add parentheses unlike when creating freestanding objects by calling the default constructor.

```
    Car carArray[] = {Car(), Car(100, 90)};
    carArray[0].TurnLeft(90);
```

Pointers and Linked Lists

A pointer may point at an object as well as a value, and a class may have a pointer to another object as a member variable, which in turn points at another object and so on. In this way, a *linked list* can be constructed. The list must end eventually, so the last pointer points at null. A pointer to the next cell in the list is called a *link*.

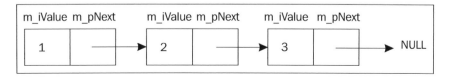

Stacks and Linked Lists

A *stack* is very valuable in a number of applications and it can be implemented with a linked list. We can add a value on top of the stack, we can inspect or remove the topmost value, and we can check whether the stack is empty. However, we cannot do anything to the values that are not on top. The method that adds a new value on top of the stack is called *push* and the method removing it is called *pop*. Let us say that we push our stack three times with the values 1, 2, and 3. Then we can only access the topmost value, 3, and not the two below, 1 or 2.

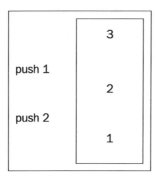

An additional point of this example is that the `Value` method is overloaded. The first version returns a reference to the value; the second version is constant and returns the value itself. This implies that the first version can be called to modify the value of the cell and the second version can be called to inspect the value of a constant cell object.

```
Cell cell1(1, NULL);
cell1.Value() = 2;

const cell2(2, NULL);
int iValue = cell2.Value();
```

Another way to archive the same functionality would be to add a get/set pair.

```
const int GetValue() const {return m_iValue;}
void SetValue(int iValue) {m_iValue = iValue;}
/// ...
Cell cell1(1, NULL);
cell1.SetValue(2);

const cell2(2, NULL);
int iValue = cell2.GetValue();
```

In order to make the `typedef` definition below work, we have to declare the class on the preceding line. It is possible to define a pointer to an unknown type as all pointers occupy the same amount of memory regardless of what they point at. However, it is not allowed to define arrays of unknown types or classes with fields of unknown types.

Cell.h

```cpp
class Cell;
typedef Cell* Link;

class Cell
{
  public:
    Cell(int iValue, Cell* pNextCell);

    int& Value() {return m_iValue;}
    const int Value() const {return m_iValue;}

    Link& NextLink() {return m_pNextLink;}
    const Link NextLink() const {return m_pNextLink;}

  private:
    int m_iValue;
    Link m_pNextLink;
};
```

Cell.cpp

```cpp
#include "Cell.h"

Cell::Cell(int iValue, Link pNextLink)
 :m_iValue(iValue),
  m_pNextLink(pNextLink)
{
  // Empty.
}
```

Main.cpp

```cpp
#include <cstdlib>
#include "Cell.h"

void main()
{
  Link pCell3 = new Cell(3, NULL);
  Link pCell2 = new Cell(2, pCell3);
  Link pCell1 = new Cell(1, pCell2);
}
```

The following structure is created by `main` above.

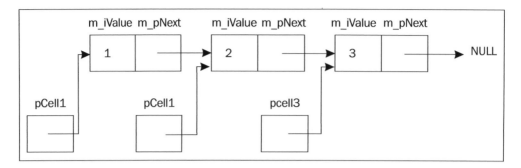

There is one more thing to think about. What happens if we run out of dynamic memory or try to access the topmost value of an empty stack? We can deal with the problem in some different ways, everything from ignoring it to aborting the execution. In this case, I have limited the handling of memory shortage to the use of the macro *assert*, as described in the previous chapter.

Stack.h

```cpp
class Stack
{
  public:
    Stack();
    ~Stack();

    void Push(int iValue);
    void Pop();

    int Top() const;
    bool IsEmpty() const;

  private:
    Cell* m_pFirstCell;
};
```

Stack.cpp

```cpp
#include <cstdlib>
#include <cassert>
#include "..\\LinkedList\\Cell.h"
#include "Stack.h"

Stack::Stack()
 :m_pFirstCell(NULL)
{
  // Empty.
}
```

```
Stack::~Stack()
{
  Cell* pCurrCell = m_pFirstCell;
  while (pCurrCell != NULL)
  {
    Cell* pRemoveCell = pCurrCell;
    pCurrCell = pCurrCell->NextLink();
    delete pRemoveCell;
  }
}
void Stack::Push(int iValue)
{
  Cell* pNewCell = new Cell(iValue, m_pFirstCell);
  assert(pNewCell != NULL);
  m_pFirstCell = pNewCell;
}
void Stack::Pop()
{
  assert(m_pFirstCell != NULL);
  Cell* pTempCell = m_pFirstCell;
  m_pFirstCell = m_pFirstCell->NextLink();
  delete pTempCell;
}
int Stack::Top() const
{
  assert(m_pFirstCell != NULL);
  return m_pFirstCell->Value();
}

bool Stack::IsEmpty() const
{
  return (m_pFirstCell == NULL);
}
```

Main.cpp

```
#include "..\\LinkedList\\Cell.h"
#include "Stack.h"
void main()
{
  Stack stack;
  stack.Push(1);
  stack.Push(2);
  stack.Push(3);
}
```

The stack in `main` above gives rise to the following structure. However, when the stack goes out of scope (at the end of `main`), the destructor deallocates the allocated memory. All memory allocated with `new` must (or at least should) be deallocated with `delete`.

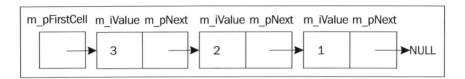

Operator Overloading

C++ supports operator overloading; that is, letting a method of a class be disguised to look like an operator. The priority and associativity of the operators are unaffected as well as their number of operands. As an example, let us look at a class handling rational numbers. A rational number is a number that can be expressed as a quotient between two integers, for instance 1/2 or 3/4. The integers are called *numerator* and *denominator*, respectively.

Rational.h

```
class Rational
{
  public:
    Rational(int iNumerator = 0, int iDenominator = 1);
    Rational(const Rational& rational);
    Rational operator=(const Rational& rational);
    bool operator==(const Rational &number) const;
    bool operator!=(const Rational &number) const;
    bool operator< (const Rational &number) const;
    bool operator<=(const Rational &number) const;
    bool operator> (const Rational &number) const;
    bool operator>=(const Rational &number) const;
    Rational operator+(const Rational &number) const;
    Rational operator-(const Rational &number) const;
    Rational operator*(const Rational &number) const;
    Rational operator/(const Rational &number) const;
    friend istream &operator>>(istream &inputStream, Rational &number);
    friend ostream &operator<<(ostream &outputStream,
                               const Rational &number);
  private:
    int m_iNumerator, m_iDenominator;
    void Normalize();
    int GreatestCommonDivider(int iNum1, int iNum2);
};
```

In the class, we again use the assert macro in the constructor to avoid division by zero, every integer is acceptable as numerator and denominator, except that the denominator cannot be zero. The zero rational number is represented by zero as numerator and one as denominator.

A rational number can be assigned another number as the class overloads the assignment operator. The operator works in a way similar to the copy constructor. One difference, however, is that while the constructor does not return a value, the assignment operator has to return its own object. One way to solve that problem is to use the `this` pointer, which is a pointer to the object. Every non-static method of the class can access it. As the object itself shall be returned rather than a pointer to the object, we first derefer the `this` pointer.

Two rational numbers are equal if their numerators and denominators are equal. Or are they? How about 1/2 and 2/4? They should be regarded as equal. So let us refine the rule to be that two rational numbers are equal if their numerators and denominators in their *normalized* forms are equal. A normalized rational number is a number where the numerator and the denominator have both been divided with their *Greatest Common Divider*, which is the greatest integer that divides both the numerator and the denominator. In every equality method of the class, we assume that the numbers are normalized.

When testing whether two rational numbers are equal or not, we do not have to re-invent the wheel. We just call the equality operator. The same goes for the less-than-or-equal-to, greater-than, and greater-than-or-equal-to operators. We just have to implement the less-than operator.

$$\frac{n_1}{d_1} < \frac{n_2}{d_2} \implies n_1 \cdot d_2 < n_2 \cdot d_1$$

The four rules of arithmetic are implemented in their traditional mathematical way. The result of each operation is normalized.

$$\frac{n_1}{d_1} + \frac{n_2}{d_2} \implies \frac{n_1 \cdot d_2 + n_2 \cdot d_1}{d_1 \cdot d_2} \quad \text{and} \quad \frac{n_1}{d_1} - \frac{n_2}{d_2} \implies \frac{n_1 \cdot d_2 - n_2 \cdot d_1}{d_1 \cdot d_2}$$

$$\frac{n_1}{d_1} \cdot \frac{n_2}{d_2} \implies \frac{n_1 \cdot n_2}{d_1 \cdot d_2} \quad \text{and} \quad \frac{n_1}{d_1} / \frac{n_2}{d_2} \implies \frac{d_1 \cdot d_2}{n_1 \cdot n_2}$$

We can also overload the stream operators to read and write whole rational numbers. The predefined classes `istream` and `ostream` are used. We read from the given input stream and write to the given output stream. In this way, we can read from and write to different sources, not only the keyboard and screen, but also different kinds of files. The stream operators are not methods of the class. Instead, they are freestanding functions. They are, however, *friends* of the class, which means that they can access the private and protected members of the class; in this case, the fields `m_iNumerator` and `m_iDenominator`. The friend feature is a rather debated way to circumvent the encapsulation rules. Therefore, I advise you to use it with care.

The *Greatest Common Divider* algorithm is known as the world's oldest algorithm, it was invented by the Greek mathematician Euclid in approximately 300 B.C. It is often abbreviated *gcd*.

$$gcd(iNum1,iNum2)= \begin{cases} gcd(iNum1-iNum2,iNum2,) & iNum1>iNum2 \\ gcd(iNum1,iNum2-iNum1,) & iNum1<iNum2 \\ lNum1,iNum1=iNum2 \end{cases}$$

Rational.cpp

```cpp
#include <iostream>
using namespace std;

#include <cstdlib>
#include <cassert>

#include "Rational.h"
Rational::Rational(int iNumerator, int iDenominator)
  :m_iNumerator(iNumerator),
   m_iDenominator(iDenominator)
{
  assert(m_iDenominator != 0);
  Normalize();
}
Rational::Rational(const Rational &rational)
  :m_iNumerator(rational.m_iNumerator),
   m_iDenominator(rational.m_iDenominator)
{
  // Empty.
}
Rational Rational::operator=(const Rational &rational)
{
  m_iNumerator = rational.m_iNumerator;
  m_iDenominator = rational.m_iDenominator;
```

```
    return *this;
}
bool Rational::operator==(const Rational &rational) const
{
    return (m_iNumerator == rational.m_iNumerator) &&
           (m_iDenominator == rational.m_iDenominator);
}
bool Rational::operator!=(const Rational &rational) const
{
    return !operator==(rational);
}
bool Rational::operator<(const Rational &rational) const
{
    return (m_iNumerator * rational.m_iDenominator) <
           (rational.m_iNumerator * m_iDenominator);
}
bool Rational::operator<=(const Rational &rational) const
{
    return operator<(rational) || operator==(rational);
}
bool Rational::operator>(const Rational &rational) const
{
    return !operator<=(rational);
}
bool Rational::operator>=(const Rational &rational) const
{
    return !operator<(rational);
}
Rational Rational::operator+(const Rational &rational) const
{
    int iResultNumerator = m_iNumerator*rational.m_iDenominator
                     + rational.m_iNumerator*m_iDenominator;
    int iResultDenominator = m_iDenominator *
                          rational.m_iDenominator;
    Rational result(iResultNumerator, iResultDenominator);
    result.Normalize();
    return result;
}
Rational Rational::operator-(const Rational &rational) const
{
    int iResultNumerator = m_iNumerator*rational.m_iDenominator-
                        rational.m_iNumerator*m_iDenominator;
```

```
    int iResultDenominator = m_iDenominator *
                          rational.m_iDenominator;
  Rational result(iResultNumerator, iResultDenominator);
  result.Normalize();
  return result;
}
Rational Rational::operator*(const Rational &rational) const
{
  int iResultNumerator = m_iNumerator * rational.m_iNumerator;
  int iResultDenominator = m_iDenominator *
                          rational.m_iDenominator;
  Rational result(iResultNumerator, iResultDenominator);
  result.Normalize();
  return result;
}
Rational Rational::operator/(const Rational &rational) const
{
  assert(rational.m_iNumerator != 0);
  int iResultNumerator=m_iDenominator*rational.m_iDenominator;
  int iResultDenominator=m_iNumerator*rational.m_iNumerator;
  Rational result(iResultNumerator, iResultDenominator);
  result.Normalize();
  return result;
}
istream &operator>>(istream &inputStream, Rational &rational)
{
  inputStream >> rational.m_iNumerator
            >> rational.m_iDenominator;
  return inputStream;
}
ostream &operator<<(ostream &outputStream,
                  const Rational &rational)
{
  if (rational.m_iNumerator == 0)
  {
    outputStream << "0";
  }
  else if (rational.m_iDenominator == 1)
  {
    outputStream << "1";
  }
```

```
  else
  {
    outputStream << "(" << rational.m_iNumerator << "/"
                  << rational.m_iDenominator << ")";
  }
  return outputStream;
}
void Rational::Normalize()
{
  if (m_iNumerator == 0)
  {
    m_iDenominator = 1;
    return;
  }
  if (m_iDenominator < 0)
  {
    m_iNumerator = -m_iNumerator;
    m_iDenominator = -m_iDenominator;
  }
  int iGcd = GreatestCommonDivider(abs(m_iNumerator),
                                    m_iDenominator);
  m_iNumerator /= iGcd;
  m_iDenominator /= iGcd;
}
int Rational::GreatestCommonDivider(int iNum1, int iNum2)
{
  if (iNum1 > iNum2)
  {
    return GreatestCommonDivider(iNum1 - iNum2, iNum2);
  }
  else if (iNum2 > iNum1)
  {
    return GreatestCommonDivider(iNum1, iNum2 - iNum1);
  }
  else
  {
    return iNum1;
  }
}
```

Main.cpp

```cpp
#include <iostream>
using namespace std;
#include "Rational.h"
void main()
{
  Rational a, b;
  cout << "Rational number 1: ";
  cin >> a;

  cout << "Rational number 2: ";
  cin >> b;
  cout << endl;
  cout << "a: " << a << endl;
  cout << "b: " << b << endl << endl;

  cout << "a == b: " << (a == b ? "Yes" : "No") << endl;
  cout << "a != b: " << (a != b ? "Yes" : "No") << endl;
  cout << "a <  b: " << (a <  b ? "Yes" : "No") << endl;
  cout << "a <= b: " << (a <= b ? "Yes" : "No") << endl;
  cout << "a >  b: " << (a >  b ? "Yes" : "No") << endl;
  cout << "a >= b: " << (a >= b ? "Yes" : "No") << endl
       << endl;
  cout << "a + b: " << a + b << endl;
  cout << "a - b: " << a - b << endl;
  cout << "a * b: " << a * b << endl;
  cout << "a / b: " << a / b << endl;
}
```

Exceptions

So far, we have handled errors in a rather crude way by using the assert macro. Another, more sophisticated, way is to use *exceptions*. The idea is that when an error occurs, the method throws an exception instead of returning a value. The calling method can choose to handle the exception or to ignore it, in which case it is in turn thrown to its calling method and so on. If no method catches the exception, the execution of the program will finally abort with an error message.

The idea behind exceptions is that the method who discovers the error just throws an exception. It is the calling method that decides what to do with it. The main advantage with exceptions is that we do not have to check for errors after every function call; an exception is thrown at one point in the code and caught at another point. There is a predefined class *exception* that can be thrown. It is also possible to throw exception of other classes, which may be a subclass of exception, but it does not have to.

Exception.cpp

```cpp
#include <iostream>
#include <exception>
using namespace std;
double divide(double dNumerator, double dDenominator)
{
  if (dDenominator == 0)
  {
    throw exception("Division by zero.");
  }
  return dNumerator / dDenominator;
}
double invers(double dValue)
{
  return divide(1, dValue);
}
void main()
{
  double dValue;
  cout << ": ";
  cin >> dValue;
  try
  {
    cout << "1 / " << dValue << " = " << invers(dValue)
         << endl;
  }
  catch (exception exp)
  {
    cout << exp.what() << endl;
  }
}
```

Templates

Suppose that we need a stack of integers in an application. We could use the one
in the previous section. Then maybe we also need a stack of characters, and maybe
another one of car objects. It would certainly be a waste of time to repeat the coding
for each type of stack. Instead, we can write a `template` class with *generic* types.
When we create an object of the class, we specify the type of the stack. The condition
is that the methods, functions, and operators used are defined on the involved types;
otherwise, a linking error will occur. Due to linking issues, both the definition of
the class and the methods shall be included in the header file. The following is a
template version of the stack.

TemplateCell.h

```cpp
template <typename Type>
class Cell
{
  public:
    Cell(Type value, Cell<Type>* pNextCell);

    Type& Value() {return m_value;}
    const Type Value() const {return m_value;}
    Cell<Type>*& Next() {return m_pNextCell;}
    const Cell<Type>* Next() const {return m_pNextCell;}

  private:
    Type m_value;
    Cell<Type>* m_pNextCell;
};

template <typename Type>
Cell<Type>::Cell(Type value, Cell<Type>* pNextCell)
 :m_value(value),
  m_pNextCell(pNextCell)
{
    // Empty.
}
```

TemplateStack.h

```cpp
template <typename Type>
class TemplateStack
{
  public:
    TemplateStack();
    ~TemplateStack();

    void Push(Type value);
    void Pop();
    Type Top();
    bool IsEmpty();

  private:
    Cell<Type>* m_pFirstCell;
};

template <typename Type>
TemplateStack<Type>::TemplateStack()
 :m_pFirstCell(NULL)
{
  // Empty.
}
```

```
template <typename Type>
TemplateStack<Type>::~TemplateStack()
{
  Cell<Type>* pCurrCell = m_pFirstCell;
  while (pCurrCell != NULL)
  {
    Cell<Type>* pRemoveCell = pCurrCell;
    pCurrCell = pCurrCell->Next();
    delete pRemoveCell;
  }
}
template <typename Type>
void TemplateStack<Type>::Push(Type value)
{
    Cell<Type>* pNewCell = new Cell<Type>(value,m_pFirstCell);
    assert(pNewCell != NULL);
    m_pFirstCell = pNewCell;
}
template <typename Type>
void TemplateStack<Type>::Pop()
{
    assert(m_pFirstCell != NULL);
    Cell<Type>* pRemoveCell = m_pFirstCell;
    m_pFirstCell = m_pFirstCell->Next();
    delete pRemoveCell;
}
template <typename Type>
Type TemplateStack<Type>::Top()
{
    assert(m_pFirstCell != NULL);
    return m_pFirstCell->Value();
}
template <typename Type>
bool TemplateStack<Type>::IsEmpty()
{
    return m_pFirstCell == NULL;
}
```

Finally, there is also a freestanding template function, in which case we do not have to state the type of the parameters before we call the function.

Main.cpp

```cpp
#include <iostream>
#include <string>
using namespace std;

#include <cstdlib>
#include <cassert>

#include "TemplateCell.h"
#include "TemplateStack.h"

template <typename Type>
Type Min(Type value1, Type value2)
{
  return (value1 < value2) ? value1 : value2;
}

void main()
{
  TemplateStack<int> intStack;
  intStack.Push(1);
  intStack.Push(2);
  intStack.Push(3);

  TemplateStack<double> doubleStack;
  doubleStack.Push(1.2);
  doubleStack.Push(2.3);
  doubleStack.Push(3.4);

  int i1 = 2, i2 = 2;
  cout << Min(i1, i2) << endl; // 2

  string s1 = "abc", s2 = "def";
  cout << Min(s1, s2) << endl; // "def"
}
```

Namespaces

Code can be placed in functions and functions can be placed in classes as methods.
The next step is to create a namespace that contains classes, functions, and
global variables.

```cpp
namespace TestSpace
{
  double Square(double dValue);

  class BankAccount
  {
    public:
      BankAccount();
```

```
      double GetSaldo() const;
      void Deposit(double dAmount);
      void Withdraw(double dAmount);
    private:
      double m_dSaldo;
  };
};
double TestSpace::Square(double dValue)
{
  return dValue * dValue;
}
TestSpace::BankAccount::BankAccount()
 :m_dSaldo(0)
{
  // Empty.
}
// ...
void main()
{
  int dSquare = TestSpace::Square(3.14);
  TestSpace::BankAccount account;
  account.Deposit(1000);
  account.Withdraw(500);
  double dSaldo = account.GetSaldo();
}
```

We could also choose to use the namespace. If so, we do not have to refer to the namespace explicitly. This is what we did with the std namespace at the beginning of Chapter 1.

```
#include <iostream>
using namespace std;
namespace TestSpace
{
  // ...
};
// ...
using namespace TestSpace;
void main()
{
  cout << square(3.14);
  BankAccount account;
  account.deposit(1000);
  account.withdraw(500);
  cout << account.getSaldo();
}
```

Finally, namespaces can be nested. A namespace may hold another namespace, which in turn can hold another namespace and so on.

```cpp
#include <iostream>
using namespace std;
namespace Space1
{
  namespace Space2
  {
    double Square(double dValue);
  };
};
double Space1::Space2::Square(double dValue)
{
  return dValue * dValue;
}
void main(void)
{
  cout << Space1::Space2::Square(3);
}
```

Streams and File Processing

We can open, write to, read from, and close files with the help of *streams*. Streams are predefined classes. ifstream is used to read from files, and ofstream is used to write to files. They are subclasses of istream and ostream in the operator overload section above. The program below reads a series of integers from the text file input. txt and writes their squares to the file output.txt. The stream operator returns false when there are no more values to be read from the file. Note that we do not have to close the file at the end of the program, the destructor will take care of that.

TextStream.cpp

```cpp
#include <iostream>
#include <fstream>
using namespace std;
void main(void)
{
  ifstream inFile("Input.txt", ios::in);
  ofstream outFile("Output.txt", ios::out);
  int iValue;
  while (inFile >> iValue)
  {
    outFile << (iValue * iValue) << endl;
  }
}
```

The text files are written in plain text and can be viewed by the editor.

Input.txt

```
1
2
3
4
5
```

Output.txt

```
1
4
9
16
25
```

We can also read and write binary data with the stream classes. The program below writes the numbers 1 to 10 to the file `Numbers.bin` and then reads the same series of values from the file. The methods `write` and `read` take the address of the value to be read or written and the size of the value in bytes. They return the number of bytes actually read or written. When reading, we can check whether we have reached the end of the file by counting the number of read bytes; if it is zero, we have reached the end. Even though we do not have to close the file, it is appropriate to do so when the file has been written so that the values are safely saved before we open the same file for reading.

BinaryStreams.cpp

```cpp
#include <iostream>
#include <fstream>
using namespace std;
void main(void)
{
  ofstream outFile("Numbers.bin", ios::out);
  for (int iIndex = 1; iIndex <= 10; ++iIndex)
  {
    outFile.write((char*) &iIndex, sizeof iIndex);
  }
  outFile.close();
  ifstream inFile("Numbers.bin", ios::in);
  int iValue;
  while (inFile.read((char*) &iValue, sizeof iValue) != 0)
  {
      cout << iValue << endl;
  }
}
```

The values are stored in compressed form in the binary file `Numbers.bin`, which is why they are not readable in the editor. Here is a screen dump of the file:

```
Numbers.bin
00000000   01 00 00 00 02 00 00 00   03 00 00 00 04 00 00 00   ................
00000010   05 00 00 00 06 00 00 00   07 00 00 00 08 00 00 00   ................
00000020   09 00 00 00 0D 0A 00 00   00                        .........
```

Even though these file processing techniques are of use in many situations, we will not use them in the applications of this book. Instead, we will use the technique of *Serialization*, described in Chapter 3.

Summary

- The object-oriented model rests on the three cornerstones *inheritance*, *encapsulation*, and *dynamic binding* as well as the five relations *instance*, *inheritance*, *aggregation*, *connection*, and *call*.

- An object can be created as an *instance* of a class. A class consists of two types of *members*: *methods* (member functions) and *fields* (member variables). A member can be *private*, *protected*, or *public*. The methods of a class can be divided into constructors, inspectors, modifications, and one destructor.

- A class can *inherit* one or more, other baseclasses with its members. A method of the baseclass can be *virtual*, resulting in *dynamic binding*.

- An array can hold a sequence of objects. The classes of those objects have to have a default constructor or no constructor at all in order for the objects to be thoroughly initialized.

- With the help of pointers and classes, we can create a linked list, which is a very useful structure. With its help, we can construct a stack.

- We can overload the usual operators so they take objects as operands. However, we cannot affect the number of operands, nor the precedence or associativity of the operators.

- We can use the *this* pointer to access our own object and we can define functions as *friends* to a class.

- Exception handling is an elegant error handling method. When an error occurs, we throw an exception. The point in the exception may or may not be handled in another part of the code. In either case, we do not have to worry about that when the error occurs.

- We can define template classes, which are instantiated with suitable types when we instantiate objects. We can also define template functions that take parameters of different types.

- We can organize our classes, freestanding functions, and global variables into namespace.

- We can read from and write to text and binary files with the predefined classes `ifstream` and `ofstream`.

3
Windows Development

The development environment of choice in this book is the Visual Studio from Microsoft. In this chapter we also study the Microsoft Foundation Classes (MFC).

- Visual Studio provides us with a few Wizards — tools that help us generate code. The Application Wizard creates an *application framework* (a skeleton application) to which we add the specific logic and behavior of our application.

- When developing a Windows application, the Document/View model comes in handy. The application is divided into a document object that holds the data and performs the logic, and one or more views that take care of user input and display information on the screen.

- When an event occurs (the user clicks the mouse, the window is resized) a *message* is sent to the application, it is caught by a view object and is passed on to the document object. There are hundreds of messages in the Windows system. However, we only catch those that interest us.

- The device context can be viewed both as a canvas to paint on and as a toolbox holding pens and brushes.

- When we finish an application, we may want it to occur in the same state when we launch it the next time. This can be archived by storing vital values in the *registry*.

- Serialization is an elegant way of storing and loading values to and from a file. The framework takes care of naming, opening, and closing the file, all we have to do is to fill in the unique values of the application.

- The cursor has different appearances on different occasions. There are several predefined cursors we can use.

Visual Studio

Visual Studio is an environment for developing applications in Windows. It has a number of tools, such as an editor, compilers, linkers, a debugger, and a project manager. It also has several *Wizards* — tools designed for rapid development. The Wizard you will first encounter is the Application Wizard. It generates code for an *Application Framework*. The idea is that we use the Application Wizard to design a skeleton application that is later completed with more application-specific code. There is no real magic about wizards, all they do is generate the skeleton code. We could write the code ourselves, but it is a rather tedious job. Moreover, an application can be run in either *debug* or *release* mode. In debug mode, additional information is added in order to allow debugging; in release mode, all such information is omitted in order to make the execution as fast as possible. The code of this book is developed with Visual Studio 2008.

The Windows 32 bits Application Programming Interface (Win32 API) is a huge C function library. It contains a couple of thousand functions for managing the Windows system. With the help of Win32 API it is possible to totally control the Windows operating system. However, as the library is written in C, it could be a rather tedious job to develop a large application, even though it is quite possible. That is the main reason for the existence of the Microsoft Foundation Classes (MFC). It is a large C++ class library containing many classes encapsulating the functionality of Win32 API. It does also hold some generic classes to handle lists, maps, and arrays. MFC combines the power of Win32 API with the advantages of C++. However, on some occasions MFC is not enough. When that happens, we can simply call an appropriable Win32 API function, even though the application is written in C++ and uses MFC.

Most of the classes of MFC belong to a class hierarchy with `CObject` at the top. On some occasions, we have to let our classes inherit `CObject` in order to achieve some special functionality. The baseclass `Figure` in the Draw and Tetris applications inherits `CObject` in order to read or write objects of unknown classes. The methods `UpdateAllViews` and `OnUpdate` communicate by sending pointers to `CObject` objects. The Windows main class is `CWnd`.

In this environment, there is no function `main`. Actually, there is a `main`, but it is embedded in the framework. We do not write our own `main` function, and there is not one generated by the Application Wizard. Instead, there is the object `theApp`, which is an instance of the application class. The application is launched by its constructor.

When the first version of MFC was released, there was no standard logical type in C++. Therefore, the type BOOL with the values TRUE and FALSE was introduced. After that, the type *bool* was introduced to C++. We must use BOOL when dealing with MFC method calls, and we could use *bool* otherwise. However, in order to keep things simple, let us use BOOL everywhere.

In the same way, there is a MFC class `CString` that we must use when calling MFC methods. We could use the C++ built-in class `string` otherwise. However, let us use `CString` everywhere. The two classes are more or less equivalent.

As mentioned in Chapter 1, there are two types for storing a character, `char` and `wchar_t`. In earlier version of Windows, you were supposed to use `char` for handling text, and In more modern versions you use `wchar_t`. In order to make our application independent of which version it is run on, there are two macros `TCHAR` and `TEXT`. `TCHAR` is the character type that replaces `char` and `wchar_t`. `TEXT` is intended to encapsulate character and string constants.

```
TCHAR *pBuffer;
stScore.Format(TEXT("Score: %d."), iScore);
```

There is also the MFC type `BYTE` which holds a value of the size of one byte, and `UINT` which is shorthand for unsigned integer. Finally, all generated framework classes have a capital C at the beginning of the name. The classes we write ourselves do not.

The Document/View Model

The applications in this book are based on the Document/View model. Its main idea is to have two classes with different responsibilities. Let us say we name the application *Demo*, the Application Wizard will name the document class `CDemoDoc` and the view class will be named `CDemoView`. The view class has two responsibilities: to accept input from the user by the keyboard or the mouse, and to repaint the client area (partly or completely) at the request of the document class or the system. The document's responsibility is mainly to manage and modify the application data.

The model comes in two forms: Single Document Interface (SDI) and Multiple Document Interface (MDI). When the application starts, a document object and a view object are created, and connected to each other. In the SDI, it will continue that way. In the MDI form, the users can then add or remove as many views they want to. There is always exactly one document object, but there may be one or more view objects, or no one at all.

The objects are connected to each other by pointers. The document object has a list of pointers to the associated view objects. Each view object has a field m_pDocument that points at the document object. When a change in the document's data has occurred, the document instructs all of its views to repaint their client area by calling the method UpdateAllViews in order to reflect the change.

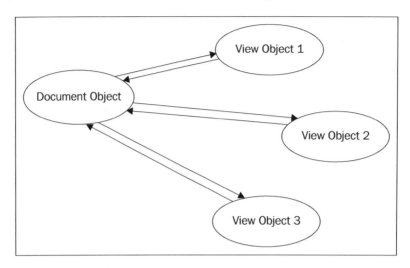

The Message System

Windows is built on messages. When the users press one of the mouse buttons or a key, when they resize a window, or when they select a menu item, a message is generated and sent to the current appropriate class.

The messages are routed by a *message map*. The map is generated by the Application Wizard. It can be modified manually or with the *Properties Window View* (the Messages or Events button).

The message map is declared in the file class' header file as follows:

```
DECLARE_MESSAGE_MAP()
```

The message map is implemented in the class' implementation file as follows:

```
BEGIN_MESSAGE_MAP(this_class, base_class)
  // Message handlers.
END_MESSAGE_MAP()
```

Each message has it own handle, and is connected to a method of a specific form that catches the message. There are different handlers for different types of messages. There are around 200 messages in Windows. Here follows a table with the most common ones. Note that we do not have to catch every message. We just catch those we are interested in, the rest will be handled by the framework.

Message	Handler/Method	Sent
WM_CREATE	ON_WM_CREATE/OnCreate	When the window is created, but not yet shown.
WM_SIZE	ON_WM_SIZE/OnSize	When the window has been resized.
WM_MOVE	ON_WM_MOVE/OnMove	When the window has been moved.
WM_SETFOCUS	ON_WM_SETFOCUS/ OnSetFocus	When the window receives input focus.
WM_KILLFOCUS	ON_WM_KILLFOCUS/ OnKillFocus	When the window loses input focus.
WM_VSCROLL	ON_WM_VSCROLL/ OnVScroll	When the user scrolls the vertical bar.
WM_HSCROLL	ON_WM_HSCROLL/ OnHScroll	When the user scrolls the horizontal bar.
WM_LBUTTONDOWN	ON_WM_LBUTTONDOWN/ OnLButtonDown	When the user presses the left, middle, or right mouse button.
WM_MBUTTONDOWN	ON_WM_MBUTTONDOWN/ OnMButtonDown	
WM_RBUTTONDOWN	ON_WM_RBUTTONDOWN/ OnRButtonDown	
WM_MOUSEMOVE	ON_WM_MOUSEMOVE/ OnMouseMove	When the user moves the mouse, there are flags available to decide whether the buttons are pressed.
WM_LBUTTONUP	ON_WM_LBUTTONUP/ OnLButtonUp	When the user releases the left, middle, or right button.
WM_MBUTTONUP	ON_WM_MUTTONUP/ OnMButtonUp	
WM_RBUTTONUP	ON_WM_RUTTONUP/ OnRButtonUp	
WM_CHAR	ON_WM_CHAR/OnChar	When the user inputs a writable character on the keyboard.

Message	Handler/Method	Sent
WM_KEYDOWN	ON_WM_KEYDOWN/ OnKeyDown	When the user presses a key on the keyboard.
WM_KEYUP	ON_WM_KEYUP/ OnKeyUp	When the user releases a key on the keyboard.
WM_PAINT	ON_WM_PAINT/OnPaint	When the client area of the window needs to be repainted, partly or completely.
WM_CLOSE	ON_WM_CLOSE/OnClose	When the user clicks at the close button in the upper right corner of the window.
WM_DESTROY	ON_WM_DESTROY/ OnDestroy	When the window is to be closed.
WM_COMMAND	ON_COMMAND(Identifier, Name)/OnName	When the user selects a menu item, a toolbar button, or an accelerator key connected to the identifier.
WM_COMMAND_ UPDATE	ON_COMMAND_ UPDATE_ UI(Identifier,Name)/ OnUpdateName	During idle time, when the system is not busy with any other task, this message is sent in order to enable/disable or to check menu items and toolbar buttons.

When a user selects a menu item, a command message is sent to the application. Thanks to MFC, the message can be routed to virtually any class in the application. However, in the applications of this book, all menu messages are routed to the document class. It is possible to connect an accelerator key or a toolbar button to the same message, simply by giving it the same identity number.

Moreover, when the system is in idle mode (not busy with any other task) the *command update* message is sent to the application. This gives us an opportunity to check or disable some of the menu items. For instance, the **Save** item in the **File** menu should be grayed (disabled) when the document has not been modified and does not have to be saved. Say that we have a program where the users can paint in one of three colors. The current color should be marked by a radio box.

The message map and its methods can be written manually or be generated with the Resource View (the **View** menu in Visual Studio) which can help us generate the method prototype, its skeleton definition, and its entry in the message map.

The *Resource* is a system of graphical objects that are linked to the application. When the framework is created by the Application Wizard, the standard menu bar and toolbar are included. We can add our own menus and buttons in Resource Editor, a graphical tool of Visual Studio.

For more information about creating a framework application and handling messages, see the Ring Application in the next chapter.

The Coordinate System

In Windows, there are device (physical) and logical coordinates. There are several logical coordinate mapping systems in Windows. The simplest one is the text system; it simply maps one physical unit to the size of a pixel, which means that graphical figures will have different size monitors with different sizes or resolutions. This system is used in the Ring and Tetris applications.

The metric system maps one physical unit to a tenth of a millimeter (low metric) or a hundredth of a millimeter (high metric). The Draw, Calc, and Word applications of this book use the high metric system. There is also the British system that maps one physical unit to a hundredth of an inch (low English) or a thousandth of an inch (high English). The British system is not used in this book.

The position of a mouse click is always given in device units. When a part of the client area is invalidated (marked for repainting), the coordinates are also given in device units, and when we create or locate the caret, we use device coordinates. Except for these events, we translate the positions into logical units of our choice. We do not have to write translation routines ourselves, there are device context methods LPtoDP (Logical Point to Device Point) and DPtoLP (Device Point to Logical Point) in the next section that do the job for us. The setting of the logical unit system is done in OnInitialUpdate and OnPrepareDC in the view classes.

In the Ring and Tetris Applications, we just ignore the coordinates system and use pixels. In the Draw application, the view class is a subclass of the MFC class CScrollView. It has a method SetScrollSizes that takes the logical coordinate system and the total size of the client area (in logical units). Then the mapping between the device and logical system is done automatically and the scroll bars are set to appropriate values when the view is created and each time its size is changed.

```
void SetScrollSizes(int nMapMode, CSize sizeTotal,
                    const CSize& sizePage = sizeDefault,
                    const CSize& sizeLine = sizeDefault);
```

In the Calc and Word Applications, however, we set the mapping between the device and logical system manually by overriding the `OnPrepareDC` method. It calls the method `SetMapMode` which sets the logical horizontal and vertical units to be equal. This ensures that circles will be kept round. The MFC device context method `GetDeviceCaps` returns the size of the screen in pixels and millimeters. Those values are used in the call to `SetWindowExt` and `SetViewportExt`, so that the logical unit is one hundredth of a millimeter also in those applications. The `SetWindowOrg` method sets the origin of the view's client area in relation to the current positions of the scroll bars, which implies that we can draw figures and text without regarding the current positions of the scroll bars.

```
int SetMapMode(int iMapMode);
int GetDeviceCaps(int iIndex) const;
CSize SetWindowExt(CSize szScreen);
CSize SetViewportExt(CSize szScreen);
CPoint SetWindowOrg(CPoint ptorigin);
```

The Device Context

The device context can be thought of as a toolbox, equipped with pens and brushes, as well as a canvas on which we can draw lines, paint figures, and write text. It also contains methods for converting between device and logical units. Finally, it can be regarded as a connection between our program and the screen or printer.

In Windows, a window usually has a frame with an icon at the top left corner, buttons to resize the window at the top right corner and, possibly a menu bar, a toolbar, and a status bar. the white area inside the frame is called the *client area*. With the help of a device context, we can paint the client area.

When the view class is created with the Application Wizard, the method `OnDraw` is included. It takes a parameter `pCD` that is a pointer to a device context. The device context class `CDC` is a very central part of a Windows application. However, `CDC` is an abstract class, a device context object is instantiated from the subclass `ClientDC`. In order to draw lines or paint areas we need a pen and a brush.

```
CPen(int iPenStyle, int iWidth, COLORREF crColor);
CBrush(COLORREF crColor);
```

The pen style can be solid, dashed, or dotted. However, in the applications of this book, we settle with the solid style. If the width of the line is set to zero, the line will be drawn as thin as possible (one pixel) on the output device (screen or printer). We also need to select the pen and brush for the device context, and when we have used them, we reset the drawing system by returning the previous ones.

```
void GraphicalClass::Draw(CDC* pDC) const
{
  CPen pen(PS_SOLID, 0, BLACK);
  CBrush brush(WHITE);

  CPen* pOldPen = pDC->SelectObject(&pen);
  CBrush* pOldBrush = pDC->SelectObject(&brush);

  // Painting the client area.

  pDC->SelectObject(&pOldBrush);
  pDC->SelectObject(&pOldPen);
}
```

For drawing and painting, there are a number of methods to call.

```
BOOL MoveTo(int x, int y);
BOOL LineTo(int x, int y);
BOOL Rectangle(int x1, int y1, int x2, int y2);
BOOL Ellipse(int x1, int y1, int x2, int y2);
```

When we write text, we do not have to select a pen or a brush. Instead, we set the text and background colors directly by calling the methods below. They return the previous set text and background color, respectively. We do not have to put back the previous colors.

```
COLORREF SetTextColor(COLORREF crColor);
COLORREF SetBkColor(COLORREF crColor);
```

DrawText does the actual writing of the text. Besides the text, it takes the rectangle where the text will be written inside. It also takes a number of flags to align the text in the rectangle. Possible flags for horizontal alignment are DT_LEFT, DT_CENTER, and DT_RIGHT, possible flags for vertical alignment are DT_TOP, DT_VCENTER, and DT_BOTTOM. If there is not enough room for the text in the given rectangle, the text is wrapped. That can be avoided with the DT_SINGLE_LINE flag. TextOut is a simpler version of DrawText. It takes a position and text that are by default written with the position at its top left corner. It can be combined with a preceding call to SetTextAlign that sets the horizontal and vertical alignment of the written text.

```
int DrawText(const CString& stText, LPRECT pRect,
             UINT uFormat);
BOOL TextOut(int xPos, int yPos, const CString& stText);
UINT SetTextAlign(UINT uFlags);
```

`SetTextJustification` is a rather special method that is used in the Calc application to write the values of cells. It ensures that the following calls to `DrawText` insert extra long spaces between the words in order to display the text in justified horizontal alignment. It takes the total width of the spaces and the number of spaces as parameters. After the writing of the text, we should reset the alignment with another call to `SetTextJustification` to prevent succeeding calls to `DrawText` to write with justified alignment. The horizontal alignment is irrelevant when the call to `DrawText` has been preceded by a call to `SetTextJustification`.

```
int SetTextJustification(int iTotalSpaceWidth,
                         int iNumberOfSpaces);
```

However, before we write text, we have to select a font. In the applications of this book, the font is represented by the `Font` class later in this chapter. Note that the font size is stored in typographical points (1/72 inch) and needs to be translated into logical units.

```
void GraphicalClass::Draw(CDC* pDC) const
{
  Font font("Times New Roman", 12);
  CFont cFont;
  cFont.CreateFontIndirect(font.PointsToMeters());
  CFont* pPrevFont = pDC->SelectObject(&cFont);

  pDC->SetTextColor(BLACK);
  pDC->SetBgColor(WHITE);

  pDC->DrawText("Hello, World!", CRect(0, 0, 1000, 1000),
              DT_SINGLELINE | DT_CENTER | DT_VCENTER);
  pDC->SelectObject(pPrevFont);
}
```

`GetTextMetrics` fills a structure with information about the average dimension of a text written in a specific font. The measured values are given in logical units.

```
typedef struct tagTEXTMETRIC
{
  LONG tmHeight;        // Height of the text.
  LONG tmAscent;        // Ascent line of the text.
  LONG tmAveCharWidth;  // Average width of the text, roughly
                        // equal to the width of the character
                        // 'z'.
  LONG tmDescent;
  LONG tmInternalLeading;
  LONG tmExternalLeading;
  LONG tmMaxCharWidth;
  LONG tmWeight;
```

```
      LONG tmOverhang;
      LONG tmDigitizedAspectX;
      LONG tmDigitizedAspectY;
      TCHAR tmFirstChar;
      TCHAR tmLastChar;
      TCHAR tmDefaultChar;
      TCHAR tmBreakChar;
      BYTE tmItalic;
      BYTE tmUnderlined;
      BYTE tmStruckOut;
      BYTE tmPitchAndFamily;
      BYTE tmCharSet;
    } TEXTMETRIC, *PTEXTMETRIC;
```

```
    BOOL GetTextMetrics(TEXTMETRIC* pTextMetrics) const;
```

Of the fields above, we will only use the first three ones in the applications of this book. This method will be called when we actually do not have any text to write (an empty cell or an empty paragraph), but when we, nevertheless, need information about the width, height, and ascent line of text in a particular font. See *The Word Application* chapter for a description of the ascent line.

When we have a text to write, we can use GetTextExtent instead. It takes a text and returns the size of it in the selected font in logical units.

```
    CSize GetTextExtent(const CString& stText) const;
```

When the user clicks the mouse on a certain position, the position is given in device coordinates that need to be translated into logical coordinates. When a part of the client area is to be marked for repainting (invalidated), the area should be given in device coordinates. DPtoLP (Device Coordinates to Logical Coordinates) and LPtoDP (Logical Coordinates to Device Coordinates) translates MFC class objects CSize, and CRect, and (one or more) CPoint objects between logical and device coordinates.

```
    void DPtoLP(CSize* pSize) const;
    void DPtoLP(CRect* pRect) const;
    void DPtoLP(CPoint* pPoints, int iNumberofPoints = 1) const;
    void LPtoDP(CSize* pSize) const;
    void LPtoDP(CRect* pRect) const;
    void LPtoDP(CPoint* pPoints, int iNumberOfPoints = 1) const;
```

IntersectClipRect limits the invalidated area (the part of the client area that is to be repainted).

```
    int IntersectClipRect(CRect* pRect);
```

All of the methods above return true if the operation was successful.

The Registry

The registry is a series of files, stored on the local hard drive, that stores application specific information. The MFC application class CWinApp has a number of methods to communicate with the registry. It is possible to read or write an integer, a block of memory, or a string. The global MFC function AfxGetApp returns a pointer to the application class object. There can only be one such object. The stSection in the methods below is usually the name of the application and the stEntry is the name of the value.

GetProfileBinary returns true if the reading was successful. GetProfileInt and GetProfileString take a default value that is returned if the entry was not found. WriteProfileBinary, WriteProfileInt, and WriteProfileString all return true on successful writing.

```
UINT GetProfileInt(CString stSection, CString stEntry, int iDefault);
CString GetProfileString(CString stSection, CString stEntry,
                    CString stDefault);
BOOL GetProfileBinary(CString stSection, CString stEntry,
                    LPBYTE* ppData, UINT* pBytes);

BOOL WriteProfileInt(CString stSection, CString stEntry, int nValue);
BOOL WriteProfileString(CString stSection, CString stEntry,
                    CString stValue);
BOOL WriteProfileBinary(CString stSection, CString stEntry,
                    LPBYTE pData, UINT nBytes);
```

The Cursor

The message WM_CURSOR is sent to the view class when the application is in idle mode (not busy with anything else). The answer to the message is handled to the preferred cursor. There are a number of standard cursors that are returned by the CWinApp method LoadStandardCursor. The global function AfxGetApp returns a pointer to the application object (there is only one). The cursor is set in the view class by the SetCursor Win32 API function.

```
CWinApp* AfxGetApp();
HCURSOR LoadStandardCursor(CString stCursorName) const;
HCURSOR SetCursor(HCURSOR hCursor);
```

The parameter `stCursorName` could be any of the following predefined constants.

IDC_ARROW	Standard arrow cursor.
IDC_IBEAM	Standard text-insertion cursor.
IDC_CROSS	Cross-hair cursor for selection.
IDC_SIZEALL	A four-pointed arrow, the cursor used to resize a window.
IDC_SIZEWE	Horizontal two-headed arrow.
IDC_SIZENS	Vertical two-headed arrow.
IDC_SIZENWSE	Two-headed arrow aimed at the upper left and lower right corner.
IDC_SIZENESW	Two-headed arrow aimed at the upper right and lower left corner.

Serialization

Serialization is the process of writing to and reading from a file. When the user chooses to open or save a file, the framework calls the method `Serialize` of the document class. Every serialized class must have a default constructor and implement the serial macro. If we read an object of an unknown class, which we do in the Tetris and Draw applications, the class must be a subclass of the MFC root class `CObject`.

We can store or load values in three ways. If we want to read or write a block of memory (such as an array), we can use the `CArchive` methods `Write` and `Read` to transfer a block between the file and the memory. `Read` takes the maximum number of bytes (the buffer size) to be read to the buffer and returns the number of bytes actually read.

```
void Write(const void* pBuffer, UINT uSize);
UINT Read(void* pBuffer, UINT uMaxSize);
```

For the basic types of C++, the stream operators are overloaded. Many classes define their own `Serialize`; in that case, we just have to call it with the archive object as parameter. The following code comes from the Tetris application.

```
void CRingDoc::Serialize(CArchive& archive)
{
  if (archive.IsStoring())
  {
    archive << m_iRow << m_iCol;
    archive.Write(&m_northArray, sizeof m_northArray);
  }
```

```
      if (archive.IsLoading())
      {
        archive >> m_iRow >> m_iCol;
        archive.Read(&m_northArray, sizeof m_northArray);
      }
      m_font.Serialize(archive);
    }
```

On some occasions, we do not know which class the object to be read or written is an instance of. In those cases, we can use the methods WriteClass, ReadClass, WriteObject, and ReadObject. When writing an object, we first write information about its class. We can extract that information with the CObject method GetRuntimeClass that returns a pointer to an object of CRuntimeClass. As GetRuntimeClass is a method of CObject, the class of the object to be read or written must be a (direct or indirect) subclass of CObject.

```
CRuntimeClass* GetRuntimeClass() const;
void WriteClass(const CRuntimeClass* pClass);
void WriteObject(const CObject* pObject);
CRuntimeClass* ReadClass(const CRuntimeClass* pClass);
CObject* ReadObject(const CRuntimeClass* pClass);
```

When writing an object, we first call WriteClass to store information about the object, and then we call WriteObject to store the object itself. Likewise, when reading an object, we first call ReadClass to read information about the next object in the file, and then we call ReadObject to read the actual object. This technique is used in the Tetris and Draw applications, the following code is from the Draw application. Figure is an abstract baseclass and we store and load objects of subclasses to Figure. In each case, we do not know which subclass, we only know that it is a subclass of Figure.

```
Figure* pFigure = m_figurePtrList.GetAt(position);
archive.WriteClass(pFigure->GetRuntimeClass());
archive.WriteObject(pFigure);

CRuntimeClass* pClass = archive.ReadClass();
Figure* pFigure = (Figure*) archive.ReadObject(pClass);
m_figurePtrList.AddTail(pFigure);
```

Summary

- The Application Wizard creates an application framework that we extend with code specific for the application. The Class Wizard helps us catch and handle messages.

- The document/view model consists of one document object, handling the application logic, and one or several view objects, handling user input and data presentation.

- Every time an event occurs, a message is sent to the application in focus. We can generate handling code with Class Wizard.

- The device context can be viewed both as a canvas to paint on, a toolbox holding pens and brushes, and a connection to the screen and printer.

- Between executions, we can store the state of the application in the registry.

- The cursor can be set to standard representations.

- We can save and load document data by the means of Serialization.

4

Ring: A Demonstration Example

This chapter presents a simple Windows application, with the purpose of introducing the features of MFC. When the user clicks the left mouse button, a ring is drawn. The user can choose the color of the next ring as well as save and load the set of rings. We will start by creating the framework with the help of the Application Wizard, and then add application specific code.

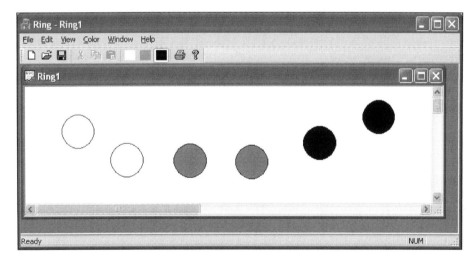

- We store the colors and positions of the ring in an array. There is a predefined type COLORREF holding a color.

- When the user presses or releases the mouse, messages are sent to the application. We use the Class Wizard to create methods that detect the messages.

- We can paint the rings by overriding the `Draw` method and using the methods of the Device Context.

- The paint area may not fit into the window. We can add scroll bars and define the size of the underlying canvas.

- As well as detecting mouse clicks, we can also write methods that detect when the user presses a keyboard key.

- In order to increase the user-friendliness of the application, we can add menus, accelerators, and toolbars.

- Using the RGB standard, we can theoretically handle more than 16 million colors. These colors are easier to handle with a Color Dialog.

- When finishing the application, we can store the latest used color in the registry. When starting the application, we read the state from the registry.

- Finally, we save and load the colors and positions of the rings by using Serialization.

The Application Wizard

Let us start by selecting **New Project** in the **File** menu and choosing **Visual C++** Projects and **MFC Application** with the name **Ring** and a suitable place on the hard drive.

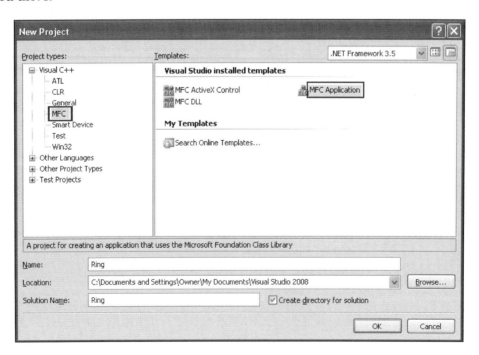

Then we get the first of several Application Wizard dialogs.

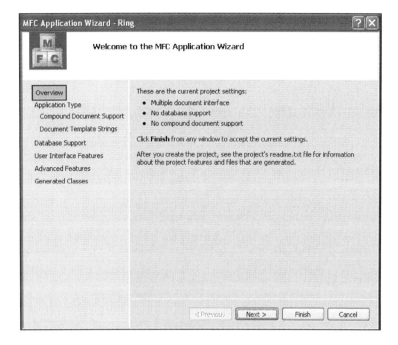

We select **Application Type** and accept the default settings.

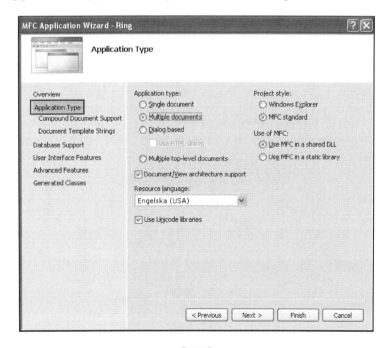

The same goes for **Compound Document Support**.

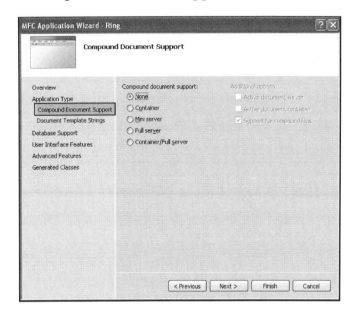

When we come to **Document Template Strings** we add **Rng** for the **File extension**. Otherwise, we accept the default settings.

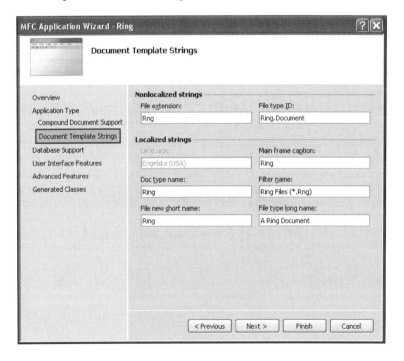

We have no **Database Support** in this application, so we accept the default settings.

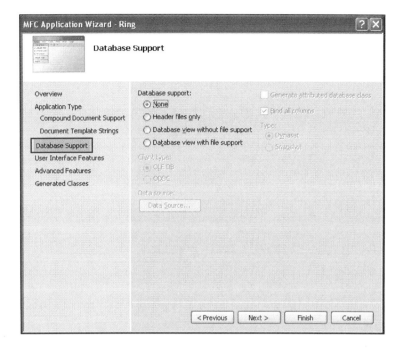

In **User Interface Features**, we accept the default settings.

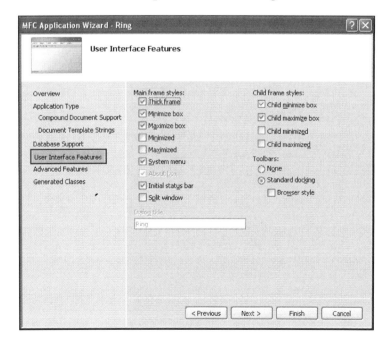

The same goes for **Advanced Features**.

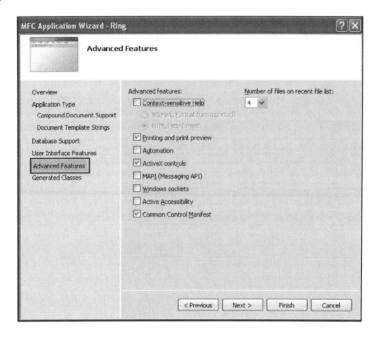

We change the base class of **CRingView** from **CView** to **CScrollView**.

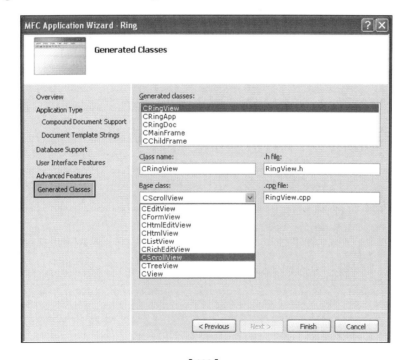

We finally choose **Finish**, and a fully functional application is generated. We can now compile and run this generated application code. Here is a snapshot of the application.

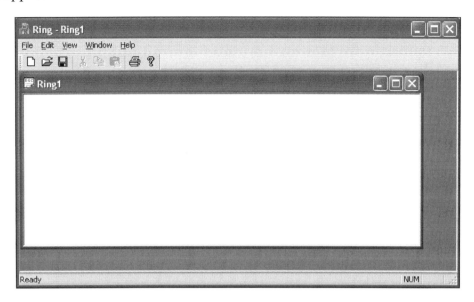

This is the main idea of the Application Framework and the Application Wizard. By now, we have generated a framework to which we will add application-specific functionality. We will only modify the classes CRingDoc and CRingView. We will not change anything in the other classes generated by the Application Wizard.

Colors and Arrays

Let us first look at CRingDoc. We start by adding two types, ColorArray and PointArray. As the names implies, they are arrays of colors and points. The Win32 API type COLORREF stores a color according to the RGB (Red, Green, Blue) standard. There is also a class CPoint defined in MFC; it handles a point in a two-dimensional coordinate system. In order to create an array, we can use the MFC template class CArray. To do so, we have to include the header file AfxTempl.h.

We will need three colors: WHITE, GREY, and BLACK. We can use the RGB macro to define them as static constants. Let us finally add two private fields to the class: m_colorArray and m_pointArray.

RingDoc.h

```cpp
// RingDoc.h : interface of the CRingDoc class
//
#include <AfxTempl.h>
typedef CArray<CPoint> PointArray;
typedef CArray<COLORREF> ColorArray;
static const COLORREF WHITE = RGB(255, 255, 255);
static const COLORREF GREY = RGB(128, 128, 128);
static const COLORREF BLACK = RGB(0, 0, 0);
class CRingDoc : public CDocument
{
protected: // create from serialization only
  CRingDoc();
  DECLARE_DYNCREATE(CRingDoc)
// Attributes
public:
// Operations
public:
// Overrides
  public:
  virtual BOOL OnNewDocument();
  virtual void Serialize(CArchive& ar);
// Implementation
public:
  virtual ~CRingDoc();
#ifdef _DEBUG
  virtual void AssertValid() const;
  virtual void Dump(CDumpContext& dc) const;
#endif
protected:

// Generated message map functions
protected:
  DECLARE_MESSAGE_MAP()

private:
  PointArray m_pointArray;
  ColorArray m_colorArray;
};
```

Catching the Mouse

When the user clicks the left mouse button, a message is sent from Windows to the application. We can catch the message by opening the file `RingView.cpp`, choosing **View** and **Properties Window,** and the **Message** button. Then we connect the function `OnLeftButtonDown` to the message `WM_LBUTTONDOWN`.

Then we have a function prototype in the RingView.h file and a skeleton function definition in the RingView.cpp file.

RingView.cpp

```
void CRingView::OnLButtonDown(UINT nFlags, CPoint point)
{
  // TODO: Add your message handler code here and/or call
  // default.
  CScrollView::OnLButtonDown(nFlags, point);
}
```

We modify the function by sending the message from the view to the document.

RingView.cpp

```
void CRingView::OnLButtonDown(UINT nFlags, CPoint point)
{
  CRingDoc* pDoc = GetDocument();
  ASSERT_VALID(pDoc);
  pDoc->MouseDown(point);
  CScrollView::OnLButtonDown(nFlags, point);
}
```

After that, we have to add the function MouseDown to the document class. We do also add two functions for accessing the point and color arrays.

RingDoc.h

```
class CRingDoc : public CDocument
{
// ...
public:
  void MouseDown(CPoint point);

  PointArray& GetPointArray() {return m_pointArray;}
  ColorArray& GetColorArray() {return m_colorArray;}
};
```

UpdateAllViews indirectly calls OnUpdate in the view class, which in turns calls OnDraw.

RingDoc.cpp

```
void CRingDoc::MouseDown(CPoint point) // CRingDoc.cpp
{
  m_pointArray.Add(point);
  m_colorArray.Add(WHITE);
  UpdateAllViews(NULL);
}
```

Drawing the Rings

So far, we cannot see any rings when we execute the program. The missing piece is the drawing function. Its name is OnDraw and it is already defined in CRingView, all we have to do is to add some painting code.

We create a pen with a one-pixel-width solid black line, and a brush with the specified color. The color of the brush is white. However, we will change that later on in the application. We use the device context to add the pen and brush; afterwards, we have to restore the old pen and brush. We also use the device context to draw the rings.

RingView.cpp

```
void CRingView::OnDraw(CDC* pDC)
{
  CRingDoc* pDoc = GetDocument();
  ASSERT_VALID(pDoc);
  if (!pDoc)
```

```
      return;
  PointArray& pointArray = pDoc->GetPointArray();
  ColorArray& colorArray = pDoc->GetColorArray();
  int iSize = (int) pointArray.GetSize();
  for (int iIndex = 0; iIndex < iSize; ++iIndex)
  {
    CPoint point = pointArray[iIndex];
    COLORREF color = colorArray[iIndex];
    CPen pen(PS_SOLID, 0, BLACK);
    CBrush brush(color);
    pDC->Ellipse(point.x - 10, point.y - 10,
                 point.x + 10, point.y + 10);
    CPen* pOldPen = pDC->SelectObject(&pen);
    CBrush* pOldBrush = pDC->SelectObject(&brush);
  }
}
```

Now, the first version of the application is finished. Please feel free to test it.

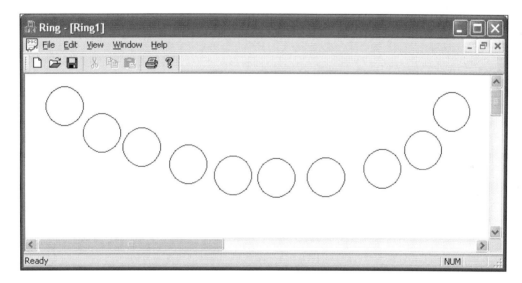

Setting the Coordinate System and the Scroll Bars

So far, the rings are drawn with a radius of 10 pixels, which means that we cannot define an exact radius measured in inches or meters (or at least not without research, the pixel size of every screen we execute the application on). We can address the problem by modifying OnInitialUpdate.

RingView.cpp

```
void CRingView::OnInitialUpdate()
{
  CScrollView::OnInitialUpdate();
  CSize sizeTotal;
  // TODO: calculate the total size of this view
  sizeTotal.cx = sizeTotal.cy = 100;
  SetScrollSizes(MM_TEXT, sizeTotal);
}
```

The function SetScrollSizes sets the scroll bars to reflect the chosen coordinate system. Let us chose the metric system with high resolution: MM_HIMETRIC; one logical unit is a hundredth of a millimeter. We set the page to correspond to a letter with a width of 216 millimetres and a height of 279 millimetres; we set the height of a line to 5 millimeters and the height of a page to 50 millimeters.

RingView.cpp

```
void CRingView::OnInitialUpdate()
{
  CScrollView::OnInitialUpdate();
  CSize sizeTotal;
  CSize sizeLine(500, 500);
  CSize sizePage(5000, 5000);
  CSize sizeTotal(216000, 27900);
  SetScrollSizes(MM_HIMETRIC, sizeTotal, sizePage, sizeLine);
}
```

We have now two problems: the first one is that the mouse handler function OnLButtonDown receives its position in physical coordinates. It must be transformed into logical coordinates. In order to do so, we first need to create and prepare our own device context. That is, an object of the class CClientDC, and call the function DPtoLP (Device Point at Logical Point).

RingView.cpp

```
void CRingView::OnLButtonDown(UINT nFlags, CPoint point)
{
  CRingDoc* pDoc = GetDocument();
  ASSERT_VALID(pDoc);
  CClientDC dc(this);
  OnPrepareDC(&dc);
  dc.DPtoLP(&point);
  pDoc->MouseDown(point);
  CScrollView::OnLButtonDown(nFlags, point);
}
```

The second problem is that we have still specified the radius of the circles to 10 units. Those units are now hundredths of millimeters, which means that the circles are hardly visible. We need to increase the radius in OnDraw. Let us define a constant for that purpose.

RingDoc.h

```
static const int RADIUS = 500;

class CRingDoc : public CDocument
{
  // ...
};
```

RingView.cpp

```
void CRingView::OnDraw(CDC* pDC)
{
  CRingDoc* pDoc = GetDocument();
  ASSERT_VALID(pDoc);
  if (!pDoc)
    return;
  PointArray& pointArray = pDoc->GetPointArray();
  ColorArray& colorArray = pDoc->GetColorArray();
  int iSize = (int) pointArray.GetSize();
  for (int iIndex = 0; iIndex < iSize; ++iIndex)
  {
    CPoint point = pointArray[iIndex];
    COLORREF color = colorArray[iIndex];

    CPen pen(PS_SOLID, 0, BLACK);
    CBrush brush(color);

    pDC->Ellipse(point.x - RADIUS, point.y - RADIUS,
                 point.x + RADIUS, point.y + RADIUS);

    CPen* pOldPen = pDC->SelectObject(&pen);
    CBrush* pOldBrush = pDC->SelectObject(&brush);
  }
}
```

Catching the Keyboard Input

When the user presses a key on the keyboard, a message is sent to the view. We can catch that message in the same manner as we caught the mouse click.

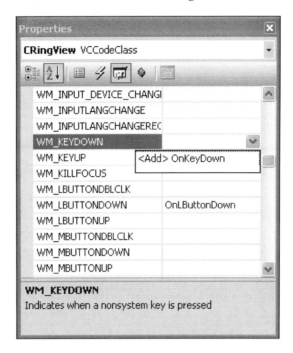

Let us use the keyboard to simulate scroll movements.

RingView.cpp

```
void CRingView::OnKeyDown(UINT nChar, UINT nRepCnt,
                          UINT nFlags)
{
  switch (nChar)
  {
    case VK_UP:
      OnVScroll(SB_LINEUP, 0, NULL);
      break;
    case VK_DOWN:
      OnVScroll(SB_LINEDOWN, 0, NULL);
      break;
    case VK_PRIOR:
      OnVScroll(SB_PAGEUP, 0, NULL);
      break;
```

```
    case VK_NEXT:
      OnVScroll(SB_PAGEDOWN, 0, NULL);
      break;

    case VK_LEFT:
      OnHScroll(SB_LINELEFT, 0, NULL);
      break;

    case VK_RIGHT:
      OnHScroll(SB_LINERIGHT, 0, NULL);
      break;

    case VK_HOME:
      OnHScroll(SB_LEFT, 0, NULL);
      break;

    case VK_END:
      OnHScroll(SB_RIGHT, 0, NULL);
      break;
  }

  CScrollView::OnKeyDown(nChar, nRepCnt, nFlags);
}
```

Menus, Accelerators, and Toolbars

So far, we could only paint rings in one color, now it is time to change that. Let us add a field m_nextColor to the document class and initialize it with the white color. We also modify the function MouseDown and OnDraw.

RingDoc.h

```
class CRingDoc : public CDocument
{
// ...

private:
  COLORREF m_nextColor;
};
```

RingDoc.cpp

```
CRingDoc::CRingDoc()
  : m_nextColor(WHITE)
{
  // Empty.
}

void CRingDoc::MouseDown(CPoint point)
{
  m_pointArray.Add(point);
  m_colorArray.Add(m_nextColor);

  UpdateAllViews(NULL);
}
```

When we created the application with theApplication Wizard, we got a standard menu bar. We can modify it by editing the resource file `resource.rc` manually, or we can use the tool Resource View.

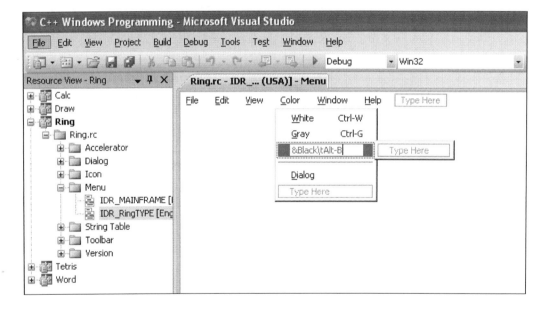

We can add mnemonic markers for the menus and items by preceding the character with an ampersand (&), and we can set a tabulator between words with \t. Then we pick a name for the menu items, lets us choose **ID_COLOR_WHITE**, **ID_COLOR_GREY**, and **ID_COLOR_BLACK**.

We can also set a corresponding accelerator for each of the items. However, we have to reuse the menu identities.

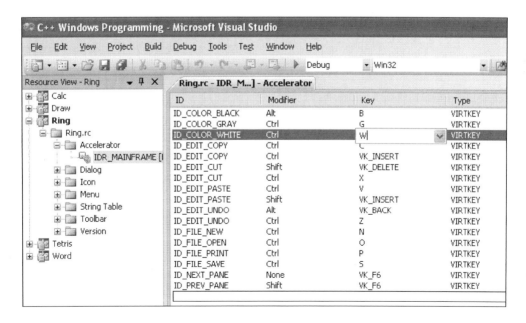

Finally, we can add buttons to the toolbar. Again, we have to reuse the menu identities.

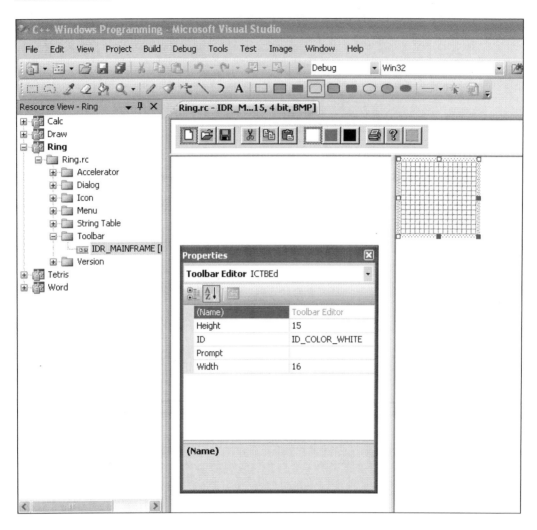

When we execute the program, we will notice that our new menu items and toolbar buttons are disabled and greyed. In order to make it work, we have to catch the messages in a manner similar to the way we caught mouse clicks and keyboard inputs. We can do that rather easily by using the **Properties** window, this time we choose the **Events** option. We choose to attach a new method **OnColorWhite** to **ID_COLOR_WHITE**. Then we do the same with **ID_COLOR_BLACK** and **ID_COLOR_GREY**.

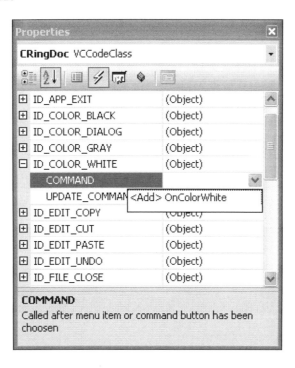

When this is done, three functions are added to the document class. We simply let them update the field m_nextColor.

RingDoc.cpp

```
void CRingDoc::OnColorWhite()
{
  m_nextColor = WHITE;
}

void CRingDoc::OnColorGray()
{
  m_nextColor = GREY;
}
```

```
void CRingDoc::OnColorBlack()
{
  m_nextColor = BLACK;
}
```

There is one more thing we can do. Suppose we want to see the color currently chosen. We can do that by attaching the method **OnUpdateColorWhite** to **UPDATE_COMMAND_UI**. The same goes with the grey and black colors.

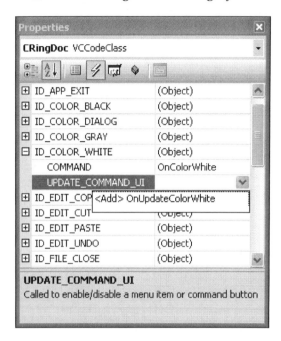

Then we have three more functions which we can modify. The function `SetRadio` takes a logical value and sets a radio marker (a small filled circle) at the chosen menu item; it also makes the toolbar button look pushed. A similar function is `SetCheck`, it sets a tick at the menu item instead of a radio button. `SetRadio` and `SetCheck` mark a toolbar button the same way. Finally, the function `Enable` sets the menu item or toolbar button to be enabled or disabled (greyed).

RingDoc.cpp

```
void CRingDoc::OnUpdateColorWhite(CCmdUI *pCmdUI)
{
  pCmdUI->SetRadio(m_nextColor == WHITE);
}


void CRingDoc::OnUpdateColorGray(CCmdUI *pCmdUI)
```

```
{
  pCmdUI->SetRadio(m_nextColor == GREY);
}
void CRingDoc::OnUpdateColorBlack(CCmdUI *pCmdUI)
{
  pCmdUI->SetRadio(m_nextColor == BLACK);
}
```

The Color Dialog

Suppose we would like to increase the color palette from three colors to every color available in the RGB standard (more than 16 millions). We can do so by adding another menu item and letting it launch the MFC color dialog.

RingDoc.cpp

```
void CRingDoc::OnColorDialog()
{
  CColorDialog colorDialog(m_nextColor);
  if (colorDialog.DoModal() == IDOK)
  {
    m_nextColor = colorDialog.GetColor();
  }
}
```

When the user chooses the color dialog menu item, the color dialog will launch.

The Registry

Suppose that we would like the current color to be saved between executions of our application. We can make that happen by calling the registry in the constructor and destructor of the document class.

RingDoc.cpp

```
CRingDoc::CRingDoc()
{
  m_nextColor = (COLORREF) AfxGetApp()->GetProfileInt
                  (TEXT("Ring"), TEXT("Color"), WHITE);
}
CRingDoc::~CRingDoc()
{
  AfxGetApp()->WriteProfileInt(TEXT("Ring"), TEXT("Color"),
                                m_nextColor);
}
```

Serialization

When the users choose the **File | Open** item, a file should be opened and read, when they choose the **File | Save** item, it should be written. Let us implement functions for loading and storing the rings. It is actually quite easy because the framework has already made most of the work. There is a function Serialize in the document class, the framework will call it for reading or writing data. We just have to add a few lines of code to Serialize in the document class. The MFC class CArray has built-in functionality to load and save the points and colors.

RingDoc.cpp

```
void CRingDoc::Serialize(CArchive& ar)
{
  m_pointArray.Serialize(ar);
  m_colorArray.Serialize(ar);

  if (ar.IsStoring())
  {
    ar << m_nextColor;
  }
  else
  {
    ar >> m_nextColor;
  }
}
```

Finally, we also ought to call the MFC method SetModifiedFlag in MouseDown in order to make sure the user cannot end the program without a warning about unsaved data.

RingDoc.cpp

```
void CRingDoc::MouseDown(CPoint point)
{
  m_pointArray.Add(point);
  m_colorArray.Add(m_nextColor);

  SetModifiedFlag(TRUE);
  UpdateAllViews(NULL);
}
```

Summary

In this chapter, we have gradually built a complete Windows application.

- We caught the mouse clicks and the keyboard inputs.
- We painted the rings.
- We added scroll bars and defined the size of the underlying canvas.
- We can add menus, accelerators, toolbars, and the color dialog.
- The state of the application was stored in the registry.
- Finally, we saved and loaded the rings by using Serialization.

5

Utility Classes

In the application of the following chapters, we will need some general container classes. MFC has many classes for developing graphical interfaces. It also has some general container classes for list and arrays. However, in some cases, a better solution is to build our own classes.

It shall also be mentioned that the **Standard Template Library (STL)** is a part of standard C++. It holds several generic container classes such as pairs, lists, and vectors. However, I found many of those classes to be rather clumsy to use, I have also found that it is not a good idea to mix MFC and STL container classes. Therefore, in this chapter we use the MFC classes useful to us, and write our own ones when necessary.

- We look at the MFC classes CPoint, CSize, and CRect. They hold a point, size, and rectangle, respectively, and they will come in handy in the following chapters.

- There is a structure LOGFONT, representing a font. However, we build the class Font to encapsulate it. In the same way, COLORREF holds a color, and we build the class Color to encapsulate it.

- When displaying text, we need to display a caret (the vertical blinking bar guiding the user when entering the next character). There is a set of functions for that purpose, which we combine into the class Caret.

- We inherit the MFC class CList to create lists and sets. The set class supports the mathematical operations union, intersection, and difference.

- Finally, we handle errors with the check and check_memory macros.

The Point, Size, and Rectangle Classes

MFC has three classes—point, size, and rectangle. The first one is the CPoint class. It holds x- and y-position. There are two constructors taking a position or another point. The x- and y-position can be extracted by accessing the public fields x and y.

```
CPoint ptMouse1(1, 2);
CPoint ptMouse2(ptMouse1);
int xMouse = ptMouse1.x, yMouse = ptMouse2.y;
```

The second class is CSize, it holds width and height. Similar to CPoint, it has two constructors and the width and height can be extracted by accessing the public fields cx and cy.

```
CSize szText1(1, 2);
CSize szText2(szText1);
int iTextWidth = szText1.cx, iTextHeight = szText2.cy;
```

The third class is CRect, it holds the dimensions of a rectangle. Its first constructor takes the positions of the four corners, the second one takes another rectangle, the third one takes two points (the top left and bottom right positions), and the fourth one takes a point (the top left position) and a size (the width and height). The width and height of the rectangle are given by the methods Width and Height. The four corners of the rectangle can be accessed by the public fields left, top, right, and bottom.

```
int xLeft = 100, xRight = 300, yTop = 200, yBottom = 500;
CRect rcArea1(xLeft, yTop, xRight, yBottom);
CRect rcArea2(rcArea1);

CPoint ptTopLeft(xLeft, yTop), ptBottomRight(xRight, yBottom);
CRect rcArea3(ptTopLeft, ptBottomRight);

CSize szArea(xRight - xLeft, yBottom - yTop);
CRect rcArea4(ptTopLeft, szArea);

int iWidth = rcArea1.Width();
int iHeight = rcArea2.Height();

xLeft = rcArea1.left;
yTop = rcArea2.top;
xRight = rcArea3.right;
yBottom = rcArea4.bottom;
```

Sometimes when we use `CRect` objects as parameters it is understood that the rectangle is normalized for the fourth-quadrant. That is, the left side is less than or equal to the right side and the top side is less than or equal to the bottom side. The `CRect` method `NormalizeRect` takes care of that.

```
CRect rcInverted(200, 500, 100, 300);
rcInverted.NormalizeRect();
```

The Color Class

In the Ring and Tetris applications, we used the type `COLORREF`, which manages a color according to the RGB standard. However, it would be nice to have a class encapsulating it, so let us write the `Color` class. `COLORREF` is a 32 bit value, even thought it only uses the lower 24 bits. A color consists of the three basic colors red (bits 0 – 7), green (bits 8 – 15), and blue (bits 16 – 23). The macro RGB puts together a `COLORREF` value given its red, green, and blue portions. There are also macros `GetRValue`, `GetGValue`, and `GetBValue` that extract the red, green, and blue parts of the color, respectively.

In the Ring and Tetris applications of this book, the type `COLORREF` is used. In the Draw, Calc, and Word applications, the class `Color` is used.

As object of this class will be serialized. The class must include a default constructor. The constructor sets the color to zero, which represents black. Moreover, there is a copy constructor, a constructor taking a `COLORREF` value, and the overloaded assignment operator. They all initialize the field `m_crRedGreenBlue` that holds the actual color.

Color.h

```
class Color
{
  public:
    Color();
    Color(const COLORREF crRedGreenBlue);
    Color(const Color& color);

    operator COLORREF() const;
    Color& operator=(const Color& color);

    void Serialize(CArchive& archive);
    Color Inverse() const;

  private:
    COLORREF m_crRedGreenBlue;
};
```

There is one rule in MFC we have to follow. When we add our own files to the project, the implementation files must begin with the inclusions of the header file `StdAfx.h`; otherwise, it will not work.

The `Inverse` method inverts the color by extracting the red, green, and blue values of the color. Then it subtracts the values from 255, and merges the modified values into the resulting color.

Color.cpp

```
#include "StdAfx.h"
#include "Color.h"

// ...
Color Color::Inverse() const
{
  int iRed = GetRValue(m_crRedGreenBlue);
  int iGreen = GetGValue(m_crRedGreenBlue);
  int iBlue = GetBValue(m_crRedGreenBlue);

  return Color(RGB(255 - iRed, 255 - iGreen, 255 - iBlue));
}
```

The Font Class

The Win32 structure LOGFONT below represents a logical font in Windows.

```
typedef struct tagLOGFONT
{
  LONG lfHeight;
  LONG lfWidth;
  LONG lfEscapement;
  LONG lfOrientation;
  LONG lfWeight;
  BYTE lfItalic;
  BYTE lfUnderline;
  BYTE lfStrikeOut;
  BYTE lfCharSet;
  BYTE lfOutPrecision;
  BYTE lfClipPrecision;
  BYTE lfQuality;
  BYTE lfPitchAndFamily;
  TCHAR lfFaceName[LF_FACESIZE];
}
LOGFONT, *PLOGFONT;
```

It might seem like a complicated task to set all the fields to their correct values. However, one benefit with the structure is that we really just have to set the lfFaceName and the lfHeight fields. If we set the rest of the fields to zero, they will be adjusted automatically. One convenient way to do is that to call the C standard function memset. In a similar manner, we can use memcmp to compare whether two fonts are equal. There is also a function memcpy to copy a memory block between two locations.

```
void *memset(void* pDestination, int iValue, size_t iSize);
void *memcpy(void* pDestination, const void* pSource,
             size_t iSize);
int memcmp(const void *pBlock1, const void *pBlock2,
           size_t iSize);
```

Let us write our own class Font, its main purpose is to wrap the functionality of the structure LOGFONT. The default constructor is necessary because the font object is loaded and stored on a CArchive stream. It is quite easy to load or save a font in *Serialize*, we call the CArchive methods Read and Write, respectively.

A point is defined as 1/72 inch. However, the logical coordinate system of choice in the applications of this book is MM_HIMETRIC, hundredths of millimetres. That is, when we draw text or calculate its size, the size of a font must be recalculated from points to hundredths of millimeters. PointsToMeters takes care of that task, it creates and returns a new CSize object with the dimensions recalculated.

The constructors of the MFC classes CFont and CFontDialog want pointers to LOGFONT structures. For convenience, we have the LOGFONT operator (which returns a LOGFONT structure) and the PLOGFONT operator (which returns a pointer to a LOGFONT structure). Technically, we would manage with one of them but the code will be clearer with both of them.

Font.h

```
class Font
{
  public:
    Font();
    Font(CString stName, int iSize);
    Font(const LOGFONT& logFont);
    Font(const Font& font);

    operator LOGFONT() {return m_logFont;}
    operator PLOGFONT() {return &m_logFont;}
    Font PointsToMeters() const;

    Font& operator=(const Font& font);
    BOOL operator==(const Font& font) const;
```

```
      BOOL operator!=(const Font& font) const;
      void Serialize(CArchive& archive);
      BOOL IsItalic() const {return m_logFont.lfItalic;}
  private:
      LOGFONT m_logFont;
};
```

In order to reset the LOGFONT structure we use the C standard memset function. With the parameter zero, it sets all bytes in the structure to zero. Then we just copy the name and set the size.

There are two C standard functions for copying string. The function strcpy takes pointers to char and wcscpy takes pointers to wchar_t. However, wcscpy_s is the type safe version. It is a macro that choose the correct type.

Font.cpp

```
Font::Font(CString stName, int iSize)
{
  ::memset(&m_logFont, 0, sizeof m_logFont);
  wcscpy_s(m_logFont.lfFaceName, stName);
  m_logFont.lfHeight = iSize;
}
```

The size of a font is normally given in typographical points. However, in order to calculate the screen size of text written in a certain font, we need to calculate its size in hundredths of millimeters. As an inch is defined to be 25.4 millimeters, to translate a point into hundredths of millimeters we multiply it with 2540 and divide by 72.

```
Font Font::PointsToMeters() const
{
  LOGFONT logFont = m_logFont;

  logFont.lfWidth = (int) ((double) 2540*logFont.lfWidth/72);
  logFont.lfHeight = (int)((double) 2540*logFont.lfHeight/72);
  return Font(logFont);
}
```

The C standard function memcmp works in a way similar to memset. It takes memory blocks of equal sizes and compares them byte by byte.

```
BOOL Font::operator==(const Font& font) const
{
  return (::memcmp(&m_logFont, &font.m_logFont,
                   sizeof m_logFont) == 0);
}
```

When it comes to serializing, the CArchive class has two methods: Write and Read. They take the address and size of a memory block, in this case the LOGFONT structure m_logfont.

```
void Font::Serialize(CArchive& archive)
{
  if (archive.IsStoring())
  {
    archive.Write(&m_logFont, sizeof m_logFont);
  }
  if (archive.IsLoading())
  {
    archive.Read(&m_logFont, sizeof m_logFont);
  }
}
```

The Caret Class

In Windows, we have two small markers that tell us the location of the mouse pointer and where the next character is going to be inserted. They are called the cursor and the caret, respectively.

The keyboard input has to be directed to one specific application, that application has *input focus*. Only one application may have focus at a time. The application receives the message WM_SETFOCUS when it gain focus and WM_KILLFOCUS when it is lost.

Caret is a class (written by us) that manages the caret. It has to address two issues. First, it has to keep track of whether the application has focus. It also has to keep track of whether the caret is visible. It has three fields: m_bVisible that decides whether the caret is visible, m_pFocusView that is a pointer to the view having the focus, and m_rcCaret that holds the dimensions of the caret (in logical units).

The functions OnSetFocus and OnKillFocus are called when the view having the focus receives the corresponding messages. Even though an application has input focus, it might not want to show the caret. For instance, in the case when text is marked in a word processor or when several cells are marked in a spreadsheet program. SetAndShowCaret shows the caret only when the field m_bVisible is true.HideCaret hides the care; however, when m_bVisible is false, it does in effect nothing. The methods of the class are calling MFC CWnd functions to create, locate, and show the caret. However, there is no MFC function to destroy the Caret. instead, we call the Win32 API function DestroyCaret. Moreover, there is not a function for hiding the caret. Therefore, we have to create a new caret and destroy the caret every time we want to show or hide it.

One final detail is that the applications using the Caret give the coordinates in logical units, units that have to be translated into device units before the actual Caret is created.

Caret.h

```
class Caret
{
  public:
    Caret();

    void SetAndShowCaret(const CRect rcCaret);
    void HideCaret();

    void OnSetFocus(CView* pView);
    void OnKillFocus();

    CView* GetView() const {return m_pFocusView;}
  private:
    BOOL m_bVisible;
    CView* m_pFocusView;
    CRect m_rcCaret;
};
```

When the Caret needs to be updated due to the user's action, SetAndShowCaret is called. It receives the new position and size of the Caret, translates the values into device coordinates, and shows the Caret by calling CreateSolidCaret, SetCaretPos, ShowCaret.

When the Caret is to be hidden, HideFocus is called, which in turn calls the Win32 API function DestroyCaret.

Caret.cpp

```
void Caret::SetAndShowCaret(const CRect rcCaret)
{
  m_rcCaret = rcCaret;

  CClientDC dc(m_pFocusView);
  m_pFocusView->OnPrepareDC(&dc);

  dc.LPtoDP(m_rcCaret);
  m_rcCaret.left = min(m_rcCaret.left, m_rcCaret.right - 1);

  if (m_rcCaret.left < 0)
  {
    m_rcCaret.right += abs(m_rcCaret.left);
    m_rcCaret.left = 0;
  }
```

```
      m_pFocusView->CreateSolidCaret(m_rcCaret.Width(),
                                      m_rcCaret.Height());
      m_pFocusView->SetCaretPos(m_rcCaret.TopLeft());
      m_bVisible = TRUE;
      m_pFocusView->ShowCaret();
  }

  void Caret::HideCaret()
  {
    if (m_pFocusView != NULL)
    {
      m_bVisible = FALSE;
      ::DestroyCaret();
    }
  }
```

Each application holds one `Caret` object, and when the application receives or loses the input focus the `Caret` is notified.

```
  void Caret::OnSetFocus(CView* pView)
  {
    m_pFocusView = pView;

    if (m_bVisible)
    {
      m_pFocusView->CreateSolidCaret(m_rcCaret.Width(),
                                      m_rcCaret.Height());
      m_pFocusView->SetCaretPos(m_rcCaret.TopLeft());
      m_pFocusView->ShowCaret();
    }
  }
```

Note that we cannot make the `Caret` invisible when we lose focus. As there is only one caret to be shared by several applications, we must destroy it. When we gain focus, we have to create a new caret.

```
  void Caret::OnKillFocus()
  {
    m_pFocusView = NULL;
    ::DestroyCaret();
  }
```

The List Class

List is a sub class of the MFC class CList. It uses the functionality of CList with some improvements. The default constructor does nothing but call the matching constructor of the base class. CList has no copy constructor, so the copy constructor of List adds the given list to its own. Nor does CList have a method Remove which takes a value and removes it from the list if it finds it.

List.h

```
template<typename T>
class List : public CList<T>
{
  public:
    List();
    List(const List<T>& list);

    void Remove(T value);
    List<T> FilterIf(BOOL Predicate(T value)) const;
    int CountIf(BOOL Predicate(T value)) const;
};
```

FilterIf takes a function Predicate that returns a logical value as parameter, applies it to every element in the list, and returns a list containing every element that satisfies Predicate (every element in the list for which Predicate returns true). CountIf does the same thing, but returns just the number of satisfied elements.

```
template<typename T>
List<T> List<T>::FilterIf(BOOL Predicate(T value)) const
{
  List<T> result;

  for (POSITION position = GetHeadPosition();
       position != NULL; GetNext(position))
  {
    T value = GetAt(position);

    if (Predicate(value))
    {
      result.AddTail(value);
    }
  }

  return result;
}
```

The Set Class

There is no MFC class `CSet`, so we have to write our own. Similar to `List`, `Set` is a sub class to `CList`. It has a default constructor and a copy constructor, two methods `Add` and `AddAll` which add a value or another set, methods `Remove` and `Exists` which remove a given element from the set and decide whether a given value is a member of the set.

Set.h

```cpp
template<typename T>
class Set : public CList<T>
{
  public:
    Set();
    Set(const Set<T>& set);
    Set<T>& operator=(const Set<T>& set);

    void Add(T value);
    void AddAll(Set<T>& set);

    void Remove(T value);
    BOOL Exists(T value) const;

    static Set<T> Merge(Set<T> leftSet, Set<T> rightSet,
                        BOOL bAddEQ, BOOL bAddLT,BOOL bAddGT,
                        BOOL bAddLeft, BOOL bAddRight);

    static Set<T> Union(Set<T> leftSet, Set<T> rightSet);
    static Set<T> Intersection(Set<T> leftSet,
                               Set<T> rightSet);
    static Set<T> Difference(Set<T> leftSet, Set<T> rightSet);
    static Set<T> SymmetricDifference(Set<T> leftSet,
                                      Set<T> rightSet);
};
```

Merge merges two sets in different manners depending on its given parameters; it is called `Union`, `Intersection`, `Difference`, and `SymmetricDifference`. In order for it to work properly, the sets have to be ordered. Therefore, `Add` takes care to add the new values in their correct positions. `AddAll` simply calls `Add` for each value in the new set. Note that `Add` does nothing if the values already exist in the set.

Set.cpp

```
template<typename T>
void Set<T>::Add(T newValue)
{
  for (POSITION position = GetHeadPosition();
       position != NULL; GetNext(position))
  {
    T value = GetAt(position);

    if (value == newValue)
    {
      return;
    }

    else if (newValue < value)
    {
      InsertBefore(position, newValue);
      return;
    }
  }

  AddTail(newValue);
}
```

The methods Union, Intersection, Difference, and SymmetricDifference work the same as their mathematical counterparts. They all take two sets and return a new one. Union returns a set containing elements occurring in at least one of the sets, without duplicates. Intersection returns the set containing elements occurring in both sets. Difference returns the set containing elements occurring in the first set but not in the second set. Finally, SymmetricDifference returns the elements occurring in one of the two sets, but not in both of them.

The methods above all call Merge, whose task is to merge two given sets into one. Merge traverses the two sets and takes action according to the parameters bAddEQ, bAddLT, and bAddGT. If bAddEQ is true and the left element is equal to the right one, the left element is added to the result (we could have added the right element instead, it does not matter since they are the same). If bAddLT is true and the left element is less that the right one, the left element is added to the result. If bAddGT is true and the left element is greater than the right one, the right element is added to the result. The traverse continues until the end of (at least) one of the sets. Thereafter, the remaining part of the left set (if it is not empty) is added if to the result if bAddLeft is true and the remaining part of the right set (if it is not empty) is added if bAddRight is true.

Set.h

```
template<typename T>
Set<T> Set<T>::Merge(Set<T> leftSet, Set<T> rightSet,
                     BOOL bAddEQ, BOOL bAddLT, BOOL bAddGT,
                     BOOL bAddLeft, BOOL bAddRight)
{
  Set<T> resultSet;

  while (!leftSet.IsEmpty() && !rightSet.IsEmpty())
  {
    T leftValue = leftSet.GetHead();
    T rightValue = rightSet.GetHead();

    if (leftValue == rightValue)
    {
      if (bAddEQ)
      {
        resultSet.AddTail(leftValue);
      }
      leftSet.RemoveHead();
      rightSet.RemoveHead();
    }
    else if (leftValue < rightValue)
    {
      if (bAddLT)
      {
        resultSet.AddTail(leftValue);
      }
      leftSet.RemoveHead();
    }
    else
    {
      if (bAddGT)
      {
        resultSet.AddTail(rightValue);
      }
      rightSet.RemoveHead();
    }
  }
  if (bAddLeft)
  {
    resultSet.AddAll(leftSet);
  }
```

```
      if (bAddRight)
      {
        resultSet.AddAll(rightSet);
      }
      return resultSet;
    }
```

By calling `Merge` with appropriate values, all four of the set methods above can be implemented.

	bAddEQ	*bAddLT*	*bAddGT*	*bAddLeft*	*bAddRight*
Union	*true*	*true*	*true*	*true*	*true*
Intersection	*true*	*false*	*false*	*false*	*false*
Difference	*false*	*true*	*false*	*true*	*false*
SymmetricDifference	*false*	*true*	*true*	*true*	*true*

As noted in the table, *Union* really wants all values, regardless of whether they are located in one of the sets or both of them. On the other hand, *Intersection* is only interested in values located in both sets. *Difference* is the only unsymmetrical method, it wants the values of the left set, but not the right. Finally, *SymmetricDifference* is really symmetric, it keeps all values except the ones located in both sets.

The Array Class

Actually, there is no `Array` class. However, there is a MFC template class `CArray`, which we use.

Error Handling

The `check` macro below comes in handy on several occasions. The macro is given a test parameter and, it displays a message box with an appropriate error message and exits the program execution. It works similarly to the `assert` macro, however, `assert` only works in debug mode while `check` works in both debug and release mode.

Check.h

```
    #define check(test)                                        \
    {                                                          \
      if (!(test))                                             \
      {                                                        \
        CString stMessage;                                     \
        stMessage.Format(TEXT("\"%s\" on line %d in file %s"), \
```

```
                        TEXT(#test), __LINE__, TEXT(__FILE__)); \
        ::MessageBox(NULL, stMessage, TEXT("Assertion"), MB_OK); \
        ::exit(-1);                                               \
    }                                                             \
}
```

It is used all over the code in this book for two kinds of situations. At the end of a method when the end point is not supposed to be reached.

```
    // ...
    check(FALSE);
    return 0;
}
```

When a row and a column is given in order to look up an object in a matrix.

```
ReferenceSet* TSetMatrix::Get(int iRow, int iCol) const
{
    check((iRow >= 0) && (iRow < ROWS));
    check((iCol >= 0) && (iCol < COLS));
    // ...
```

These checks are introduced for debugging purposes only. They are not supposed to occur.

Moreover, there is a MFC macro ASSERT_VALID that checks that a given MFC class object has been properly initialized. In this book, it is used to check the document class object in the view class of each application.

```
CRingDoc* pDoc = GetDocument();
check(pDoc != NULL);
ASSERT_VALID(pDoc);
```

If we run out of dynamic memory, new throws an exception. The check_memory macro catches it and aborts the execution with an error message.

Check.h

```
#define check_memory(alloc_code)
{
    try
    {
        alloc_code;
    }
    catch (CException*)
    {
        CString stMessage;
        stMessage.Format(TEXT("Out of memory \"%s\" ")
                         TEXT("on line %d in file %s"),
```

```
                      TEXT(#alloc_code), __LINE__,
                      TEXT(__FILE__));
      ::MessageBox(NULL,stMessage,TEXT("Memory Check"),MB_OK);
      ::exit(-1);
    }
  }
}
```

The `check_memory` macro is used every time we try to allocate dynamic memory.

```
check_memory(m_pFigure = new LineFigure());
```

However, if the user makes a mistake we cannot just abort the execution. Instead, we use exceptions that are thrown and caught. They are used on two occasions in *The Calc Application*. When the user inputs an invalid formula, then a message box with an error message is displayed, and when the value of a formula cannot be evaluated, then a message is displayed in the cell.

Summary

- There are small MFC classes `CPoint`, `CSize`, and `CRect` holding a point (x and y), a size (width and height), and a rectangle (the four corners of). These classes will be thoroughly used in the following chapters.

- We build our own classes `Color` and `Font` based upon the Win32 API types `COLORREF` and `LOGFONT`.

- In every application, except Tetris, we display text. In order for the user to know where to enter the next character, we need a caret (a blinking vertical bar). The class `Caret` handles that.

- The classes `List` and `Set` inherit the MFC class `CList` to handle list and sets, respectively. The `Set` class supports the mathematical operations union, intersection, and difference.

- In the application of this book, two kinds of errors may occur: internal errors, such as an index out of bounds, or a user errors, such as entering an incorrect formula. In the former case, we use the `check` macro to stop the execution with an error message; in the latter case, we throw an error exception that eventually will be displayed for the user in a cell or a message box. The `check_memory` macro handles allocation of dynamic memory in a similar way.

6

The Tetris Application

Tetris is a classic game. In this chapter, we will develop a version very similar to the original version. Seven figures of different shapes and colors fall down and the player's job is to move and rotate them into positions so that as many rows as possible are completely filled. When a row is filled, it disappears. Every removed row gives one point.

This application is the only one in this book that supports the single document interface, which implies that we have one document class object and one view class object. The other applications support the multiple document interface, they have one document class object and zero or more view class objects. The following screenshot depicts a classic example of the Tetris Application:

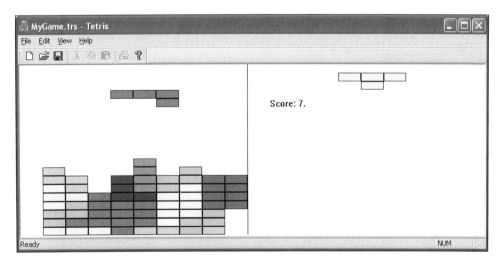

- We start by generating the application's skeleton code with The Application Wizard. The process is similar to the Ring application code.
- There is a small class Square holding the position of one square and a class ColorGrid managing the game grid.

- The document class manages the data of the game and handles the active (falling down) figure and the next (shown to the right of the game grid) figure.

- The view class accepts input from the keyboard and draws the figures and the game grid.

- The Figure class manages a single figure. It is responsible for movements and rotations.

- There are seven kinds of figures. The *Figure Info* files store information pertaining to their colors and shapes.

The Tetris Files

We start by creating a MFC application with the name Tetris and follow the steps of the Ring application. The classes CTetrisApp, CMainFrame, CTetrisDoc, CTetrisView, and CAboutDlg are then created and added to the project.

There are only two differences. We need to state that we are dealing with a "Single Document Application Type", that the file extension is "Trs" and that the file type long name is "A Game of Tetris". Otherwise, we just accept the default settings. Note that in this application we accept the CView base class instead of the CScrollView like we did in the Ring application.

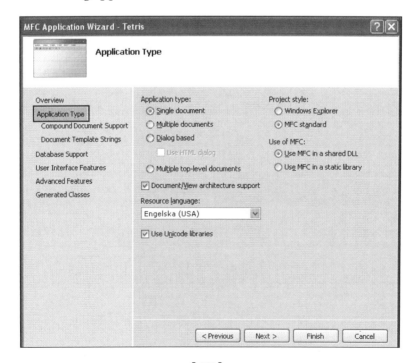

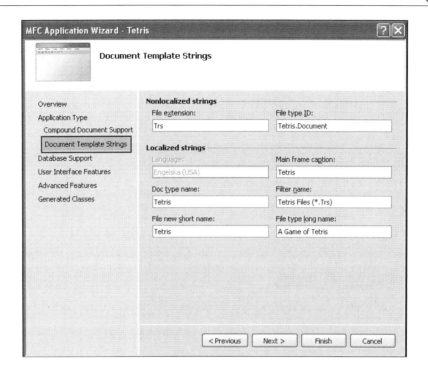

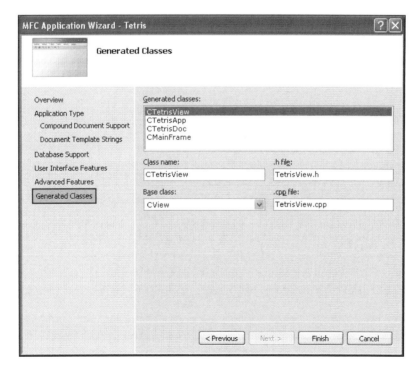

We add the marked lines below. In all other respects, we leave the file unmodified. We will not need to modify the files `Tetris.h`, `MainFrm.h`, `MainFrm.cpp`, `StdAfx.h`, `StdAfx.cpp`, `Resource.h`, and `Tetris.rc`.

```
#include "stdafx.h"

#include "Square.h"
#include "Figure.h"
#include "ColorGrid.h"

#include "Tetris.h"
#include "MainFrm.h"
#include "TetrisDoc.h"
#include "TetrisView.h"

// ...
```

The Square Class

`Square` is a small class holding a row and column position. It is used by the `figureInfo` class in this application.

Square.h

```
class Square
{
  public:
    Square();
    Square(int iRow, int iCol);

    int Row() const {return m_iRow;}
    int Col() const {return m_iCol;}
  private:
    int m_iRow, m_iCol;
};
```

The Color Grid Class

The `ColorGrid` handles the background game grid of twenty rows and twenty columns. Each square can have a color. At the beginning, every square is initialized to the default color white. The `Index` method is overloaded with a constant version that returns the color of the given square, and a non-constant version that returns a reference to the color. The latter version makes it possible to change the color of a square.

ColorGrid.h

```
const int ROWS = 20;
const int COLS = 10;

class ColorGrid
{
  public:
    ColorGrid();
    void Clear();

    COLORREF& Index(int iRow, int iCol);
    const COLORREF Index(int iRow, int iCol) const;

    void Serialize(CArchive& archive);
  private:
    COLORREF m_buffer[ROWS * COLS];
};
```

There are two `Index` methods, the second one is intended to be called on a constant object. Both methods check that the given row and position have valid values. The checks are, however, for debugging purposes only. The methods are always called with valid values. Do not forget to include the file `StdAfx.h`.

ColorGrid.cpp

```
#include "StdAfx.h"

COLORREF& ColorGrid::Index(int iRow, int iCol)
{
  check((iRow >= 0) && (iRow < ROWS));
  check((iCol >= 0) && (iCol < COLS));
  return m_buffer[iRow * COLS + iCol];
}

const COLORREF ColorGrid::Index(int iRow, int iCol) const
{
  check((iRow >= 0) && (iRow < ROWS));
  check((iCol >= 0) && (iCol < COLS));
  return m_buffer[iRow * COLS + iCol];
}
```

The Document Class

`CTetrisDoc` is the document class of this application. When created, it overrides `OnNewDocument` and `Serialize` from its base class `CDocument`.

We add to the CTetrisDoc class a number of fields and methods. The field m_activeFigure is active figure, that is the one falling down during the game. The field m_nextFigure is the next figure, that is the one showed in the right part of the game view. They both are copies of the objects in the m_figureArray, which is an array figure object. There is one figure object of each kind (one figure of each color). The integer list m_scoreList holds the ten top list of the game. It is loaded from the file ScoreList.txt by the constructor and saved by the destructor. The integer field m_iScore holds the score of the current game. GetScore, GetScoreList, GetActiveFigure, GetNextFigure, and GetGrid are called by the view class in order to draw the game grid. They simply return the values of the corresponding fields.

The field m_colorGrid is an object of the class ColorGrid, which we defined in the previous section. It is actually just a matrix holding the colors of the squares of the game grid. Each square is intialized to the color white and a square is considered to be empty as long as it is white.

When the application starts, the constructor calls the C standard library function srand. The name is an abbreviation for sowing a random seed. By calling srand with an integer seed, it will generate a series of random number. In order to find a new seed every time the application starts, the C standard library function time is called, which returns the number of seconds elapsed since January 1, 1970. In order to obtain the actual random number, we call rand that returns a number in the interval from zero to the predefined constant RAND_MAX. The prototypes for these functions are defined in time.h (time) and stdlib.h (rand and srand), respectively.

```
#include <time.h>
#include <stdlib.h>
time_t time(time_t *pTimer);
void srand(unsigned int uSeed);
int rand();
```

When the user presses the space key and the active figure falls down or when a row is filled and is flashed, we have to slow down the process in order for the user to apprehand the event. There is a Win32 API function Sleep that pauses the application for the given amount of milliseconds.

```
void Sleep(int iMilliSeconds);
```

The user can control the horizontal movement and rotation of the falling figures by pressing the arrow keys. Left and right arrow keys move the figure to the left or right. The up and down arrow key rotates the figure clockwise or counterclockwise, respectively. Every time the user presses one of those keys, a message is sent to the view class object and caught by the method OnKeyDown, which in turn calls one of the methods LeftArrowKey, RightArrowKey, UpArrowKey, DownArrowKey to deal with the message. They all work in a similar fashion. They try to execute the movement or rotation in question. If it works, both the old and new area of the figure is repainted by making calls to UpdateAllViews.

The view class also handles a timer that sends a message every second the view is in focus. The message is caught by the view class method OnTimer that in turn calls Timer. It tries to move the active figure one step downwards. If that is possible, the area of the figure is repainted in the same way as in the methods above. However, if it is not possible, the squares of the figure are added to the game grid. The active figure is assigned to the next figure, and the next figure is assigned a copy of a randomly selected figure in m_figureArray. We also check whether any row has been filled. In that case, it will be removed and we will check to see if the game is over.

The user can speed up the game by pressing the space key. The message is caught and sent to SpaceKey. It simply calls OnTimer as many times as possible at intervals of twenty milliseconds in order to make the movement visible to the user.

When a figure has reached its end position and any full rows have been removed, the figure must be valid. That is, its squares are not allowed to occupy any already colored position. If it does, the game is over and GameOver is called. It starts by making the game grid gray and asks the users whether they want to play another game. If they do, the game grid is cleared and set back to colored mode and a new game starts. If they do not, the application exits.

NewGame informs the players whether they made to the top ten list and inquires about another game by displaying a message box. AddToScore examines whether the player has made to the ten top list. If so, the score is added to the list and the ranking is returned, if not, zero is returned.

DeleteFullRows traverses the game grid from top to bottom flashing and removing every full row. IsRowFull traverses the given row and returns true if no square has the default color (white). FlashRow flashes the row by showing it three times in grayscale and color at intervals of twenty milliseconds. DeleteRow removes the row by moving all rows above one step downwards and inserting an empty row (all white squares) at top.

The next figure and the current high score are painted at specific positions on the client area, the rectangle constants NEXT_AREA and SCORE_AREA keep track of those positions.

TetrisDoc.h

```cpp
typedef CList<int> IntList;
const int FIGURE_ARRAY_SIZE = 7;
class CTetrisDoc : public CDocument
{
  protected:
    CTetrisDoc();
  public:
    virtual ~CTetrisDoc();
    void SaveScoreList();
  protected:
    DECLARE_MESSAGE_MAP()
    DECLARE_DYNCREATE(CTetrisDoc)
  public:
    virtual void Serialize(CArchive& archive);
    int GetScore() const {return m_iScore;}
    const IntList* GetScoreList() {return &m_scoreList;}
    const ColorGrid* GetGrid() {return &m_colorGrid;}
    const Figure& GetActiveFigure() const {return
                                        m_activeFigure;}
    const Figure& GetNextFigure() const {return m_nextFigure;}
  public:
    void LeftArrowKey();
    void RightArrowKey();
    void UpArrowKey();
    void DownArrowKey();

    BOOL Timer();
    void SpaceKey();
  private:
    void GameOver();
    BOOL NewGame();
    int AddScoreToList();
    void DeleteFullRows();
    BOOL IsRowFull(int iRow);

    void FlashRow(int iFlashRow);
    void DeleteRow(int iDeleteRow);
  private:
    ColorGrid m_colorGrid;
    Figure m_activeFigure, m_nextFigure;

    int m_iScore;
    IntList m_scoreList;
```

```
const CRect NEXT_AREA, SCORE_AREA;
static Figure m_figureArray[FIGURE_ARRAY_SIZE];
};
```

The field `m_figureArray` holds seven figure objects, one of each color. When we need a new figure, we just randomly copy one of them.

TetrisDoc.cpp

```
Figure redFigure(NORTH, RED, RedInfo);
Figure brownFigure(EAST, BROWN, BrownInfo);
Figure turquoiseFigure(EAST, TURQUOISE, TurquoiseInfo);
Figure greenFigure(EAST, GREEN, GreenInfo);
Figure blueFigure(SOUTH, BLUE, BlueInfo);
Figure purpleFigure(SOUTH, PURPLE, PurpleInfo);
Figure yellowFigure(SOUTH, YELLOW, YellowInfo);

Figure CTetrisDoc::m_figureArray[] = {redFigure, brownFigure,
                    turquoiseFigure, greenFigure, yellowFigure,
                    blueFigure, purpleFigure};
```

When the user presses the left arrow key, the view class object catches the message and calls `LeftArrowKey` in the document class object. We try to move the active figure one step to the left. It is not for sure that we succeed. The figure may already be located at the left part of the game grid. However, if the movement succeeds, the figure's position is repainted and true is returned. In that case, we repaint the figure's old and new graphic areas in order to repaint the figure. Finally, we set the modified flag since the figure has been moved. The method `RightArrowKey` works in a similar way.

```
void CTetrisDoc::LeftArrowKey()
{
  CRect rcOldArea = m_activeFigure.GetArea();
  if (m_activeFigure.MoveLeft())
  {
    CRect rcNewArea = m_activeFigure.GetArea();
    UpdateAllViews(NULL, COLOR, (CObject*) &rcOldArea);
    UpdateAllViews(NULL, COLOR, (CObject*) &rcNewArea);
    SetModifiedFlag();
  }
}
```

Timer is called every time the active figure is to moved one step downwards. That is, each second when the application has focus. If the downwards movement succeeds, then the figure is repainted in a way similar to LeftArrowKey above. However, if the movement does not succeed, the movement of the active figure has come to an end. We call AddToGrid to color the squares of the figure. Then we copy the next figure to the active figure and randomly copy a new next figure. The next figure is the one shown to the right of the game grid.

However, the case may occur that the game grid is full. That is the case if the new active figure is not valid, that is, the squares occupied by the figure are not free. If so, the game is over, and the user is asked whether he wants a new game.

```
BOOL CTetrisDoc::Timer()
{
  SetModifiedFlag();
  CRect rcOldArea = m_activeFigure.GetArea();

  if (m_activeFigure.MoveDown())
  {
    CRect rcNewArea = m_activeFigure.GetArea();

    UpdateAllViews(NULL, COLOR, (CObject*) &rcOldArea);
    UpdateAllViews(NULL, COLOR, (CObject*) &rcNewArea);

    return TRUE;
  }
  else
  {
    m_activeFigure.AddToGrid();
    m_activeFigure = m_nextFigure;
    CRect rcActiveArea = m_activeFigure.GetArea();
    UpdateAllViews(NULL, COLOR, (CObject*) &rcActiveArea);
    m_nextFigure = m_figureArray[rand() % FIGURE_ARRAY_SIZE];
    UpdateAllViews(NULL, COLOR, (CObject*) &NEXT_AREA);
    DeleteFullRows();

    if (!m_activeFigure.IsFigureValid())
    {
      GameOver();
    }
    return FALSE;
  }
}
```

If the user presses the space key, the active figure falling will fall faster. The `Timer` method is called every 20 milisseconds.

```
void CTetrisDoc::SpaceKey()
{
  while (Timer())
  {
    Sleep(20);
  }
}
```

When the game is over, the users are asked whether they want a new game. If so, we clear the grid, randomly select the the next active and next figure, and repaint the whole client area.

```
void CTetrisDoc::GameOver()
{
  UpdateAllViews(NULL, GRAY);
  if (NewGame())
  {
    m_colorGrid.Clear();
    m_activeFigure = m_figureArray[rand() %FIGURE_ARRAY_SIZE];
    m_nextFigure = m_figureArray[rand() % FIGURE_ARRAY_SIZE];
    UpdateAllViews(NULL, COLOR);
  }
  else
  {
    SaveScoreList();
    exit(0);
  }
}
```

Each time a figure is moved, one or more rows may be filled. We start by checking the top row and then go through the rows downwards. For each full row, we first flash it and then remove it.

```
void CTetrisDoc::DeleteFullRows()
{
  int iRow = ROWS - 1;
  while (iRow >= 0)
  {
    if (IsRowFull(iRow))
    {
      FlashRow(iRow);
      DeleteRow(iRow);

      ++m_iScore;
      UpdateAllViews(NULL, COLOR, (CObject*) &SCORE_AREA);
```

```
        }
      else
      {
        --iRow;
      }
    }
  }
}
```

When a row is completely filled, it will flash before it is removed. The flash effect is executed by redrawing the row in color and in grayscale three times with an interval of 50 milliseconds.

```
void CTetrisDoc::FlashRow(int iRow)
{
  for (int iCount = 0; iCount < 3; ++iCount)
  {
    CRect rcRowArea(0, iRow, COLS, iRow + 1);
    UpdateAllViews(NULL, GRAY, (CObject*) &rcRowArea);
    Sleep(50);
    CRect rcRowArea2(0, iRow, COLS, iRow + 1);
    UpdateAllViews(NULL, COLOR, (CObject*) &rcRowArea2);
    Sleep(50);
  }
}
```

When a row is removed, we do not really remove it. If we did, the game grid would shrink. Instead, we copy the squares above it and clear the top row.

```
void CTetrisDoc::DeleteRow(int iMarkedRow)
{
  for (int iRow = iMarkedRow; iRow > 0; --iRow)
  {
    for (int iCol = 0; iCol < COLS; ++iCol)
    {
      m_colorGrid.Index(iRow, iCol) =
      m_colorGrid.Index(iRow - 1, iCol);
    }
  }
  for (int iCol = 0; iCol < COLS; ++iCol)
  {
    m_colorGrid.Index(0, iCol) = WHITE;
  }
  CRect rcArea(0, 0, COLS, iMarkedRow + 1);
  UpdateAllViews(NULL, COLOR, (CObject*) &rcArea);
}
```

The View Class

CTetrisView is the view class of the application. It receives system messages and (completely or partly) redraws the client area.

The field m_iColorStatus holds the painting status of the view. Its status can be either color or grayscale. The color status is the normal mode, m_iColorStatus is initialized to color in the constructor. The grayscale is used to flash rows and to set the game grid in grayscale while asking the user for another game.

OnCreate is called after the view has been created but before it is shown. The field m_pTetrisDoc is set to point at the document class object. It is also confirmed to be valid. OnSize is called each time the size of the view is changed. It sets the global variables g_iRowHeight and g_iColWidth (defined in Figure.h), which are used by method of the Figure and ColorGrid classes to paint the squares of the figures and the grid.

OnSetFocus and OnKillFocus are called when the view receives and loses the input focus. Its task is to handle the timer. The idea is that the timer shall continue to send timer messages every second as long as the view has the input focus. Therefore, OnSetFocus sets the timer and OnKillFocus kills it. This arrangement implies that OnTimer is called each second the view has input focus.

In Windows, the timer cannot be turned off temporarily; instead, we have to set and kill it. The base class of the view, CWnd, has two methods: SetTimer that initializes a timer and KillTimer that stops the timer. The first parameter is a unique identifier to distinguish this particular timer from any other one. The second parameter gives the time interval of the timer, in milliseconds. When we send a null pointer as the third parameter, the timer message will be sent to the view and caught by OnTimer. KillTimer simply takes the identity of the timer to finish.

```
UINT_PTR SetTimer(UINT_PTR iIDEvent, UINT iElapse,
                  void (CALLBACK* lpfnTimer)
                       (HWND, UINT, UINT_PTR, DWORD));
BOOL KillTimer(UINT_PTR nIDEvent);
```

OnKeyDown is called every time the user presses a key on the keyboard. It analizes the pressed key and calls suitable methods in the document class if the left, right, up, or down arrow key or the space key is pressed.

When a method of the document class calls `UpdateAllViews`, `OnUpdate` of the view class object connected to the document object is called. As this is a single view application, the application has only one view object on which `OnUpdate` is called. `UpdateAllViews` takes two extra parameters, hints, which are sent to `OnUpdate`. The first hint tells us whether the next repainting shall be done in color or in grayscale, the second hint is a pointer to a rectangle holding the area that is to be repainted. If the pointer is not null, we calculate the area and repaint it. If it is null, the whole client area is repainted.

`OnUpdate` is also called by `OnInitialUpdate` of the base class `CView` with both hints set to zero. That is not a problem because the `COLOR` constant is set to zero. The effect of this call is that the whole view is painted in color.

`OnUpdate` calls `UpdateWindow` in `CView` that in turn calls `OnPaint` and `OnDraw` with a device context. `OnPaint` is also called by the system when the view (partly or completely) needs to be repainted. `OnDraw` loads the device context with a black pen and then draws the grid, the score list, and the active and next figures.

TetrisView.h

```
const int TIMER_ID = 0;
enum {COLOR = 0, GRAY = 1};
class CTetrisDoc;
COLORREF GrayScale(COLORREF rfColor);
class CTetrisView : public CView
{
  protected:
    CTetrisView();

    DECLARE_DYNCREATE(CTetrisView)
    DECLARE_MESSAGE_MAP()
  public:
    afx_msg int OnCreate(LPCREATESTRUCT lpCreateStruct);
    afx_msg void OnSize(UINT nType, int iClientWidth,
                        int iClientHeight);

    afx_msg void OnSetFocus(CWnd* pOldWnd);
    afx_msg void OnKillFocus(CWnd* pNewWnd);
    afx_msg void OnKeyDown(UINT nChar, UINT nRepCnt,
                           UINT nFlags);
    afx_msg void OnTimer(UINT nIDEvent);
    void OnUpdate(CView* /* pSender */, LPARAM lHint,
                  CObject* pHint);
    void OnDraw(CDC* pDC);
```

```
   private:
     void DrawGrid(CDC* pDC);

     void DrawScoreAndScoreList(CDC* pDC);

     void DrawActiveAndNextFigure(CDC* pDC);

   private:
     CTetrisDoc* m_pTetrisDoc;
     int m_iColorStatus;
};
```

TetrisView.cpp

This application catches the messsages WM_CREATE, WM_SIZE, WM_SETFOCUS, WM_KILLFOCUS, WM_TIMER, and WM_KEYDOWN.

```
BEGIN_MESSAGE_MAP(CTetrisView, CView)
  ON_WM_CREATE()
  ON_WM_SIZE()
  ON_WM_SETFOCUS()
  ON_WM_KILLFOCUS()
  ON_WM_TIMER()
  ON_WM_KEYDOWN()
END_MESSAGE_MAP()
```

When the view object is created, is connected to the document object by the pointer m_pTetrisDoc.

```
int CTetrisView::OnCreate(LPCREATESTRUCT lpCreateStruct)
{
  // We check that the view has been correctly created.
  if (CView::OnCreate(lpCreateStruct) == -1)
  {
    return -1;
  }
  m_pTetrisDoc = (CTetrisDoc*) m_pDocument;
  check(m_pTetrisDoc != NULL);
  ASSERT_VALID(m_pTetrisDoc);
  return 0;
}
```

The game grid is dimensioned by the constants ROWS and COLS. Each time the user changes the size of the application window, the global variables g_iRowHeight and g_iColWidth, which are defined in Figure.h, store the height and width of one square in pixels.

```
void CTetrisView::OnSize(UINT /* uType */,int iClientWidth,
                                            int iClientHeight)
{
  g_iRowHeight = iClientHeight / ROWS;
  g_iColWidth = (iClientWidth / 2) / COLS;
}
```

OnUpdate is called by the system when the window needs to be (partly or completely) repainted. In that case, the parameter pHint is zero and the whole client area is repainted. However, this method is also indirectly called when the document class calls UpdateAllView. In that case, lHint has the value color or gray, depending on whether the client area shall be repainted in color or in a grayscale.

If pHint is non-zero, it stores the coordinates of the area to be repainted. The coordinates are given in grid coordinates that have to be translated into pixel coordinates before the area is invalidated.

The method first calls Invalidate or InvalidateRect to define the area to be repainted, then the call to UpdateWindow does the actual repainting by calling OnPaint in CView, which in turn calls OnDraw below.

```
void CTetrisView::OnUpdate(CView* /* pSender */, LPARAM lHint,
                            CObject* pHint)
{
  m_iColorStatus = (int) lHint;
  if (pHint != NULL)
  {
    CRect rcArea = *(CRect*) pHint;
    rcArea.left *= g_iColWidth;
    rcArea.right *= g_iColWidth;
    rcArea.top *= g_iRowHeight;
    rcArea.bottom *= g_iRowHeight;
    InvalidateRect(&rcArea);
  }
  else
  {
    Invalidate();
  }
  UpdateWindow();
}
```

`OnDraw` is called when the client area needs to be repainted, by the system or by `UpdateWindow` in `OnUpdate`. It draws a vertical line in the middle of the client area, and then draws the game grid, the high score list, and the current figures.

```
void CTetrisView::OnDraw(CDC* pDC)
{
  CPen pen(PS_SOLID, 0, BLACK);
  CPen* pOldPen = pDC->SelectObject(&pen);

  pDC->MoveTo(COLS * g_iColWidth, 0);
  pDC->LineTo(COLS * g_iColWidth, ROWS * g_iRowHeight);

  DrawGrid(pDC);
  DrawScoreAndScoreList(pDC);
  DrawActiveAndNextFigure(pDC);

  pDC->SelectObject(&pOldPen);
}
```

`DrawGrid` traverses through the game grid and paints each non-white square. If a square is not occupied, it has the color white and it not painted. The field `m_iColorStatus` decides whether the game grid shall be painted in color or in grayscale.

```
void CTetrisView::DrawGrid(CDC* pDC)
{
  const ColorGrid* pGrid = m_pTetrisDoc->GetGrid();
  for (int iRow = 0; iRow < ROWS; ++iRow)
  {
    for (int iCol = 0; iCol < COLS; ++iCol)
    {
      COLORREF rfColor = pGrid->Index(iRow, iCol);
      if (rfColor != WHITE)
      {
        CBrush brush((m_iColorStatus == COLOR)
                ? rfColor :GrayScale(rfColor));
        CBrush* pOldBrush = pDC->SelectObject(&brush);
        DrawSquare(iRow, iCol, pDC);
        pDC->SelectObject(pOldBrush);
      }
    }
  }
}
```

GrayScale returns the grayscale of the given color, which is obtained by mixing the average of the red, blue, and green component of the color.

```
COLORREF GrayScale(COLORREF rfColor)
{
  int iRed = GetRValue(rfColor);
  int iGreen = GetGValue(rfColor);
  int iBlue = GetBValue(rfColor);

  int iAverage = (iRed + iGreen + iBlue) / 3;
  return RGB(iAverage, iAverage, iAverage);
}
```

The active figure (m_activeFigure) is the figure falling down on the game grid. The next figure (m_nextFigure) is the figure announced at the right side of the client area. In order for it to be painted at the right-hand side, we alter the origin to the middle of the client area, and one row under the upper border by calling SetWindowOrg.

```
void CTetrisView::DrawActiveAndNextFigure(CDC* pDC)
{
  const Figure activeFigure = m_pTetrisDoc->GetActiveFigure();
  activeFigure.Draw(m_iColorStatus, pDC);

  const Figure nextFigure = m_pTetrisDoc->GetNextFigure();
  CPoint ptOrigin(-COLS * g_iColWidth, -g_iRowHeight);
  pDC->SetWindowOrg(ptOrigin);
  nextFigure.Draw(m_iColorStatus, pDC);
}
```

The Figure Class

All figures can be moved to the left or the right as well as be rotated clockwise or counterclockwise as a response to the user's requests. They can also be moved downwards as a response to the timer. The crossed square in the figures of this section marks the center of the figure, that is, the position the fields m_iRow and m_iCol of the Figure class refer to.

All kinds of figures are in fact objects of the Figure class. What differs between the figures are their colors and their shapes. The files FigureInfo.h and FigureInfo. cpp holds the information specific for each kind of figure, see the next section.

The field m_rfColor holds the color of the figure, m_pColorGrid is a pointer to the color grid of the game grid, m_iRow, m_iCol, and m_iDirection are the positions and the directions of the figure, respectively. The figure can be rotated into the directions north, east, south, and west. However, the red figure is a square, so it cannot be rotated at all. Moreover, the brown, turquoise, and green figures can only be rotated into vertical and horizontal directions, which implies that the north and south directions are the same for these figures, as are the east and west directions.

The second constructor takes a parameter of the type FigureInfo, which holds the shape of the figure in all four directions. They hold the position of the squares of the figure relative to the middle squares referred to by m_iRow and m_iCol for each of the four directions. The FigureInfo type consists of four arrays, one for each direction. The arrays in turn hold four positions, one for each square of the figure. The first position is always zero since it refers to the center square. For instance, let us look at the yellow figure in south direction.

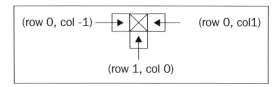

The crossed square above is the one referred to by m_iRow and m_iCol. The south array for the yellow figure is initialized as follows.

```
SquareArray YellowSouth = {Square(0, 0), Square(0, -1),
                           Square(1, 0), Square(0, 1)};
```

The first square object refers to the center square, so it always holds zero. The other square objects holds the position of one square each relative to the center square. The second square object refers to the square to the left of the center square in the figure. Note that the row numbers increase downward and the column numbers increase to the right. Therefore, the relative column is negative. The third square object refers to the square below the crossed one, one row down and the same column, and the fourth square object refers to the square to the right, the same row and one column to the right.

The methods RotateClockwiseOneQuarter and RotateCounterclockwiseOneQuarter move the direction 90 degrees. MoveLeft, MoveRight, RotateClockwise, RotateCounterclockwise, and MoveDown all works in the same way. They execute the operation in question, test whether the figure is still valid (its squares are not already occupied), and return true if it is. Otherwise, they undo the operation and return false. Again, note that row numbers increase downwards and column numbers increase to the right.

IsSquareValid tests whether the given position is on the game grid and not occupied by a color other then white. IsFigureValid tests whether the four squares of the whole figure are valid at their current position and in their current direction.

GetArea returns the area currently occupied by the figure. Note that the area is returned in color grid coordinates (rows and columns). The coordinates are translated into pixel coordinates by OnUpdate in the view class before the figure is repainted.

When a figure is done falling, its squares shall be added to the grid. AddToGrid takes care of that, it sets the color of this figure to the squares currently occupied of the figure in the color grid.

Draw is called by the view class when the figure needs to be redrawn. It draws the four squares of the figure in color or grayscale. DrawSquare is called by Draw and does the actual drawing of each square. It is a global function because it is also called by the ColorGrid class to draw the squares of the grid. The global variables g_iRowHeight and g_iColWidth are set by the view class method OnSize every time the user changes the size of the view. They are used to calculate the positions and dimensions of the squares in DrawSquare.

Serialize stores and loads the current row, column, and direction of the figure as well as its color. It also writes and reads the four direction arrays.

The two global C standard library methods memset and memcpy come in handy when we want to copy a memory block or turn it to zero. They are used by the constructors to copy the directions arrays and turn them to zero.

```
void *memset(void* pDestination, int iValue, size_t iSize);
void *memcpy(void* pDestination, const void* pSource,
             size_t iSize);
```

Figure.h

```
const COLORREF BLACK = RGB(0, 0, 0);
const COLORREF WHITE = RGB(255, 255, 255);
const COLORREF DEFAULT_COLOR = WHITE;

class ColorGrid;
extern int g_iRowHeight, g_iColWidth;
enum {NORTH = 0, EAST = 1, SOUTH = 2, WEST = 3};

const int SQUARE_ARRAY_SIZE = 4;
const int SQUARE_INFO_SIZE = 4;

typedef Square SquareArray[SQUARE_ARRAY_SIZE];
typedef SquareArray SquareInfo[SQUARE_INFO_SIZE];
```

```
class Figure
{
  public:
    Figure();
    Figure(int iDirection, COLORREF rfColor,
           const SquareInfo& squareInfo);

    Figure operator=(const Figure& figure);
    void SetColorGrid(ColorGrid* pColorGrid) {m_pColorGrid =
                                                pColorGrid;};

  private:
    BOOL IsSquareValid(int iRow, int iCol) const;

  public:
    BOOL IsFigureValid() const;

    BOOL MoveLeft();
    BOOL MoveRight();

  private:
    void RotateClockwiseOneQuarter();
    void RotateCounterclockwiseOneQuarter();

  public:
    BOOL RotateClockwise();
    BOOL RotateCounterclockwise();
    BOOL MoveDown();

    void AddToGrid();
    CRect GetArea() const;

  public:
    void Draw(int iColorStatus, CDC* pDC) const;
    friend void DrawSquare(int iRow, int iCol, CDC* pDC);

  public:
    void Serialize(CArchive& archive);

  private:
    COLORREF m_rfColor;
    ColorGrid* m_pColorGrid;
    int m_iRow, m_iCol, m_iDirection;
    SquareInfo m_squareInfo;
};

typedef CArray<const Figure> FigurePtrArray;
```

Figure.cpp

`Figure.cpp` the main constructor. It initializes the direction (north, east, south, or west), the color (red, brown, turquoise, green, yellow, blue, or purple), the pointer to `ColorGrid`, and the specific figure information. The red figure sub class will initialize all four direction arrays with the same values because it cannot be rotated. The brown, turquoise, and green figure sub classes will initialize both the north and south arrays to its vertical direction as well as the east and west directions to its horizontal direction. Finally, the yellow, blue, and purple figure sub classes will initialize all four arrays with different values because they can be rotated in all four directions.

The C standard funtion `memcpy` is used to copy the figure specific information.

```
Figure::Figure(int iDirection, COLORREF rfColor,
               const SquareInfo & squareInfo)
 :m_iRow(0),
  m_iCol(COLS / 2),
  m_iDirection(iDirection),
  m_rfColor(rfColor),
  m_pColorGrid(NULL)
{
   ::memcpy(&m_squareInfo, &squareInfo, sizeof m_squareInfo);
}
```

`IsSquareValid` is called by `IsFigureValid` below. It checks whether the given square is on the grid and that it is not already occupied by another color.

```
BOOL Figure::IsSquareValid(int iRow, int iCol) const
{
   return (iRow >= 0) && (iRow < ROWS) &&
          (iCol >= 0) && (iCol < COLS) &&
          (m_pColorGrid->Index(iRow, iCol) == DEFAULT_COLOR);
}
```

`IsFigureValid` checks whether the figure is at a valid position by examining the four squares of the figure. It is called by `MoveLeft`, `MoveRight`, `Rotate`, and `MoveDown` below:

```
BOOL Figure::IsFigureValid() const
{
   SquareArray* pSquareArray = m_squareInfo[m_iDirection];
   for (int iIndex = 0; iIndex < SQUARE_ARRAY_SIZE; ++iIndex)
   {
     Square& square = (*pSquareArray)[iIndex];
     if (!IsSquareValid(m_iRow + square.Row(), m_iCol + square.Col()))
```

```
    {
      return FALSE;
    }
  }
  return TRUE;
}
```

`RotateClockwiseOneQuarter` rotates the direction clockwise one quarter of a complete turn. `RotateCounterclockwiseOneQuarter` works in a similar way.

```
void Figure::RotateClockwiseOneQuarter()
{
    switch (m_iDirection)
    {
      case NORTH:
        m_iDirection = EAST;
        break;
      case EAST:
        m_iDirection = SOUTH;
        break;
      case SOUTH:
        m_iDirection = WEST;
        break;
      case WEST:
        m_iDirection = NORTH;
        break;
    }
}
```

`MoveLeft` moves the figure one step to the left. If the figure then is valid it returns true. If it is not, it puts the figure to back in origional position and returns false. `MoveRight`, `RotateClockwise`, `RotateCounterclockwise`, and `MoveDown` work in a similar way. Remember that the rows increase downwards and the columns increase to the right.

```
BOOL Figure::MoveLeft()
{
    --m_iCol;
    if (IsFigureValid())
    {
      return TRUE;
    }
    else
    {
```

```
            ++m_iCol;
            return FALSE;
        }
    }
```

`AddToGrid` is called by the document class when the figure cannot be moved another step downwards. In that case, a new figure is introduced and the squares of the figure are added to the grid, that is, the squares currently occupied by the figure are the to the figure's color.

```
void Figure::AddToGrid()
{
    SquareArray* pSquareArray = m_squareInfo[m_iDirection];
    for (int iIndex = 0; iIndex < SQUARE_ARRAY_SIZE; ++iIndex)
    {
        Square& square = (*pSquareArray)[iIndex];
        m_pColorGrid->Index(m_iRow + square.Row(),
                            m_iCol + square.Col()) = m_rfColor;
    }
}
```

When a figure has been moved and rotated, it needs to be repainted. In order to do so without having to repaint the whole game grid we need the figures area. We calculate it by comparing the values of the squares of the figure in its current direction. The rectangle returned holds the coordinates of the squares, not pixel coordinates. The translation is done by `OnUpdate` in the `view` class.

```
CRect Figure::GetArea() const
{
    int iMinRow = 0, iMaxRow = 0, iMinCol = 0, iMaxCol = 0;
    SquareArray* pSquareArray = m_squareInfo[m_iDirection];
    for (int iIndex = 0; iIndex < SQUARE_ARRAY_SIZE; ++iIndex)
    {
        Square& square = (*pSquareArray)[iIndex];
        int iRow = square.Row();
        iMinRow = (iRow < iMinRow) ? iRow : iMinRow;
        iMaxRow = (iRow > iMaxRow) ? iRow : iMaxRow;

        int iCol = square.Col();
        iMinCol = (iCol < iMinCol) ? iCol : iMinCol;
        iMaxCol = (iCol > iMaxCol) ? iCol : iMaxCol;
    }
    return CRect(m_iCol + iMinCol, m_iRow + iMinRow,
                 m_iCol + iMaxCol + 1, m_iRow + iMaxRow + 1);
}
```

Draw is called when the figure needs to be repainted. It selects a black pen and a brush with the figure's color. Then it draws the four squares of the figure. The iColorStatus parameter makes the figure appear in color or in grayscale.

```
void Figure::Draw(int iColorStatus, CDC* pDC) const
{
  CPen pen(PS_SOLID, 0, BLACK);
  CPen* pOldPen = pDC->SelectObject(&pen);
  CBrush brush((iColorStatus == COLOR) ? m_rfColor : GrayScale(
                                              m_rfColor));
  CBrush* pOldBrush = pDC->SelectObject(&brush);
  SquareArray* pSquareArray = m_squareInfo[m_iDirection];
  for (int iIndex = 0; iIndex < SQUARE_ARRAY_SIZE; ++iIndex)
  {
    Square& square = (*pSquareArray)[iIndex];
    DrawSquare(m_iRow + square.Row(), m_iCol + square.Col(), pDC);
  }
  pDC->SelectObject(&pOldBrush);
  pDC->SelectObject(&pOldPen);
}
```

The Figure Information

There are seven figures, each of them has their own color: red, brown, turquoise, green, yellow, blue, and purple. Each of them also has a unique shape. However, they all consist of four squares. They can further be divided into three groups based on the ability to rotate. The red figure is the simplest one, as it does not rotate at all. The brown, turquoise, and green figures can be rotated in vertical and horizontal directions while the yellow, blue, and purple figures can be rotated in north, east, south, and west directions.

As seen above, the document class creates one object of each figure. When doing so, it uses the information stored in FigureInfo.h and FigureInfo.cpp.

In this section, we visualize every figure with a sketch like the one in the previous section. The crossed square is the center position referred to by the fields m_iRow and m_iCol in Figure. The positions of the other squares relative to the crossed one are given by the integer pairs in the directions arrays.

First of all, we need do define the color of each figure. We do so by using the COLORREF type.

FigureInfo.cpp

```
const COLORREF RED = RGB(255, 0, 0);
const COLORREF BROWN = RGB(255, 128, 0);
const COLORREF TURQUOISE = RGB(0, 255, 255);
const COLORREF GREEN = RGB(0, 255, 0);
const COLORREF BLUE = RGB(0, 0, 255);
const COLORREF PURPLE = RGB(255, 0, 255);
const COLORREF YELLOW = RGB(255, 255, 0);
```

The Red Figure

The red figure is one large square, built up by four regular squares. It is the simplest figure of the game since it does not change shape when rotating. This implies that we just need to look at one figure.

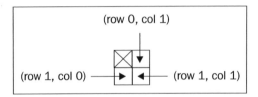

In this case, it is enough to define the squares for one direction and use it to define the shape of the figure in all four directions.

```
SquareArray RedGeneric = {Square(0, 0), Square(0, 1),
                          Square(1, 1), Square(1, 0)};
SquareInfo RedInfo = {&RedGeneric, &RedGeneric,
                      &RedGeneric, &RedGeneric};
```

The Brown Figure

The brown figure can be oriented in horizontal and vertical directions. It is initialized by the constructor to a vertical direction. As it can only be rotated into two directions, the north and south array will be initialized with the vertical array and the east and west array will be initialized with the horizontal array.

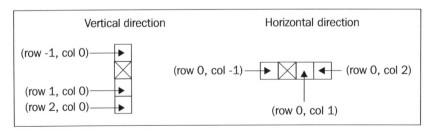

```
SquareArray BrownVertical = {Square(0, 0), Square(-1, 0),
                             Square(1, 0), Square(2, 0)};
SquareArray BrownHorizontal = {Square(0, 0), Square(0, -1),
                               Square(0, 1), Square(0, 2)};
SquareInfo BrownInfo = {&BrownVertical, &BrownHorizontal,
                        &BrownVertical, &BrownHorizontal};
```

The Turquoise Figure

Similar to the brown figure, the turquoise figure can be rotated in the vertical and horizontal directions.

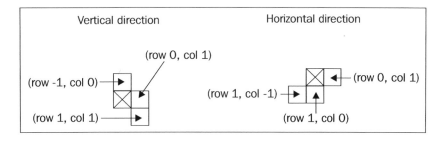

```
SquareArray TurquoiseVertical = {Square(0, 0), Square(-1, 0),
                                 Square(0, 1), Square(1, 1)};
SquareArray TurquoiseHorizontal = {Square(0, 0), Square(1, -1),
                                   Square(1, 0), Square(0, 1)};
SquareInfo TurquoiseInfo = {&TurquoiseVertical, &TurquoiseHorizontal,
                            &TurquoiseVertical,&TurquoiseHorizontal};
```

The Green Figure

The green figure is a mirror image of the turquoise figure.

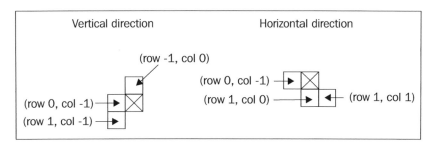

```
SquareArray GreenVertical = {Square(0, 0), Square(1, -1),
                             Square(0, -1), Square(-1, 0)};
SquareArray GreenHorizontal = {Square(0, 0), Square(0, -1),
                               Square(1, 0), Square(1, 1)};

SquareInfo GreenInfo = {&GreenVertical, &GreenHorizontal,
                        &GreenVertical, &GreenHorizontal};
```

The Yellow Figure

The yellow figure can be rotated in the north, east, south, and west directions. It is initialized by the `Figure` class constructor to the south direction.

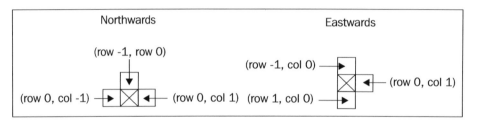

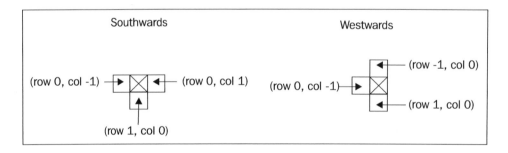

```
SquareArray YellowNorth = {Square(0, 0), Square(0, -1),
                           Square(-1, 0), Square(0, 1)};
SquareArray YellowEast = {Square(0, 0), Square(-1, 0),
                          Square(0, 1), Square(1, 0)};
SquareArray YellowSouth = {Square(0, 0), Square(0, -1),
                           Square(1, 0), Square(0, 1)};
SquareArray YellowWest = {Square(0, 0), Square(-1, 0),
                          Square(0, -1), Square(1, 0)};
SquareInfo YellowInfo = {&YellowNorth, &YellowEast,
                         &YellowSouth, &YellowWest};
```

The Blue Figure

The blue figure can also be in all four directions. It is initialized to the south direction.

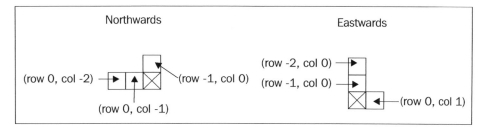

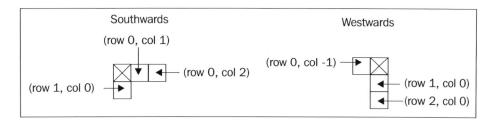

```
SquareArray BlueNorth = {Square(0, 0), Square(0, -2),
                         Square(0, -1),Square(-1, 0)};
SquareArray BlueEast = {Square(0, 0), Square(-2, 0),
                        Square(-1, 0), Square(0, 1)};
SquareArray BlueSouth = {Square(0, 0), Square(1, 0),
                         Square(0, 1), Square(0, 2)};
SquareArray BlueWest = {Square(0, 0), Square(0, -1),
                        Square(1, 0), Square(2, 0)};
SquareInfo BlueInfo = {&BlueNorth, &BlueEast,
                       &BlueSouth, &BlueWest};
```

The Purple Figure

The purple figure, finally, is a mirror image of the blue figure, it is also initialized into the south direction.

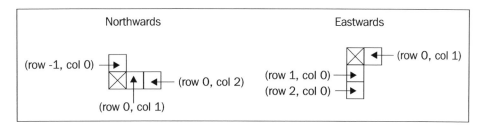

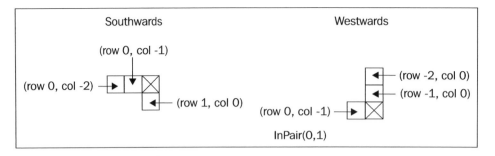

```
SquareArray PurpleNorth = {Square(0, 0), Square(-1, 0),
                           Square(0, 1), Square(0, 2)};
SquareArray PurpleEast = {Square(0, 0), Square(1, 0),
                          Square(2, 0), Square(0, 1)};
SquareArray PurpleSouth = {Square(0, 0), Square(0, -2),
                           Square(0, -1), Square(1, 0)};
SquareArray PurpleWest = {Square(0, 0), Square(0, -1),
                          Square(-2, 0), Square(-1, 0)};
SquareInfo PurpleInfo = {&PurpleNorth, &PurpleEast,
                         &PurpleSouth, &PurpleWest};
```

Summary

- We have generated a framework for the application with the Application Wizard.

- We added the classes Square and ColorGrid that keep track of the game grid.

- We defined the document class. It holds the data of the game and keeps track of when the game is over.

- We defined the view class, it accepts keyboard input and draws the figures and the game grid.

- The Figure class manages a single figure, it keeps track of its position and decides whether it is valid to move it into another position.

- The Figure info files store information of the seven kinds of figures.

The Draw Application

7

In this chapter, we will deal with a drawing program. It is capable of drawing lines, arrows, rectangles, and ellipses. It is also capable of writing and editing text, cut-and-paste figures as well as saving and loading the drawings. The following screenshot depicts a classic example of the Draw Application:

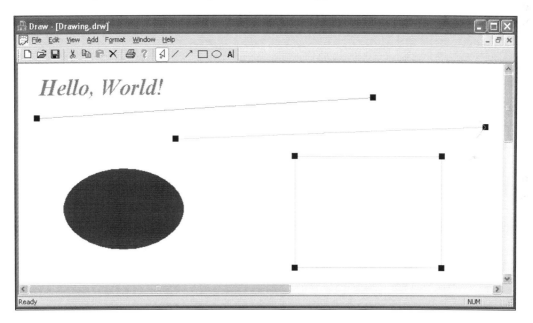

- We start by generating the application's skeleton code with the Application Wizard. The process is similar to the Ring application code.
- The figures are represented by a class hierarchy. The root class is Figure. It is abstract and has a set of pure virtual methods that are to be defined by its sub classes. It has one abstract sub class TwoDimensionalFigure.

- There are five concrete sub classes in the hierarchy: `LineFigure`, `ArrowFigure`, `RectangleFigure`, `EllipseFigure`, and `TextFigure`. There is also the class `FigureFileManager` that handles the file management of the figures.

- The `document` class manages the data of the drawing. It has a list to keep track of the figure objects and several fields to keep track of the state of the application.

- The `view` class accepts input from the mouse and keyboard and draws the figures.

The Application Wizard process generates the classes `CDrawApp`, `CMainFrame`, `CAboutDlg`, `CDrawDoc`, and `CDrawView`. The skeleton source code for these classes is automatically generated by Visual Studio. As before, among these classes we will only modify `CDrawDoc` and `CDrawView`. However, we will create and add the class `Figure`, which is an abstract base class handling general functionality of the figures. The classes `LineFigure`, `ArrowFigure`, `RectangleFigure`, `EllipseFigure`, and `TextFigure` define the functionality of the figures. `TwoDimensionalFigure` is an abstract help class. The classes `Color`, `Font`, and `Caret` from Chapter 5 will also be used in this application.

Let us start by creating the application with the Application Wizard. The generation process is almost identical to the one of the Ring application in Chapter 4. The only difference is the **Document Template Strings** option; we state **drw** as the **File extension**, and **A Draw Application Document** as **File type long name**. This implies that we can start the application in Windows Explorer by choosing the application, or by choosing one of the documents (a file with the extension `.drw`) of the application. The application will be launched and (in the latter case) open the document.

Similar to the Ring application, but unlike the Tetris application, we choose
CSCrollView as the view base class.

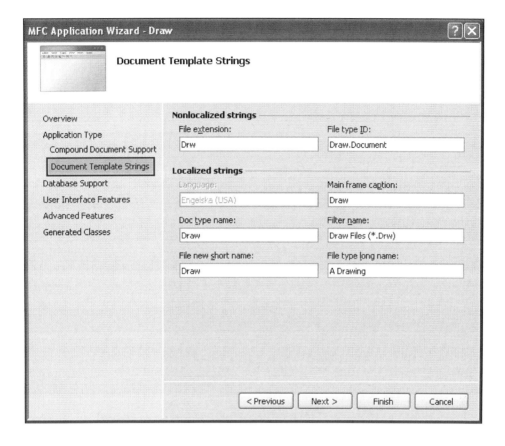

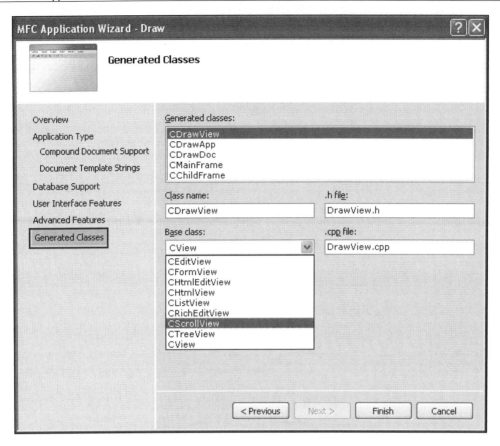

When the generation process is finished, it has generated the classes CDrawApp, CMainFrame, CChildFrame, CDrawDoc, CDrawView, and CAboutDlg. We add a few include lines to Draw.cpp below. Otherwise, we will only modify CDrawDoc and CDrawView as we develop the application, the rest of the classes will remain unmodified.

Draw.cpp

```
#include "MainFrm.h"
#include "ChildFrm.h"
#include "..\\List.h"
#include "..\\Color.h"
#include "..\\Font.h"
#include "..\\Caret.h"
#include "Figure.h"
#include "TwoDimensionalFigure.h"
#include "RectangleFigure.h"
#include "TextFigure.h"
```

The Resource

The Application Wizard creates a basic set of menus, which are used by the Application Framework. We add the menus **Add** and **Format** to the resource with the help of the Resource Editor.

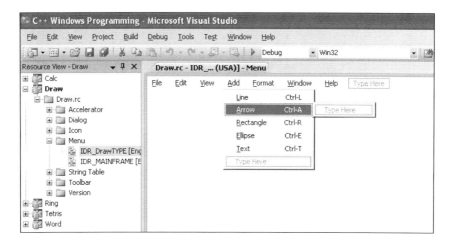

It is also possible to use the Resource Editor to add accelerators. The Application Wizard has already added accelerators to some of the menu items it generated. We will add accelerators to the menu item we have added. One advantage is that we can reuse the menu item identifiers above to represent accelerators. This means that the Application Framework will call the same method, no matter if the user has selected the menu item or the accelerator. We can also reuse the same identifiers to represent a button in a toolbar. The Application Wizard creates a default toolbar we can increase.

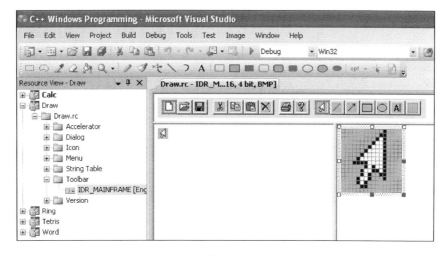

We can also add a status line and a tool tip with the help of the string table. The string connected to the identifier is divided into two parts by a new line (\n). The first part is the status line and the second part is the tool tip. A status line is shown at the lower edge of the window when the user selects a menu item or holds the mouse pointer at a toolbar button. A tool tip is shown as a little box when the user holds the mouse pointer at a toolbar button.

Here is a summarization of the added menus, accelerators, toolbar buttons, and strings.

Id	Menu Item	Accelerator Toolbar	String Table
ID_EDIT_CUT	Edit\Cut	Ctrl-X	Cut the selection and put it on the Clipboard \nCut
ID_EDIT_COPY	Edit\Copy	Ctrl-C	Copy the selection and put it on the Clipboard \nCopy
ID_EDIT_PASTE	Edit\Paste	Ctrl-V	Insert Clipboard contents\ nPaste
ID_EDIT_DELETE	Edit\Delete	Delete	Delete a Figure in the Drawing\nDelete Figure
ID_ADD_LINE	Add\Line	Ctrl-L	Add a Line to the Drawing\nAdd Line
ID_ADD_ARROW	Add\Arrow	Ctrl-A	Add an Arrow to the Drawing\nAdd Arrow
ID_ADD_RECTANGLE	Add\Rectangle	Ctrl-R	Add a Rectangle to the Drawing\nAdd Rectangle
ID_ADD_ELLIPSE	Add\Ellipse	Ctrl-E	Add an Ellipse to the Drawing\nAdd Ellipse
ID_ADD_TEXT	Add\TextFigure	Ctrl-T	Add a TextFigure to the Drawing\nAdd TextFigure
ID_FORMAT_MODIFY	Format\Modify	Ctrl-M	Modify a Figure in the Drawing\nModify Figure
ID_FORMAT_COLOR	Format\Color	Alt-C	Set the Color of a Figure\ nFigure
ID_FORMAT_FONT	Format\Font	Ctrl-F	Set the Font of a TextFigure\nFont
ID_FORMAT_FILL	Format\Fill	Alt-I	Fill a Figure\nFill

The underlines in the menu items are designated by an ampersand (&) before the underlined letter. For instance, **Arrow** is written as **&Arrow**. They are used as shortcut commands. The Edit menu is generated by the Application Wizard and is included in the table because we will use it in the document class. These items will be caught with the help of a message map.

There is an important identifier IDR_DRAWTYPE. It reflects the information we added when we created the project.

```
\nDraw\nDraw\nDraw Files (*.drw)\n.drw\nDraw.Document\n
A Draw Application Document
```

We can also use the Version Resource to define the name of the application.

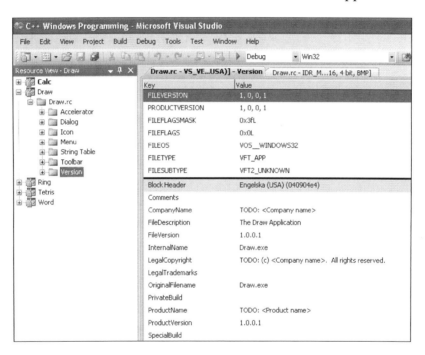

The Class Hierarchy

Now we are ready to start building the real application. We are going to construct a drawing program. The user will be able to draw lines, arrows, rectangles, ellipses, and will be able to write text. Do not confuse the Figure class of this application with the Figure class of the Tetris application. In this application, Figure is an **abstract base class**, it works as a blue print for the sub classes. Figure only handles the color and mark status of the figure. Otherwise, it consists of pure virtual methods that are to be defined by the sub classes.

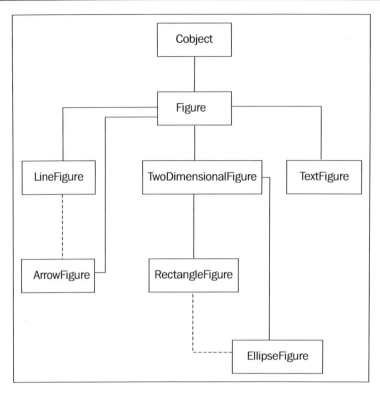

As is custom in MFC, we let Cobject to be the root class of the hierarchy. The dashed lines in the diagram denote private inheritance, which means that all public and protected members in the base class become private in the sub class. Private inheritance is not a part of the object-oriented model, but it comes in handy when we want to reuse code in the base class.

The Figure Class

The default constructor of Figure is used only in connection with serialization. The second constructor is called by the sub classes in order to initialize the figure's color and mark status. The third constructer is called by the Copy function, which in turn is called by the document class when the user wants to copy or paste a figure. It returns a pointer to a copy of the figure object. It is defined in each sub class in such a way that Copy calls the copy constructor. The copy constructor itself would not be sufficient because we want to copy a figure given only a pointer to a Figure object; that is, without knowing the class of the object.

All figures have two things in common: they have a color, and they may be marked. The class has two fields `m_bMarked` and `m_figureColor` reflecting these features. It also has the functions `IsMarked`, `Mark`, `SetColor`, and `GetColor` to inspect and modify the fields.

`Serialize` is called by the framework when a user chooses to save or open a drawing. The framework creates a `CArchive` object and connects it to the file. Our function just has to read or write the values of its fields. In the `Figure` case, we just have to deal with the color of the figure, we do not serialize the mark status. The `Serialize` versions of the sub class functions work similar ways, they call `Serialize` of the nearest base class, and then serialize their own values.

Then we have the two pure virtual functions `Click` and `DoubleClick`. They are called by the document object when a user clicks or double-clicks with the mouse. Their task is first to decide whether a user has clicked on the figure and secondly to decide if the user has hit one of the modified squares. Exactly where those squares are located relative to the figure varies between the figures. Besides, the class `TextFigure` has no such squares, even though they are drawn when the text is marked. `Inside` is a similar function. It takes a rectangle object and decides if the figure is completely enclosed by the rectangle. It is called when the user wants to mark an area. Each class sets internal fields in accordance to these findings, in order to modify the position, size, and color of the figure when `MoveOrModify` and `Move` is called.

`MoveOrModify` is called by the document class when the user has marked a figure and moves it. As the name implies, the figure is either moved or modified depending on the preceding calls to `Click`, `DoubleClick`, or `Inside`. `Move` is a simpler version; it does always move the figure, regardless of what the call to the preceding function has decided. It is called when the user moves several figures.

`Draw` is called by the view class for each figure to draw their physical shape. It is given a device context connected to the calling view object. `GetArea` returns a `CRect` object containing the figure's physical measurements in logical units.

Finally, we have the constant `SQUARE_SIDE` that defines the size of the black squares marking the figures. It is initialized to the value of `200`. The measurement given in logical coordinates. As 200 logical units is equivalent to 200 hundredths of a millimeter, each square will have a side of two millimeters.

Figure.h

```
class Figure : public CObject
{
  public:
    Figure();
    Figure(const Color& color, BOOL bMarked = FALSE);

    Figure(const Figure& figure);
    virtual Figure* Copy() const = 0;

    BOOL IsMarked() const {return m_bMarked;}
    void Mark(const BOOL bMarked) {m_bMarked = bMarked;}

    Color GetColor() const {return m_figureColor;}
    void SetColor(const Color& color) {m_figureColor = color;}

    virtual void Serialize(CArchive& archive);
    virtual HCURSOR GetCursor() const = 0;

    virtual BOOL Click(const CPoint& ptMouse) = 0;
    virtual BOOL DoubleClick(const CPoint& ptMouse) = 0;
    virtual BOOL Inside(const CRect& rcInside) const = 0;

    virtual void MoveOrModify(const CSize& szDistance) = 0;
    virtual void Move(const CSize& szDistance) = 0;

    virtual void Draw(CDC* pDC) const = 0;
    virtual CRect GetArea() const = 0;

  private:
    BOOL m_bMarked;
    Color m_figureColor;

  protected:
    static const int SQUARE_SIDE = 200;
};

typedef List<Figure*> FigurePointerList;
```

In this application, we use our generic list class `List`. We define the type `FigurePointerList` from it. A figure list will be added to and removed from as the user adds or removes figures from the drawing. We also need means to iterate the list in both directions.

Figure.cpp

```
#include "StdAfx.h"

#include "..\\List.h"
#include "..\\Color.h"
#include "..\\Font.h"

#include "Figure.h"
```

```
Figure::Figure()
 :m_figureColor(0),
  m_bMarked(FALSE)
{
    // Empty.
}
Figure::Figure(const Figure& figure)
 :m_figureColor(figure.m_figureColor),
  m_bMarked(figure.m_bMarked)
{
    // Empty.
}
Figure::Figure(const Color& color, BOOL bMark /* = FALSE */)
 :m_figureColor(color),
  m_bMarked(bMark)
{
    // Empty.
}
void Figure::Serialize(CArchive& archive)
{
  CObject::Serialize(archive);
  m_figureColor.Serialize(archive);
}
```

The TwoDimensionalFigure Class

TwoDimensionalFigure is a sub class of Figure and the base class of
RectangleFigure and EllipseFigure. A two-dimensional figure can be filled or
unfilled. TwoDimensionalFigure has the field m_bFilled with their methods Fill
and IsFilled to keep track of the fill status.

TwoDimensionalFigure.h

```
class TwoDimensionalFigure : public Figure
{
  public:
    TwoDimensionalFigure();
    TwoDimensionalFigure(const Color& color, BOOL bFilled);
    BOOL IsFilled() const {return m_bFilled;}
    void Fill(const BOOL bFill) {m_bFilled = bFill;}
    void Serialize(CArchive& archive);
  private:
    BOOL m_bFilled;
};
```

The implementation of `Figure` is rather straightforward. Remember that each time we introduce a new class to the application we have to include the header file `StdAfx.h` at the beginning of the implementation file. Otherwise, the application will not work.

TwoDimensionalFigure.cpp

```
#include "StdAfx.h"

#include "..\\List.h"
#include "..\\Color.h"
#include "..\\Font.h"

#include "Figure.h"
#include "TwoDimensionalFigure.h"

TwoDimensionalFigure::TwoDimensionalFigure() :m_bFilled(FALSE)
{
  // Empty.
}

TwoDimensionalFigure::TwoDimensionalFigure(const Color& color,
                                           BOOL bFilled)
 :Figure(color),
  m_bFilled(bFilled)
{
  // Empty.
}

void TwoDimensionalFigure::Serialize(CArchive& archive)
{
  Figure::Serialize(archive);

  if (archive.IsStoring())
  {
    archive << m_bFilled;
  }

  if (archive.IsLoading())
  {
    archive >> m_bFilled;
  }
}
```

The LineFigure Class

LineFigure is a direct sub class of Figure. Its task is to draw a line between two points, represented by m_ptFirst to m_ptLast. The fields are protected as they are reused by the ArrowFigure, which privately inherits LineFigure.

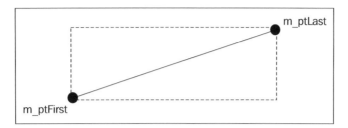

The default constructor is necessary due to serialization. The second constructor initializes the object when the user adds a new line to the drawing. The line's color is given, and so is its start point. Both the fields m_ptFirst and m_ptLast are set to the start point. When the line is created, it has the same start and end point.

The field m_eDragMode is originally set to CREATE_LINE by the constructor and to MODIFY_FIRST, MODIFY_LAST, or MOVE_LINE by Click, DoubleClick, or Inside depending whether the user clicks on one of the end points of the line or on the line itself. Observe that there is no enumeration constant for the case when the user misses the line. In that case, the functions simply return false and ModifyOrMove or Move will not be called.

As both LineFigure and ArrowFigure are direct sub classes of Figure and ArrowFigure inherits LineFigure privately, a **repeated inheritance** has occurred. An object of ArrowFigure would have two instances of Figure's field m_rfColor. It is called **redundancy**, which is something we should avoid. The solution is **virtual inheritance**. It gives the effect that there is only way from ArrowFigure to Figure. The way over LineFigure is in effect cut off. In order for this to work, we have to let LineFigure inherit Figure virtually.

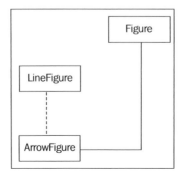

In the next section, we will also see that `ArrowFigure` inherits `Figure` virtually.

LineFigure.h

```
class LineFigure: public virtual Figure
{
  public:
    LineFigure();
    LineFigure(const Color& color, const CPoint& ptMouse);
    LineFigure(const LineFigure& line);
    Figure* Copy() const;

    void Serialize(CArchive& archive);
    HCURSOR GetCursor() const;

    BOOL Click(const CPoint& ptMouse);
    BOOL DoubleClick(const CPoint& ptMouse);
    BOOL Inside(const CRect& rcInside) const;

    void MoveOrModify(const CSize& szDistance);
    void Move(const CSize& szDistance);

    void Draw(CDC* pDC) const;
    CRect GetArea() const;

  protected:
    CPoint m_ptFirst, m_ptLast;
    enum {CREATE_LINE, MODIFY_FIRST, MODIFY_LAST, MOVE_LINE}
        m_eDragMode;
};
```

`Click` is a rather complicated function that decides whether the user has clicked on the line. First, we examine whether the user has hit the start point by defining a small square centered around the start point of the line. We use `SQUARE_SIDE` in `Figure` to define the square. This means that a mouse click one millimeter away from the actual start point counts as a hit. If we have a hit, we know that the user wants to modify the start point of the line, and we set `m_eDragMode` to `MODIFY_FIRST` in accordance to this. If it does not work, we try the same process with the end point.

If the mouse click does not hit the start or end point, we continue by investigating if the user instead has hit the actual line between the points. First, we have to investigate whether the line is vertical (`m_ptFirst.x == m_ptLast.x`). If it is, we have a special case. Then we construct a small rectangle around the line and test whether the mouse position is in it.

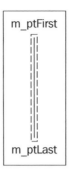

If the line is not vertical, we start by constructing a surrounding rectangle and test if the mouse point is on it. If it is, we let the leftmost point of `m_ptFirst` and `m_ptLast` equal `ptMin` and the rightmost point equal `ptMax`. Then we calculate the width (`cxLine`) and height (`cyLine`) of the surrounding rectangle as well as the distance between the `ptMin` and `ptMouse` in x- and y-direction (`cxMouse` and `cyMouse`).

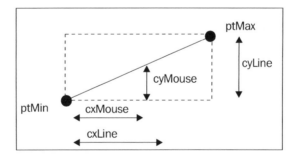

Due to uniformity, the following equation is true if the mouse point hits the line.

$$\frac{cyMouse}{cxMouse} = \frac{cyLine}{cxLine}$$

This implies that

$$cyMouse = \frac{cyLine}{cxLine}\, cxMouse$$

And that

$$cyMouse - \frac{cyLine}{cxLine} \; cxMouse = 0.$$

Let us allow for a small tolerance, say that the user is allowed to miss the line by a millimeter. If we reuse the SQUARE_SIDE constant, as the side of the square is two millimeters, it would change the last equation to:

$$\left| cyMouse - \frac{cyLine}{cxLine} \; cxMouse \right| \leq \frac{SQUARE\_SIDE}{2}$$

LineFigure.cpp

```
BOOL LineFigure::Click(const CPoint& ptMouse)
{
  // Did the user click on the first end point?
  CRect rcFirst(m_ptFirst.x - (SQUARE_SIDE / 2),
                m_ptFirst.y - (SQUARE_SIDE / 2),
                m_ptFirst.x + (SQUARE_SIDE / 2),
                m_ptFirst.y + (SQUARE_SIDE / 2));
  if (rcFirst.PtInRect(ptMouse))
  {
      m_eDragMode = MODIFY_FIRST;
      return TRUE;
  }
  // Or the second one?
  CRect rcLast(m_ptLast.x - (SQUARE_SIDE / 2),
               m_ptLast.y - (SQUARE_SIDE / 2),
               m_ptLast.x + (SQUARE_SIDE / 2),
               m_ptLast.y + (SQUARE_SIDE / 2));
  if (rcLast.PtInRect(ptMouse))
  {
    m_eDragMode = MODIFY_LAST;
    return TRUE;
  }
  m_eDragMode = MOVE_LINE;
  // If the line completely vertical?
  if (m_ptFirst.x == m_ptLast.x)
  {
    CRect rcLine(m_ptFirst.x - (SQUARE_SIDE / 2), m_ptFirst.y,
                 m_ptLast.x + (SQUARE_SIDE / 2), m_ptLast.y);
```

```
      rcLine.NormalizeRect();
      return rcLine.PtInRect(ptMouse);
    }
    // Or not?
    else
    {
      CRect rcLine(m_ptFirst, m_ptLast);
      rcLine.NormalizeRect();
      if (rcLine.PtInRect(ptMouse))
      {
        CPoint ptMin = (m_ptFirst.x < m_ptLast.x)
                     ? m_ptFirst : m_ptLast;
        CPoint ptMax = (m_ptFirst.x < m_ptLast.x)
                     ? m_ptLast : m_ptFirst;
        int cxLine = ptMax.x - ptMin.x;
        int cyLine = ptMax.y - ptMin.y;
        int cxMouse = ptMouse.x - ptMin.x;
        int cyMouse = ptMouse.y - ptMin.y;
        return fabs(cyMouse - cxMouse * (double) cyLine /
                 cxLine) <= (SQUARE_SIDE / 2);
      }
      return FALSE;
    }
  }
}
```

When the user drags the mouse over a marked figure, it is supposed to be moved or modified. The document class calls MoveOrModify, but it does not really know whether the user has hit on the endpoints (modify) or the line itself (move), that information is stored locally by the line object. The document class just calls MoveOrModify, and the line object takes care of the rest.

MoveOrModify takes the distance of the mouse transfer since the previous call. If we are in the process of creating the line, the distance shall affect the last end point of the line. If the users clicked on one of the end points, we modify that end point. If they click on the line, it moves the line by calling Move, which is easy to define, we just modify both the end points.

```
    void LineFigure::MoveOrModify(const CSize& szDistance)
    {
      switch (m_eDragMode)
      {
        case CREATE_LINE:
          m_ptLast += szDistance;
```

```
            break;

         case MODIFY_FIRST:
            m_ptFirst += szDistance;
            break;

         case MODIFY_LAST:
            m_ptLast += szDistance;
            break;

         case MOVE_LINE:
            Move(szDistance);
            break;
      }
   }

   void LineFigure::Move(const CSize& szDistance)
   {
      m_ptFirst += szDistance;
      m_ptLast += szDistance;
   }
```

Draw is called every time the figure needs to be repainted, partly or completely. If the line is unmarked, we just select our pen and draw the line. When we select a new pen we save the old one, which is to be later restored. If the line is marked, we add two squares at each end point. For that, we need a brush. We create and select our brush in a way similar to the pen. We create and paint the squares by calling Rectangle, there is no function in the CDC class to paint a square.

LineFigure.cpp

```
   void LineFigure::Draw(CDC *pDC) const
   {
      CPen pen(PS_SOLID, 0, (COLORREF) GetColor());
      CPen* pOldPen = pDC->SelectObject(&pen);

      pDC->MoveTo(m_ptFirst.x, m_ptFirst.y);
      pDC->LineTo(m_ptLast.x, m_ptLast.y);
      pDC->SelectObject(pOldPen);

      if (IsMarked())
      {
         CPen pen(PS_SOLID, 0, BLACK);
         CPen* pOldPen = pDC->SelectObject(&pen);

         CBrush brush(BLACK);
         CBrush* pOldBrush = pDC->SelectObject(&brush);

         CRect rcFirst(m_ptFirst.x - (SQUARE_SIDE / 2),
                       m_ptFirst.y - (SQUARE_SIDE / 2),
                       m_ptFirst.x + (SQUARE_SIDE / 2),
```

```
                       m_ptFirst.y + (SQUARE_SIDE / 2));
        pDC->Rectangle(rcFirst);
        CRect rcLast(m_ptLast.x - (SQUARE_SIDE / 2),
                     m_ptLast.y - (SQUARE_SIDE / 2),
                     m_ptLast.x + (SQUARE_SIDE / 2),
                     m_ptLast.y + (SQUARE_SIDE / 2));
        pDC->Rectangle(rcLast);

        pDC->SelectObject(pOldPen);
        pDC->SelectObject(pOldBrush);
    }
}
```

GetArea calculates the area of the line by creating a rectangle with the end points of the line as opposite corners. If the line is marked, we need to slightly increase the rectangle in order to fit in the squares at the end points.

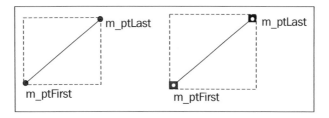

LineFigure.cpp

```
CRect LineFigure::GetArea() const
{
  CRect rcLine(m_ptFirst, m_ptLast);
  rcLine.NormalizeRect();

  if (IsMarked())
  {
    rcLine.left   -= (SQUARE_SIDE / 2);
    rcLine.right  += (SQUARE_SIDE / 2);
    rcLine.top    -= (SQUARE_SIDE / 2);
    rcLine.bottom += (SQUARE_SIDE / 2);
  }

  return rcLine;
}
```

The ArrowFigure Class

ArrowFigure is a direct sub class of Figure and it inherits LineFigure privately, and reuses most of the functionality. Similar to LineFigure, it draws a line, and then adds the extension of two extra lines that constitutes an arrowhead. The class has two fields of its own, m_ptLeft and m_ptRight, which holds the end points of the arrowhead. It also reuses the fields m_ptFirst and m_ptLast of LineFigure. Moreover, it has a constant ARROW_LENGTH; it is initialized to 500, which means that the extra lines constituting the arrowhead are five millimeters long, regardless of the length of the arrow itself.

The constructors just call the corresponding constructors in their base class LineFigure. GetArea calculates the area of the arrow by calling its analogous function in LineFigure. In addition to that, it also calculates the area of the arrowhead. The resulting area is the smallest rectangle containing the whole arrow.

Copy creates and returns a pointer to an identical arrow object. ModifyOrMove and Move calls their matching functions in LineFigure, and then calls SetArrowPoints in order to evaluate the positions of the arrowhead. Draw also has a rather simple implementation as we just have to draw three straight lines and, in case the arrow is marked, draw the squares at the arrowhead's end points. DoubleClick switches the endpoints of the arrow, so it points in the opposite direction.

In the previous section, we let LineFigure inherit Figure virtually. In this section, we also let ArrowFigure inherit Figure virtually. In that way, the real base class of ArrowFigure is Figure. The only purpose behind the private inheritance between ArrowFigure and LineFigure is to let ArrowFigure reuse LineFigure's code. As you can see in the class definition below, GetCursor, Click, and Inside just call their counterparts in LineFigure.

ArrowFigure.h

```
class ArrowFigure: public virtual Figure, private LineFigure
{
  public:
    ArrowFigure();
    ArrowFigure(const Color& color, const CPoint& ptMouse);
    ArrowFigure(const ArrowFigure& arrow);
    Figure* Copy() const;
    void Serialize(CArchive& archive);
    HCURSOR GetCursor() const
            {return LineFigure::GetCursor();}
    BOOL Click(const CPoint& ptMouse)
            {return LineFigure::Click(ptMouse);}
    BOOL DoubleClick(const CPoint& ptMouse);
```

```
    BOOL Inside(const CRect& rcInside) const
              {return LineFigure::Inside(rcInside);}
  void MoveOrModify(const CSize& szDistance);
  void Move(const CSize& szDistance);
  void Draw(CDC *pDC) const;
  CRect GetArea() const;
private:
  void SetArrowPoints();
  CPoint m_ptLeft, m_ptRight;
  static const int ARROW_LENGTH = 500;
};
```

As ArrowFigure inherits Figure virtually, its constructor must call Figure's constructor directly as well as LineFigure's constructor.

ArrowFigure.cpp

```
ArrowFigure::ArrowFigure(const ArrowFigure& arrow)
 :Figure(arrow),
  LineFigure(arrow)
{
  m_ptLeft = arrow.m_ptLeft;
  m_ptRight = arrow.m_ptRight;
}
```

When the user double-clicks on a line, nothing happens. However, when they double-click on an arrow, its head is reversed.

```
BOOL ArrowFigure::DoubleClick(const CPoint& ptMouse)
{
  if (LineFigure::Click(ptMouse))
  {
    CPoint ptTemp = m_ptFirst;
    m_ptFirst = m_ptLast;
    m_ptLast = ptTemp;

    SetArrowPoints();
    return TRUE;
  }

  return FALSE;
}
```

Most of the drawing is done in `LineFigure`. The `ArrowFigure` method just adds the arrow head.

```
void ArrowFigure::Draw(CDC *pDC) const
{
  LineFigure::Draw(pDC);
  CPen pen(PS_SOLID, 0, (COLORREF) Figure::GetColor());
  CPen* pOldPen = pDC->SelectObject(&pen);

  pDC->MoveTo(m_ptLast);
  pDC->LineTo(m_ptLeft);

  pDC->MoveTo(m_ptLast);
  pDC->LineTo(m_ptRight);

  pDC->SelectObject(pOldPen);
}
```

In the same way, the area of the line is calculated in `LineFigure`. The `GetArea` method of this class just adds the area of the arrow head. The method `UnionRect` takes two rectangles and returns the smallest rectangle surrounding them both. In order for that to work, the rectangles have to be *normalized*. This means that this left corner must be less than or equal to the right one and the top corner has to be less than or equal to the bottom one. *Normalize* takes care of that.

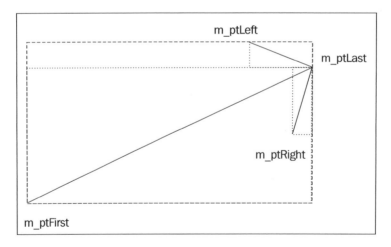

```
CRect ArrowFigure::GetArea() const
{
  CRect rcLine = LineFigure::GetArea();
  CRect rcLeftArrow(m_ptLast, m_ptLeft);
  rcLeftArrow.NormalizeRect();
  rcLine.UnionRect(rcLine, rcLeftArrow);
```

```
    CRect rcRightArrow(m_ptLast, m_ptRight);
    rcRightArrow.NormalizeRect();
    rcLine.UnionRect(rcLine, rcRightArrow);
    return rcLine;
}
```

`SetArrowPoints` is a private help method, called by `DoubleClick`, `MoveOrModify`, and `Move`. Its task is to calculate the positions of the head of the arrow when it has been modified. We will use the following relations to calculate the fields `m_ptLeft` and `m_ptRight`.

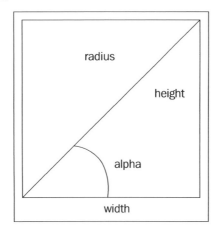

$$\sin \text{ angle} = \frac{\text{height}}{\text{radius}}$$

$$\cos \text{ angle} = \frac{\text{Width}}{\text{radius}}$$

$$\text{width} = \text{radius cos angle}$$

$$\text{height} = \text{radius sin angle}$$

$$\text{radius} = \sqrt{\text{width}^2 + \text{height}^2}$$

$$\text{angle} = \arctan \frac{\text{height}}{\text{width}}$$

The calculation is performed in three steps. First we calculate the `dAlpha` and `dBeta` angles illustrated in the figure on next page.

$$\text{iHeight} = \text{m\_ptLast.y - m\_pt.First.y}$$

$$\text{iWidth} = \text{m\_ptLast.x - m\_ptFirst.x}$$

$$\text{dAlpha} = \arctan \frac{\text{iHeight}}{\text{iwidth}}$$

$$\text{dBeta} = \text{dAlpha} + \pi$$

Then we calculate `dLeftAngle` and `dRightAngle` and use their values to calculate the value of `m_ptLeft` and `m_ptRight`. The angle between the line and the arrow head parts is 45 degrees, which is equivalent to $\pi/2$ radians. So in order to determine the angles for the arrow head parts, we simply subtract and add $\pi/2$ to `dBeta`, respectively.

$$\text{dLeftAngle} = \text{dBeta} - \frac{\pi}{2}$$

$$\text{dRightAngle} = \text{dBeta} + \frac{\pi}{2}$$

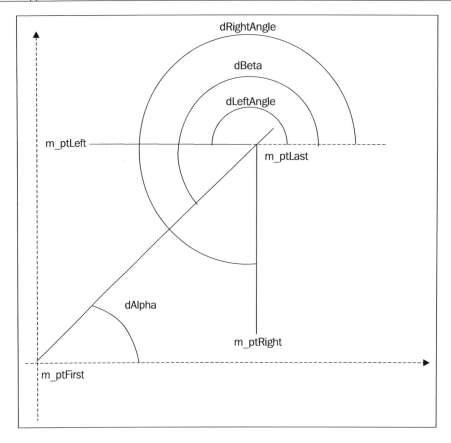

Then we use the formulas below to finally determine m_ptLeft and m_ptRight.

m_ptLeft.x = m_ptLast.x + ARROW_LENGTH cos dLeftAngle

m_ptLeft.y = m_ptLast.y + ARROW_LENGTH sin dLeftAngle

m_ptRight.x = m_ptLast.x + ARROW_LENGTH cos dRightAngle

m_ptRight.y = m_ptLast.y + ARROW_LENGTH sin dRightAngle

The trigonometric functions are available in the C standard library (include file cmath). However, we need to define our value for π. The function atan2 calculates the tangent value for the quota of iHeight and iWidth, and takes into consideration the possibility that iWidth might be zero.

```
void ArrowFigure::SetArrowPoints()
{
  int iHeight = m_ptLast.y - m_ptFirst.y;
  int iWidth = m_ptLast.x - m_ptFirst.x;
  const double PI = 3.14159265;
```

```
   double dAlpha = atan2((double) iHeight, (double) iWidth);
   double dBeta = dAlpha + PI;

   double dLeftAngle = dBeta - PI / 4;
   double dRightAngle = dBeta + PI / 4;

   m_ptLeft.x = m_ptLast.x +
                (int) (ARROW_LENGTH * cos(dLeftAngle));
   m_ptLeft.y = m_ptLast.y +
                (int) (ARROW_LENGTH * sin(dLeftAngle));

   m_ptRight.x = m_ptLast.x +
                 (int) (ARROW_LENGTH * cos(dRightAngle));
   m_ptRight.y = m_ptLast.y +
                 (int) (ARROW_LENGTH * sin(dRightAngle));
}
```

The RectangleFigure Class

RectangleFigure manages a rectangle. It is a direct sub class of
TwoDimensionalFigure. It has two fields m_ptTopLeft and m_ptBottomRight
for the opposite corners. The fields are protected as they are accessed by
EllipseFigure, which privately inherits RectangleFigure. RectangleFigure
inherits TwoDimensionalFigure virtually in the same way as LineFigure inherits
Figure virtually.

RectangleFigure.h

```
class RectangleFigure: public virtual TwoDimensionalFigure
{
  public:
    RectangleFigure();
    RectangleFigure(const Color& color, const CPoint&
                    ptTopLeft, BOOL bFilled);
    RectangleFigure(const RectangleFigure& rectangle);
    Figure* Copy() const;
    void Serialize(CArchive& archive);
    HCURSOR GetCursor() const;
    BOOL Click(const CPoint& ptMouse);
    BOOL DoubleClick(const CPoint& ptMouse);
    BOOL Inside(const CRect& rcInside) const;
    void MoveOrModify(const CSize& szDistance);
    void Move(const CSize& szDistance);
    void Draw(CDC* pDC) const;
    CRect GetArea() const;
  private:
    enum {CREATE_RECTANGLE, MODIFY_TOPLEFT, MODIFY_TOPRIGHT,
          MODIFY_BOTTOMRIGHT, MODIFY_BOTTOMLEFT,
```

```
                MOVE_RECTANGLE} m_eDragMode;
    protected:
      CPoint m_ptTopLeft, m_ptBottomRight;
};
```

When the user clicks on a rectangle, `Click` is called. The user may hit one of the four corners of the rectangle, the borders of the rectangle, or, if the rectangle is filled, the interior of the rectangle. The field `m_eDragMode` is set to an appropriate value.

`Click` works in a way similar to its equivalent function in the line class. It tests in turn the four corners of the rectangle. If that fails and if the rectangle is filled, it tests if the user has clicked in the rectangle. If the rectangle is unfilled, it tests if the user has clicked on any of the four lines constituting the rectangle by constructing a slightly small rectangle and a slightly larger one. If the mouse position is included in the larger rectangle but not in the smaller one, the user has hit the rectangle.

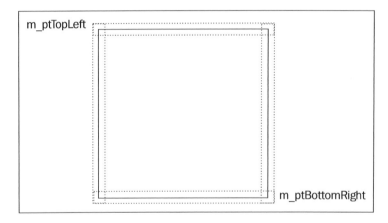

RectangleFigure.cpp

```cpp
BOOL RectangleFigure::Click(const CPoint& ptMouse)
{
  // Did the user click on the top left corner?
  CRect rcTopLeft(m_ptTopLeft.x - (SQUARE_SIDE / 2),
                  m_ptTopLeft.y - (SQUARE_SIDE / 2),
                  m_ptTopLeft.x + (SQUARE_SIDE / 2),
                  m_ptTopLeft.y + (SQUARE_SIDE / 2));
  if (rcTopLeft.PtInRect(ptMouse))
  {
    m_eDragMode = MODIFY_TOPLEFT;
    return TRUE;
  }
  // Or the top right corner?
  CRect rcTopRight(m_ptBottomRight.x - (SQUARE_SIDE / 2),
                   m_ptTopLeft.y - (SQUARE_SIDE / 2),
```

```
                  m_ptBottomRight.x + (SQUARE_SIDE / 2),
                  m_ptTopLeft.y + (SQUARE_SIDE / 2));
  if (rcTopRight.PtInRect(ptMouse))
  {
    m_eDragMode = MODIFY_TOPRIGHT;
    return TRUE;
  }
  // Or the bottom right corner?
  CRect rcBottomRight(m_ptBottomRight.x - (SQUARE_SIDE / 2),
                      m_ptBottomRight.y - (SQUARE_SIDE / 2),
                      m_ptBottomRight.x + (SQUARE_SIDE / 2),
                      m_ptBottomRight.y + (SQUARE_SIDE / 2));
  if (rcBottomRight.PtInRect(ptMouse))
  {
    m_eDragMode = MODIFY_BOTTOMRIGHT;
    return TRUE;
  }
  // Or the bottom left corner?
  CRect rcBottomLeft(m_ptTopLeft.x - (SQUARE_SIDE / 2),
                     m_ptBottomRight.y - (SQUARE_SIDE / 2),
                     m_ptTopLeft.x + (SQUARE_SIDE / 2),
                     m_ptBottomRight.y +(SQUARE_SIDE / 2));
  if (rcBottomLeft.PtInRect(ptMouse))
  {
    m_eDragMode = MODIFY_BOTTOMLEFT;
    return TRUE;
  }
  CRect rcArea(m_ptTopLeft, m_ptBottomRight);
  rcArea.NormalizeRect();
  // Is the rectangle filled?
  if (IsFilled())
  {
    m_eDragMode = MOVE_RECTANGLE;
    return rcArea.PtInRect(ptMouse);
  }
  // Or is it unfilled?
  else
  {
    CSize szMargin((SQUARE_SIDE / 2), (SQUARE_SIDE / 2));
    CRect rcSmallArea(rcArea.TopLeft() + szMargin,
                      rcArea.BottomRight() - szMargin);
    CRect rcLargeArea(rcArea.TopLeft() - szMargin,
                      rcArea.BottomRight() + szMargin);
    m_eDragMode = MOVE_RECTANGLE;
    return rcLargeArea.PtInRect(ptMouse) &&
           !rcSmallArea.PtInRect(ptMouse);
  }
}
```

GetArea simply creates and returns a CRect object with m_ptTopLeft and m_ptBottomRight as its corners. If the rectangle is marked, we increase the surrounding area in order to include the four squares.

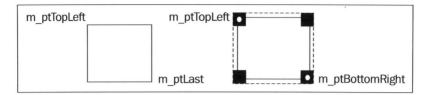

RectangleFigure.cpp

```
CRect RectangleFigure::GetArea() const
{
  CRect rcRectangle(m_ptTopLeft, m_ptBottomRight);
  rcRectangle.NormalizeRect();

  if (IsMarked())
  {
    rcRectangle.left   -= (SQUARE_SIDE / 2);
    rcRectangle.right  += (SQUARE_SIDE / 2);
    rcRectangle.top    -= (SQUARE_SIDE / 2);
    rcRectangle.bottom += (SQUARE_SIDE / 2);
  }

  return rcRectangle;
}
```

The EllipseFigure Class

EllipseFigure manages an ellipse and is a direct sub class of TwoDimensionalFigure. It also privately inherits RectangleFigure, from which it reuses a large part of functionality. The user may re-shape the ellipse by seizing the ellipse at its leftmost, rightmost, uppermost, or lowermost point. The class reuses the fields m_ptTopLeft and m_ptBottomRight from RectangleFigure. Serialize, DoubleClick, Inside and GetArea simply call their counterparts in *RectangleClass*.

EllipseFigure.h

```
class EllipseFigure: public virtual TwoDimensionalFigure,
                     private RectangleFigure
{
  public:
    EllipseFigure();
```

```
      EllipseFigure(const Color& color, const CPoint& ptTopLeft,
                    BOOL bFilled);
      EllipseFigure(const EllipseFigure& ellipse);
      Figure* Copy() const;
      void Serialize(CArchive& archive)
          {return RectangleFigure::Serialize(archive);}
      HCURSOR GetCursor() const;
      BOOL Click(const CPoint& ptMouse);
      BOOL DoubleClick(const CPoint& ptMouse)
          {return RectangleFigure::DoubleClick(ptMouse);}
      BOOL Inside(const CRect& rcInside) const
          {return RectangleFigure::Inside(rcInside);}
      void MoveOrModify(const CSize& szDistance);
      void Move(const CSize& szDistance)
          {return RectangleFigure::Move(szDistance);}
      void Draw(CDC* pDC) const;
      CRect GetArea() const
            {return RectangleFigure::GetArea();}
    private:
      enum {CREATE_ELLIPSE, MODIFY_LEFT, MODIFY_RIGHT,
            MODIFY_TOP, MODIFY_BOTTOM, MOVE_ELLIPSE}
            m_eDragMode;
  };
```

Just as in the rectangle case, `Click` first decides if the user has clicked on one of the four end points, the only difference is that the positions are different in relation to the figure.

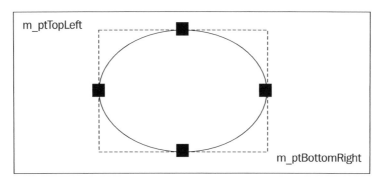

If the user has not clicked on one of the modifying positions, we have to decide if the user has clicked on the ellipse itself. It is rather easy if the ellipse is filled, we create an elliptic region by using the MFC class CRgn and test if the mouse position is in it. If the ellipse is not filled, we create two regions, one slightly smaller than the ellipse and on slightly larger. If the mouse position is included in the larger region but not in the smaller one, we have a hit.

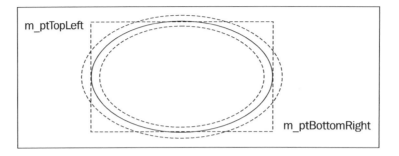

EllipseFigure.cpp

```
BOOL EllipseFigure::Click(const CPoint& ptMouse)
{
  int xCenter = (m_ptTopLeft.x + m_ptBottomRight.x) / 2;
  int yCenter = (m_ptTopLeft.y + m_ptBottomRight.y) / 2;

  // Has the user clicked at the leftmost point?
  CRect rcLeft(m_ptTopLeft.x - (SQUARE_SIDE / 2),
               yCenter - (SQUARE_SIDE / 2),
               m_ptTopLeft.x + (SQUARE_SIDE / 2),
               yCenter + (SQUARE_SIDE / 2));

  if (rcLeft.PtInRect(ptMouse))
  {
    m_eDragMode = MODIFY_LEFT;
    return TRUE;
  }

  // Or the rightmost point?
  CRect rcRight(m_ptBottomRight.x - (SQUARE_SIDE / 2),
                yCenter - (SQUARE_SIDE / 2),
                m_ptBottomRight.x + (SQUARE_SIDE / 2),
                yCenter + (SQUARE_SIDE / 2));

  if (rcRight.PtInRect(ptMouse))
  {
    m_eDragMode = MODIFY_RIGHT;
    return TRUE;
  }
```

```
// Or the topmost point?
CRect rcTop(xCenter - (SQUARE_SIDE / 2),
            m_ptTopLeft.y - (SQUARE_SIDE / 2),
            xCenter + (SQUARE_SIDE / 2),
            m_ptTopLeft.y + (SQUARE_SIDE / 2));
if (rcTop.PtInRect(ptMouse))
{
  m_eDragMode = MODIFY_TOP;
  return TRUE;
}
// Or the bottommost point?
CRect rcBottom(xCenter - (SQUARE_SIDE / 2),
               m_ptBottomRight.y - (SQUARE_SIDE / 2),
               xCenter + (SQUARE_SIDE / 2),
               m_ptBottomRight.y + (SQUARE_SIDE / 2));
if (rcBottom.PtInRect(ptMouse))
{
  m_eDragMode = MODIFY_BOTTOM;
  return TRUE;
}
CRgn rgArea;
rgArea.CreateEllipticRgn(m_ptTopLeft.x, m_ptTopLeft.y,
                         m_ptBottomRight.x,
                         m_ptBottomRight.y);
// Is the ellipse filled?
if (IsFilled())
{
  m_eDragMode = MOVE_ELLIPSE;
  return rgArea.PtInRegion(ptMouse);
}
// Or unfilled?
else
{
  int xMin = min(m_ptTopLeft.x, m_ptBottomRight.x);
  int xMax = max(m_ptTopLeft.x, m_ptBottomRight.x);
  int yMin = min(m_ptTopLeft.y, m_ptBottomRight.y);
  int yMax = max(m_ptTopLeft.y, m_ptBottomRight.y);
  CRgn rgSmallArea, rgLargeArea;
  rgSmallArea.CreateEllipticRgn(xMin + (SQUARE_SIDE / 2),
                                yMin + (SQUARE_SIDE / 2),
```

```
                              xMax - (SQUARE_SIDE / 2),
                              yMax - (SQUARE_SIDE / 2));
      rgLargeArea.CreateEllipticRgn(xMin - (SQUARE_SIDE / 2),
                              yMin - (SQUARE_SIDE / 2),
                              xMax + (SQUARE_SIDE / 2),
                              yMax + (SQUARE_SIDE / 2));
    m_eDragMode = MOVE_ELLIPSE;
    return rgLargeArea.PtInRegion(ptMouse) &&
           !rgSmallArea.PtInRegion(ptMouse);
  }
}
```

The TextFigure Class

TextFigure is a direct sub class of Figure. It manages the text. The users can move and edit the text, they can also change the font of the text.

The field m_ptText represents the upper left corner of the text, in logical units. m_szText is the size of the text, also in logical units. The field m_stText is the actual text; m_stPreviousText is used to resume the original text in case the user aborts the editing by pressing the *Esc* key. GenererateCaretArray is called every time the text is changed (change of font or addition or removal of a character) and calculates the size and position for each character in the text. The horizontal positions (x values) relative to the beginning of the text are stored in m_caretArray. The field m_font is the font of the text and m_iAverageWidth holds the average width of the font, roughly the width of the **z** character. It is used by the caret in the keyboard overwrite state. Finally, m_eDragMode is used to give the cursor the correct form.

TextFigure.h

```
    typedef CArray<int> IntArray;
    enum KeyboardState {KS_INSERT, KS_OVERWRITE};
    class TextFigure: public Figure
    {
      public:
        TextFigure();
        TextFigure(const Color& color, const CPoint& ptMouse,
                   const Font& font, CDC* pDC);
        TextFigure(const TextFigure& text);
        Figure* Copy() const;

        void Serialize(CArchive& archive);

        BOOL Click(const CPoint& ptMouse);
        BOOL DoubleClick(const CPoint& ptMouse);
```

```
     BOOL Inside(const CRect& rcInside) const;
     void MoveOrModify(const CSize& szDistance);
     void Move(const CSize& szDistance);
     BOOL KeyDown(UINT uChar, CDC* pDC);
     void CharDown(UINT uChar, CDC* pDC,
                 KeyboardState eKeyboardState);
     void SetPreviousText(CDC* pDC);
     void Draw(CDC* pDC) const;
     CRect GetArea() const;
     Font* GetFont();
     void SetFont(const Font& font, CDC* pDC);
  private:
     void GenerateCaretArray(CDC* pDC);
  public:
     CRect GetCaretArea(KeyboardState eKeyboardState);
     HCURSOR GetCursor() const;
  private:
     enum {CREATE_TEXT, MOVE_TEXT, EDIT_TEXT, NONE_TEXT}
          m_eDragMode;
     CPoint m_ptText;
     CSize m_szText;
     CString m_stText, m_stPreviousText;
     int m_iAverageWidth;
     Font m_font;
     int m_iEditIndex;
     IntArray m_caretArray;
};
```

TextFigure.cpp

`Serialize` loads and stores the position of the text and the text itself as well as the size of the text. Storing and saving the size of the text may seem as an unnecessary measure as we can calculate the size of the given text and its font. However, that requires access to a device context, which `Serialize` does not have. So, instead of a rather complicated process of letting the document class create a device context without access to a view object, we just load and store the size of the text. Remember that the size is given in logical units, so the text will have the same size on screens with different size and resolution.

We have to call `Serialize` in `Figure` to store and load the color of the figure. It is possible to serialize `m_caretArray` since it holds objects. It would not be possible if it held pointers to objects.

```
void TextFigure::Serialize(CArchive& archive)
{
  Figure::Serialize(archive);
  m_font.Serialize(archive);
  m_caretArray.Serialize(archive);

  if (archive.IsStoring())
  {
    archive << m_ptText << m_stText << m_szText
            << m_iAverageWidth;
  }

  if (archive.IsLoading())
  {
    archive >> m_ptText >> m_stText >> m_szText
            >> m_iAverageWidth;
    m_iEditIndex = 0;
  }
}
```

`Click` is rather straightforward as we do not have to check whether the user has clicked at any of the text's squares or on the text itself. We just create a `CRect` object with the text's coordinates and check if the mouse click position fits inside it. `Inside` is also quite straightforward, we just check if the top-left and bottom-right corner of the text is enclosed by the given rectangle.

```
BOOL TextFigure::Click(const CPoint& ptMouse)
{
  m_eDragMode = MOVE_TEXT;
  CRect rcText(m_ptText, m_szText);
  return rcText.PtInRect(ptMouse);
}

BOOL TextFigure::Inside(const CRect& rcInside) const
{
  CRect rcText(m_ptText, m_szText);
  rcText.NormalizeRect();
  return rcInside.PtInRect(rcText.TopLeft()) &&
         rcInside.PtInRect(rcText.BottomRight());
}
```

DoubleClick, on the other hand, is more complicated. First, we decide if the user has clicked on the text at all. In that case, we have to find out where in the text the user has clicked in order to set the caret marker at the correct position. The vector m_caretArray has been initialized to the start positions of characters in the text by a previous call to GenerateCaretArray. We traverse that vector and define the start and end position (iFirstPos and iLastPos) of every character. When we find the correct character (the character the user has clicked on), we have to decide if the user has clicked on its left or right side. If they have clicked on the left side, we return the characters position, if they have clicked on the right side, we return the position of the character on the right. Since we know that the user has clicked on the text, we do not have to consider any case where the user has clicked on the left of the leftmost character or on the right of the rightmost character.

```
BOOL TextFigure::DoubleClick(const CPoint& ptMouse)
{
  CRect rcText(m_ptText, m_szText);
  if (rcText.PtInRect(ptMouse))
  {
    CPoint ptTextMouse = ptMouse - m_ptText;
    int iSize = m_stText.GetLength();
    for (int iIndex = 0; iIndex < iSize; ++iIndex)
    {
      int iFirstPos = m_caretArray[iIndex];
      int iLastPos = m_caretArray[iIndex + 1] - 1;
      if ((ptTextMouse.x >= iFirstPos) &&
          (ptTextMouse.x <= iLastPos))
      {
        if ((ptTextMouse.x - iFirstPos) <
            (iLastPos - ptTextMouse.x))
        {
          m_iEditIndex = iIndex;
        }
        else
        {
          m_iEditIndex = iIndex + 1;
        }
        break;
      }
    }

    m_eDragMode = EDIT_TEXT;
    m_stPreviousText = m_stText;
    return TRUE;
  }
```

As we always find the character clicked on this point of the method is never reached. The check is for debugging purposes only.

```
    check(FALSE);
    return FALSE;
}
```

KeyDown and CharDown are called by one of the view objects as a response to the WM_KEYDOWN and WM_CHAR messages. As the name implies, WM_CHAR is called when the user presses a non-system character (writable character with ASCII number 32 – 122), while WM_KEYDOWN is sent for every key on the keyboard. There is also a message WM_KEYUP that is sent when the user releases the key. We have, however, no need for that message.

KeyDown catches the *Home* and *End* keys as well as the left and right arrow keys. These keys all set the carat index to an appropriate value. Furthermore, KeyDown catches the *Delete* key, which, unless the caret index is already at the end of the text, erases the current character (the character after the caret index) and re-calculates the size of the text and the start position of every character in the text by calling GenerateCaretArray. KeyDown also catches the *Backspace* key in a similar manner; it erases the character at the left of the caret index and re-calculates the text calling GenerateCaretArray unless the caret index is already at the beginning of the text.

```
    BOOL TextFigure::KeyDown(UINT uChar, CDC* pDC)
    {
      int iLength = m_stText.GetLength();
      switch (uChar)
      {
        case VK_HOME:
          if (m_iEditIndex > 0)
          {
            m_iEditIndex = 0;
          }
          break;
        // ...
      }
      return FALSE;
    }
```

`CharDown` is called by one of the view objects when the user presses a regular key. We restrict the acceptable set of keys to the printable characters. If the caret index is located at the end of the text, we just add the character to the text regardless of the keyboard input state. Otherwise, we insert or overwrite the character at the caret position. In either case, we increment the caret index by one and re-calculate the text by calling `GenerateCaretArray`.

```
void TextFigure::CharDown(UINT uChar, CDC* pDC,
                          KeyboardState eKeyboardState)
{
  if (m_iEditIndex == m_stText.GetLength())
  {
    m_stText.AppendChar((TCHAR) uChar);
  }
  else
  {
    switch (eKeyboardState)
    {
      case KS_INSERT:
        m_stText.Insert(m_iEditIndex, (TCHAR) uChar);
        break;
      case KS_OVERWRITE:
        m_stText.SetAt(m_iEditIndex, (TCHAR) uChar);
        break;
    }
  }
  ++m_iEditIndex;
  GenerateCaretArray(pDC);
}
```

`Draw` writes the text by calling the CDC method `TextOut`. It writes the text with its top-left corner at the given position. When it comes to writing text, we do not have to select a pen, we just set the color by calling `SetTextColor`. However, we need to select a font. The font is stored as points (1 point = 1/72 inch, 1 inch = 25.4 millimeters), so we convert the size of the font to hundredths of millimeters by calling `PointToMeters` in the `Font` class.

Finally, if the text is marked, we need to calculate, create, and paint the squares marking the text. We create four rectangles centered on each of the four corners and paint them by calling `Rectangle`.

```
void TextFigure::Draw(CDC* pDC) const
{
  CFont cFont;
  cFont.CreateFontIndirect(m_font.PointsToMeters());
```

```
  CFont* pPrevFont = pDC->SelectObject(&cFont);
  pDC->SetTextColor((COLORREF) GetColor());
  pDC->TextOut(m_ptText.x, m_ptText.y + m_szText.cy,
               m_stText);
  pDC->SelectObject(pPrevFont);
  if (IsMarked())
  {
    CPen pen(PS_SOLID, 0, BLACK);
    CPen* pOldPen = pDC->SelectObject(&pen);
    CBrush brush(BLACK);
    CBrush* pOldBrush = pDC->SelectObject(&brush);
    int xLeft = m_ptText.x;
    int xRight = m_ptText.x + m_szText.cx;
    int yTop = m_ptText.y;
    int yBottom = m_ptText.y + m_szText.cy;
    int xCenter = m_ptText.x + m_szText.cx / 2;
    int yCenter = m_ptText.y + m_szText.cy / 2;
    CRect rcLeft(xLeft - (SQUARE_SIDE / 2),
                 yCenter - (SQUARE_SIDE / 2),
                 xLeft + (SQUARE_SIDE / 2),
                 yCenter + (SQUARE_SIDE / 2));
    CRect rcRight(xRight - (SQUARE_SIDE / 2),
                  yCenter - (SQUARE_SIDE / 2),
                  xRight + (SQUARE_SIDE / 2),
                  yCenter + (SQUARE_SIDE / 2));
    CRect rcTop(xCenter - (SQUARE_SIDE / 2),
                yTop - (SQUARE_SIDE / 2),
                xCenter + (SQUARE_SIDE / 2),
                yTop + (SQUARE_SIDE / 2));
    CRect rcBottom(xCenter - (SQUARE_SIDE / 2),
                   yBottom - (SQUARE_SIDE / 2),
                   xCenter + (SQUARE_SIDE / 2),
                   yBottom + (SQUARE_SIDE / 2));
    pDC->Rectangle(rcLeft);
    pDC->Rectangle(rcRight);
    pDC->Rectangle(rcTop);
    pDC->Rectangle(rcBottom);
    pDC->SelectObject(pOldPen);
    pDC->SelectObject(pOldBrush);
  }
}
```

`GetArea` starts by calculating the unmarked size. It is an easy task to create a `CRect` object because we already have to top left position (`m_ptText`) and its size (`m_szText`). In case the text is marked, we add margins for the squares.

```
CRect TextFigure::GetArea() const
{
  CRect rcText(m_ptText, m_szText);
  rcText.NormalizeRect();

  if (IsMarked())
  {
    rcText.left   -= (SQUARE_SIDE / 2);
    rcText.right  += (SQUARE_SIDE / 2);

    rcText.top    -= (SQUARE_SIDE / 2);
    rcText.bottom += (SQUARE_SIDE / 2);
  }

  return rcText;
}
```

`SetFont` sets the font of the text. We need to recalculate the characters positions by calling `GenerateCaretArray`.

```
void TextFigure::SetFont(const Font& font, CDC* pDC)
{
  m_font = font;
  GenerateCaretArray(pDC);
}
```

`GenerateCaretArray` determines the size and position of each character in the text. The positions relative the beginning of the text (the x-position) for each character is stored in `m_caretArray`. The size of the text is stored in `m_szText` and the average character width with the given font is stored in `m_iAverageWidth`.

First, we need to select a font with coordinates given in logical units. The translation from typographical points to hundredths of millimeters is done by `PointsToMetrics` in the `Font` class.

To find the size of the text we need to consider two cases. If the text is non-empty, we call `GetTextExtent` to receive the size of the text. If the text is empty, we use the field `tmHeight` of the `TEXTMETRIC` structure and set the width of the text to zero. A call to `GetTextExtent` in this case would return a zero size. The size is given in logical units because the function calling `GenerateCaretArray` has initialized the device context with the logical coordinate system.

After the size of the whole text is set, we need to find the horizontal starting position (the x-position) of each character in the text. We traverse through the text and find the width of each character by calling GetTextExtent. We set the size of the vector m_caretArray to one more than the size of the text, in order to be able to store the rightmost position of the text.

```
void TextFigure::GenerateCaretArray(CDC* pDC)
{
  CFont cFont;
  cFont.CreateFontIndirect(m_font.PointsToMeters());
  CFont* pPrevFont = pDC->SelectObject(&cFont);

  TEXTMETRIC textMetric;
  pDC->GetTextMetrics(&textMetric);
  m_iAverageWidth = textMetric.tmAveCharWidth;

  if (!m_stText.IsEmpty())
  {
    m_szText = pDC->GetTextExtent(m_stText);
  }
  else
  {
    m_szText.SetSize(0, textMetric.tmHeight);
  }

  int iWidth = 0, iSize = m_stText.GetLength();
  m_caretArray.SetSize(iSize + 1);

  for (int iIndex = 0; iIndex < iSize; ++iIndex)
  {
    CSize szChar = pDC->GetTextExtent
                         (m_stText.Mid(iIndex, 1));
    m_caretArray[iIndex] = iWidth;
    iWidth += szChar.cx;
  }

  m_caretArray[iSize] = m_szText.cx;
  pDC->SelectObject(pPrevFont);
}
```

GetCaretArea calculates and returns the size and position of the caret. First we define the top-left position of the character the caret marker is set to. Then we have two cases to consider depending on the input state of the keyboard. In an insert state, the caret shall be a thin vertical blinking line. We set the width to one and the height to the height of the text. Remember that we are dealing with logical coordinates (hundredths of millimeters), so the width will most likely be rounded down to zero when translated to device coordinates. However, the function OnUpdate in the view class will take this into consideration and set the width to at least one device unit. If the keyboard is set to overwrite the input state, the caret marker should be a small blinking rectangle whose width should be the width of an average character in the current font. We use the value of m_iAverageWidth, which was assessed by a previous call to GenerateCaretArray.

```
CRect TextFigure::GetCaretArea(KeyboardState eKeyboardState)
{
  CPoint ptCaret(m_ptText.x + m_caretArray[m_iEditIndex],
                 m_ptText.y);

  switch (eKeyboardState)
  {
    case KS_INSERT:
      {
        CSize szCaret(1, m_szText.cy);
        return CRect(ptCaret, ptCaret + szCaret);
      }
      break;

    case KS_OVERWRITE:
      {
        CSize szCaret(m_iAverageWidth, m_szText.cy);
        return CRect(ptCaret, ptCaret + szCaret);
      }
      break;
  }

  return CRect();
}
```

The FigureFileManager Class

Since the user can save and load drawings, we need to manage the saving and loading of figure class objects. There is really no problem in saving them, we just call Serialize for each figure class object. However, when it comes to loading figures, we must know which concrete class has been saved. Here is where FigureFileManager comes into the picture. Before the figure object is saved, a FigureFileManager is created, it saves an identity value connected to the figure class before the contents of the figure are saved. When a file is loaded, first the identity value is read by the FigureFileManager. It then creates an object of the class connected to the identity value. After that, we just serialize the object.

One advantage of this system is that if we would like to add another figure to our drawing program, we just need to modify this class, figure classes do not need to be modified. A similar effect can be archived by the use of the CArchive classes WriteClass, WriteObject, ReadClass, and ReadObject. However, they do not work well together with repeated inheritance.

FigureFileManager.h

```
class FigureFileManager : public CObject
{
  public:
    FigureFileManager(Figure* pFigure = NULL);
    Figure* GetFigure() const {return m_pFigure;}
  private:
    int GetId() const;
    void CreateFigure(int iId);
  public:
    void Serialize(CArchive& archive);
  private:
    enum {LINE, ARROW, RECTANGLE, ELLIPSE, TEXT};
    Figure* m_pFigure;
};
```

The FigureFileManager uses the language construct dynamic_cast to decide the class the object is an instanse of. We can use dynamic_cast to perform safe pointer type conversion. If m_pFigure points at an ArrowFigure object, the address of that object will be returned in a pointer to ArrowFigure. If it does not, null is returned.

Note the reversed order of GetId. If we first tried dynamic cast with LineFigure, it would also catch the case of ArrowFigure, as it is a private sub class of LineFigure.

FigureFileManager.cpp

```
int FigureFileManager::GetId() const
{
  if (dynamic_cast<ArrowFigure*>(m_pFigure) != NULL)
  {
    return ARROW;
  }
  else if (dynamic_cast<LineFigure*>(m_pFigure) != NULL)
  {
    return LINE;
  }
  // ...
```

```
   else
   {
     check(FALSE);
     return 0;
   }
}
void FigureFileManager::CreateFigure(int iId)
{
     case LINE:
       check_memory(m_pFigure = new LineFigure());
       break;
     // ...
     default:
       check(FALSE);
   }
}
void FigureFileManager::Serialize(CArchive& archive)
{
   CObject::Serialize(archive);
   if (archive.IsStoring())
   {
     archive << GetId();
   }
   if (archive.IsLoading())
   {
     int iId;
     archive >> iId;
     CreateFigure(iId);
   }
}
```

The Document Class

CDrawDoc is the document class. Its task is to accept mouse and keyboard input from the CDrawView view objects, to manage the document's data, to load and save data, to alert the view object about changes in the data, and to accept input from the menus. This implies that the class is rather large.

One central point of this application is its states. The application can be in a number of different states. For the application to keep up with them there is a set of fields. First, we have m_eNextActionState. It keeps track of the user's next move. It can be set to adding a line, adding an arrow, adding a rectangle, adding an ellipse, adding text, or modifying a figure. It has the enumeration type NextActionState.

```
enum NextActionState {ADD_LINE, ADD_ARROW, ADD_RECTANGLE,
                        ADD_ELLIPSE, ADD_TEXT, MODIFY_FIGURE};
```

The constructor and destructor access its current value from the registry. The last parameter to GetProfileInt is the default value in case the value is not stored in the registry.

```
CDrawDoc::CDrawDoc()
{
  m_eNextActionState = (NextActionState) AfxGetApp()->
                        GetProfileInt(TEXT("Draw"),
                        TEXT("ActionMode"), MODIFY_FIGURE);
  // ...
}
CDrawDoc::~CDrawDoc()
{
  AfxGetApp()->WriteProfileInt(TEXT("Draw"),
              TEXT("ActionMode"), (int) m_eNextActionState);
  // ...
}
```

Second, we have m_eApplicationState. It keeps track of the user's activity. The user may be involved in moving or modifying a single figure, moving several figures, surrounding figures inside a rectangle, editing text, or doing nothing at all. m_eApplicationState has the enumeration type ApplicationState.

```
enum ApplicationState {SINGLE_DRAG, MULTIPLE_DRAG,
                        RECTANGLE_DRAG, EDIT_TEXT, IDLE};
```

m_eApplicationState is initialized to the idle state by the constructor. When m_eApplicationState is in the edit-text state, m_pEditText points at the text being edited. The caret class object m_caret keeps track of the caret. When m_eApplicationState is in single-drag state m_pSingleFigure points at the figure being dragged, and when it is in rectangle-drag state, m_pDragRectangle points at the surrounding rectangle.

As the user adds figure to and removes figure from the drawing, the figure objects are dynamically created and pointers to them are stored in m_figurePtrList. When the user marks and copies a set of figures, the figures are copied with the Copy of the Figure class in question, and the pointers are stored in m_copyPtrList.

The field `m_nextColor` stores the color of the next figure to be added to the drawing, `m_nextFont` stores the font of the next text, and `m_bNextFill` stores the fill status of the next two-dimensional figure (rectangle or ellipse). The fields are set by the user and are used when a new figure is added to the drawing. Similar to `m_iApplicationState`, the values of `m_nextColor` and `m_bNextFill` are accessed by the constructor and destructor from the registry.

```
CDrawDoc::CDrawDoc()
{
  // ...
  m_nextColor = (COLORREF) AfxGetApp()->GetProfileInt
                (TEXT("Draw"), TEXT("CurrentColor"), BLACK);
  m_bNextFill = (BOOL) AfxGetApp()->GetProfileInt
                (TEXT("Draw"),TEXT("CurrentFill"), TRUE);
}
CDrawDoc::CDrawDoc()
{
  // ...
  m_nextColor = (COLORREF) AfxGetApp()->GetProfileInt
                (TEXT("Draw"), TEXT("CurrentColor"), BLACK);
  m_bNextFill = (BOOL) AfxGetApp()->GetProfileInt
                (TEXT("Draw"), TEXT("CurrentFill"), TRUE);
}
```

If one figure is marked, it is moved or modified depending on how it was marked. If several figures a marked, they are always moved. Each time the user moves the mouse the `WM_MOUSEMOVE` message is sent to the `view` object and transferred to the `document` class object. In order to determine the distance between two consecutive mouse movements, we need to compare the position of the current mouse position to the position of the mouse pointer when the previous message was sent. The previous position is stored in `m_ptPrevMouse`.

When the user types text on the keyboard, the keyboard may be in *insert* or *overwrite* state. Unfortunately, there is no way to find out which one by calling some system function, so the application must keep track of it. It uses `m_eKeyboardMode` of the enumeration type `KeyboardState`.

```
enum KeyboardState {KS_INSERT, KS_OVERWRITE};
```

As `KeyboardState` is used by the text figure, it is defined in `TextFigure.h`.

Finally, the two constants `TOTAL_WIDTH` and `TOTAL_HEIGHT` holds the dimensions of a letter (216 millimeters width and 297 millimeters height) in logical units (hundredths of millimeters).

DrawDoc.h

```
const int TOTAL_WIDTH = 21600, TOTAL_HEIGHT = 27900;
enum ApplicationState {SINGLE_DRAG, MULTIPLE_DRAG,
                       RECTANGLE_DRAG, EDIT_TEXT, IDLE};
enum NextActionState {ADD_LINE, ADD_ARROW, ADD_RECTANGLE,
                      ADD_ELLIPSE, ADD_TEXT, MODIFY_FIGURE};
class CDrawDoc: public CDocument
{
  private:
    DECLARE_DYNCREATE(CDrawDoc)
    DECLARE_MESSAGE_MAP()

    CDrawDoc();
    ~CDrawDoc();

  public:
    void Serialize(CArchive& ar);
    void MouseDown(CPoint ptMouse, BOOL bControlKeyDown,
                   CDC* pDC);
    void MouseDrag(const CPoint& ptMouse);
    void MouseUp();

    void DoubleClick(const CPoint& ptMouse);
    BOOL KeyDown(UINT cChar, CDC* pDC);
    void CharDown(UINT cChar, CDC* pDC);

    const FigurePointerList* GetFigurePtrList() const
                             {return &m_figurePtrList;}
    const RectangleFigure* GetInsideRectangle() const
                             {return m_pDragRectangle;}

    Caret* GetCaret() {return &m_caret;}
    const HCURSOR GetCursor() const;

    afx_msg void OnUpdateAddLine(CCmdUI *pCmdUI);
    afx_msg void OnUpdateAddArrow(CCmdUI *pCmdUI);
    afx_msg void OnUpdateAddRectangle(CCmdUI *pCmdUI);
    afx_msg void OnUpdateAddEllipse(CCmdUI *pCmdUI);
    afx_msg void OnUpdateAddText(CCmdUI *pCmdUI);
    afx_msg void OnUpdateModifyFigure(CCmdUI *pCmdUI);

    afx_msg void OnAddLine();
    afx_msg void OnAddArrow();
    afx_msg void OnAddRectangle();
    afx_msg void OnAddEllipse();
    afx_msg void OnAddText();
    afx_msg void OnModifyFigure();

    afx_msg void OnUpdateCut(CCmdUI *pCmdUI);
```

```
    afx_msg void OnCut();

    afx_msg void OnUpdateCopy(CCmdUI *pCmdUI);
    afx_msg void OnCopy();
    afx_msg void OnUpdatePaste(CCmdUI *pCmdUI);
    afx_msg void OnPaste();

    afx_msg void OnUpdateDelete(CCmdUI *pCmdUI);
    afx_msg void OnDelete();

    afx_msg void OnUpdateColor(CCmdUI *pCmdUI);
    afx_msg void OnColor();

    afx_msg void OnUpdateFont(CCmdUI *pCmdUI);
    afx_msg void OnFont();

    afx_msg void OnUpdateFill(CCmdUI *pCmdUI);
    afx_msg void OnFill();
  private:
    static BOOL IsMarked(Figure* pFigure);
    static BOOL IsMarkedText(Figure* pFigure);
    static BOOL IsMarkedAndFilled(Figure* pFigure);
    static BOOL IsMarkedAndNotFilled(Figure* pFigure);

    void UnmarkAllFigures();
    void ClearCopyList();

  private:
    Caret m_caret;

    ApplicationState m_eApplicationState;
    NextActionState m_eNextActionState;
    KeyboardState m_eKeyboardState;

    Color m_nextColor;
    Font m_nextFont;
    BOOL m_bNextFill;

    Figure *m_pSingleFigure;
    TextFigure* m_pEditText;
    RectangleFigure *m_pDragRectangle;
    FigurePointerList m_figurePtrList, m_copyPtrList;
    CPoint m_ptPrevMouse;
};
```

Serialize loads and stores the figures in m_figurePtrList. We cannot serialize the list itself because it contains pointers to the figure objects, not the objects themselves. Therefore, we have to traverse the list and store the objects one by one. In order for the function to correctly read the objects, we also have to store information about the class. We know that the class is a sub class of Figure, but we do not know which one.

This is when the `FigureFileManager` class steps into action. When storing, before serializing each `Figure` class object, we first create a `FigureFileManager` object that looks up and saves the identity value of the figure. When loading, we also create a `FigureFileManager` that reads the identity value and dynamically creates an appropriate `Figure` class object by calling its default constructor. Then we serialize the fields of the figure.

DrawDoc.cpp

```
void CDrawDoc::Serialize(CArchive& archive)
{
  CDocument::Serialize(archive);
  if (archive.IsStoring())
  {
    archive << (int) m_figurePtrList.GetSize();
    for (POSITION position =m_figurePtrList.GetHeadPosition();
         position != NULL; m_figurePtrList.GetNext(position))
    {
      Figure* pFigure = m_figurePtrList.GetAt(position);
      FigureFileManager manager(pFigure);
      manager.Serialize(archive);
      pFigure->Serialize(archive);
    }
  }
  if (archive.IsLoading())
  {
    int iSize;
    archive >> iSize;
    for (int iIndex = 0; iIndex < iSize; ++iIndex)
    {
      FigureFileManager manager;
      manager.Serialize(archive);
      Figure* pFigure = manager.GetFigure();
      pFigure->Serialize(archive);
      m_figurePtrList.AddTail(pFigure);
    }
  }
}
```

`MouseDown` can together with `MouseMove` and `MouseUp` be considered the heart of the application. It is called by `OnLButtonDown` in the `view` class when it receives the `WM_LBUTTONDOWN` message.

We start by storing the mouse position, because we will need to keep track of mouse movements. In case the application is in the state of editing a text, we finish that process by simulating a `Return` key.

```
void CDrawDoc::MouseDown(CPoint ptMouse, BOOL bControlKeyDown,
                         CDC* pDC)
{
  m_ptPrevMouse = ptMouse;
  if (m_eApplicationState == EDIT_TEXT)
  {
    KeyDown(VK_RETURN, pDC);
  }
```

If `m_eNextActionState` is set to add a figure, we simply add the figure in question. We create the figure object and add its address to the figure list. In every case, except text, we set `m_eApplicationState` to the drag-mouse state, which it will remain in as long as the user is holding the mouse button down (`MouseUp` is called when the user releases the mouse button). In these cases, we also set `m_eDragState` to the single-drag state, as we only operate on one new figure. Note that we check the allocated memory with the `check_memory` macro.

```
switch (m_eNextActionState)
{
  case ADD_LINE:
    check_memory(m_pSingleFigure =
                   new LineFigure(m_nextColor, ptMouse));
    m_figurePtrList.AddTail(m_pSingleFigure);
    m_eApplicationState = SINGLE_DRAG;
    SetModifiedFlag();
    break;
  case ADD_ARROW:
    // ...
```

In the case of adding text, we set `m_eApplicationState` to the edit-text state. It will remain in that state until the user types the `Return` or `Escape`. It will also exit that state if the user clicks the mouse, in which case we simulate a `Return` key, see the beginning of this method. In the case of creating text, we also set and show the caret marker at an appropriate size and position by calling `GetCaretArea` on the text object.

```
case ADD_TEXT:
  {
    check_memory(m_pEditText = new TextFigure(m_nextColor,
                                  ptMouse, m_nextFont, pDC));
    m_figurePtrList.AddTail(m_pEditText);
    m_eApplicationState = EDIT_TEXT;
```

```
        CRect rcCaret = m_pEditText->GetCaretArea
                                      (m_eKeyboardState);
        m_caret.SetAndShowCaret(rcCaret);
        SetModifiedFlag();
    }
    break;
```

In the case of modifying a figure, we have two different situations. If the control key(*Ctrl*) is pressed, we will mark the figure pointed as if it is unmarked, and vice versa. If the control key(*Ctrl*) is not pressed, we will mark the figure pointed regardless of whether it is already marked and unmarked for all other figures.

So, if the control key(*Ctrl*) is not pressed, we start by unmarking all figures. Then we traverse the figure list and break if we find a figure hit by the click. We traverse the list from start to end, which corresponds to examining the topmost figure first. Note that we need not know which kind of figure we are testing, its up to the sub classes of Figure to implement the pure virtual method Click.

```
case MODIFY_FIGURE:
    if (!bControlKeyDown)
    {
        UnmarkAllFigures();
    }
    Figure* pClickedFigure = NULL;
    for (POSITION position =
            m_figurePtrList.GetTailPosition();
            position != NULL;m_figurePtrList.GetPrev(position))
    {
        Figure* pFigure = m_figurePtrList.GetAt(position);
        if (pFigure->Click(ptMouse))
        {
            pClickedFigure = pFigure;
            break;
        }
    }
```

If we find a figure, we have two cases to consider. If the *Ctrl* key is pressed, we mark or unmark the figure depending on its current mark status. If the figure is already marked, we unmark it and put the application in the idle state. If the figure is not already marked, we mark it and move it to the end of the figure list (which makes it appear on top of the other figures). We then put the application in the multiple-drag state, which means that one or more figures are marked and ready to be moved, but not modified.

```
        if (pClickedFigure != NULL)
        {
            CRect rcOldFigure = pClickedFigure->GetArea();
            if (bControlKeyDown)
```

```
  {
    if (pClickedFigure->IsMarked())
    {
      pClickedFigure->Mark(FALSE);
      m_eApplicationState = IDLE;
    }
    else
    {
      pClickedFigure->Mark(TRUE);
      m_figurePtrList.Remove(pClickedFigure);
      m_figurePtrList.AddTail(pClickedFigure);

      m_eApplicationState = MULTIPLE_DRAG;
      SetModifiedFlag();
    }
  }
```

If the *Ctrl* key is not pressed, we mark the figure (all figures have been unmarked if the control key is not pressed, see the beginning of this case statement) and set the field `m_pSingleFigure` to point at it. We put it last in the figure list (which makes it appear on top of the other figures), and put the application in the single-drag state. Finally, we update the views by calling `UpdateAllFigures`.

```
      else
      {
        m_pSingleFigure = pClickedFigure;
        m_pSingleFigure->Mark(TRUE);
        m_figurePtrList.Remove(m_pSingleFigure);
        m_figurePtrList.AddTail(m_pSingleFigure);
        CRect rcFigure = m_pSingleFigure->GetArea();
        UpdateAllViews(NULL, (LPARAM) &rcFigure);
        m_eApplicationState = SINGLE_DRAG;
        SetModifiedFlag();
      }
      CRect rcNewFigure = pClickedFigure->GetArea();
      UpdateAllViews(NULL, (LPARAM) &rcOldFigure);
      UpdateAllViews(NULL, (LPARAM) &rcNewFigure);
    }
```

If we did not find a figure, we initialize the inside rectangle and and put the application in the rectangle-drag state.

```
      else
      {
        check_memory(m_pDragRectangle = new
                     RectangleFigure(GRAY, ptMouse, FALSE));
        m_eApplicationState = RECTANGLE_DRAG;
      }
      break;
    }
  }
```

MouseDrag is called when the user moves the mouse with the left button pressed. The distance since the last call to MouseDown or MouseDrag is stored in szDistance.

```
void CDrawDoc::MouseDrag(const CPoint& ptMouse)
{

  CSize szDistance = ptMouse - m_ptPrevMouse;
  m_ptPrevMouse = ptMouse;
```

If the application is in the single-drag state, we call MoveAndModify on the single figure. Whether the figure will be moved of modified depends on the setting of the previous call to Click. We do not really need to know, as the information is stored in the figure object. When the figure has been moved or modified, we update its old and new area by calling UpdateAllViews.

```
switch (m_eApplicationState)
{
  case SINGLE_DRAG:
    {
      CRect rcOldFigure = m_pSingleFigure->GetArea();
      m_pSingleFigure->MoveOrModify(szDistance);
      CRect rcNewFigure = m_pSingleFigure->GetArea();
      UpdateAllViews(NULL, (LPARAM) &rcOldFigure);
      UpdateAllViews(NULL, (LPARAM) &rcNewFigure);
    }
    break;
```

If the application is in the multiple-drag state, we traverse the figure list and for each marked figure, we call Move on the figure. Note that we do not modify the figures in this case. It would be illogical to modify several figures at the same time.

```
  case MULTIPLE_DRAG:
    {
      for (POSITION position = m_figurePtrList.
           GetHeadPosition(); position != NULL;
           m_figurePtrList.GetNext(position))
      {
        Figure* pFigure = m_figurePtrList.GetAt(position);
        if (pFigure->IsMarked())
        {
          CRect rcOldFigure = pFigure->GetArea();
          pFigure->Move(szDistance);
          CRect rcNewFigure = pFigure->GetArea();
          UpdateAllViews(NULL, (LPARAM) &rcOldFigure);
```

```
                UpdateAllViews(NULL, (LPARAM) &rcNewFigure);
          }
        }
      }
    break;
```

If the application is in the rectangle-drag state, we modify the rectangle. Even though we call `MoveOrModify`, the rectangle will be modified (not moved) because it was created by the call to `MouseDown` above, which puts the rectangle in the modify state.

```
    case RECTANGLE_DRAG:
      {
        CRect rcOldInside = m_pDragRectangle->GetArea();
        m_pDragRectangle->MoveOrModify(szDistance);
        CRect rcNewInside = m_pDragRectangle->GetArea();
        UpdateAllViews(NULL, (LPARAM) &rcOldInside);
        UpdateAllViews(NULL, (LPARAM) &rcNewInside);
      }
    break;
```

If the application is in the edit-text or in the idle state, we do nothing.

```
    case EDIT_TEXT:
    case IDLE:
        break;
  }
}
```

In `MouseUp`, we only do something if the application is in the rectangle-drag state. If it is, we have to find the figures enclosed by the rectangle. We do that by traversing the figure list and calling `Inside` on every figure. The figures found are marked and put at the end of the figure list (on top of the non-marked figures). The surrounding rectangle is deleted and the application is set to the idle state.

Note that the application can be set in the rectangle-drag state only if the *Ctrl* key was not pressed. If it was not, all figures were unmarked at the beginning of `MouseDown`.

```
    void CDrawDoc::MouseUp()
    {
      switch (m_eApplicationState)
      {
        case RECTANGLE_DRAG:
          CRect rcArea = m_pDragRectangle->GetArea();
          rcArea.NormalizeRect();
          POSITION position = m_figurePtrList.GetTailPosition();
```

```
        while (position != NULL)
        {
          Figure* pFigure = m_figurePtrList.GetPrev(position);
          if (pFigure->Inside(rcArea))
          {
            pFigure->Mark(TRUE);
            m_figurePtrList.Remove(pFigure);
            m_figurePtrList.AddTail(pFigure);
          }
        }
        delete m_pDragRectangle;
        m_pDragRectangle = NULL;
        UpdateAllViews(NULL, (LPARAM) &rcArea);
        m_eApplicationState = IDLE;
        break;
```

If the application is in the single-drag or the multiple-drag state, we just set the application to the idle state. Otherwise, we are done because the movement or modification of the figures has been made by the call to MouseMove.

```
      case SINGLE_DRAG:
      case MULTIPLE_DRAG:
        m_eApplicationState = IDLE;
        break;
      case EDIT_TEXT:
      case IDLE:
        break;
    }
}
```

DoubleClick is called by OnLDblClick in the view class when it receives the WM_LDBLCLICK message. This call is only interesting when then application state is in the modify-figure state. If it is not, we do nothing.

However, if it is in the modify-figure state, we first unmark all figures, then we traverse the figure list backwards trying to find a figure that is hit by the mouse by calling DoubleClick on each figure.

```
    void CDrawDoc::DoubleClick(const CPoint& ptMouse)
    {
      switch (m_eNextActionState)
      {
        // ...
```

```
case MODIFY_FIGURE:
  UnmarkAllFigures();
  m_eApplicationState = IDLE;
  CRect rcOldArea;
  Figure* pClickedFigure = NULL;
  for (POSITION position = m_figurePtrList.
       GetTailPosition(); position != NULL;
       m_figurePtrList.GetPrev(position))
  {
    Figure* pFigure = m_figurePtrList.GetAt(position);
    rcOldArea = pFigure->GetArea();

    if (pFigure->DoubleClick(ptMouse))
    {
      pClickedFigure = pFigure;
      break;
    }
  }
```

If we find a figure, we place the figure on top of the other figures by placing it at the end of the figure list. Then we have two cases depending on whether it is text or not. If it is text, we set the edit-text pointer to the figure and set the caret. Then we set the application state to the edit-text state.

We can use dynamic_cast to perform safe pointer type conversion between Figure and TextFigure. If pClickedFigure points at a TextFigure object, the address of that object will be returned in a pointer to TextFigure, on which we can call TextFigure specific methods. If it does not point at a TextFigure object, null is returned.

```
if (pClickedFigure != NULL)
{
  m_figurePtrList.Remove(pClickedFigure);
  m_figurePtrList.AddTail(pClickedFigure);

  m_pEditText = dynamic_cast<TextFigure*>
                  (pClickedFigure);
  if (m_pEditText != NULL)
  {
    CRect rcCaret = m_pEditText->GetCaretArea
                              (m_eKeyboardState);
    m_caret.SetAndShowCaret(rcCaret);
    m_eApplicationState = EDIT_TEXT;
  }
```

If the figure is not text, we settle with putting it on top and updating its area as the modification of the figure has taken place in the call to `DoubleClick`.

```
    else
    {
      CRect rcNewArea = pClickedFigure->GetArea();
      UpdateAllViews(NULL, (LPARAM) &rcOldArea);
      UpdateAllViews(NULL, (LPARAM) &rcNewArea);
    }
  }
  break;
}
}
```

When the user presses and releases a key, the two messages WM_KEYDOWN and WM_KEYUP are sent. They are sent for every key, including *Insert, Delete, Home, End, PageUp, PageDown,* and the arrow keys. In addition to that, WM_CHAR is sent between them for every writeable key (ASCII table value 32 – 122).

First, if the *Insert* is pressed, we set m_eKeyboardState to its reverse value. If the application is in the edit-text state, we update the caret marker.

Otherwise, if the application is in the edit-text state we examine the input character. If there is an editing (Left Arrow, Right Arrow, Home, End, Delete, or Backspace) character, we edit the text and set the modified flag if the KeyDown method to return true.

In case the Return key is pressed, we finish the editing process by unmarking and updating the text. Then we set the application to the idle state. In case the *Esc* key is pressed, we resume the original text and simulate a Return key.

```
BOOL CDrawDoc::KeyDown(UINT uChar, CDC* pDC)
{
  // ...
  int iMarked = m_figurePtrList.CountIf(IsMarked);
  if ((uChar == VK_DELETE) && (iMarked > 0))
  {
    OnDelete();
    return TRUE;
  }
  return FALSE;
}
```

Finally, if the *Delete* key is pressed, the application is in the modifying state and at least one figure is marked, we simulate the menu option **Delete**. We determine the number of marked figures by calling `CountIf` on the figure pointer list. `CountIf` is a higher ordered method, which means it takes a function as parameter. In this case it takes `IsMarked`, which returns true if a given figure is marked.

```
BOOL CDrawDoc::IsMarked(Figure* pFigure)
{
  return pFigure->IsMarked();
}
```

`CharDown` checks that the state of the application is in the text-edit state and that the character is printable. If it is, it adds the character to the text currently being edited and sets the modified flag.

```
void CDrawDoc::CharDown(UINT uChar, CDC* pDC)
{
  if ((m_eApplicationState == EDIT_TEXT) && isprint(uChar))
  {
    m_pEditText->CharDown(uChar, pDC, m_eKeyboardState);
    CRect rcText = m_pEditText->GetArea();
    UpdateAllViews(NULL, (LPARAM) &rcText);

    CRect rcCaret = m_pEditText->GetCaretArea
                              (m_eKeyboardState);
    m_caret.SetAndShowCaret(rcCaret);
    SetModifiedFlag();
  }
}
```

`OnUpdateAddLine` is called when the application receives the `ON_UPDATE_COMMAND_UI` message, which happens when the application is not busy doing something else. In this way, we can prepare the menu items, toolbar buttons, and accelerators before the user chooses them.

It is possible for the user to choose to add a line if the application is in the idle state. The **Add | Line** menu item is radio checked if this action is chosen.

```
void CDrawDoc::OnUpdateAddLine(CCmdUI *pCmdUI)
{
  pCmdUI->Enable(m_eApplicationState == IDLE);
  pCmdUI->SetRadio(m_eNextActionState == ADD_LINE);
}
```

If the user choses the add-line state, all figures will be unmarked and the next-action state is set to the add-line state.

```
void CDrawDoc::OnAddLine()
{
  UnmarkAllFigures();
  m_eNextActionState = ADD_LINE;
}
```

It is possible for the user to cut or copy if the application is in the idle state and at least one figure is marked.

```
void CDrawDoc::OnUpdateCut(CCmdUI *pCmdUI)
{
  int iMarked = m_figurePtrList.CountIf(IsMarked);
  pCmdUI->Enable((m_eApplicationState == IDLE) &&
                (iMarked > 0));
}
void CDrawDoc::OnUpdateCopy(CCmdUI *pCmdUI)
{
  int iMarked = m_figurePtrList.CountIf(IsMarked);
  pCmdUI->Enable((m_eApplicationState == IDLE) &&
                (iMarked > 0));
}
```

OnCut is quite easy, it just calls OnCopy and OnDelete. OnCopy clears the copy list and copies the marked figures in the figure list.

```
void CDrawDoc::OnCut()
{
  OnCopy();
  OnDelete();
}
void CDrawDoc::OnCopy()
{
  ClearCopyList();
  for (POSITION position = m_figurePtrList.GetHeadPosition();
       position != NULL; m_figurePtrList.GetNext(position))
  {
    Figure* pFigure = m_figurePtrList.GetAt(position);
    if (pFigure->IsMarked())
    {
      Figure* pCopiedFigure = pFigure->Copy();
      m_copyPtrList.AddTail(pCopiedFigure);
    }
  }
}
```

It is possible for the user to paste if at least one figure has been copied and the application is in the idle state. The OnPaste method copies the figures in the copy list and adds the copies to the figure list. It also moves them ten millimeters (1000 logical units is eqivialent to 1000 hundredths of millimeters).

```
void CDrawDoc::OnUpdatePaste(CCmdUI *pCmdUI)
{
  pCmdUI->Enable(!m_copyPtrList.IsEmpty() &&
                (m_eApplicationState == IDLE));
}

void CDrawDoc::OnPaste()
{
  CSize szDistance(1000, -1000);
  for (POSITION position = m_copyPtrList.GetHeadPosition();
       position != NULL; m_copyPtrList.GetNext(position))
  {
    Figure* pCopiedFigure = m_copyPtrList.GetAt(position);
    pCopiedFigure->Move(szDistance);

    Figure* pPastedFigure = pCopiedFigure->Copy();
    m_figurePtrList.AddTail(pPastedFigure);

    CRect rcFigure = pPastedFigure->GetArea();
    UpdateAllViews(NULL, (LPARAM) &rcFigure);
  }

  SetModifiedFlag();
}
```

If the next-action state is in the modify-figure state, then it is possible for the user to update the color if the application is in the idle state and at least one figure is marked. If the next-action state is not in the modify-figure state, it is enough if the application is in the idle state.

The same goes for the font update method, with the only difference being that at least one of the marked figures should be text. In the case of updating the fill status, at least one of the marked figures should be two-dimensional.

The OnColor and OnFont methods use the MFC color dialog and font dialog classes to let the user chose a color or font, respectively. If the next-action state is the modify-figure state, the marked figures are affected. If it is another state, the fields m_nextColor or m_nextFont are updated. Note that it is possible to modify the color of a font in the font dialog.

If the next-action state is the modify-figure state, the majority rules when it comes to the fill status. That is, if at least half of the marked two-dimensional figures are filled, the fill menu option will be checked. The option is enabled if at least one two-dimensional figure is marked.

```
void CDrawDoc::OnUpdateFill(CCmdUI *pCmdUI)
{
  switch (m_eNextActionState)
  {
    // ...
    case MODIFY_FIGURE:
      int iFilled = m_figurePtrList.CountIf
                                  (IsMarkedAndFilled);
      int iNotFilled = m_figurePtrList.CountIf
                                    (IsMarkedAndNotFilled);
      BOOL bAtLeastOne = ((iFilled > 0) || (iNotFilled > 0));
      pCmdUI->Enable(bAtLeastOne);
      pCmdUI->SetCheck(bAtLeastOne &&
                      (iFilled >= iNotFilled));
      break;
  }
}
```

GetCursor is called when the application is not busy doing something else. Its task is to make sure the cursor has the correct appearance. If one single figure is being dragged, we let it pick the cursor by calling GetCursor in the figure class pointed at. If there are several figures being dragged, we pick the size all cursor (four arrows). If the surrounding rectangle is being dragged, we pick the hair cross. If text is being edited, we pick the hair vertical line. Finally, if the application is in idle mode, we pick the regular arrow cursor.

```
const HCURSOR CDrawDoc::GetCursor() const
{
  switch (m_eApplicationState)
  {
    case SINGLE_DRAG:
      return m_pSingleFigure->GetCursor();
    case MULTIPLE_DRAG:
      return AfxGetApp()->LoadStandardCursor(IDC_SIZEALL);
    case RECTANGLE_DRAG:
      return AfxGetApp()->LoadStandardCursor(IDC_CROSS);
    case EDIT_TEXT:
      return AfxGetApp()->LoadStandardCursor(IDC_IBEAM);
    case IDLE:
      return AfxGetApp()->LoadStandardCursor(IDC_ARROW);
  }
```

As all possible cases have been covered above, this point of the code will never be reached. The check is for debugging purposes only.

```
    check(FALSE);
    return NULL;
}
```

The View Class

The class CDrawView is a direct sub class of the MFC class CScrollView. Its task is to alert the document object about mouse and keyboard input from the user, and to (partly or completely) repaint the client area at the request of the document object or the system as well as handle scroll movements. Its only field m_pDrawDoc is a pointer to the document class object. It is initialized by OnCreate.

DrawView.h

```
class CDrawDoc;

class CDrawView: public CScrollView
{
  private:
    DECLARE_DYNCREATE(CDrawView)
    DECLARE_MESSAGE_MAP()
    CDrawView();

  public:
    afx_msg int OnCreate(LPCREATESTRUCT lpCreateStruct);

    afx_msg void OnSetFocus(CWnd* pOldWnd);
    afx_msg void OnKillFocus(CWnd* pNewWnd);
    afx_msg BOOL OnSetCursor(CWnd* pWnd, UINT nHitTest,
                             UINT message);

    afx_msg void OnLButtonDown(UINT uFlags, CPoint ptMouse);
    afx_msg void OnMouseMove(UINT uFlags, CPoint ptMouse);
    afx_msg void OnLButtonUp(UINT uFlags, CPoint ptMouse);
    afx_msg void OnLButtonDblClk(UINT uFlags, CPoint ptMouse);

    afx_msg void OnChar(UINT uChar, UINT nRepCnt,UINT uFlags);
    afx_msg void OnKeyDown(UINT uChar, UINT nRepCnt,
                           UINT uFlags);

    void OnUpdate(CView* pSender, LPARAM lHint,
                  CObject* pHint);
    void OnDraw(CDC* pDC);

  private:
    CDrawDoc* m_pDrawDoc;
};
```

OnCreate is called after the view is created but before it is shown. It sets and checks the m_pDrawDoc field. It also loads the scroll view with the logical coordinates of a letter (216 millimeters width and 279 millimeters height). The TOTAL_WIDTH and TOTAL_HEIGHT constants was initialized to 21600 and 27900 hundredths of millimeters in DrawDoc.h

CDrawView.cpp

```
int CDrawView::OnCreate(LPCREATESTRUCT lpCreateStruct)
{
  // We check that the view has been correctly created.
  if (CScrollView::OnCreate(lpCreateStruct) == -1)
  {
    return -1;
  }
  m_pDrawDoc = (CDrawDoc*) m_pDocument;
  ASSERT_VALID(m_pDrawDoc);
  CSize szTotal(TOTAL_WIDTH, TOTAL_HEIGHT);
  SetScrollSizes(MM_HIMETRIC, szTotal);
  return 0;
}
```

The methods OnLButtonDown, OnMouseMove, OnLButtonUp, and OnLButtonDblClk call MouseDown, MouseMove, MouseUp, and DoubleClick of the document class.

The mouse point is given in device coordinates. We need to translate it into logical coordinates by creating and preparing a device context and calling DPtoLP. The flags hold information about the mouse clicks. The constant MK_CONTROL is useful for checking whether the user is pressing the *Ctrl* key.

```
void CDrawView::OnLButtonDown(UINT uFlags, CPoint ptMouse)
{
  CClientDC dc(this);
  OnPrepareDC(&dc);
  dc.DPtoLP(&ptMouse);
  BOOL bControlKeyDown = (uFlags & MK_CONTROL);
  m_pDrawDoc->MouseDown(ptMouse, bControlKeyDown, &dc);
}
```

OnKeyDown is called when the user presses a key on the keyboard. First it is sent to the document class method KeyDown. If it has no use for the character, false is returned and we can instead use it for scrolling.

```
void CDrawView::OnKeyDown(UINT uChar, UINT /* uRepCnt */,
                          UINT /* uFlags */)
{
  CClientDC dc(this);
  OnPrepareDC(&dc);
```

```
    switch (uChar)
    {
      case VK_HOME:
        if (!m_pDrawDoc->KeyDown(VK_HOME, &dc))
        {
          OnVScroll(SB_TOP, 0, NULL);
          OnHScroll(SB_LEFT, 0, NULL);
        }
        break;
      // ...
    }
}
```

The methods `OnSetFocus` and `OnKillFocus` are called when the input view gains or looses the focus. They notify the caret object of the document class object about the change.

```
void CDrawView::OnSetFocus(CWnd* /* pOldWnd */)
{
  Caret* pCaret = m_pDrawDoc->GetCaret();
  pCaret->OnSetFocus(this);
}

void CDrawView::OnKillFocus(CWnd* /* pNewWnd */)
{
  Caret* pCaret = m_pDrawDoc->GetCaret();
  pCaret->OnKillFocus();
}
```

`OnUpdate` is indirectly called by `UpdateAllViews` in the document class. If the first parameter `lHint` is not null, it is a pointer to a rectangle containing the area to update. It is given in logical coordinates that need to be translated into device coordinates. In order to be sure the area is properly updated, we add a small margin.

```
void CDrawView::OnUpdate(CView* /* pSender */, LPARAM lHint,
                         CObject* /* pHint */)
{
  if (lHint != NULL)
  {
    CRect rcClip = *(CRect*) lHint;
    int cxMargin = (int) (0.05 * rcClip.Width());
    int cyMargin = (int) (0.05 * rcClip.Height());
    rcClip.left   -= cxMargin;
    rcClip.right  += cxMargin;
    rcClip.top    -= cyMargin;
    rcClip.bottom += cyMargin;
```

```
        CClientDC dc(this);
        OnPrepareDC(&dc);
        dc.LPtoDP(rcClip);
        InvalidateRect(rcClip);
    }
```

OnUpdate is also called by OnIntialUpdate in CScrollView with a zero hint, in which case we invalidate the whole client area before we update the window by calling UpdateWindow, which in turn indirectly calls OnDraw.

```
    else
    {
        Invalidate();
    }
    UpdateWindow();
}
```

OnDraw traverses the figure list and draws the figures. It also draw the inside rectangle unless its pointer is null.

```
    void CDrawView::OnDraw(CDC* pDC)
    {
      const FigurePointerList* pFigurePtrList =
                            m_pDrawDoc->GetFigurePtrList();
      for (POSITION position = pFigurePtrList->GetHeadPosition();
           position != NULL; pFigurePtrList->GetNext(position))
      {
        Figure* pFigure = pFigurePtrList->GetAt(position);
        CRect rcFigure = pFigure->GetArea();
        pFigure->Draw(pDC);
      }
      const RectangleFigure* pInsideRectangle =
                            m_pDrawDoc->GetInsideRectangle();
      if (pInsideRectangle != NULL)
      {
          pInsideRectangle->Draw(pDC);
      }
    }
```

Summary

- We started by generating the application's skeleton code with The Application Wizard.

- Figure is the root class of our class hierarchy. It is abstract and has the abstract sub class TwoDimensionalFigure.

- It also has five concrete sub classes: LineFigure, ArrowFigure, RectangleFigure, EllipseFigure, and TextFigure. There is also the class FigureFileManager that handles the file management of the figures.

- The document class manages the data of the drawing. Its most central part is the MouseDown, MouseDrag, and MouseUp methods that keep track of the user's mouse movements.

- The view class accepts mouse keyboard inputs. It also draws the figures and the surrounding rectangle when the user is marking figures.

8

The Calc Application

Calc is a spreadsheet program. The code is divided into several classes. It has the functionality to handle text, numerical values, and formulas composed by the four arithmetic operators. It also has the ability to change the font and color and the horizontal and vertical alignment. It also supports cut and paste as well as load and save. The references of a formula are relative, which means they are updated when the user cuts and pastes a block of cells to another location. The following screenshot depicts a classic example of the Calc Application:

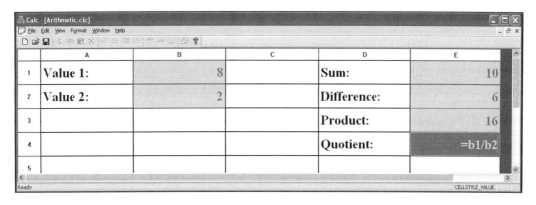

- We start by generating the code with the help of the Application Wizard.

- We need the class Reference to keep track of references in the spreadsheet.

- Then we look into formula generation. First we write the *scanner*, whose task is to put together sequences of characters into *tokens*, the smallest significant part of the formula.

- Then we write the *parser*. Given a list of tokens, its task is to determine whether the formula is correct and to generate a *syntax tree*.

- Then we continue to define the class for the spreadsheet *cell*. It shall hold functionality to handle and display user input and formula values.

- The cells are organized in a *matrix*. The size of a matrix is statically set to ten rows and five columns. It can be altered. However, the logical limit of the number of columns is 26, the number of letters in the alphabet.

- When a formula is input into a cell, the formula is assigned a set of *sources* and *targets*. The sets form a directed acyclic graph. It would be illogical to introduce cycles into the graph. So, every time a formula is altered, we check that no cycles are introduced.

- The document class handles the logic of the spreadsheet, such as cut and paste and re-evaluations of affected cells.

- Finally, the view class handles the user input as well as the scrolling and displaying of the spreadsheet.

We use the Application Wizard to generate the classes CCalcApp, CMainFrame, CChildFrame, CCalcDoc, CCalcView, and CAboutDlg. We will modify CCalcDoc and CCalcView as we develop the application, the rest of the classes will be left unmodified. The process is very similar to those of previous chapters. The only difference is that we set the **File extension** to **Clc** and the **File type long name** to **A Calc Document**. In this application, we use CView as the base class of our view class.

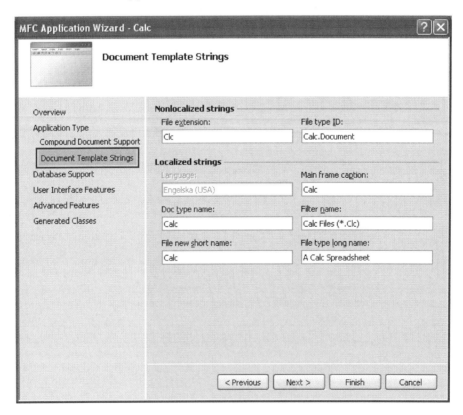

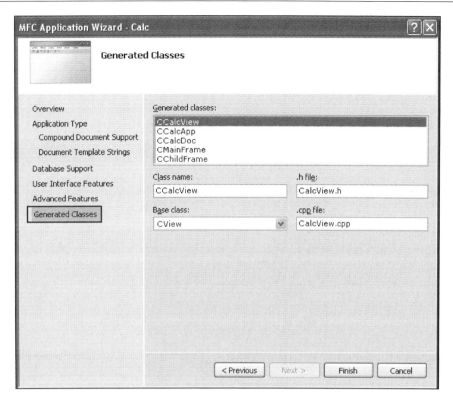

We leave `CMainFrame` and `CChildFrame` unmodified. `CCalcDoc` and `CCalcView` will be modified later on. Regarding `CCalcApp`, we only add the following include lines.

Calc.cpp

```
#include "MainFrm.h"
#include "ChildFrm.h"

#include "..\\Set.h"
#include "..\\List.h"
#include "..\\Color.h"
#include "..\\Font.h"
#include "..\\Caret.h"

#include "Reference.h"
#include "SyntaxTree.h"

#include "Cell.h"
#include "CellMatrix.h"
#include "TSetMatrix.h"

#include "CalcDoc.h"
#include "CalcView.h"
```

The Resource

The Application Wizard creates the basic set of menus, which are used by the Application Framework. We add the menu *Format* to the resource with the help of the Resource Editor. Here follows a summarization of the added menus, accelerators, toolbar buttons, and strings.

Id	Menu Item	Accelerator Toolbar	String Table
ID_EDIT_CUT	Edit | Cut	Ctrl-X ✂	Cut the selection and put it on the Clipboard \nCut
ID_EDIT_COPY	Edit | Copy	Ctrl-C 📋	Copy the selection and put it on the Clipboard \nCopy
ID_EDIT_PASTE	Edit | Paste	Ctrl-V 📋	Insert Clipboard contents\nPaste
ID_FORMAT_FONT	Format | Font	Ctrl-F	Set the Font\nFont
ID_ALIGN_HORZ_LEFT	Format | Align-ment | Horizontal | Left		Horizontal Alignment Left\nLeft
ID_ALIGN_HORZ_CENTER	Format | Align-ment | Horizontal | Center		Horizontal Alignment Center\nCenter
ID_ALIGN_HORZ_RIGHT	Format | Align-ment | Horizontal | Right		Horizontal Alignment Right\n Right
ID_ALIGN_HORZ_JUSTIFIED	Format | Align-ment | Horizontal | Justified		Horizontal Alignment Justified\nJustified
ID_ALIGN_VERT_TOP	Format | Align-ment | Vertical | Top		Vertical Alignment Top \nTop
ID_ALIGN_VERT_CENTER	Format | Align-ment | Vertical | Center		Vertical Alignment Center\nCenter
ID_ALIGN_VERT_BOTTOM	Format | Align-ment | Vertical | Bottom		Vertical Alignment Bottom\nBottom
ID_COLOR_TEXT	Format | Color | Text		Set the Text Color\nText Color
ID_COLOR_BACKGROUND	Format | Color | Background		Set the Background Color\nBackground Color

Formula Interpretation

The core of a spreadsheet program is its ability to interpret formulas. When the user inputs a formula in a cell, it has to be interpreted and its value has to be evaluated. The process is called *formula interpretation*, and is divided into three separate steps. First, given the input string, the *scanner* generates a list of *tokens*, then the *parser* generates a *syntax tree*, and, finally, the *evaluator* determines the value of the formula.

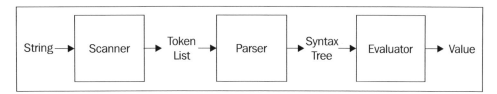

A token is the smallest significant part of the formula. For instance, the text "a1" is interpreted as a token representing a reference, the text "1.2" is interpreted as the value 1.2. Assume that the cells have values according the sheet below, the formula interpretation process will be as follows.

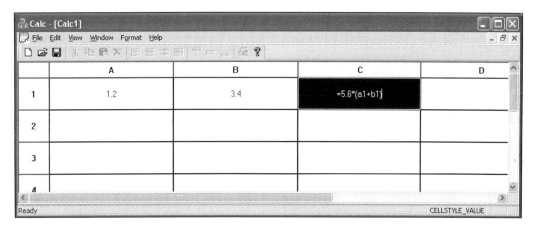

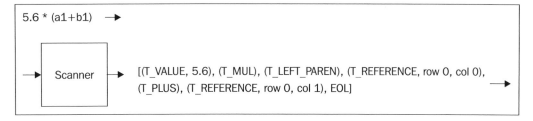

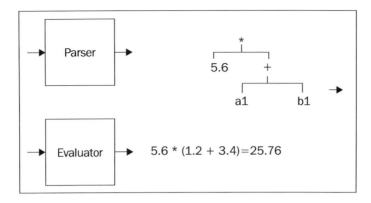

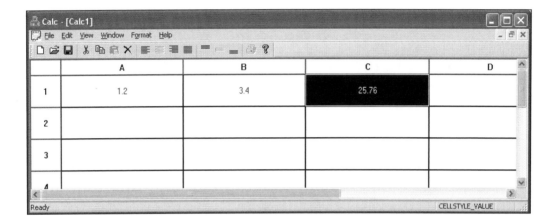

The Tokens

The scanner takes a string as input, traverses it, and finds its least significant parts, its tokens. Blanks are ignored, and the scanner sees no difference between capital and small letters. The token T_VALUE needs an extra piece of information to keep track of the actual value; it is called an *attribute*. T_REFERENCE also needs an attribute to keep track of its row and column. In this application, there are ten different tokens:

`T_ADD, T_SUB,` `T_MUL, T_DIV`	The four arithmetic operators: '+', '-', '*', and '/'.
`T_LEFT_PAREN,` `T_RIGHT_PAREN`	Left and right parenthesis: '(' and ')'.
`T_VALUE`	A numerical value, for instance: 123, -3.14, or +0.45. It does not matter whether the value is integral or decimal. Nor does it matter if the decimal point (if present) is preceded or succeeded by digits. However, the value must contain at least one digit.
	Attribute: a value of type double.
`T_REFERENCE`	Reference, for instance: a12, b22.
	Attribute: an object of the Reference class.
`T_EOL`	The end of the line, there is no more characters in the string.

As stated above, the string "2 * (a1 + b1)" generates the tokens in the table on the next page. The end-of-line token is added to the list.

Text	Token	Attribute
2.5	T_VALUE	2.5
*	T_MUL	
(	T_LEFT_PAREN	
a1	T_REFERENCE	row 0, col 0
+	T_ADD	
b1	T_REFERENCE	row 0, col 1
)	T_RIGHT_PAREN	
	T_EOL	

The class `Token` handles a token `TokenIdentity` which is an enumeration of the tokens in the table above. The token is identified by `m_eTokenId`. The class also has attribute fields `m_dValue` and `m_reference`. As we do not differ between integral and decimal values, the value has double type. The reference is stored in an object of the `Reference` class, see the next section.

There are five constructors altogether. The default constructor is necessary because we store tokens in a list, which requires a default constructor. The other three constructors are used by the scanner to create tokens with or without attributes.

Token.h

```
enum TokenIdentity {T_ADD, T_SUB, T_MUL, T_DIV, T_LEFT_PAREN,
                    T_RIGHT_PAREN, T_REFERENCE, T_VALUE, T_EOL};

class Token
{
  public:
    Token();
    Token(const Token& token);
    Token operator=(const Token& token);

    Token(double dValue);
    Token(Reference reference);
    Token(TokenIdentity eTokenId);

    TokenIdentity GetId() const {return m_eTokenId;}
    double GetValue() const {return m_dValue;}
    Reference GetReference() const {return m_reference;}
  private:
    TokenIdentity m_eTokenId;
    double m_dValue;
    Reference m_reference;
};
typedef List<Token> TokenList;
```

The Reference Class

The class `Reference` identifies the cell's position in the spreadsheet. It is also used by the `scanner`, `parser`, and `syntax` tree classes to identify a reference of a formula.

The row and column of the reference are zero-based value integers. The column 'a' corresponds to row 0, 'b' to 1, and so on. For instance, the reference "b3" will generate the fields $m\_iRow = 2$, $m\_iCol = 1$, and the reference "c5" will generate the fields $m\_iRow = 4$, $m\_iCol = 2$.

The default constructor is used for serialization purposes and for storing references in sets. The copy constructor and the assignment operator are necessary for the same reason. The second constructor initializes the field with the given row and column.

Reference.h

```
class Reference
{
  public:
    Reference();
    Reference(int iRow, int iCol);

    Reference(const Reference& reference);
    Reference operator=(const Reference& reference);

    int GetRow() const {return m_iRow;}
    int GetCol() const {return m_iCol;}

    void SetRow(int iRow) {m_iRow = iRow;}
    void SetCol(int iCol) {m_iCol = iCol;}

    friend BOOL operator==(const Reference &ref1,
                           const Reference &ref2);
    friend BOOL operator<(const Reference& ref1,
                          const Reference& ref2);

    CString ToString() const;
    void Serialize(CArchive& archive);
  private:
    int m_iRow, m_iCol;
};

typedef Set<Reference> ReferenceSet;
```

The equality operator regards the left and right references to be equal if their rows and columns are equal. The left reference is less than the right reference if its row is less than the right ones, or if the rows are equal the left column is less than the right one. The method ToString returns the reference as a string. The zero row is written as one and the zero column is written as a small 'a'.

Reference.cpp

```
BOOL operator==(const Reference& rfLeft,
                const Reference& rfRight)
{
  return (rfLeft.m_iRow == rfRight.m_iRow) &&
         (rfLeft.m_iCol == rfRight.m_iCol);
}
BOOL operator<(const Reference& rfLeft,
               const Reference& rfRight)
{
  return (rfLeft.m_iRow < rfRight.m_iRow) ||
         ((rfLeft.m_iRow == rfRight.m_iRow) &&
          (rfLeft.m_iCol < rfRight.m_iCol));
}
```

```
CString Reference::ToString() const
{
  CString stBuffer;
  stBuffer.Format(TEXT("%c%d"), (TCHAR) (TEXT('a') + m_iCol),
                  m_iRow + 1);
  return stBuffer;
}
```

The Scanner—Generating the List of Tokens

The `Scanner` class handles the scanning. Its task is to group together characters into a token. For instance, the text "12.34" is interpreted as the value 12.34.

Scanner.h

```
class Scanner
{
  public:
    Scanner(const CString& stBuffer);
    TokenList* GetTokenList() {return &m_tokenList;}
  private:
    Token NextToken();
    BOOL ScanValue(double& dValue);
    BOOL ScanReference(Reference& reference);
  private:
    CString m_stBuffer;
    TokenList m_tokenList;
};
```

The constructor takes a string as parameter and generates `m_tokenList` by repeatedly calling `NextToken` until the input string is empty. A null character ($\backslash$0) is added to the string by the constructor in order not to have to check for the end of the text. `NextToken` returns `EOL` (End of Line) when it encounters the end of the string.

Scanner.cpp

```
Scanner::Scanner(const CString& m_stBuffer)
 :m_stBuffer(m_stBuffer + TEXT('\0'))
{
  Token token;
  do
  {
    token = NextToken();
    m_tokenList.AddTail(token);
  }
  while (token.GetId() != T_EOL);
}
```

`NextToken` does the actual work of the scanner and divides the text into token, one by one. First, we skip any preceding blanks and tabulators (tabs), these are known as **white spaces**. It is rather simple to extract the token regarding the arithmetic symbols and the parentheses. We just have to check the next character of the buffer.

It becomes more difficult when it comes to numerical values, references, or text. We have two auxiliary functions for that purpose, `ScanValue` and `ScanReference`.

```
Token Scanner::NextToken()
{
  while ((m_stBuffer[0] == TEXT(' ')) ||
         (m_stBuffer[0] == TEXT('\t')))
  {
    m_stBuffer.Delete(0);
  }
  switch (m_stBuffer[0])
  {
    case TEXT('\0'):
      return Token(T_EOL);
    case TEXT('+'):
      {
        double dValue;
        if (ScanValue(dValue))
        {
          return Token(dValue);
        }
        else
        {
          m_stBuffer.Delete(0);
          return Token(T_ADD);
        }
      }
    }
    // ...
```

If none of the above cases apply, the token may be a value or a reference. The two methods `ScanValue` and `ScanReference` find out if that is the case. If not, the scanner has encountered an unknown character and an exception is thrown.

```
default:
  double dValue;
  Reference reference;
  if (ScanValue(dValue))
  {
    return Token(dValue);
  }
  else if (ScanReference(reference))
  {
    return Token(reference);
  }
```

```
      else
      {
        CString stMessage;
        stMessage.Format(TEXT("Unknown character: \"%c\"."),
                         m_stBuffer[0]);
        throw stMessage;
      }
      break;
    }
  }
}
```

ScanValue first scans for a possible plus or minus sign and then for digits. If the last digit is followed by a decimal point it scans for more digits. Thereafter, if it has found at least one digit, its value is converted into a double and true is returned.

```
BOOL Scanner::ScanValue(double& dValue)
{
  CString stValue = ScanSign();
  stValue.Append(ScanDigits());

  {
    m_stBuffer.Delete(0);
    stValue += TEXT('.') + ScanDigits();
  }

  if (stValue.FindOneOf(TEXT("0123456789")) != -1)
  {
    dValue = _tstof(stValue);
    return TRUE;
  }
  else
  {
    m_stBuffer.Insert(0, stValue);
    return FALSE;
  }
}
```

ScanReference checks that the next character is a letter and that the characters thereafter are a sequence of at least one digit. If so, we extract the column and the row of the reference.

```
BOOL Scanner::ScanReference(Reference& reference)
{
  if (isalpha(m_stBuffer[0]) && isdigit(m_stBuffer[1]))
  {
    reference.SetCol(tolower(m_stBuffer[0]) - TEXT('a'));
    m_stBuffer.Delete(0);
```

```
        CString stRow = ScanDigits();
        reference.SetRow(_tstoi(stRow) - 1);
        return TRUE;
    }

    return FALSE;
}
```

The Parser—Generating the Syntax Tree

The users write a formula by beginning the input string with an equals sign (=). The parser's task is to translate the scanner's token list into a syntax tree, or, more exactly, to check the formula's syntax and to generate an object of the class SyntaxTree. The expression's value will be evaluated when the cell's value needs to be re-evaluated.

The syntax of a valid formula may be defined by a *grammar*. Let us start with one that handles expressions that make use of the basic rules of arithmetic operators:

1. Formula → Expression EOL

2. Expression → Expression+ Expression

3. Expression → Expression- Expression

4. Expression → Expression* Expression

5. Expression → Expression / Expression

7. Expression → (Expression)

8. Expression → REFERENCE

9. Expression → VALUE

A grammar is a set of *rules*. In the grammar above, each line represents a rule. *Formula* and *Expression* in the grammar are called **non-terminals**. EOL, VALUE and the characters '+', '-', '*', and '/'are called **terminals**. Terminals and non-terminals are called **symbols**. One of the rules is defined as the grammar's *start rule*, in our case the first rule. The symbol on the start rule's left side is called the grammar's *start symbol*, in our case *Formula*.

The arrow can be read as **is**. The grammar above can be read as:

> *A formula is an expression followed by end of line. An expression is the sum of two expressions, the difference of two expressions, the product of two expressions, the quotient of two expressions, an expression surrounded by parentheses, an reference, or a numerical value.*

This is a good start, but there are a few problems. Let us test if the string "1 * 2 + 3" is accepted by the grammar. We can test that by doing a *derivation*, where we start with the start symbol (*Formula*) and apply rules until we have only terminals. The digits in the following derivation refer to the grammar rules.

Formula $\overset{1}{\Rightarrow}$ Expression EOL $\overset{2}{\Rightarrow}$ Expression + Expression EOL $\overset{4}{\Rightarrow}$

Expression* Expression + Expression EOL $\overset{9}{\Rightarrow}$ VALUE(1)* Expression + Expression EOL $\overset{9}{\Rightarrow}$

VALUE(1)* VALUE(2) + Expression EOL $\overset{9}{\Rightarrow}$ VALUE(1)* VALUE(2) + VALUE(3) EOL

The derivation can be illustrated by the development of a *parse tree*.

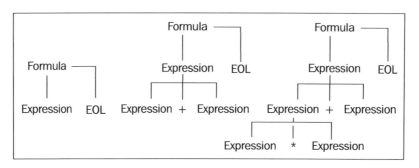

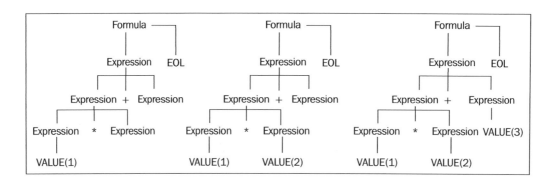

Let us try another derivation of the same string, with the rules applied in a different order.

Formula $\overset{1}{\Rightarrow}$ Expression EOL $\overset{4}{\Rightarrow}$ Expression • Expression EOL $\overset{2}{\Rightarrow}$

Expression* Expression + Expression EOL $\overset{9}{\Rightarrow}$ VALUE(1) • Expression + Expression EOL $\overset{9}{\Rightarrow}$

VALUE(1)* VALUE(2) + Expression EOL $\overset{9}{\Rightarrow}$ VALUE(1)* VALUE(2) + VALUE(3) EOL

This derivation will generate a different parse tree.

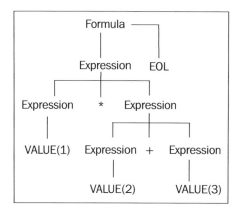

A grammar is said to be *ambiguous* if it can generate two different parse trees for the same input string, which is something we should avoid. The second tree above is of course a violation of the laws of mathematics, which says that multiplication should be evaluated before addition, that multiplication has a higher *priority* than addition. However, the grammar does not know that. One way to avoid ambiguity is to introduce one new set of rules in the grammar for each priority level:

1. Formula ➔ Expression EOL

2. Expression ➔ Expression + Term

3. Expression ➔ Expression - Term

4. Expression ➔ Term

5. Term ➔ Term · Factor

6. Term ➔ Term / Factor

7. Term ➔ Factor

8. Factor ➔ VALUE

9. Factor ➔ REFERENCE

10. Factor ➔ (Expression)

This new grammar is not ambiguous, if we try our string with this grammar, we can only generate one parse tree, regardless of which order we choose to apply the rules.

$$\text{Formula} \overset{1}{\Rightarrow} \text{Expression EOL} \overset{2}{\Rightarrow} \text{Expression + Term EOL} \overset{4}{\Rightarrow} \text{Term + Term EOL} \overset{5}{\Rightarrow}$$

$$\text{Term+Term} \cdot \text{Factor EOL} \overset{7}{\Rightarrow} \text{Factor+Term} \cdot \text{Factor EOL} \overset{8}{\Rightarrow} \text{VALUE(1)+Term} \cdot \text{Factor EOL} \overset{7}{\Rightarrow}$$

$$\text{VALUE(1)+Factor} \cdot \text{Factor EOL} \overset{8}{\Rightarrow} \text{VALUE(1)+VALUE(2)} \cdot \text{Factor EOL} \overset{8}{\Rightarrow}$$

$$\text{VALUE(1)+VALUE(2)} \cdot \text{VALUE(3)}$$

This derivation gives the following tree. It is not possible to derivate a different tree from the same input string.

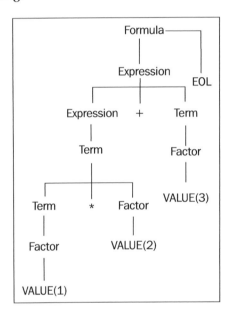

Now we are ready to write a parser. Essentially, there are two types of parsers: **top-down** and **bottom-up**. As the terms imply, a top-down parser starts by the grammar's start symbol together with the input string, and tries to apply rules until we have only terminals left. A bottom-up parser starts by the input strings and tries to apply rules backward, *reduce* the rules, until we reach the start symbol.

It is a complicated matter to construct a bottom-up parser. It is usually not done by hand; instead, there are parser generators that construct a *parser table* for the given grammar and the skeleton of the implementation of the parser. However, the theory of bottom-up passing is outside the scope of this book.

One way to construct a very simple, but unfortunately also a very inefficient, top-down parser would be to apply all possible rules in random order. If we reach a dead end, we simply backtrack and try another rule. A more efficient, but still rather simple, parser would be a **look-ahead** parser. Given a suitable grammar, we only need to look at the next token in order to uniquely determine which rule to apply. If we reach a dead end, we do not have to backtrack; we simply state that the input string is incorrect according to the grammar.

A first attempt to implement a look-ahead parser could be to write a method for each rule in the grammar. Unfortunately, we cannot do that quite yet, because that would result in a method *Expression* like:

```
CSyntaxTree* CSyntaxTree::Expression()
{
    switch (nextToken.GetId())
    {
        case PLUS:
            Expression();
            break;
        // ...
    }
}
```

Do you see the problem? The method calls itself without any change of the input stream, which would result in an infinitive loop. This is called **left recursion**. We can solve the problem, however, with the help of a simple translation. The rules:

Expression ➔ Expression+Term

Expression ➔ Expression-Term

Expression ➔ Term

Can be translated to the equivalent set of rules:

Expression ➔ Term NextExpression

NextExpression ➔ +Term NextExpression

NextExpression ➔ -Term NextExperssion

NextExpression ➔ ε

Epsilon ε denotes the empty string. If we apply this transformation to the *Expression* and *Term* rules in the grammar above, we receive the following grammar:

1. Formula → Expression EOL

2. Expression → Term NextExpression

3. NextExpression → +Term NextExpression

4. NextExpression → -Term NextExperssion

5. NextExpression → ε

6. Term → Factor NextTerm

7. NextTerm → +Factor NextTerm

8. NextTerm → -Factor NextTerm

9. NextTerm → ε

10. Factor → VALUE

11. Factor → REFERENCE

12. Factor → (Expression)

Let us try this new grammar with our string "1 * 2 + 3":

Formula $\overset{1}{\Rightarrow}$ Expression EOL $\overset{2}{\Rightarrow}$ Term NextExpression EOL $\overset{3}{\Rightarrow}$ Term + Term NextExpression EOL

$\overset{5}{\Rightarrow}$ Term + Term EOL $\overset{6}{\Rightarrow}$ Factor NextTerm + Term EOL $\overset{7}{\Rightarrow}$ Factor* Factor NextTerm + Term EOL $\overset{9}{\Rightarrow}$

Factor* Factor + Term EOL $\overset{10}{\Rightarrow}$ VALUE(1)* Factor + Term EOL $\overset{10}{\Rightarrow}$ VALUE(1)* VALUE(2) + Term

EOL $\overset{6}{\Rightarrow}$ VALUE(1)* VALUE(2) + Factor NextTerm EOL $\overset{9}{\Rightarrow}$ VALUE(1)* VALUE(2) + Factor EOL $\overset{10}{\Rightarrow}$

VALUE(1)* VALUE(2) + VALUE(3) EOL

This will generate the following parse tree.

The requirement for a grammar to be suitable for a look-ahead parser is that every set of rules with the same left-hand side symbol must have at most one empty rule or at most one rule with a non-terminal as the first symbol on the right-hand side. Our grammar above meets those requirements.

Now we are ready to write the parser. The parser should also generate some kind of output, representing the string. One such representation is the syntax tree. A syntax tree can be viewed as an abstract parse tree; we keep only the essential information. For instance, the parse tree above has a matching syntax tree on the text page.

The idea is that we write a method for every set of rules with the same left hand symbol, each such method generates a part of the resulting syntax tree. For this purpose, we create the class `Parser`. *Formula* takes the text to parse, places it in `m_stBuffer`, generates a list of token with the `Scanner` class, starts the parsing process, and returns the generated syntax tree. If an error occurs during the parsing process, an exception is thrown. The message of the exception is eventually displayed to the user by a message box

The field `m_ptokenList` is generated by the scanner. The field `m_nextToken` is the next token, we need it to decide which grammar rule to apply. As constructors cannot return a value, they are omitted in this class. In this class, *Formula* does the job of the constructor.

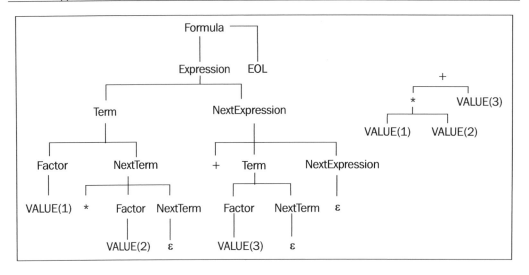

Parser.h

```
class Parser
{
  public:
    SyntaxTree Formula(const CString& stBuffer);

  private:
    void Match(TokenIdentity eTokenId);

    SyntaxTree* Expression();
    SyntaxTree* NextExpression(SyntaxTree* pLeftTerm);
    SyntaxTree* Term();
    SyntaxTree* NextTerm(SyntaxTree* pLeftFactor);
    SyntaxTree* Factor();

  private:
    CString m_stBuffer;
    Token m_nextToken;
    TokenList* m_ptokenList;
};
```

Parser.cpp

`Formula` is the start method of the class. It is called in order to interpret the text the user has input. The input string is saved in case we need it in an error messages. We scan the input string, receive the token list, and initialize the first token in the list. Even if the input string is completely empty, there is still the token `T_EOL` in the list.

We parse the token list and receive a pointer to a syntax tree. If there was a parse error, an exception is thrown instead. When the token list has been parsed, we have to make sure there are no extra tokens left in the list except the end-of-line token.

For the purpose of avoiding a classic mistake (dangling pointers), we create and return a static syntax tree, which is initialized with the pointer generated from the parsing. We also delete the generated syntax tree in order to avoid another classic mistake (memory leaks).

```
SyntaxTree Parser::Formula(const CString& stBuffer)
{
  m_stBuffer = stBuffer;

  Scanner scanner(m_stBuffer);
  m_ptokenList = scanner.GetTokenList();
  m_nextToken = m_ptokenList->GetHead();

  SyntaxTree* pExpr = Expression();
  Match(T_EOL);

  SyntaxTree syntaxTree(*pExpr);
  delete pExpr;
  return syntaxTree;
}
```

`Match` is used to match the next token with the expected one. If they do not match, an exception is thrown. Otherwise, the next token is removed from the list and if there is another token in the list, is becomes the next one.

```
void Parser::Match(TokenIdentity eTokenId)
{
  if (m_nextToken.GetId() != eTokenId)
  {
    CString stMessage;
    stMessage.Format(TEXT("Invalid Expression: \"") +
                     m_stBuffer + TEXT("\"."));
    throw stMessage;
  }

  m_tokenList->RemoveHead();
  if (!m_ptokenList->IsEmpty())
  {
    m_nextToken = m_ptokenList->GetHead();
  }
}
```

The rest of the methods implement the grammar above. There is one function for each for the symbols `Formula`, `Expression`, `NextExpression`, `Term`, `NextTerm`, and `Factor`.

```
SyntaxTree* Parser::Expression()
{
  SyntaxTree* pTerm = Term();
  SyntaxTree* pNextExpression = NextExpression(pTerm);
  return pNextExpression;
}
```

The method `NextExpression` takes care of addition and subtraction. If the next token is `T_ADD` or `T_SUB`, we match the operator and parse its right operand. Then we create and return a new syntax tree with the operator in question. If the next token is neither `T_ADD` nor `T_SUB`, we just assume that this rule does not apply and return the given left syntax tree.

```
SyntaxTree* Parser::NextExpression(SyntaxTree* pLeftTerm)
{
  switch (m_nextToken.GetId())
  {
    case T_ADD:
      {
        Match(T_ADD);
        SyntaxTree *pRightTerm = Term(), *pResult;
        check_memory(pResult = new
                    SyntaxTree(ST_ADD,pLeftTerm,pRightTerm));
        SyntaxTree* pNextExpression = NextExpression(pResult);
        return pNextExpression;
      }
      break;
    case T_SUB:
      // ...
    default:
      return pLeftTerm;
  }
}
```

The method `Factor` parses values, references, and expression surrounded by parentheses. If the next token is a left parenthesis, we match it and parse the following expression as well as the closing right parenthesis. If the next token is a reference or a value, we match it.

We receive the reference attribute with its row and column and match the reference token. If the user has given a reference outside the spreadsheet, an exception is thrown.

We create and return a new syntax tree holding the reference. If none of the tokens above applies, the user has input an invalid expression.

```
SyntaxTree* Parser::Factor()
{
  switch (m_nextToken.GetId())
  {
    case T_LEFT_PAREN:
      // ...
    case T_REFERENCE:
      {
        Reference reference = m_nextToken.GetReference();
        Match(T_REFERENCE);

        int iRow = reference.GetRow();
        int iCol = reference.GetCol();
        if ((iRow < 0) || (iRow >= ROWS) ||
            (iCol < 0) || (iCol >= COLS))
        {
          CString stMessage=TEXT("Reference Out Of Range: \"")
                          + m_stBuffer + TEXT("\".");
          throw stMessage;
        }

        check_memory(return (new SyntaxTree(reference)));
      }
      break;

    case T_VALUE:
      {
        double dValue = m_nextToken.GetValue();
        Match(T_VALUE);
        check_memory(return (new SyntaxTree(dValue)));
      }
      break;

    default:
      CString stMessage = TEXT("Invalid Expression: \"") +
                          m_stBuffer + TEXT("\".");
      throw stMessage;
      break;
  }
}
```

The Syntax Tree—Representing the Formula

The class `SyntaxTree` is used to build a syntax tree and to evaluate its value. For instance, the formula "a1 / (b2 - 1.5) + 2.4 + c3 * 3.6" generates the syntax tree on the next page.

The class `SyntaxTree` manages a syntax tree. There are seven different types of trees, and the enumeration type `SyntaxTreeIdentity` keeps track of them. First, we have the four arithmetic operators, then the case of an expression in brackets, and finally the reference and the numerical value. We do not really need the parentheses sub tree as the priority of the expression is stored in the syntax tree itself. However, we need it to generate the original string from the syntax tree when written in the cell.

The field `m_eTreeId` is used to identify the class of the tree in accordance with the classes above. The fields `m_pLeftTree` and `m_pRightTree` are used to store sub trees for the arithmetic operators. In the case of surrounding parentheses, only the left tree is used. The fields `m_reference` and `m_dValue` are used for references and values, respectively.

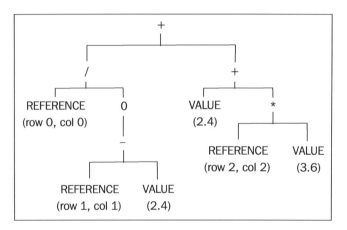

SyntaxTree.h

```
class CellMatrix;
enum SyntaxTreeIdentity {ST_EMPTY, ST_ADD, ST_SUB, ST_MUL,
                         ST_DIV, ST_PARENTHESES,
                         ST_REFERENCE, ST_VALUE};

class SyntaxTree
{
  public:
    SyntaxTree();
```

```
    SyntaxTree(const SyntaxTree& syntaxTree);
    SyntaxTree& operator=(const SyntaxTree& syntaxTree);
    void CopySyntaxTree(const SyntaxTree& syntaxTree);
    SyntaxTree(SyntaxTreeIdentity eTreeId,
               SyntaxTree* pLeftTree,
               SyntaxTree* pRightTree);
    SyntaxTree(double dValue);
    SyntaxTree(Reference& reference);
    ~SyntaxTree();
    double Evaluate(BOOL bRecursive,
                    const CellMatrix* pCellMatrix) const;
    ReferenceSet GetSourceSet() const;
    void UpdateReference(int iRows, int iCols);
    CString ToString() const;
    void Serialize(CArchive& archive);
  private:
    SyntaxTreeIdentity m_eTreeId;
    double m_dValue;
    SyntaxTree *m_pLeftTree, *m_pRightTree;
    Reference m_reference;
};
```

The `SyntaxTree` must have a default constructor as it is serialized. The identity `ST_EMPTY` is not used in any other part of the application. Its only purpose is to represent an empty syntax tree in the case of a cell holding a text or value instead of a formula. As the syntax tree is dynamically created, the destructor de-allocates all memory of the tree.

SyntaxTree.cpp

```
SyntaxTree::SyntaxTree(int eTreeId, SyntaxTree* pLeftTree,
                       SyntaxTree* pRightTree)
 :m_eTreeId(eTreeId),
  m_pLeftTree(pLeftTree),
  m_pRightTree(pRightTree)
{
  // Empty.
}
SyntaxTree::~SyntaxTree()
{
  switch (m_eTreeId)
  {
    case ST_ADD:
    case ST_SUB:
    case ST_MUL:
    case ST_DIV:
      delete m_pLeftTree;
      delete m_pRightTree;
```

```
        break;
    case ST_PARENTHESES:
      delete m_pLeftTree;
      break;
  }
}
```

When the user inputs new data into a cell, the values of the cells referring to that cell (its target set) need to be evaluated. Evaluate is called on each referring cell. It calculates the value depending on the structure of the tree. If the formula of the cell has a reference, we need to look up its value. That's why pCellMatrix is given as a parameter. If the cell referred to does not have a value, an exception is thrown. An exception is also thrown in the case of division by zero. If the parameter bRecursive is true, the user has cut and pasted a block of cells, in which case we have to recursively evaluate the values of the cells referred to by this syntax tree to catch the correct values. In the case of addition, subtraction, or multiplication, we extract the values of the left and right operand by calling Evaluate on one the sub trees. Then we carry out the operation and return the result.

```
double SyntaxTree::Evaluate(BOOL bRecursive,
                         const CellMatrix* pCellMatrix) const
{
  switch (m_eTreeId)
  {
    case ST_ADD:
      {
        double dLeftValue =
              m_pLeftTree->Evaluate(bRecursive, pCellMatrix);
        double dRightValue=
              m_pRightTree->Evaluate(bRecursive,pCellMatrix);
        return dLeftValue + dRightValue;
      }
      break;
    // ...
    case ST_DIV:
      {
        double dLeftValue =
              m_pLeftTree->Evaluate(bRecursive, pCellMatrix);
        double dRightValue=
              m_pRightTree->Evaluate(bRecursive,pCellMatrix);
        if (dRightValue != 0)
        {
          return dLeftValue / dRightValue;
        }
```

```
      else
      {
        CString stMessage = TEXT("#DIVISION_BY_ZERO");
        throw stMessage;
      }
    }
    break;
```

In the case of parenthesis, we just return the value. However, we still need the parentheses case in order to generate the string of the syntax tree.

```
    case ST_PARENTHESES:
      return m_pLeftTree->Evaluate(bRecursive, pCellMatrix);
```

If the referred cell has a value, it is returned. If not, an exception is thrown.

```
    case ST_REFERENCE:
      {
        int iRow = m_reference.GetRow();
        int iCol = m_reference.GetCol();
        Cell* pCell = pCellMatrix->Get(iRow, iCol);
        if (pCell->HasValue(bRecursive))
        {
          return pCell->GetValue();
        }
        else
        {
          CString stMessage = TEXT("#MISSING_VALUE");
          throw stMessage;
        }
      }
      break;
    case ST_VALUE:
      return m_dValue;
  }
```

As all possible cases have been covered above, this point of the code will never be reached. The check is for debugging purposes only.

```
  check(FALSE);
  return 0;
}
```

The source set of a formula is the union of all its references. In the case of addition, subtraction, multiplication, and division, we return the union of the source sets of the two sub trees.

```
ReferenceSet SyntaxTree::GetSourceSet() const
{
  switch (m_eTreeId)
  {
    case ST_ADD:
    case ST_SUB:
    case ST_MUL:
    case ST_DIV:
      {
        ReferenceSet leftSet = m_pLeftTree->GetSourceSet();
        ReferenceSet rightSet = m_pRightTree->GetSourceSet();
        return ReferenceSet::Union(leftSet, rightSet);
      }
    case ST_PARENTHESES:
      return m_pLeftTree->GetSourceSet();
    case ST_REFERENCE:
      {
        ReferenceSet resultSet;
        resultSet.Add(m_reference);
        return resultSet;
      }
    default:
      ReferenceSet emptySet;
      return emptySet;
  }
}
```

When the user cuts or copies a block of cells, and pastes it at another location in the spreadsheet, the references shall be updated as they are relative. The method UpdateReference takes care of that task. When it comes to the arithmetic operators, it just calls itself recursively on the left and right tree. The same goes for the expression surrounded by brackets, with the difference that it only examines the left tree. In the case of a reference, the row and column are updated and then the method checks than the reference remains inside the spreadsheet.

```
void SyntaxTree::UpdateReference(int iRows, int iCols)
{
  switch (m_eTreeId)
  {
    case ST_ADD:
```

```
      case ST_SUB:
      case ST_MUL:
      case ST_DIV:
        m_pLeftTree->UpdateReference(iRows, iCols);
        m_pRightTree->UpdateReference(iRows, iCols);
        break;

      case ST_PARENTHESES:
        m_pLeftTree->UpdateReference(iRows, iCols);

      case ST_REFERENCE:
        int iRow = m_reference.GetRow();
        int iCol = m_reference.GetCol();

        int iNewRow = iRow + iRows;
        int iNewCol = iCol + iCols;

        if ((iNewRow < 0) || (iNewRow >= ROWS) ||
            (iNewCol < 0) || (iNewCol >= COLS))
        {
          CString stMessage;
          stMessage.Format(TEXT("Invalid reference: \"%c%d\"."),
                           (TCHAR) (TEXT('a') + iNewCol),
                           iNewRow + 1);
          throw stMessage;
        }

        m_reference.SetRow(iNewRow);
        m_reference.SetCol(iNewCol);
        break;
    }
  }
```

When the user has cut and pasted a cell, and by that action updated the rows and columns of the references in the formula of the cell, we need to generate a new string representing the formula. That is the task of `ToString`. It traverses the tree and generates a string for each part tree, which are joined into the final string.

```
CString SyntaxTree::ToString() const
{
  CString stResult;
  switch (m_eTreeId)
  {
    case ST_ADD:
      {
        CString stLeftTree = m_pLeftTree->ToString();
        CString stRightTree = m_pRightTree->ToString();
        stResult.Format(TEXT("%s+%s"), stLeftTree,
                        stRightTree);
```

```
          }
        break;
      case ST_REFERENCE:
        stResult = m_reference.ToString();
        break;
      case ST_VALUE:
        {
          stResult.Format(TEXT("%f"), m_dValue);
          stResult.TrimRight(TEXT('0'));
          stResult.TrimRight(TEXT('.'));
        }
        break;
    }
  return stResult;
}
```

The Spreadsheet

The spreadsheet of the application is represented by the classes Cell, CellMatrix, and TSetMatrix.

The Cell—Holding Text, Value, or Formula

The information of a spreadsheet is organized in *cells*. Each cell contains a text representing a numerical value, a formula, or (possibly empty) plain text. The value of the cell may affect the values in other cells. If the cell contains a formula, its value may depend on the values in other cells. This implies that each cell has a set of cells whose values it depends on, a *source set*, and a set of cells. The set's values depend on the cell's value and are called its *target set*.

There are three classes in this section: Cell, which handles a single cell, CellMatrix, which handles the whole spreadsheet, and TSetMatrix, which handles the target set for all cells. You may wonder why there is a matrix for the target sets, but not for the source sets. The answer is that the cell itself decides its source set. Only formulas have a source set, texts and values do not, and the source set is the union of all references of the formula.

The target set, on the other hand, is more complicated. The cell does not decide its own target set, it is set indirectly by the formulas of another cells. Lifting the target set out of the cell and storing it in a target set matrix of its own simplifies the matter, especially when it comes to cut and paste.

To put it in mathematical terms, the cells and its sets constitute a *directed graph*. When the user inputs a formula, we have to a check that the formula does not give rise to a circular reference. This implies that the graph never contains a cycle, meaning the graph is *acyclic*.

For instance, in the screenshot below the source set of *c2* holds *b1* and *a2* because the formula of *c2* includes *b1* and *b2*. In the same way, the source set of *b3* holds *a2* because the formula of *b3* includes *a2*. The source set of *b1* and *a2* are empty because they do not hold formulas.

As *a2* is included in both the formulas of *b3* and *c2*, the value of *a2* affects the values of *b3* and *c2*. This implies that the target set of *a2* holds *b3* and *c2*. In the same way, as *a2* is included in the formula of *b3*, the target set of *b3* holds *a2*. As the values of *b3* and *c2* do not affect the values of any other cells, their target sets are empty.

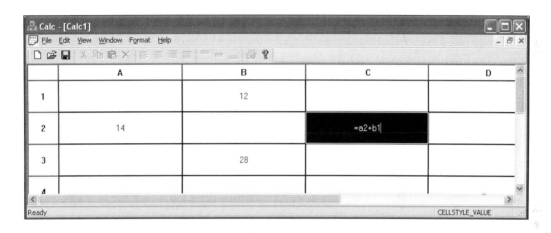

The first of the following diagrams shows the acyclic graph of the source sets of the spreadsheet above, the second diagram shows the acyclic graph of the target sets. As shown by the graphs, the source and targets sets are actually inverses of each other. Technically, we could manage with only one of the sets. However, as the sets are needed on different occasions the code will be clearer.

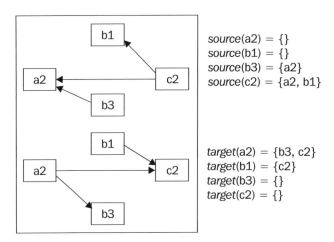

source(a2) = {}
source(b1) = {}
source(b3) = {a2}
source(c2) = {a2, b1}

target(a2) = {b3, c2}
target(b1) = {c2}
target(b3) = {}
target(c2) = {}

When the value of a cell is changed, its target set is traversed and the values of those cells are updated. Thereafter the target sets of these cells are traversed, and so on. The traversal is executed in a *breadth-first* manner, see the `EvaluateTargets` method in the `TSetMatrix` class. As there are no circular references in the spreadsheet, the search will always terminate.

Cell.h

```
static const int CELL_MARGIN = 100;
enum CellState {CELL_TEXT, CELL_VALUE, CELL_FORMULA};
typedef CArray<CRect> RectArray;
enum Alignment {HALIGN_LEFT = DT_LEFT,
    HALIGN_CENTER = DT_CENTER, HALIGN_RIGHT = DT_RIGHT,
    HALIGN_JUSTIFIED = DT_LEFT + DT_CENTER + DT_RIGHT,
    VALIGN_TOP = DT_TOP, VALIGN_CENTER = DT_VCENTER,
    VALIGN_BOTTOM = DT_BOTTOM};
enum KeyboardState {KM_INSERT, KM_OVERWRITE};
enum Direction {HORIZONTAL, VERTICAL};
enum ColorStatus {TEXT, BACKGROUND};
class CellMatrix;
class TSetMatrix;
class CCalcDoc;
```

```
class Cell
{
  public:
    Cell();
    Cell(const Cell& cell);
    Cell& operator=(const Cell& cell);
    void CopyCell(const Cell& cell);
    void SetCellMatrix(CellMatrix* pCellMatrix)
                    {m_pCellMatrix = pCellMatrix;}
    void SetTargetSetMatrix(TSetMatrix* pTargetSetMatrix)
                    {m_pTargetSetMatrix = pTargetSetMatrix;}
    BOOL IsEmpty() const
        {return (m_eCellState == CELL_TEXT) &&
                m_stText.IsEmpty();}
    void Clear(Reference home);
    void Serialize(CArchive& archive);
    void CharDown(UINT cChar, int iEditIndex,
                    KeyboardState eKeyBoardMode);
    void GenerateCaretArray(CDC* pDC);
    CString GetInputText() {return m_stInput;}
    void SetInputText(CString stInput) {m_stInput = stInput;}
    int MouseToIndex(CPoint ptMouse);
    CRect IndexToCaret(int iIndex);
    void Draw(CPoint ptTopLeft, BOOL bEdit, BOOL bMarked,
            CDC *pDC);
    Font GetFont() const {return m_font;}
    void SetFont(const Font& font) {m_font = font;}
    Color GetColor(int iColorType) const;
    void SetColor(int iColorType, const Color& textColor);
    Alignment GetAlignment(Direction eDirection) const;
    void SetAlignment(Direction eDirection,
                    Alignment eAlignment);
    void GenerateInputText();
    void EndEdit(Reference home);
    BOOL IsNumeric(CString stText);
    BOOL HasValue(BOOL bRecursive);
    double GetValue() const {return m_dValue;}
    void EvaluateValue(BOOL bRecursive);
    void UpdateSyntaxTree(int iAddRows, int iAddCols);
    ReferenceSet GetSourceSet() const {return m_sourceSet;};
  private:
    CellState m_eCellState;
    CString m_stText;
```

```
        double m_dValue;
        SyntaxTree m_syntaxTree;
        BOOL m_bHasValue;
        RectArray m_caretRectArray;
        CString m_stInput, m_stOutput;
        Font m_font;
        Color m_textColor, m_backgroundColor;
        Alignment m_eHorizontalAlignment, m_eVerticalAlignment;
        ReferenceSet m_sourceSet;
        CellMatrix* m_pCellMatrix;
        TSetMatrix* m_pTargetSetMatrix;
    };
```

The user inputs a (possible empty) text, and the text is interpreted as a (possible empty) plain text, a numerical value, or a formula. The interpretation is saved in m_eCellState, the possible state of the cell is text, value, or formula.

When the user inputs plain text (m_eCellState == CS_TEXT), the text is stored in m_stText. If the user inputs a numerical value (m_eCellState == CS_VALUE), the value is stored in m_dValue, and if the user inputs a formula beginning with an equal sign (m_eCellState == CS_FORMULA), the formula is scanned, parsed, and stored in m_syntaxTree.

When a text is inserted or edited, it is stored in m_stInput. When the input process is finished (the user presses the return or escape key (*Esc*) or clicks with the mouse) the text is interpreted and stored in the fields described above. The field m_stOutput holds a string representation of the cell contents (a possibly empty text, a numerical value, or a formula).

The field m_bHasValue is true if the cell contains a numerical value (m_eCellState == CS_VALUE) or a formula (m_eCellState == CS_FORMULA) that has been successfully evaluated (without throwing an exception) to a numerical value. If so, m_dValue holds the actual value that can be accessed by other formulas to evaluate their values.

When the user inputs text, the caret marks the place of insertion in the text. Every time the user adds or removes a character, m_caretRectArray is recalculated. It contains a rectangle for each character in the text (m_stInput) as well as an extra rectangle for the case when the user places the caret at the end of the text. If the cell contains a formula which is not correctly evaluated (an exception has been thrown), the error message will be stored in m_stDisplay.

If the application is in the edit state (m_eCalcStatus == CS_EDIT) and this particular cell is being edited, m_stInput is displayed. Otherwise (m_eCalcStatus == CS_MARK or another cell is being edited), m_stOutput is displayed.

The text may be aligned in both horizontal and vertical directions. The fields m_eHorizontalAlignment and m_eVerticalAlignment have the enumeration type Alignment. The DT values below refer to alignment in call to CDC text printing methods.

```
enum Alignment {HALIGN_LEFT = DT_LEFT,
    HALIGN_CENTER = DT_CENTER, ALIGN_RIGHT = DT_RIGHT,
    HALIGN_JUSTIFIED = DT_LEFT + DT_CENTER + DT_RIGHT,
    VALIGN_TOP = DT_TOP, VALIGN_CENTER = DT_VCENTER,
    VALIGN_BOTTOM = DT_BOTTOM};
```

The text may be set to a specific font as well as foreground and background colors. The fields m_font, m_textColor, and m_backgroundColor store the current settings. This goes for the whole of the text of the cell. It is not possible to set a font or a color for an individual character in the text. However, it is possible to set the size and font of a single character in *The Word Application* of the next chapter.

If the cell holds a formula with references to other cells, the references are stored in m_sourceSet. Each cell in the set has the cell in question as a target, which means it will notify the cell when a change has occurred, so that the value of the cell can be re-evaluated. When the contents of the cell are changed, the source cells are notified that they should remove the cell from their target sets. Then a new source set is generated and the sources in the new set are notified that they should add this cell as a target.

For each spreadsheet, there is a cell matrix and a target set matrix. Each cell has the pointers m_pCellMatrix and m_pTargetSetMatrix to keep track of them.

The constructor initializes the fields to the appropriate values. Before the cell is used, m_pCellMatrix and m_pTargetSetMatrix will be set by a call to SetCellMatrix and SetTargetSetMatrix, respectively. An empty rectangle is added to m_caretRectArray as we need an extra caret for the position to the right of the text. Before the cell is edited, m_caretRectArray will be initialized by a call to GenerateCaretArray.

The copy constructor just calls the assignment operator, which copies the values of the fields. The process of copying and serialization is quite straightforward as no fields are pointers to dynamically allocated memory.

The method Clear is called by OnDelete in the document class. The cell is set to an empty text. The parameter *home* is a reference representing the cell's position in the spreadsheet. Every cell has the (possibly empty) set or sources m_sourceSet. The set is generated from the syntax tree if the cell has a formula; otherwise, it is empty. RemoveTargets in TSetMatrix goes through the set and for each source it removes the target, which is the cell in question.

The method `Serialize` is called for each cell in the cell matrix when the user saves or loads the spreadsheet. The method `CharDown` is called as a response to the `WM_CHAR` message. It inserts or overwrites a character depending on the caret position and the keyboard state.

The method `GenerateCaretArray` generates the caret array in order for the caret to appear at the correct position when the user edits the text of the cell.

The method `MouseToIndex` takes a mouse position and decides which character is hit by the mouse. The *x* position of the mouse can be to the left of the text (zero is returned), at the text, or to the right of the text (the length of the text is returned). `IndexToCaret` works in an opposite manner, it takes a text index and returns the caret rectangle.

The method `Draw` is called when the contents of the cell are to be drawn. The cell may be edited or marked; the parameters `bEdit` and `bMarked` indicate that. If the cell is edited or marked the pen and brush color are inverted.

The method `GetAlignment` and `SetAlignment` return and set the horizontal or vertical alignment. The method `GetColor` and `SetColor` return and set the text and background color. The method `GenerateInputText` is called when the user want to input or edit text in this cell. It prepares `m_stInput` to hold a string representation of the cell.

The method `EndEdit` is called when the user presses return or clicks in a cell. The field `m_stText` is interpreted as a text, a numerical value (an integer or a decimal number) and `m_stOutput` is set to represent the value of the cell.

The method `IsNumeric` returns true if the given text can be interpreted as a numerical value (a possible plus or minus sign, a possible empty sequence of digits, a possible decimal point, a possible empty sequence of digits, at least one digit altogether).

The method `HasValue` returns true if the cell has a valid value (a numerical value or a formula correctly evaluated). The method `EvaluateValue` is called when the value of the cell needs to be re-evaluated; that is, when the value of a cell in the source set has been changed. For every cell in the cell's source set, the cell in question is included in the cell's target set.

The references in a formula of a cell are relative. This means that when the user cuts or copies and then pastes a block of cells, the references are updated. This is taken care of by `UpdateReferences` in the syntax tree. It returns true if all goes well and false if any reference is placed outside the spreadsheet. The source set is also updated by a call to `GetSourceSet`.

A newly created cell is empty, has cell style text, is centered both in the horizontal and vertical view, and has black text color on white background. Remember that the caret array contains one rectangle for each character together with one extra for the caret position one step to the right of the text. So even though the text is empty, we add one empty rectangle to the caret array. The cell font's default constructor is called, which loads the font with the system font.

Cell.cpp

```
Cell::Cell()
 :m_eCellState(CELL_TEXT),
  m_eHorizontalAlignment(DT_CENTER),
  m_eVerticalAlignment(DT_VCENTER),
  m_textColor(BLACK),
  m_backgroundColor(WHITE),
  m_pCellMatrix(NULL),
  m_pTargetSetMatrix(NULL)
{
  m_caretRectArray.Add(CRect(0, 0, 0, 0));
}
```

The copy constructor and the assignment operator simply call the copy method, which copies every field. As every field is static (there are no pointers in this class and there is no need for dynamically created memory) we can just copy the fields one by one. The MFC class CArray, however, does not have an overloaded assignment operator. Instead, we call Copy, which copies the array.

```
void Cell::CopyCell(const Cell& cell)
{
  m_eCellState = cell.m_eCellState;
  m_syntaxTree = cell.m_syntaxTree;
  m_sourceSet = cell.m_sourceSet;

  m_stText = cell.m_stText;
  m_dValue = cell.m_dValue;
  m_stInput = cell.m_stInput;
  m_stOutput = cell.m_stOutput;

  m_eHorizontalAlignment = cell.m_eHorizontalAlignment;
  m_eVerticalAlignment = cell.m_eVerticalAlignment;

  m_textColor = cell.m_textColor;
  m_backgroundColor = cell.m_backgroundColor;

  m_font = cell.m_font;
  m_caretRectArray.Copy(cell.m_caretRectArray);
}
```

The method `Clear` clears the cell. It is called when the user deletes one or more cells. If the cell contains a formula, we first have to go through its source set and, for each source cell in the set, remove this cell as a target by calling `RemoveTargets`.

```
void Cell::Clear(Reference home)
{
  if (m_eCellState == CELL_FORMULA)
  {
    m_pTargetSetMatrix->RemoveTargets(home);
  }
  m_eCellState = CELL_TEXT;
  m_stText = TEXT("");
  m_stOutput = TEXT("");
}
```

The method `CharDown` is called every time the user presses a printable character. If the input edit index is at the end of the text (that is, one step to the right of the text), we just add the character. If not, we have to take into consideration the keyboard state. It can be in either insert or the overwrite state. In the case of the insert state, we insert the character. In case of the overwrite state, we overwrite the old character at the edit index by calling `SetAt`.

```
void Cell::CharDown(UINT uNewChar, int iInputIndex,
                    KeyboardState eKeyBoardMode)
{
  if (iInputIndex == m_stInput.GetLength())
  {
    m_stInput.AppendChar((TCHAR) uNewChar);
  }
  else
  {
    switch (eKeyBoardMode)
    {
      case KM_INSERT:
        m_stInput.Insert(iInputIndex, (TCHAR) uNewChar);
        break;
      case KM_OVERWRITE:
        m_stInput.SetAt(iInputIndex, (TCHAR) uNewChar);
        break;
    }
  }
}
```

The method `GenerateCaretArray` is a central method to the application. When the user adds or removes a character of the text of a cell, the position of the caret must be updated. `GenerateCaretArray` takes care of that, it is a more advanced version of `GenerateCaretArray` in the `Draw` application. Note that this is necessary only when the cell has input focus. We create, initialize, and select the font of the cell text. Remember that the font is stored in typographical point, which have to be converted to logical units (hundredths of millimeters) by calling `PointsToMeters`.

First, we need the width and height of the text (in logical units). If the text is non-empty, we call `GetTextExtent` to measure the input text. If the text is empty, the width is zero and the height is set to the height of the font by calling `GetTextMetric`.

```
void Cell::GenerateCaretArray(CDC* pDC)
{
  CFont cFont;
  cFont.CreateFontIndirect(m_font.PointsToMeters());
  CFont* pPrevFont = pDC->SelectObject(&cFont);
  int iTextWidth, iTextHeight;
  if (!m_stInput.IsEmpty())
  {
    CSize szText = pDC->GetTextExtent(m_stInput);
    iTextWidth = szText.cx;
    iTextHeight = szText.cy;
  }
  else
  {
    TEXTMETRIC textMetric;
    pDC->GetTextMetrics(&textMetric);
    iTextWidth = 0;
    iTextHeight = textMetric.tmHeight;
  }
```

The writable part of the cell area is slightly smaller than the cell area in order to prevent the text from overwriting the cell borders. The margin is subtracted from the width and height of the cell.

```
  const int CELL_WIDTH = COL_WIDTH - 2 * CELL_MARGIN;
  const int CELL_HEIGHT = ROW_HEIGHT - 2 * CELL_MARGIN;
```

The beginning of the text (`xLeftPos`) should be decided. The horizontal alignment can be set in four different states: left, centered, right, and justified state. The variables are initialized in order to avoid compiler warnings.

```
  int xLeftPos = 0;      // The start position of the text in
                         // horizontal direction.
```

```
int iSpaceWidth = 0; // The width of a space in justified
                     // horizontal alignment.
int yTopPos = 0;     // The start position of the text in
                     // vertical direction.
```

In the case of left alignment, the text starts at the beginning of the cell; so the position is set to zero. In the case of centered alignment, the text should be placed in the middle of the cell. In case of right alignment, the text should be placed at the end of the cell.

```
switch (m_eHorizontalAlignment)
{
  case DT_LEFT:
    xLeftPos = 0;
    break;
  case DT_CENTER:
    xLeftPos = (CELL_WIDTH - iTextWidth) / 2;
    break;
  case DT_RIGHT:
    xLeftPos = CELL_WIDTH - iTextWidth;
    break;
```

In the case of justified alignment, the text should be equally divided along the cell by stretching the spaces in the text. For that purpose, we need to count the number of spaces in the text by calling Remove.

If there is at least one space in the text, we decide the width of each space by subtracting the width of the text without spaces from the area width and then dividing it by the number of spaces. If there are no spaces in the text, we regard the alignment to be left, so the start position is zero.

```
  case DT_JUSTIFIED:
    CString stInputNoSpaces = m_stInput;
    int iSpaceCount = stInputNoSpaces.Remove(TEXT(' '));
    if (iSpaceCount > 0)
    {
      xLeftPos = 0;
      CSize szInputNoSpaces =
            pDC->GetTextExtent(stInputNoSpaces );
      iSpaceWidth = (CELL_WIDTH  - szInputNoSpaces.cx) /
                    iSpaceCount;
    }
    else
    {
      xLeftPos = 0;
    }
    break;
}
```

The top position of the text (yTopPos) is assessed in a way similar to the horizontal alignment. The vertical alignment can be set in three different states: top, centered, and bottom state. In case of top alignment, the text starts at the beginning of the cell, so the position is set to zero.

```
switch (m_eVerticalAlignment)
{
  case DT_TOP:
    yTopPos = 0;
    break;
  case DT_VCENTER:
    yTopPos = (CELL_HEIGHT - iTextHeight) / 2;
    break;
  case DT_BOTTOM:
    yTopPos = CELL_HEIGHT - iTextHeight;
    break;
}
```

The text is traversed and the rectangle for each character is calculated. The start position in the y direction and the height of the text is the same for all characters. The position in the x direction starts by the position calculated above, and is increased for each character. If the character is a space and the text has justified horizontal alignment, we use the space width calculated above. Otherwise, we call GetTextExtent to get the size width of the character.

```
int xPos = xLeftPos;
int iLength = m_stInput.GetLength();
m_caretRectArray.SetSize(iLength + 1);
for (int iIndex = 0; iIndex < iLength; ++iIndex)
{
  CString stChar = m_stInput.Mid(iIndex, 1);
  int iCharWidth;
  if ((stChar == TEXT(" ")) &&
      (m_eHorizontalAlignment == DT_JUSTIFIED))
  {
    iCharWidth = iSpaceWidth;
  }
  else
  {
    iCharWidth = pDC->GetTextExtent(stChar).cx;
  }
  CRect rcChar(xPos, yTopPos, xPos + iCharWidth,
               yTopPos + iTextHeight);
  m_caretRectArray[iIndex] = rcChar;
  xPos += iCharWidth;
}
```

Finally, we add the size of a character of average size because the user may put the caret marker to the right of the last character.

```
TEXTMETRIC textMetric;
pDC->GetTextMetrics(&textMetric);
int iAverageCharWidth = textMetric.tmAveCharWidth;
CRect rcLastChar(xPos, yTopPos, xPos + iAverageCharWidth,
                 yTopPos + iTextHeight);
m_caretRectArray[iLength] = rcLastChar;
pDC->SelectObject(pPrevFont);
}
```

The method `MouseToIndex` examines the text of the cell with the help of the caret array and finds the index of the matching character. If the mouse position in the x direction is to the left of the leftmost character, we return index zero. We traverse the rectangle array of the text, and return the index for the character whose rectangle includes the x position of the mouse. If we have not found the index so far, it is located to the right of the text, so we return the length of the text (the position to the right of the text).

```
int Cell::MouseToIndex(CPoint ptMouse)
{
  ptMouse -= CSize(CELL_MARGIN, CELL_MARGIN);
  int iLength = m_stInput.GetLength();
  if (ptMouse.x < m_caretRectArray[0].left)
  {
    return 0;
  }
  for (int iIndex = 0; iIndex < iLength; ++iIndex)
  {
    if ((ptMouse.x >= m_caretRectArray[iIndex].left) &&
        (ptMouse.x < m_caretRectArray[iIndex].right))
    {
      return iIndex;
    }
  }
  return iLength;
}
```

The drawing of the text is rather straightforward, we just simply state the horizontal and vertical alignment together with the dimensions of the cell when we call `DrawText`. However, there is one exception—the justified alignment. In order to obtain justified horizontal alignment, we call the device context method `SetTextJustification` that makes the text in the `DrawText` call be equally distributed in the cell.

In order not to overwrite the border of the cell, we introduce a cell margin. The pen and brush are selected and attached to the device context, and the cell is painted. The pen and background colors are inversed if the cell is in the edit state (the application is in the edit state and this particular cell is being edited, m_rfEditCell referees to this cell) or the mark state (the application is in the mark state and this particular cell is marked, it is inside the block referred to by m_rfFirstMark and m_rfLastMark). When the pen and brush have been used, we will select the previous pen and brush to the device context.

```
void Cell::Draw(CPoint ptTopLeft, BOOL bEdit, BOOL bMarked,
                CDC *pDC)
{
  CRect rcCell(ptTopLeft, CSize(COL_WIDTH, ROW_HEIGHT));
  CRect rcMargin(rcCell.left + CELL_MARGIN,
                 rcCell.top + CELL_MARGIN,
                 rcCell.right - CELL_MARGIN,
                 rcCell.bottom - CELL_MARGIN);
  Color penColor = (bEdit || bMarked) ? m_textColor.Inverse()
                                       : m_textColor;
  Color brushColor  = (bEdit || bMarked)
                        ? m_backgroundColor.Inverse()
                        : m_backgroundColor;
  CPen pen(PS_SOLID, 0, penColor);
  CPen* pPrevPen = pDC->SelectObject(&pen);
  CBrush brush(brushColor);
  CBrush* pPrevBrush = pDC->SelectObject(&brush);
  pDC->Rectangle(rcCell);
  pDC->SelectObject(pPrevPen);
  pDC->SelectObject(pPrevBrush);
```

In order to draw the text we set the text and background color instead of selecting a pen and brush. We also need to set the text font. As the size of the font is stored in typographical points, we convert the size to logical units (hundredths of millimeters) by calling PointsToMeters before we select the font to the device context. If the cell is in the edit state, we choose to display the input text; otherwise, we display the output text.

```
  pDC->SetTextColor(penColor);
  pDC->SetBkColor(brushColor);
  CFont cFont;
  cFont.CreateFontIndirect(m_font.PointsToMeters());
  CFont* pPrevFont = pDC->SelectObject(&cFont);
  CString stDisplay = bEdit ? m_stInput : m_stOutput;
```

If the text has justified horizontal alignment, we have to set the space distribution by calling `SetTextJustification`. After the call to `DrawText`, we should reset the space distribution. If the cell has left, center, or right horizontal alignment, we just draw the text with the horizontal and vertical alignment of the cell. Similar to the pen and brush above, we finally select the previous font.

```
  if (m_eHorizontalAlignment == DT_JUSTIFIED)
  {
    CString stTemp = stDisplay;
    int iSpaceCount = stTemp.Replace(TEXT(' '), TEXT('.'));
    CSize szDisplay = pDC->GetTextExtent(stDisplay);
    pDC->SetTextJustification(rcMargin.Width() - szDisplay.cx,
                              iSpaceCount);
    pDC->DrawText(stDisplay, &rcMargin,
                  DT_SINGLELINE | m_eVerticalAlignment);
    pDC->SetTextJustification(0, 0);
  }
  else
  {
    pDC->DrawText(stDisplay, &rcMargin, DT_SINGLELINE |
                  m_eHorizontalAlignment |
                  m_eVerticalAlignment);
  }

  pDC->SelectObject(pPrevFont);
}
```

The method `GenerateInputText` is called by the document class when the user wants to start editing a cell. We have to find the input text of the cell, which we store in the field `m_stInput`. If the cell is in the text state, we just use the value of `m_stText`. If it is in the value state, we convert the value to a text by calling `Format` in the MFC `CString` class. We also remove ending zeros and the decimal point if there are no significant decimals. If the cell is in the formula state, we call the syntax tree to evaluate a string matching the formula. We also introduce an equals sign.

```
void Cell::GenerateInputText()
{
  switch (m_eCellState)
  {
    case CELL_TEXT:
      m_stInput = m_stText;
      break;

    case CELL_VALUE:
      m_stInput.Format(TEXT("%f"), m_dValue);
      m_stInput.TrimRight(TEXT('0'));
```

```
      m_stInput.TrimRight(TEXT('.'));
      break;

    case CELL_FORMULA:
      m_stInput = TEXT("=") + m_syntaxTree.ToString();
      break;
  }
}
```

The method EditEnd is called by the document class when the user presses the
return or *Tab* key, or presses the mouse (it does not matter whether the user presses
the mouse on this cell or any other position in the spreadsheet). We then interpret the
input text of the cell. Depending on the text, the input cell may be set to text, value,
or formula state. First, we get rid of trailing blanks in order to decide whether the
first character is an equals sign. If the text without trailing blanks is non-empty and
begins with an equals sign, we treat it as a formula.

```
    void Cell::EndEdit(Reference home)
    {
      CString stTrimInput = m_stInput;
      stTrimInput.Trim();
      if ((!stTrimInput.IsEmpty()) &&
          (stTrimInput[0] == TEXT('=')))
      {
        Parser parser;
        SyntaxTree newSyntaxTree =
                  parser.Formula(stTrimInput.Mid(1));
        ReferenceSet newSourceSet = newSyntaxTree.GetSourceSet();
        m_pTargetSetMatrix->CheckCircular(home, newSourceSet);
        m_eCellState = CELL_FORMULA;
        m_pTargetSetMatrix->RemoveTargets(home);
        m_syntaxTree = newSyntaxTree;
        m_sourceSet = newSourceSet;
        m_pTargetSetMatrix->AddTargets(home);
      }
      else if (IsNumeric(stTrimInput))
      {
        m_eCellState = CELL_VALUE;
        m_dValue = _tstof(stTrimInput);
        m_stOutput.Format(TEXT("%f"), m_dValue);
        m_stOutput.TrimRight(TEXT('0'));
        m_stOutput.TrimRight(TEXT('.'));

        m_pTargetSetMatrix->RemoveTargets(home);
        m_sourceSet.RemoveAll();
      }
```

```
      else
      {
        m_eCellState = CELL_TEXT;
        m_stText = m_stInput;
        m_stOutput = m_stText;
        m_pTargetSetMatrix->RemoveTargets(home);
        m_sourceSet.RemoveAll();
      }
    }
```

The method `HasValue` is called when the value of a formula in another cell is to be evaluated. A cell has a value, it holds a numerical value of a formula that has been successfully evaluated (`m_bHasValue` is true).

This method is called on two occasions. The first case is when the user ends editing a cell either by pressing return or *Tab*, or by pressing the mouse. In that case, we do only have to evaluate the value of this cell because no other cell has been updated (bRecursive is false). However, it is also called when the user has pasted a block of cells. In that case, we have to evaluate the values of the cells in the source set recursively because their values might have been updated too (bRecursive is true).

Naturally, a text is never interpreted as a value and a value is always interpreted as a value. A cell in formula state may or may not have a valid value depending on whether the formula was correctly evaluated; `m_bHasValue` holds the status of the evaluation.

```
      BOOL Cell::HasValue(BOOL bRecursive)
      {
        switch (m_eCellState)
        {
          case CELL_TEXT:
            return FALSE;
          case CELL_VALUE:
            return TRUE;
          case CELL_FORMULA:
            if (bRecursive)
            {
              EvaluateValue(TRUE);
            }
            return m_bHasValue;
        }
```

As the cell always is in text, value, or formula state, this part of the method will never be reached. However, in order to avoid compilation warnings, we return false.

```
        return FALSE;
      }
```

The method `EvaluateValue` is called when some of the source cell of the call has been altered. If the cell holds a formula, its value is evaluated by calling `Evaluate` method of its syntax tree. If the value of the formula is successfully evaluated, the value flag (`m_bHasValue`) is set to true and the evaluated value is converted to the output text (`m_stOutput`).

If the text cannot be evaluated due to division by zero or a missing value, an exception is thrown. The output text (`m_stOutput`) is set to the error message and the value flag (`m_bHasValue`) is set to false.

```
void Cell::EvaluateValue(BOOL bRecursive)
{
  if (m_eCellState == CELL_FORMULA)
  {
    try
    {
      m_dValue = m_syntaxTree.
                  Evaluate(bRecursive, m_pCellMatrix);
      m_bHasValue = TRUE;
      m_stOutput.Format(TEXT("%f"), m_dValue);
      m_stOutput.TrimRight(TEXT('0'));
      m_stOutput.TrimRight(TEXT('.'));
    }
    catch (const CString& stMessage)
    {
      m_bHasValue = FALSE;
      m_stOutput = stMessage;
    }
  }
}
```

Finally, `UpdateSyntaxTree` is called when a block of cells has been copied and pasted into another location in the spreadsheet. If the cell holds a formula, it calls the `UpdateReference` method of its syntax tree and sets a new source set.

```
void Cell::UpdateSyntaxTree(int iRows, int iCols)
{
  if (m_eCellState == CELL_FORMULA)
  {
    m_syntaxTree.UpdateReference(iRows, iCols);
    m_sourceSet = m_syntaxTree.GetSourceSet();
  }
}
```

The Cell Matrix—Managing Rows and Columns

The cells of the spreadsheet are organized in a matrix. The size of the matrix is determined by the constants ROWS and COLS. The fields m_buffer is a two-dimensional array holding the cells.

The default constructor sets the pointer to this cell matrix for each cell. The copy constructor and the assignment operator copy the cells one by one and set the cell matrix pointer for each cell. This shows that every cell has a pointer to the matrix it belongs to as well as the associated target set matrix.

Serialize is called when the user chooses the save or open menu item. It serializes the matrix, one cell at a time. In the case of loading, it also sets the cell matrix pointer of the cell.

CellMatrix.h

```
class TSetMatrix;
const int ROWS = 10;
const int COLS = 5;
class CellMatrix
{
  public:
    CellMatrix();
    CellMatrix(const CellMatrix& cellMatrix);
    CellMatrix operator=(const CellMatrix& cellMatrix);
    void SetTargetSetMatrix(TSetMatrix* pTargetSetMatrix);

    Cell* Get(int iRow, int iCol) const;
    Cell* Get(Reference home) const;

    void Serialize(CArchive& archive);
  private:
    Cell m_buffer[ROWS][COLS];
};
```

The copy constructor copies the cells one by one and sets the cell matrix pointer for each cell. This shows that every cell has a pointer to the matrix it belongs to.

CellMatrix.cpp

```
CellMatrix::CellMatrix(const CellMatrix& cellMatrix)
{
  for (int iRow = 0; iRow < ROWS; ++iRow)
  {
    for (int iCol = 0; iCol < COLS; ++iCol)
    {
```

```
        m_buffer[iRow][iCol] = cellMatrix.m_buffer[iRow][iCol];
        m_buffer[iRow][iCol].SetCellMatrix(this);
      }
    }
  }
```

The method `Get` comes in two forms, it returns a pointer to the cell indicated by the given row and column or by the given reference. The row and column are checked to be inside the limits of the matrix. However, the check is for debugging purpose only, the method will never be called with invalid parameters.

```
Cell* CellMatrix::Get(int iRow, int iCol) const
{
  check((iRow >= 0) && (iRow < ROWS));
  check((iCol >= 0) && (iCol < COLS));
  return (Cell*) &m_buffer[iRow][iCol];
}
Cell* CellMatrix::Get(Reference home) const
{
  return Get(home.GetRow(), home.GetCol());
}
```

The Target Set Matrix Class

The `TSetMatrix` class keeps track of the target set for each cell. It is connected to a cell matrix by m_pCellMatrix, and m_pBuffer stores the target set for each cell. Note the difference between source and target sets. While only formula cells can have non-empty source sets, all kinds of cells (even empty cells) can have non-empty target sets. Another difference between the two sets is that the target sets are defined indirectly by a formula in another set. If a formula of another cell holds a reference to a particular cell, the reference to the formula cell is added to the target set of the original cell. In the same way, when a formula is altered or cleared, the reference to the formula cell is removed from the target set of all its source cells. When a cell is updated, all its targets are evaluated, either recursively (the targets cells are re-evaluated, and before that their target cell are re-evaluated, and so on) when a block of cells are pasted or not (only the evaluated values of the target cells are interesting) when a single cell is modified.

The sources and targets are searched and evaluated in two ways: *depth-first* and *breadth-first*. As the name implies, depth-first tries to search as deep as possible. When it has reached a dead end, it backtracks and tries another way, if there is one. Breadth-first on the other hand, evaluates all cells at the same distance from the start cell. Not until then, it examines cells at a larger distance. The following pseudo code illustrates the search algorithms. The depth-first algorithm is simpler as we can take advantage of recursive calls. It is implemented in the CheckCircular method. The breadth-first algorithm is on the other hand necessary in order to evaluate the targets of a modified cell. It is implemented in the EvaluateTargets method.

```
Depth-First(Set sourceSet)
{
  Set resultSet = sourceSet;
  for (each cell in the source set)
  {
    resultSet = union(resultSet,
                      Depth-First(the source set of the cell))
  }
  return resultSet;
}
Breadth-First(Set sourceSet)
{
  Set resultSet = sourceSet;
  while (!resultSet.isEmpty())
  {
    extract and remove a cell from the search set
    add its source set to the result set
  }
  return resultSet;
}
```

TSetMatrix.h

```
class TSetMatrix
{
  public:
    TSetMatrix();
    TSetMatrix(const TSetMatrix& tSetMatrix);
    TSetMatrix operator=(const TSetMatrix& tSetMatrix);
    void SetCellMatrix(CellMatrix* pCellMatrix);
    void Serialize(CArchive& archive);
    ReferenceSet* Get(int iRow, int iCol) const;
    ReferenceSet* Get(Reference home) const;
    void CheckCircular(Reference home,
                       ReferenceSet sourceSet);
    ReferenceSet EvaluateTargets(Reference home);
    void AddTargets(Reference home);
    void RemoveTargets(Reference home);
  private:
    ReferenceSet m_buffer[ROWS][COLS];
    CellMatrix* m_pCellMatrix;
};
```

TSetMatrix.cpp

Similar to the `CellMatrix` case, `Get` comes in two forms. It returns a pointer to the target set indicated by the given row and column or by the given reference. The row and column are checked to be inside the limits of the matrix. However, again similar to the `CellMatrix` above, the check is for debugging purposes only. The method will never be called with invalid parameters.

```cpp
ReferenceSet* TSetMatrix::Get(int iRow, int iCol) const
{
  check((iRow >= 0) && (iRow < ROWS));
  check((iCol >= 0) && (iCol < COLS));
  return (ReferenceSet*) &m_buffer[iRow][iCol];
}

ReferenceSet* TSetMatrix::Get(Reference home) const
{
  return Get(home.GetRow(), home.GetCol());
}
```

When the user adds or alters a formula, it is essential that no cycles are added to the graph. `CheckCircular` throws an exception when it finds a cycle. It performs a depth-first search backwards by following the source set.

```cpp
void TSetMatrix::CheckCircular(Reference home,
                              ReferenceSet sourceSet)
{
  for (POSITION position = sourceSet.GetHeadPosition();
       position != NULL; sourceSet.GetNext(position))
  {
    Reference source = sourceSet.GetAt(position);
    if (source == home)
    {
      CString stMessage = TEXT("Circular Reference.");
      throw stMessage;
    }
    Cell* pCell = m_pCellMatrix->Get(source);
    ReferenceSet nextSourceSet = pCell->GetSourceSet();
    CheckCircular(home, nextSourceSet);
  }
}
```

When the value of a cell is modified, it is essential that the formulas having references to the cell are notified and that their values are re-evaluated. The method `EvaluateTargets` performs a breadth-first search by following the target sets forward. Unlike the check for circular cycles above, we cannot perform a depth-first search. That would introduce the risk of the cells being evaluated in the wrong order.

```
ReferenceSet TSetMatrix::EvaluateTargets(Reference home)
{
  Cell* pHome = m_pCellMatrix->Get(home);
  pHome->EvaluateValue(FALSE);

  ReferenceSet resultSet;
  resultSet.Add(home);

  ReferenceSet* pTargetSet = Get(home);
  ReferenceSet updateSet = *pTargetSet;

  while (!updateSet.IsEmpty())
  {
    Reference target = updateSet.GetHead();
    resultSet.Add(target);
    updateSet.Remove(target);

    Cell* pTarget = m_pCellMatrix->Get(target);
    pTarget->EvaluateValue(FALSE);

    ReferenceSet* pNextTargetSet = Get(target);
    updateSet.AddAll(*pNextTargetSet);
  }

  return resultSet;
}
```

The method `AddTargets` traverses the source set of the cell with the given reference in the cell matrix and, for each source cell, adds the given cell as a target in the target set of the source cell.

```
void TSetMatrix::AddTargets(Reference home)
{
  Cell* pCell = m_pCellMatrix->Get(home);
  ReferenceSet sourceSet = pCell->GetSourceSet();

  for (POSITION position = sourceSet.GetHeadPosition();
       position != NULL; sourceSet.GetNext(position))
  {
    Reference source = sourceSet.GetAt(position);
    ReferenceSet* pTargetSet = Get(source);
    pTargetSet->Add(home);
  }
}
```

RemoveTargets traverses the source set of the cell with the given reference in the cell matrix and, for each source cell, removes the given cell as a target in the target set of the source cell.

```
void TSetMatrix::RemoveTargets(Reference home)
{
  Cell* pCell = m_pCellMatrix->Get(home);
  ReferenceSet sourceSet = pCell->GetSourceSet();
  for (POSITION position = sourceSet.GetHeadPosition();
       position != NULL; sourceSet.GetNext(position))
  {
    Reference source = sourceSet.GetAt(position);
    ReferenceSet* pTargetSet = Get(source);
    pTargetSet->Remove(home);
  }
}
```

The Document/View Model

This application supports the Document/View model. CCalcDoc is the document class and CCalcView is the view class.

The Document Class

The class CCalcDoc is generated by the Application Wizard. We add the document's data and methods to handle the data. The class is inherited from the MFC class CDocument.

The field m_CalcState represents the status of the current spreadsheet. The user can choose to edit a specific cell or to mark one or more cells. The application always has to be in one of the two modes. When in the mark state, at least one cell is always marked. When the application starts, it is in the mark state and the top left cell is marked.

There is also the field m_iKeyboardState. It keeps track of the insert state of the keyboard. It can hold the insert and overwrite state. The fields have the enumeration types CalcState and KeyboardState. As KeyboardState is used by the cell class, it is defined in Cell.h.

```
enum CalcState {CS_MARK, CS_EDIT};
enum KeyboardState{KM_INSERT, KM_OVERWRITE};
```

If the users edit one cell, the cell's coordinates are placed in the CReference field m_rfEdit. The index of the character being edited is placed in m_iEditIndex. If the users choose to mark a block of cells, the coordinates of the block's first corner are placed in m_rfFirstMark and the coordinates of the block's last corner are placed in m_rfLastMark. Note that we do not know these references relation to each other. On several occasions, we have to find the top-left and bottom-right corner of the marked block.

The field m_cellMatrix contains all cells of the spreadsheet. If the user marks and copies a block of cells, the block will be placed in m_copyMatrix, and the coordinates of the marked block's top-left corner are placed in m_rfMinCopy. Its bottom-right corner is placed in m_rfMaxCopy. Note the difference between m_rfFirstMark/ m_rfLastMark and m_rfMinCopy/m_rfMaxCopy. In the m_rfMinCopy/m_rfMaxCopy case, we know that m_rfMinCopy holds the top-left corner and m_rfMaxCopy holds the bottom-right corner.

The field m_tSetMatrix holds the target set matrix of the spreadsheet. The field m_caret keeps track of the caret of the application. The caret is visible in the edit state if the cell is visible in the view and the view has input focus. It is never visible in the mark state.

The size of a cell is given by the constants ROW_HEIGHT and COL_WIDTH; all cells have the same size. The user cannot change the size of a cell nor the number of cells. The application is in the mark state when one or more cells are marked. It is in the edit state when the user edit the input text of a cell. The fields HEADER_WIDTH and HEADER_HEIGHT hold the size of the row and column bars. The fields TOTAL_WIDTH and TOTAL_HEIGHT give the total size of the spreadsheet, including the size of the headers.

As this is a multiple view application, the same spreadsheet may be visible in several views. However, the caret can only be visible in one view at a time. Therefore, m_caret needs to be notified of the current view focus status. The methods OnSetFocus and OnKillFocus notify the caret, which is used to create device contexts and to check whether the current cell is visible in its current view.

CalcDoc.h

```
const int HEADER_WIDTH = 1000;
const int HEADER_HEIGHT = 500;
const int COL_WIDTH = 4000;
const int ROW_HEIGHT = 1000;
const int TOTAL_WIDTH = HEADER_WIDTH + COLS * COL_WIDTH;
const int TOTAL_HEIGHT = HEADER_HEIGHT + ROWS * ROW_HEIGHT;
enum CalcState {CS_MARK, CS_EDIT};
```

```
class CCalcDoc : public CDocument
{
  protected:
    DECLARE_DYNCREATE(CCalcDoc)
    DECLARE_MESSAGE_MAP()
    CCalcDoc();

  public:
    virtual void Serialize(CArchive& archive);
    CellMatrix* GetCellMatrix() {return &m_cellMatrix;}

    int GetCalcStatus() {return m_eCalcStatus;}
    Caret* GetCaret() {return &m_caret;}

    Reference GetEdit() const {return m_rfEdit;}
    Reference GetFirstMark() const {return m_rfFirstMark;}
    Reference GetLastMark() const {return m_rfLastMark;}

    void RepaintEditArea();
    void RepaintMarkedArea();
    void RepaintSet(const ReferenceSet& referenceSet);

    void DoubleClick(Reference rfCell, CPoint ptMouse,
      CDC* pDC);
    void MakeCellVisible(Reference rfCell);
    void MakeCellVisible(int iRow, int iCol);
    void UpdateCaret();

    void UnmarkAndMark(int iMinRow, int iMinCol,
      int iMaxRow, int iMaxCol);

    void KeyDown(UINT uChar, CDC* pDC, BOOL bShiftKeyDown);
    void CharDown(UINT uChar, CDC* pDC);

    void LeftArrowKey(BOOL bShiftKeyDown);
    void RightArrowKey(BOOL bShiftKeyDown);
    void UpArrowKey(BOOL bShiftKeyDown);
    void DownArrowKey(BOOL bShiftKeyDown);
    void HomeKey(BOOL bShiftKeyDown);
    void EndKey(BOOL bShiftKeyDown);

    void DeleteKey(CDC* pDC);
    void BackspaceKey(CDC* pDC);

    afx_msg void OnUpdateCopy(CCmdUI *pCmdUI);
    afx_msg void OnCopy();

    afx_msg void OnUpdateCut(CCmdUI *pCmdUI);
    afx_msg void OnCut();

    afx_msg void OnUpdatePaste(CCmdUI *pCmdUI);
    afx_msg void OnPaste();

    afx_msg void OnUpdateDelete(CCmdUI *pCmdUI);
    afx_msg void OnDelete();
```

```
    afx_msg void OnUpdateAlignmentHorizontalLeft
                (CCmdUI *pCmdUI);
    afx_msg void OnUpdateAlignmentHorizontalCenter
                (CCmdUI *pCmdUI);
    afx_msg void OnUpdateAlignmentHorizontalRight
                (CCmdUI *pCmdUI);
    afx_msg void OnUpdateAlignmentHorizontalJustified
                (CCmdUI *pCmdUI);
    afx_msg void OnUpdateAlignmentVerticalTop(CCmdUI *pCmdUI);
    afx_msg void OnUpdateAlignmentVerticalCenter
                (CCmdUI *pCmdUI);
    afx_msg void OnUpdateAlignmentVerticalBottom
                (CCmdUI *pCmdUI);
    void UpdateAlignment(Direction eDirection, Alignment
                        eAlignment, CCmdUI *pCmdUI);
    BOOL IsAlignment(Direction eDirection,
                    Alignment eAlignment);
    afx_msg void OnAlignmentHorizontalLeft();
    afx_msg void OnAlignmentHorizontalCenter();
    afx_msg void OnAlignmentHorizontalRight();
    afx_msg void OnAlignmentHorizontalJustified();
    afx_msg void OnAlignmentVerticalTop();
    afx_msg void OnAlignmentVerticalCenter();
    afx_msg void OnAlignmentVerticalBottom();
    void SetAlignment(Direction eDirection,
                    Alignment eAlignment);
    afx_msg void OnUpdateColorText(CCmdUI *pCmdUI);
    afx_msg void OnUpdateColorBackground(CCmdUI *pCmdUI);
    afx_msg void OnTextColor();
    afx_msg void OnBackgroundColor();
    void OnColor(int iColorType);
    afx_msg void OnUpdateFont(CCmdUI *pCmdUI);
    afx_msg void OnFont();
  private:
    Caret m_caret;
    CalcState m_eCalcStatus;
    KeyboardState m_eKeyboardState;
    int m_iInputIndex;
    Reference m_rfEdit, m_rfFirstMark, m_rfLastMark,
            m_rfMinCopy, m_rfMaxCopy;
    CellMatrix m_cellMatrix, m_copyMatrix;
    TSetMatrix m_tSetMatrix;
};
```

When a new spreadsheet is created, the application is in the mark state and the keyboard is in the insert state. The upper left cell (row 0 and column 0) is marked. The cell matrix and the target set matrix are connected to each other.

CalcDoc.cpp

```
CCalcDoc::CCalcDoc()
 :m_eCalcStatus(CS_MARK),
  m_iKeyboardState(KM_INSERT),
  m_rfMinCopy(-1, -1),
  m_rfMaxCopy(-1, -1)
{
  m_cellMatrix.SetTargetSetMatrix(&m_tSetMatrix);
  m_tSetMatrix.SetCellMatrix(&m_cellMatrix);
}
```

The methods `RepaintEditArea`, `RepaintMarkedArea`, and `RepaintSet` all update one or more cells of the spreadsheet. That is, the views are instructed to repaint the client area of the cells. When the user has modified the text of a cell, the cell has to be updated.

```
void CCalcDoc::RepaintEditArea()
{
  CPoint ptTopLeft(m_rfEdit.GetCol() * COL_WIDTH,
                   m_rfEdit.GetRow() * ROW_HEIGHT);
  CSize szEditCell(COL_WIDTH, ROW_HEIGHT);
  CRect rcEditCell(ptTopLeft, szEditCell);
  UpdateAllViews(NULL, (LPARAM) &rcEditCell);
}
```

Similar to the `RepaintEditArea` method above, we must repaint the client area of the marked cells when their mark status has changed. Remember that `m_rdEdit` only represents one cell while `m_rfFirstMark` and `m_rfLastMark` represent a block of cells.

```
void CCalcDoc::RepaintMarkedArea()
{
  int iMinMarkedRow = min(m_rfFirstMark.GetRow(),
                          m_rfLastMark.GetRow());
  int iMaxMarkedRow = max(m_rfFirstMark.GetRow(),
                          m_rfLastMark.GetRow());
  int iMinMarkedCol = min(m_rfFirstMark.GetCol(),
                          m_rfLastMark.GetCol());
  int iMaxMarkedCol = max(m_rfFirstMark.GetCol(),
                          m_rfLastMark.GetCol());
```

```
            CPoint ptTopLeft(iMinMarkedCol * COL_WIDTH,
                             iMinMarkedRow * ROW_HEIGHT);
            CPoint ptBottomRight((iMaxMarkedCol + 1) * COL_WIDTH,
                                 (iMaxMarkedRow + 1) * ROW_HEIGHT);
            CRect rcMarkedBlock(ptTopLeft, ptBottomRight);
            UpdateAllViews(NULL, (LPARAM) &rcMarkedBlock);
    }
```

When the user modifies the value of a cell, its target needs to be notified, re-evaluated, and updated. Even though the set might hold many cells, they are not bound in a block. Therefore, we have to repaint the areas of the cells one by one.

```
    void CCalcDoc::RepaintSet(const ReferenceSet& repaintSet)
    {
      for (POSITION position = repaintSet.GetHeadPosition();
           position != NULL; repaintSet.GetNext(position))
      {
        Reference reference = repaintSet.GetAt(position);
        int iRow = reference.GetRow();
        int iCol = reference.GetCol();

        CPoint ptCell(iCol * COL_WIDTH, iRow * ROW_HEIGHT);
        CSize szCell(COL_WIDTH, ROW_HEIGHT);
        CRect rcCell(ptCell, szCell);

        UpdateAllViews(NULL, (LPARAM) &rcCell);
      }
    }
```

The method DoubleClick is called by the view class when the user double-clicks with the left mouse button. We start by setting the application in the edit state, and generate the input text of the cell in question. We also determine the index of the current character by subtracting the mouse position from the upper left corner of the cell. Finally, we generate the caret array of the cell and update the caret.

```
    void CCalcDoc::DoubleClick(Reference rfCell, CPoint ptMouse,
                               CDC* pDC)
    {
      UnmarkAndMark(rfCell.GetRow(), rfCell.GetCol(),
                    rfCell.GetRow(), rfCell.GetCol());
      m_eCalcStatus = CS_EDIT;
      m_rfEdit = rfCell;
      Cell* pEditCell = m_cellMatrix.Get(m_rfEdit.GetRow(),
                                         m_rfEdit.GetCol());
      pEditCell->GenerateInputText();
```

```
        CPoint ptTopLeft(m_rfEdit.GetCol() * COL_WIDTH,
                         m_rfEdit.GetRow() * ROW_HEIGHT);
    m_iInputIndex = pEditCell->MouseToIndex
                                (ptMouse - ptTopLeft);

    pEditCell->GenerateCaretArray(pDC);
    RepaintEditArea();
    UpdateCaret();
}
```

When the user starts to edit a cell, the cell might be outside the visible part of the view of the spreadsheet due to scrolling or resizing of the window. The two versions of MakeCellVisible take care of that by notifying the current view about the cell's area.

```
void CCalcDoc::MakeCellVisible(Reference rfCell)
{
    MakeCellVisible(rfCell.GetRow(), rfCell.GetCol());
}
void CCalcDoc::MakeCellVisible(int iRow, int iCol)
{
  CPoint ptTopLeft(iCol * COL_WIDTH, iRow * ROW_HEIGHT);
  CRect rcCell(ptTopLeft, CSize(COL_WIDTH, ROW_HEIGHT));
  CCalcView* pCalcView = (CCalcView*) m_caret.GetView();
  pCalcView->MakeCellVisible(rcCell);
}
```

When the application is in the edit state and the edited cell is visible in the view, the caret should be visible too. If the keyboard is in the overwrite state, the caret is given the size of the current character. If it is in the insert state, the caret is a vertical line.

The caret marker is never visible when the application is in the mark state. In the edit state, the caret is visible if the cell currently being edited is visible in the view currently holding the input focus. If it is visible, we need the rectangle of the caret relative its top left corner.

```
void CCalcDoc::UpdateCaret()
{
  switch (m_eCalcStatus)
  {
    case CS_MARK:
      m_caret.HideCaret();
      break;
    case CS_EDIT:
      CCalcView* pCalcView = (CCalcView*) m_caret.GetView();
```

```
        if (pCalcView->IsCellVisible(m_rfEdit.GetRow(),
                                     m_rfEdit.GetCol()))
        {
          Cell* pEditCell = m_cellMatrix.Get(m_rfEdit);
          CPoint ptTopLeft(m_rfEdit.GetCol() * COL_WIDTH,
                           m_rfEdit.GetRow() * ROW_HEIGHT);
          CRect rcCaret = ptTopLeft + pEditCell->
                          IndexToCaret(m_iInputIndex);
```

If the keyboard is in the insert state, we trim the caret to a vertical line. We need to transform the coordinates of the caret to sheet point coordinates in case the view has been scrolled. Finally, we show the caret.

```
          if (m_iKeyboardState == KM_INSERT)
          {
            rcCaret.right = rcCaret.left + 1;
          }
          pCalcView->SheetPointToLogicalPoint(rcCaret);
          m_caret.SetAndShowCaret(rcCaret);
        }
```

If the current cell is not visible in the view, we hide the caret.

```
        else
        {
          m_caret.HideCaret();
        }
        break;
    }
}
```

The method UnmarkAndMark is a central and rather complex method. Its purpose is to unmark the marked cells and to mark the new block given by the parameters without any unnecessary updating. That is, new cells already marked will not be updated. Note that the first and last marked cells refer to when they were marked rather than their positions in the spreadsheet. The last row or column may be less than the first one. Therefore, we need to find the minimum and maximum value in order to traverse through the block.

```
void CCalcDoc::UnmarkAndMark(int iNewFirstMarkedRow,
                             int iNewFirstMarkedCol,
                             int iNewLastMarkedRow,
                             int iNewLastMarkedCol)
{
  int iOldMinMarkedRow = min(m_rfFirstMark.GetRow(),
                             m_rfLastMark.GetRow());
```

```
int iOldMaxMarkedRow = max(m_rfFirstMark.GetRow(),
                           m_rfLastMark.GetRow());
int iOldMinMarkedCol = min(m_rfFirstMark.GetCol(),
                           m_rfLastMark.GetCol());
int iOldMaxMarkedCol = max(m_rfFirstMark.GetCol(),
                           m_rfLastMark.GetCol());
int iNewMinMarkedRow = min(iNewFirstMarkedRow,
                           iNewLastMarkedRow);
int iNewMaxMarkedRow = max(iNewFirstMarkedRow,
                           iNewLastMarkedRow);
int iNewMinMarkedCol = min(iNewFirstMarkedCol,
                           iNewLastMarkedCol);
int iNewMaxMarkedCol = max(iNewFirstMarkedCol,
                           iNewLastMarkedCol);
m_rfFirstMark.SetRow(iNewFirstMarkedRow);
m_rfLastMark.SetRow(iNewLastMarkedRow);
m_rfFirstMark.SetCol(iNewFirstMarkedCol);
m_rfLastMark.SetCol(iNewLastMarkedCol);
```

If the application is in the edit state, we need to finish the editing and evaluate the value of the cell. After the editing has been finished, we need to evaluate and repaint all targets of the cell by calling EvaluateTargets and RepaintSet.

```
switch (m_eCalcStatus)
{
  case CS_EDIT:
    {
      Cell* pCell = m_cellMatrix.Get(m_rfEdit);
      m_eCalcStatus = CS_MARK;
      try
      {
        pCell->EndEdit(m_rfEdit);
        pCell->EvaluateValue(FALSE);
        ReferenceSet repaintSet =
                    m_tSetMatrix.EvaluateTargets(m_rfEdit);
        RepaintSet(repaintSet);
        SetModifiedFlag();
      }
      catch (const CString stMessage)
      {
        AfxGetApp()->GetMainWnd()->
              MessageBox(stMessage, TEXT("Parse Error."));
        RepaintEditArea();
      }
      UpdateCaret();
    }
    break;
```

If the application is in the mark state, we need to unmark the cells not included in the new marked cell block.

```
case CS_MARK:
  for (int iRow = iOldMinMarkedRow;
       iRow <= iOldMaxMarkedRow; ++iRow)
  {
    for (int iCol = iOldMinMarkedCol;
         iCol <= iOldMaxMarkedCol; ++iCol)
    {
      if ((iRow < iNewMinMarkedRow) ||
          (iRow > iNewMaxMarkedRow) ||
          (iCol < iNewMinMarkedCol) ||
          (iCol > iNewMaxMarkedCol))
      {
        CPoint ptTopLeft(iCol * COL_WIDTH,
                         iRow * ROW_HEIGHT);
        CRect rcCell(ptTopLeft,
                     CSize(COL_WIDTH, ROW_HEIGHT));
        UpdateAllViews(NULL, (LPARAM) &rcCell);
      }
    }
  }
  break;
}
```

Finally, we traverse the new marked cell block and repaint all cells not already marked in the previous marked cell block.

```
for (int iRow = iNewMinMarkedRow;
     iRow <= iNewMaxMarkedRow; ++iRow)
{
  for (int iCol = iNewMinMarkedCol;
       iCol <= iNewMaxMarkedCol; ++iCol)
  {
    if ((iRow < iOldMinMarkedRow) ||
        (iRow > iOldMaxMarkedRow) ||
        (iCol < iOldMinMarkedCol) ||
        (iCol > iOldMaxMarkedCol))
    {
      CPoint ptTopLeft(iCol * COL_WIDTH, iRow * ROW_HEIGHT);
      CRect rcCell(ptTopLeft,
                   CSize(COL_WIDTH, ROW_HEIGHT));
      UpdateAllViews(NULL, (LPARAM) &rcCell);
    }
  }
}
```

The method `KeyDown` is called when the user presses a special character, regular characters are handled by `CharDown` below. The method `InsertKey` simply changes the state of the keyboard.

```
void CCalcDoc::KeyDown(UINT uChar, CDC* pDC, BOOL bShiftKeyDown)
{
  switch (uChar)
  {
    case VK_LEFT:
        LeftArrowKey(bShiftKeyDown);
        break;
    // ...
    case VK_INSERT:
        m_iKeyboardState = (m_iKeyboardState == KM_INSERT) ?
                           KM_OVERWRITE : KM_INSERT;
        break;
```

The return key finishes the editing session. The user can also finish by pressing the *Tab* key or pressing the mouse. In either case, `MarkAndUnmark` above takes care of finishing the editing process. When the editing is finished, we try to mark the cell below. The *Tab* key does almost the same thing as the return key. The difference is that the next marked cell is, if possible, the cell to right, or the cell to the left if the user pressed the *Shift* key.

```
    case VK_RETURN:
        {
          int iNewFirstMarkedRow =
              min(m_rfFirstMark.GetRow() + 1, ROWS - 1);
          UnmarkAndMark(iNewFirstMarkedRow,
                        m_rfFirstMark.GetCol(),
                        iNewFirstMarkedRow,
                        m_rfFirstMark.GetCol());
          MakeCellVisible(iNewFirstMarkedRow,
                          m_rfFirstMark.GetCol());
        }
        break;
  }
  UpdateCaret();
}
```

The method `CharDown` is called when the user presses a regular key (ASCII number between 32 and 122). If the application is in the mark state, we mark the first marked cell, change to the edit state, and clear the input text before adding the character. We make sure the edited cell is visible. We add the character and generate a new caret array. Finally, we repaint the edit area (the cell being edited) and the caret.

```
void CCalcDoc::CharDown(UINT uChar, CDC* pDC)
{
  if (m_eCalcStatus == CS_MARK)
  {
    UnmarkAndMark(m_rfFirstMark.GetRow(),
                  m_rfFirstMark.GetCol(),
                  m_rfFirstMark.GetRow(),
                  m_rfFirstMark.GetCol());
    m_eCalcStatus = CS_EDIT;
    m_rfEdit = m_rfFirstMark;
    m_iInputIndex = 0;
    Cell* pCell = m_cellMatrix.Get(m_rfEdit);
    pCell->SetInputText(TEXT(""));
  }
  MakeCellVisible(m_rfEdit);
  Cell* pCell = m_cellMatrix.Get(m_rfEdit);
  pCell->CharDown(uChar, m_iInputIndex++, m_iKeyboardState);
  pCell->GenerateCaretArray(pDC);
  RepaintEditArea();
  UpdateCaret();
}
```

LeftArrowKey is called when the user presses the Left Arrow key. We have three different cases to consider, depending on whether the application is in the edit or the mark state and on whether the user pressed the *Shift* key.

If the application is in the edit state, we make sure the current cell is visible, move the current index one step to the left if it is not already at the leftmost index, and update the caret.

```
void CCalcDoc::LeftArrowKey(BOOL bShiftKeyDown)
{
  switch (m_eCalcStatus)
  {
    case CS_EDIT:
      MakeCellVisible(m_rfEdit);
      m_iInputIndex = max(0, m_iInputIndex - 1);
      UpdateCaret();
      break;
```

If the application is in the mark state, we have to take into consideration whether the *Shift* key was pressed at the same time. If it was not, we place the marked block one step to the left of the first marked cell if it is not already at the leftmost column. In that case, we place the marked block at the first marked cell.

```
case CS_MARK:
  if (!bShiftKeyDown)
  {
    int iNewFirstMarkedCol =
        max(0, m_rfFirstMark.GetCol() - 1);
    MakeCellVisible(m_rfFirstMark.GetRow(),
                    iNewFirstMarkedCol);
    UnmarkAndMark(m_rfFirstMark.GetRow(),
                  iNewFirstMarkedCol,
                  m_rfFirstMark.GetRow(),
                  iNewFirstMarkedCol);
  }
```

If the *Shift* key was pressed, we move the last marked cell one step to the left unless it is already at the leftmost position. The first marked cell is not affected.

```
  else
  {
    int iNewLastMarkedCol =
        max(0, m_rfLastMark.GetCol() - 1);
    MakeCellVisible(m_rfLastMark.GetRow(),
                    iNewLastMarkedCol);
    UnmarkAndMark(m_rfFirstMark.GetRow(),
                  m_rfFirstMark.GetCol(),
                  m_rfLastMark.GetRow(),
                  iNewLastMarkedCol);
  }
  break;
  }
}
```

The method `DeleteKey` is called when the user presses the *Delete* key to delete a character in the edit state or, in the mark state, the contents of a block of one or several cells in the marked block. In the edit state, we delete the character on the edit index unless it is at the end of the text.

```
void CCalcDoc::DeleteKey(CDC* pDC)
{
  switch (m_eCalcStatus)
  {
```

```
case CS_EDIT:
  {
    Cell* pCell = m_cellMatrix.Get(m_rfEdit);
    CString stInput = pCell->GetInputText();

    if (m_iInputIndex < stInput.GetLength())
    {
      stInput.Delete(m_iInputIndex);
      pCell->SetInputText(stInput);
      pCell->GenerateCaretArray(pDC);
      RepaintEditArea();
      SetModifiedFlag();
    }
  }
  break;
```

If the application is in the mark state, we just call OnDelete to remove the marked cells.

```
case CS_MARK:
  OnDelete();
  break;
  }
}
```

The copy menu item, toolbar button, and accelerator are enabled when the application is in the mark state, and disabled in the edit state.

```
void CCalcDoc::OnUpdateCopy(CCmdUI *pCmdUI)
{
  pCmdUI->Enable(m_eCalcStatus == CS_MARK);
}
```

The method OnCopy is called when the user chooses the **Copy** menu item or Copy button on the toolbar. It copies the marked block into the copy cell matrix.

```
void CCalcDoc::OnCopy()
{
  m_rfMinCopy.SetRow(min(m_rfFirstMark.GetRow(),
                         m_rfLastMark.GetRow()));
  m_rfMinCopy.SetCol(min(m_rfFirstMark.GetCol(),
                         m_rfLastMark.GetCol()));
  m_rfMaxCopy.SetRow(max(m_rfFirstMark.GetRow(),
                         m_rfLastMark.GetRow()));
  m_rfMaxCopy.SetCol(max(m_rfFirstMark.GetCol(),
                         m_rfLastMark.GetCol()));
```

```
  for (int iRow = m_rfMinCopy.GetRow();
       iRow <= m_rfMaxCopy.GetRow(); ++iRow)
  {
    for (int iCol = m_rfMinCopy.GetCol();
         iCol <= m_rfMaxCopy.GetCol();++iCol)
    {
      *m_copyMatrix.Get(iRow, iCol) =
      *m_cellMatrix.Get(iRow, iCol);
    }
  }
}
```

The **Cut** menu item, toolbar button, and accelerator are enabled when the application is in the mark state, similar to OnUpdateCopy above. OnCut simply calls OnCopy and OnDelete.

```
void CCalcDoc::OnUpdateCut(CCmdUI *pCmdUI)
{
  pCmdUI->Enable(m_eCalcStatus == CS_MARK);
}
void CCalcDoc::OnCut()
{
  OnCopy();
  OnDelete();
}
```

The **Paste** menu item, toolbar button, and accelerator are disabled when the application is in the edit state. In the mark state, it is enabled if there is a block of cells copied (m_rfMinCopy.GetRow() != -1) and if exactly one cell is marked or if a block of the same size as the copied block is marked.

```
void CCalcDoc::OnUpdatePaste(CCmdUI *pCmdUI)
{
  switch (m_eCalcStatus)
  {
    case CS_EDIT:
      pCmdUI->Enable(FALSE);
      break;
    case CS_MARK:
      if (m_rfMinCopy.GetRow() != -1)
      {
        int iCopiedRows = abs(m_rfMaxCopy.GetRow() -
                              m_rfMinCopy.GetRow()) + 1;
        int iCopiedCols = abs(m_rfMaxCopy.GetCol() -
                              m_rfMinCopy.GetCol()) + 1;
```

```
if ((m_rfFirstMark.GetRow()==m_rfLastMark.GetRow())&&
    (m_rfFirstMark.GetCol() == m_rfLastMark.GetCol()))
{
  int iMinMarkedRow = min(m_rfFirstMark.GetRow(),
                          m_rfLastMark.GetRow());
  int iMinMarkedCol = min(m_rfFirstMark.GetCol(),
                          m_rfLastMark.GetCol());
  pCmdUI->Enable
          (((iMinMarkedRow + iCopiedRows) <= ROWS) &&
          ((iMinMarkedCol + iCopiedCols) <= COLS));
}
else
{
  int iMarkedRows = abs(m_rfLastMark.GetRow() -
                        m_rfFirstMark.GetRow()) + 1;
  int iMarkedCols = abs(m_rfLastMark.GetCol() -
                        m_rfFirstMark.GetCol()) + 1;
  pCmdUI->Enable((iMarkedRows == iCopiedRows) &&
                 (iMarkedCols == iCopiedCols));
}
}
else
{
  pCmdUI->Enable(FALSE);
}
break;
}
}
```

When we paste a cell block into the spreadsheet, we have to check that it does not introduce a cycle into the cell matrix. Then we paste and parse the cells one by one. We start by defining a test cell matrix and a test target set matrix, which are copies of the document fields m_cellMatrix and m_tSetMatrix.

Then we paste the cells one by one. Before we paste a cell, we have to remove it as a target for each of its sources. For each pasted cell, we adjust its references, check for cycles, and evaluates its value recursively. That is, each time we find a reference in a formula, we evaluate that reference and if it is a formula itself, its references are evaluated, and so on. As we do not have any cyclic references, the recursive evaluation has to terminate. This is necessary in order for the cells in the pasted block to receive their correct values. Otherwise, we cannot be sure that the value of a reference is the correct one or if it is the previous value of the cell, before the paste.

If there are any problems, an exception is thrown, a message box reports the error to the user, and the method returns. The cell and target set matrices are only set at the end of the method if every cell has been pasted without any problems.

First, we need to find the difference between the copy and paste location of the block in order to update the references of the block. We also introduce test matrices to protect the original ones in case of cyclic references.

```
void CCalcDoc::OnPaste()
{
  int iMinMarkedRow = min(m_rfFirstMark.GetRow(),
                          m_rfLastMark.GetRow());
  int iMinMarkedCol = min(m_rfFirstMark.GetCol(),
                          m_rfLastMark.GetCol());
  int iRowDiff = iMinMarkedRow - m_rfMinCopy.GetRow();
  int iColDiff = iMinMarkedCol - m_rfMinCopy.GetCol();
  TSetMatrix testTSetMatrix(m_tSetMatrix);
  CellMatrix testCellMatrix(m_cellMatrix);
  testTSetMatrix.SetCellMatrix(&testCellMatrix);
  testCellMatrix.SetTargetSetMatrix(&testTSetMatrix);
  ReferenceSet totalRepaintSet;
  BOOL bModified = FALSE;
  for (int iSourceRow = m_rfMinCopy.GetRow();
       iSourceRow <= m_rfMaxCopy.GetRow(); ++iSourceRow)
  {
    for (int iSourceCol = m_rfMinCopy.GetCol();
         iSourceCol <= m_rfMaxCopy.GetCol();++iSourceCol)
    {
      int iTargetRow = iSourceRow + iRowDiff;
      int iTargetCol = iSourceCol + iColDiff;
      Reference mark(iTargetRow, iTargetCol);
      testTSetMatrix.RemoveTargets(mark);
      Cell* pSourceCell =
            m_copyMatrix.Get(iSourceRow, iSourceCol);
      Cell* pTargetCell =
            testCellMatrix.Get(iTargetRow, iTargetCol);
      *pTargetCell = *pSourceCell;
      if (!pSourceCell->IsEmpty() && !pTargetCell->IsEmpty())
      {
        bModified = TRUE;
      }
```

We update the references of the cell's formula, if it has one. Then we check for cyclic references. If it goes well, we add the cell as a target for each cell in its source set by calling `AddTargets` and adding its area to the total set of cell client areas to be updated.

```
try
{
  pTargetCell->UpdateSyntaxTree(iRowDiff, iColDiff);
  testTSetMatrix.CheckCircular(mark,
                pTargetCell->GetSourceSet());
  testTSetMatrix.AddTargets(mark);
  pTargetCell->EvaluateValue(TRUE);
  ReferenceSet repaintSet =
                testTSetMatrix.EvaluateTargets(mark);
  totalRepaintSet.AddAll(repaintSet);
}
```

If we find a cyclic reference, an exception is thrown. We report the error and return the method. Note that as we have been working on copies of the original cell and target set matrix, nothing has actually been pasted.

```
catch (const CString stMessage)
{
  AfxGetApp()->GetMainWnd()->MessageBox(stMessage,
                        TEXT("Parse Error."));
  return;
}
  }
}
```

If everything worked and at least one cell has been changed, we set the modified flag. Note that we could not set the flag immediately as we did not know if the block really was to be pasted.

```
if (bModified)
{
  SetModifiedFlag();
}
```

Finally, if we make it this far without finding any cyclic references, we replace the original cell and target set matrices and repaint the client areas of the pasted cells.

```
m_cellMatrix = testCellMatrix;
m_tSetMatrix = testTSetMatrix;
RepaintSet(totalRepaintSet);
}
```

The update alignment methods are called during the process idle time. They simply call `UpdateAlignment` below. The alignments are enabled if the application is in the mark state and if not all the marked cells already have the alignment in question. If all cells have the alignment, the menu item is also marked with a radio dot.

```
void CCalcDoc::OnUpdateAlignmentHorizontalLeft(CCmdUI *pCmdUI)
{
  UpdateAlignment(HORIZONTAL, DT_LEFT, pCmdUI);
}
// ...
void CCalcDoc::UpdateAlignment(Direction eDirection, Alignment
                               eAlignment, CCmdUI *pCmdUI)
{
  switch (m_eCalcStatus)
  {
    case CS_MARK:
      pCmdUI->Enable(!IsAlignment(eDirection, eAlignment));
      pCmdUI->SetRadio(IsAlignment(eDirection, eAlignment));
      break;
    case CS_EDIT:
      pCmdUI->Enable(FALSE);
      pCmdUI->SetRadio(FALSE);
      break;
  }
}
```

The method `IsAlignment` goes through all the marked cells and returns false if at least one of them does not have the given alignment. It returns true only if all cells in the marked block have the alignment. If we find one cell without the alignment, we return false.

```
BOOL CCalcDoc::IsAlignment(Direction eDirection,
                           Alignment eAlignment)
{
  int iMinMarkedRow = min(m_rfFirstMark.GetRow(),
                          m_rfLastMark.GetRow());
  int iMaxMarkedRow = max(m_rfFirstMark.GetRow(),
                          m_rfLastMark.GetRow());
  int iMinMarkedCol = min(m_rfFirstMark.GetCol(),
                          m_rfLastMark.GetCol());
  int iMaxMarkedCol = max(m_rfFirstMark.GetCol(),
                          m_rfLastMark.GetCol());
  for (int iRow = iMinMarkedRow; iRow <= iMaxMarkedRow;
       ++iRow)
  {
```

```
        for (int iCol = iMinMarkedCol; iCol <= iMaxMarkedCol;
             ++iCol)
        {
          Cell* pCell = m_cellMatrix.Get(iRow, iCol);
```

If one of the cells does not have the given alignment, we return false.

```
          if (eAlignment != pCell->GetAlignment(eDirection))
          {
            return FALSE;
          }
        }
      }
    }
```

If all cells have the given alignment, we return true.

```
    return TRUE;
  }
```

The alignment methods simply call `SetAlignment`, which sets the given alignment for all cells in the marked block. Remember that `SetAlignment` is called only if the application is in the mark state and at least one cell does not already have the alignment in question.

```
    void CCalcDoc::OnAlignmentHorizontalLeft()
    {
      SetAlignment(HORIZONTAL, DT_LEFT);
    }
    // ...
    void CCalcDoc::SetAlignment(Direction eDirection,
                               Alignment eAlignment)
    {
      int iMinMarkedRow = min(m_rfFirstMark.GetRow(),
                              m_rfLastMark.GetRow());
      int iMaxMarkedRow = max(m_rfFirstMark.GetRow(),
                              m_rfLastMark.GetRow());
      int iMinMarkedCol = min(m_rfFirstMark.GetCol(),
                              m_rfLastMark.GetCol());
      int iMaxMarkedCol = max(m_rfFirstMark.GetCol(),
                              m_rfLastMark.GetCol());
      for (int iRow = iMinMarkedRow; iRow <= iMaxMarkedRow;
           ++iRow)
      {
        for (int iCol = iMinMarkedCol; iCol <= iMaxMarkedCol;
             ++iCol)
        {
```

```
      Cell* pCell = m_cellMatrix.Get(iRow, iCol);
      pCell->SetAlignment(eDirection, eAlignment);
    }
  }
  RepaintMarkedArea();
  SetModifiedFlag();
}
```

The View Class

`CCalcView` is the view class of the Calc application. It handles messages (mouse and keyboard) and repainting of the client area.

The field `m_pCalcDoc` is a pointer to the document class object that is initialized and tested in `OnCreate`. We also need the field `m_bDoubleClick` to distinguish between single and double-clicks. When the user releases the mouse key, we mark the cell if they have not double-clicked. If they have double-clicked, we shall just leave the cell in the edit state.

The user may mark one or more positions of the spreadsheet. If they mark all the area at the top left corner of the spreadsheet, all cells are marked (`MS_ALL`). If they mark at the row header, all columns on that row are marked (`MS_ROW`). If they mark the column header, all rows at that column are marked, and if they mark a cell, that cell is marked. The field `m_rfFirstCell` keeps track of the cells first marked by the user. In this way, we can build a marked block and not notify the document class until the user release the mouse button.

CalcView.h

```
enum SpreadSheetArea {MS_ALL, MS_ROW, MS_COL, MS_SHEET};
class CCalcView : public CView
{
  protected:
    DECLARE_DYNCREATE(CCalcView)
    DECLARE_MESSAGE_MAP()

    CCalcView();

  public:
    afx_msg int OnCreate(LPCREATESTRUCT lpCreateStruct);
    virtual void OnInitialUpdate();

    afx_msg void OnSize(UINT nType, int cx, int cy);
    virtual void OnPrepareDC(CDC* pDC,
                             CPrintInfo* pInfo = NULL);

    afx_msg void OnSetFocus(CWnd* pOldWnd);
```

```
    afx_msg void OnKillFocus(CWnd* pNewWnd);

    void LogicalPointToSheetPoint(CPoint& ptPoint);
    void LogicalPointToSheetPoint(CRect& rcRect);

    void SheetPointToLogicalPoint(CPoint& ptPoint);
    void SheetPointToLogicalPoint(CRect& rcRect);

    void MakeCellVisible(CRect rcArea);
    BOOL IsCellVisible(int iRow, int iCol);

    afx_msg void OnVScroll(UINT nSBCode, UINT nPos,
                           CScrollBar* pScrollBar);
    afx_msg void OnHScroll(UINT nSBCode, UINT nPos,
                           CScrollBar* pScrollBar);

  private:
    SpreadSheetArea GetMouseLocation(CPoint ptMouse,
                                     Reference& rcCell);

  public:
    afx_msg void OnLButtonDown(UINT uFlags, CPoint ptMouse);
    afx_msg void OnMouseMove(UINT uFlags, CPoint ptMouse);
    afx_msg void OnLButtonDblClk(UINT nFlags, CPoint ptMouse);

    afx_msg void OnKeyDown(UINT uChar, UINT nRepCnt,
                           UINT uFlags);
    afx_msg void OnChar(UINT uChar, UINT nRepCnt,
                        UINT uFlags);

    virtual void OnUpdate(CView* pSender, LPARAM lHint,
                          CObject* pHint);
    virtual void OnDraw(CDC* pDC);

  private:
    CCalcDoc* m_pCalcDoc;
    BOOL m_bDoubleClick;
    Reference m_rfFirstCell;
};
```

The method OnCreate is called when a view is created, but before it is visible. It sets the value of m_pCalcDoc, the pointer to the document object. Remember that an application may have several view objects, but only one document object.

CalcView.cpp

```
int CCalcView::OnCreate(LPCREATESTRUCT lpCreateStruct)
{
  // We check that the view has been correctly created.
  if (CView::OnCreate(lpCreateStruct) == -1)
  {
    return -1;
  }
```

```
    m_pCalcDoc = (CCalcDoc*) m_pDocument;
    ASSERT_VALID(m_pCalcDoc);

    return 0;
}
```

The method `OnInitialUpdate` is called when the view is first visible. It sets the scroll views. It is slightly complicated as we have to take the row and column headers into consideration.

```
void CCalcView::OnInitialUpdate()
{
  CClientDC dc(this);
  OnPrepareDC(&dc);
```

We convert the device coordinates (pixels) of the client area to logical coordinates (hundredths of millimeters).

```
  CRect rcClient;
  GetClientRect(rcClient);
  dc.DPtoLP(&rcClient);
```

The width and height of the client area that is to the cells disposal are the size of the client area minus the size of the row and column headers.

```
  int iPageWidth = rcClient.right - HEADER_WIDTH;
  int iPageHeight = rcClient.bottom - HEADER_HEIGHT;
```

The size of the horizontal scroll bar is the size of the columns plus the rest between the page and column width. This make sure the cells will fit nicely into the client area.

```
  SCROLLINFO scrollInfo;
  scrollInfo.fMask = SIF_ALL;
  scrollInfo.nPos = 0;
  scrollInfo.nMin = 0;
  scrollInfo.nPage = rcClient.right - HEADER_WIDTH;
  scrollInfo.nMax = COLS * COL_WIDTH +
                    iPageWidth % COL_WIDTH - 1;
  SetScrollInfo(SB_HORZ, &scrollInfo);
```

In the same way, the size of the scroll bar is the size of the rows plus the rest between the page and row height.

```
  scrollInfo.fMask = SIF_ALL;
  scrollInfo.nPos = 0;
  scrollInfo.nMin = 0;
```

```
            scrollInfo.nPage = rcClient.bottom - HEADER_HEIGHT;
            scrollInfo.nMax = ROWS * ROW_HEIGHT +
                               iPageHeight % ROW_HEIGHT - 1;
            SetScrollInfo(SB_VERT, &scrollInfo);
            m_pCalcDoc->UpdateCaret();
        }
```

The method OnSize is called every time the user changes the size of the window. It sets the scroll bars to reflect the new size. We convert the device coordinates (pixels) of the client area to logical coordinates (hundredths of millimeters).

```
    void CCalcView::OnSize(UINT /* uType */, int cxClient,
                           int cyClient)
    {
      CClientDC dc(this);
      OnPrepareDC(&dc);
      CRect rcClient(0, 0, cxClient, cyClient);
      dc.DPtoLP(&rcClient);
      SCROLLINFO scrollInfo;
      scrollInfo.fMask = SIF_PAGE;
      scrollInfo.nPage = rcClient.right - HEADER_WIDTH;
      SetScrollInfo(SB_HORZ, &scrollInfo);
      scrollInfo.fMask = SIF_PAGE;
      scrollInfo.nPage = rcClient.bottom - HEADER_HEIGHT;
      SetScrollInfo(SB_VERT, &scrollInfo);
      m_pCalcDoc->UpdateCaret();
    }
```

The method OnPrepareDC is called directly after a device context has been created. It sets the coordinate mapping of the application. The isotropic mode means that the horizontal and vertical units are equal (circles are round). GetDeviceCaps gives the size of the screen in pixels and millimeters. With that information, we set the logical unit to one hundredth millimeters.

```
    void CCalcView::OnPrepareDC(CDC* pDC, CPrintInfo* /* pInfo */)
    {
      pDC->SetMapMode(MM_ISOTROPIC);
      CSize szWindow(100 * pDC->GetDeviceCaps(HORZSIZE),
                     100 * pDC->GetDeviceCaps(VERTSIZE));
      CSize szViewport(pDC->GetDeviceCaps(HORZRES),
                       pDC->GetDeviceCaps(VERTRES));
      pDC->SetWindowExt(szWindow);
      pDC->SetViewportExt(szViewport);
    }
```

The method `LogicalPointToSheetPoint` translates a logical point to a logical point with regards to the scrollbars' current positions.

```
void CCalcView::LogicalPointToSheetPoint(CPoint& ptPoint)
{
  ptPoint.x += GetScrollPos(SB_HORZ) - HEADER_WIDTH;
  ptPoint.y += GetScrollPos(SB_VERT) - HEADER_HEIGHT;
}
void CCalcView::LogicalPointToSheetPoint(CRect& rcRect)
{
  LogicalPointToSheetPoint(rcRect.TopLeft());
  LogicalPointToSheetPoint(rcRect.BottomRight());
}
```

The method `SheetPointToLogicalPoint` translates a logical point with regards to the scrollbars' current positions to a regular logical point. That is, a logical point without regards to the scroll bars.

```
void CCalcView::SheetPointToLogicalPoint(CPoint& ptPoint)
{
  ptPoint.x += HEADER_WIDTH - GetScrollPos(SB_HORZ);
  ptPoint.y += HEADER_HEIGHT - GetScrollPos(SB_VERT);
}
void CCalcView::SheetPointToLogicalPoint(CRect& rcRect)
{
  SheetPointToLogicalPoint(rcRect.TopLeft());
  SheetPointToLogicalPoint(rcRect.BottomRight());
}
```

The method `OnSetFocus` and `OnKillFocus` are called when the view receives or loses the input focus, respectively. They notify the caret connected to the document about the event.

```
void CCalcView::OnSetFocus(CWnd* /* pOldWnd */)
{
  Caret* pCaret = m_pCalcDoc->GetCaret();
  pCaret->OnSetFocus(this);
}
void CCalcView::OnKillFocus(CWnd* /* pNewWnd */)
{
  Caret* pCaret = m_pCalcDoc->GetCaret();
  pCaret->OnKillFocus();
}
```

The method `IsCellVisible` decides whether the given cell is located in the part of the spreadsheet visible in the client area. With the scroll bar settings we find the first and last visible row and column in the client area and compare them to the given row and column.

```
BOOL CCalcView::IsCellVisible(int iRow, int iCol)
{
  SCROLLINFO scrollInfo;
  GetScrollInfo(SB_VERT, &scrollInfo, SIF_POS | SIF_PAGE);
  int iFirstVisibleRow = scrollInfo.nPos / ROW_HEIGHT;
  int iLastVisibleRow = iFirstVisibleRow +
                        scrollInfo.nPage / ROW_HEIGHT;
  GetScrollInfo(SB_HORZ, &scrollInfo, SIF_POS | SIF_PAGE);
  int iFirstVisibleCol = scrollInfo.nPos / COL_WIDTH;
  int iLastVisibleCol = iFirstVisibleCol +
                        scrollInfo.nPage / COL_WIDTH;
  return ((iRow >= iFirstVisibleRow) &&
          (iRow <= iLastVisibleRow) &&
          (iCol >= iFirstVisibleCol) &&
          (iCol <= iLastVisibleCol));
}
```

`OnVScroll` is called when the user scrolls vertically directly with the mouse, or indirectly with the Up Arrow, Down Arrow, *Home*, *End*, *Page Up*, and *Page Down* keys. First, we extract all information about the vertical scroll bar and find the current scroll position and the current top row.

```
void CCalcView::OnVScroll(UINT uSBCode, UINT /* yThumbPos */,
                          CScrollBar* /* pScrollBar */)
{
  SCROLLINFO scrollInfo;
  GetScrollInfo(SB_VERT, &scrollInfo);
  int yPos = scrollInfo.nPos;
  int iOldRow = yPos / ROW_HEIGHT;
```

We increase or decrease the line and check that the scroll position has not exceeded the scroll limits. The scroll position cannot be less than zero and it cannot be greater than the height of the spreadsheet minus the height of the client area.

```
  switch (uSBCode)
  {
    case SB_LINEUP:
      yPos = max(0, yPos - ROW_HEIGHT);
      break;
    case SB_LINEDOWN:
      yPos = min(yPos + ROW_HEIGHT, scrollInfo.nMax);
      break;
```

We scroll one page up or down. Note the difference between scrolling a line. A line always has the same height (ROW_HEIGHT), but a page is defined by the current size of the client area (scrollInfo.nMax), excluding the headers.

```
      case SB_PAGEUP:
        yPos = max(0, yPos - (int) scrollInfo.nPage);
        break;
      case SB_PAGEDOWN:
        yPos = min(yPos + (int) scrollInfo.nPage,
                   scrollInfo.nMax);
        break;
      case SB_THUMBPOSITION:
        yPos = scrollInfo.nTrackPos;
        break;
    }
    int iNewRow = (int) ((double) yPos / ROW_HEIGHT + 0.5);
```

If the top visible row has been altered, we need to repaint the client area. We need a device context to transform the headers to device coordinates. We invalidate the client area in device coordinates, excluding the header. Finally, we update the caret as the scroll position has been altered.

```
    if (iOldRow != iNewRow)
    {
      SetScrollPos(SB_VERT, iNewRow * ROW_HEIGHT);
      CRect rcClient;
      GetClientRect(&rcClient);
      CClientDC dc(this);
      OnPrepareDC(&dc);
      CSize szHeader(HEADER_WIDTH, HEADER_HEIGHT);
      dc.LPtoDP(&szHeader);
      CRect rcUpdate(0, szHeader.cy, rcClient.right,
                     rcClient.bottom);
      InvalidateRect(rcUpdate);
      m_pCalcDoc->UpdateCaret();
    }
  }
```

The method GetMouseLocation takes the position of a mouse click (in device coordinates) and returns one of four areas of the client window: the top left corner, the row header, the column header, or a cell in the spreadsheet.

Below is an outline of the different parts of the spreadsheet.

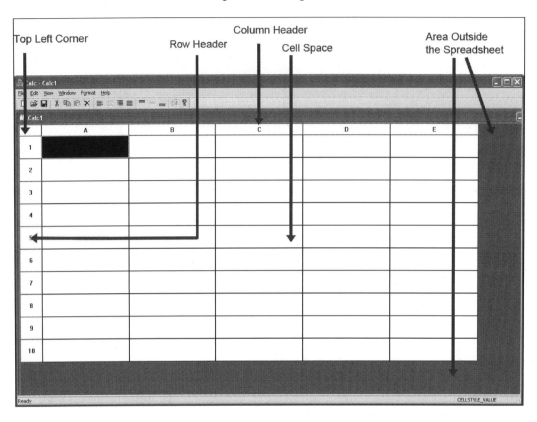

```
SpreadSheetArea CCalcView::GetMouseLocation(CPoint ptMouse,
                                            Reference& rfCell)
{
  CClientDC dc(this);
  OnPrepareDC(&dc);
  dc.DPtoLP(&ptMouse);
  // Is the mouse if the top left header box?
  if ((ptMouse.x <= HEADER_WIDTH) &&
      (ptMouse.y <= HEADER_HEIGHT))
  {
    rfCell.SetRow(0);
    rfCell.SetCol(0);
    return MS_ALL;
  }
  // Or is it in the row header?
  else if (ptMouse.x <= HEADER_WIDTH)
  {
    LogicalPointToSheetPoint(ptMouse);
```

```
      rfCell.SetRow(min(ROWS - 1, ptMouse.y / ROW_HEIGHT));
      rfCell.SetCol(0);
      return MS_ROW;
    }
    // Or is it in the column header?
    else if (ptMouse.y <= HEADER_HEIGHT)
    {
      LogicalPointToSheetPoint(ptMouse);
      rfCell.SetRow(0);
      rfCell.SetCol(min(COLS - 1, ptMouse.x / COL_WIDTH));
      return MS_COL;
    }
    // If not, is has to be in the actual cell space.
    else
    {
      LogicalPointToSheetPoint(ptMouse);
      rfCell.SetRow(min(ROWS - 1, ptMouse.y / ROW_HEIGHT));
      rfCell.SetCol(min(COLS - 1, ptMouse.x / COL_WIDTH));
      return MS_SHEET;
    }
  }
```

When the user clicks the mouse, two messages are sent: WM_LBUTTONDOWN followed by WM_LBUTTONUP. In practice, however, it is virtually impossible for the user to press and release the button without moving the mouse at least one pixel first, WM_LBUTTON is sent, which is caught by OnLButtonDown, then one or more WM_MOUSEMOVE messages are sent, which are caught by OnMouseMove. Finally WM_LBUTTONDOWN is sent, which is ignored in this application.

When we catch the mouse click, we have to find out where it hit. We have five parts of the client area to examine: the top left corner, the row header, the column header, and the cell space. If user clicks in the top left corner, all cells in the spreadsheet are marked. If they click in the row header, the whole row is marked. If they click in the column header, the whole column is marked. If they click in a cell in the cell space, that particular cell is marked.

```
    void CCalcView::OnLButtonDown(UINT /* uFlags */,
                                  CPoint ptMouse)
  {
    m_bDoubleClick = FALSE;
    SpreadSheetArea eArea = GetMouseLocation
                              (ptMouse, m_rfFirstCell);

    switch (eArea)
    {
```

```
    case MS_ALL:
      m_pCalcDoc->UnmarkAndMark(0, 0, ROWS - 1, COLS - 1);
      break;
    case MS_ROW:
      m_pCalcDoc->UnmarkAndMark(m_rfFirstCell.GetRow(), 0,
                          m_rfFirstCell.GetRow(), COLS - 1);
      break;
    case MS_COL:
      m_pCalcDoc->UnmarkAndMark(0, m_rfFirstCell.GetCol(),
                          ROWS - 1, m_rfFirstCell.GetCol());
      break;
    case MS_SHEET:
      m_pCalcDoc->UnmarkAndMark(m_rfFirstCell.GetRow(),
                            m_rfFirstCell.GetCol(),
                            m_rfFirstCell.GetRow(),
                            m_rfFirstCell.GetCol());
      break;
  };
  m_pCalcDoc->UpdateCaret();
}
```

One important detail is the `m_bDoubleClick` field. It is set to false in `OnLButtonDown`
above simply because the user has not yet double-clicked. However, if the user
double-clicks and move the mouse, it will be ignored. This is due to the fact that the
user pressing and dragging the mouse causes one or more cells to become marked.
However, when the user double-clicks, the application should enter the edit state.
Therefore, `m_bDoubleClick` is set to true in `OnLDoubleClick` below.

```
  void CCalcView::OnMouseMove(UINT uFlags, CPoint ptMouse)
  {
    BOOL bLeftButtonDown = (uFlags & MK_LBUTTON);
    if (bLeftButtonDown && !m_bDoubleClick)
    {
      Reference rcCurrCell;
      SpreadSheetArea eArea = GetMouseLocation
                              (ptMouse, rcCurrCell);
      switch (eArea)
      {
        case MS_ALL:
          m_pCalcDoc->UnmarkAndMark(0, 0, ROWS - 1, COLS - 1);
          break;
        case MS_ROW:
          m_pCalcDoc->UnmarkAndMark(rcCurrCell.GetRow(), 0,
                              rcCurrCell.GetRow(), COLS - 1);
```

```
          break;
      case MS_COL:
        m_pCalcDoc->UnmarkAndMark(0, rcCurrCell.GetCol(),
                            ROWS - 1, rcCurrCell.GetCol());
          break;
      case MS_SHEET:
        m_pCalcDoc->UnmarkAndMark(m_rfFirstCell.GetRow(),
                              m_rfFirstCell.GetCol(),
                              rcCurrCell.GetRow(),
                              rcCurrCell.GetCol());
          break;
    }
  }
}
```

`OnLButtonDblClk` is called when the user double-clicks the left mouse button.

```
    void CCalcView::OnLButtonDblClk(UINT /* nFlags */,
                                CPoint ptMouse)
  {
    m_bDoubleClick = TRUE;
    Reference rfCell;
    SpreadSheetArea eArea = GetMouseLocation(ptMouse, rfCell);
    if (eArea == MS_SHEET)
    {
      CClientDC dc(this);
      OnPrepareDC(&dc);
      dc.DPtoLP(&ptMouse);
      LogicalPointToSheetPoint(ptMouse);
      m_pCalcDoc->DoubleClick(rfCell, ptMouse, &dc);
    }
  }
```

`OnKeyDown` is called every time the user presses a keyboard key, and in the case of Left Arrow, Right Arrow, *Page Up, Page Down, Home, End, Return, Tab, Insert, Delete,* or *Backspace* keys the document class object is notified. We need not create a device context as the character may alter the text of a cell, which results in regeneration of the caret array for that cell.

We do also need to find out whether the *Shift* key was pressed at the same time as the keyboard key. The Win32 API function `GetKeyState` called with the parameter `VK_SHIFT` returns a negative value if the *Shift* key is pressed. It can also be called with the parameters `VK_CONTROL` (*Ctrl* key) and `VK_MENU` (Menu key). If we would need more specific information about which key is pressed, we can also use `VK_LSHIFT` (Left *Shift* key), `VK_RSHIFT` (Right *Shift* key), `VK_LCONTROL` (Left *Ctrl* key), `VK_RCONTROL` (Right *Ctrl* key), `VK_LMENU` (Left Menu key), and `VK_RMENU` (Right Menu key).

```
void CCalcView::OnKeyDown(UINT uChar, UINT /* uRepCnt */,
                          UINT /* uFlags*/)
{
  switch (uChar)
  {
    case VK_LEFT:
    case VK_RIGHT:
    case VK_UP:
    case VK_DOWN:
    case VK_HOME:
    case VK_END:
    case VK_RETURN:
    case VK_ESCAPE:
    case VK_TAB:
    case VK_INSERT:
    case VK_DELETE:
    case VK_BACK:
      CClientDC dc(this);
      OnPrepareDC(&dc);
      BOOL bShiftKeyDown = (::GetKeyState(VK_SHIFT) < 0);
      m_pCalcDoc->KeyDown(uChar, &dc, bShiftKeyDown);
      break;
  }
}
```

The method `OnChar` is called every time the user presses a key at the keyboard. If the character is printable it notifies the document class. A character is printable if its ASCII value is between 32 and 122; that is, if it is letter, a digit, an arithmetic character, or a punctuation mark.

```
void CCalcView::OnChar(UINT uChar, UINT  /* uRepCnt */,
                       UINT /* uFlags */)
{
  if (isprint(uChar))
  {
    CClientDC dc(this);
    OnPrepareDC(&dc);
    m_pCalcDoc->CharDown(uChar, &dc);
  }
}
```

The method `MakeCellVisible` is called by the document class on several occasions. Its task is to make the given area visible.

```
void CCalcView::MakeCellVisible(CRect rcArea)
{
  CClientDC dc(this);
  OnPrepareDC(&dc);

  SCROLLINFO scrollInfo;
  GetScrollInfo(SB_HORZ, &scrollInfo);

  int xFirst = scrollInfo.nPos;
  int xPage = scrollInfo.nPage;
  int xLast = xFirst + xPage;
```

If the cell is to the left of the first visible cell, we scroll the horizontal bar to the left border of the cell and repaint the window and the caret.

```
  if (rcArea.left < xFirst)
  {
    SetScrollPos(SB_HORZ, rcArea.left);
    CRect rcUpdate(HEADER_WIDTH, 0, TOTAL_WIDTH,
                   TOTAL_HEIGHT);
    dc.LPtoDP(rcUpdate);
    InvalidateRect(rcUpdate);
    UpdateWindow();
    m_pCalcDoc->UpdateCaret();
  }
```

If the cell is to the right of the last visible cell, we scroll the horizontal bar to the first visible cell added with the distance between the given cell and the last cell and repaint the window and the caret.

```
  if (rcArea.right > xLast)
  {
    int iDistance = rcArea.right - xLast;
    iDistance += COL_WIDTH - iDistance % COL_WIDTH;
    SetScrollPos(SB_HORZ, xFirst + iDistance);
    CRect rcUpdate(HEADER_WIDTH, 0, TOTAL_WIDTH,
                   TOTAL_HEIGHT);
    dc.LPtoDP(rcUpdate);
    InvalidateRect(rcUpdate);
    UpdateWindow();
    m_pCalcDoc->UpdateCaret();
  }

  GetScrollInfo(SB_VERT, &scrollInfo);
```

```
int yFirst = scrollInfo.nPos;
int yPage = scrollInfo.nPage;
int yLast = yFirst + yPage;
```

If the cell is above the top visible cell, we scroll the vertical bar to the top border of the cell and repaint the window and the caret.

```
if (rcArea.top < yFirst)
{
  SetScrollPos(SB_VERT, rcArea.top);
  CRect rcUpdate(0, HEADER_HEIGHT, TOTAL_WIDTH,
                TOTAL_HEIGHT);
  dc.LPtoDP(rcUpdate);
  InvalidateRect(rcUpdate);
  UpdateWindow();
  m_pCalcDoc->UpdateCaret();
}
```

If the cell is below the last visible cell, we scroll the vertical bar to top visible cell added with the distance between the given cell and the bottom cell and repaint the window and the caret.

```
if (rcArea.bottom > yLast)
{
  int iDistance = rcArea.bottom - yLast;
  iDistance += ROW_HEIGHT - iDistance % ROW_HEIGHT;
  SetScrollPos(SB_VERT, yFirst + iDistance);
  CRect rcUpdate(0, HEADER_HEIGHT, TOTAL_WIDTH,
                TOTAL_HEIGHT);
  dc.LPtoDP(rcUpdate);
  InvalidateRect(rcUpdate);
  UpdateWindow();
  m_pCalcDoc->UpdateCaret();
}
}
```

The method `OnUpdate` is indirectly called by `UpdateAllViews` in the document class when one or more cells need to be repainted. It is called on two occasions. It is called indirectly by `UpdateAllViews` in the document class with `lHint` pointed to a `CRect` object holding the area to be updateed in the client area of the view. It is also called by `OnInitialUpdate` in the MFC class `CView` with `lHint` set to null. In that case, we do nothing.

```
void CCalcView::OnUpdate(CView* /* pSender */, LPARAM lHint,
                         CObject* /* pHint */)
{
```

```
    if (lHint != NULL)
    {
      CClientDC dc(this);
      OnPrepareDC(&dc);
      CRect rcUpdate = *(CRect*) lHint;
      SheetPointToLogicalPoint(rcUpdate);
      dc.LPtoDP(&rcUpdate);
      InvalidateRect(&rcUpdate);
      UpdateWindow();
    }
  }
```

The method OnDraw is called when the view needs to be re-painted, partly or
completely. Several areas will need to be repainted. The client area can be divided
into five parts: the top left corner, the row header, the column header, the cell space,
and the area outside the spreadsheet (which is visible if the window is maximized on
a large screen).

```
void CCalcView::OnDraw(CDC* pDC)
{
  CRect rcClient;
  GetClientRect(&rcClient);
  pDC->DPtoLP(&rcClient);
  CPen pen(PS_SOLID, 0, LIGHT_GRAY);
  CPen *pOldPen = pDC->SelectObject(&pen);
  CBrush grayBrush(LIGHT_GRAY);
  CBrush *pOldBrush = pDC->SelectObject(&grayBrush);
  int iTotalWidth = HEADER_WIDTH + COLS * COL_WIDTH;
  int iTotalHeight = HEADER_HEIGHT + ROWS*ROW_HEIGHT;
  // The area outside the spreadsheet.
  pDC->Rectangle(iTotalWidth, 0, rcClient.right,
                 iTotalHeight);
  pDC->Rectangle(0, iTotalHeight,
                 rcClient.right,rcClient.bottom);
  // The headers have white background color.
  CBrush whiteBrush(WHITE);
  pDC->SelectObject(&whiteBrush);
  // Top left corner of the spreadsheet (the all button).
  pDC->Rectangle(0, 0, HEADER_WIDTH, HEADER_HEIGHT);
  // The row header of the spreadsheet.
  int xScrollPos = GetScrollPos(SB_HORZ);
  int yScrollPos = GetScrollPos(SB_VERT);
  int iStartRow = yScrollPos / ROW_HEIGHT;
  int iStartCol = xScrollPos / COL_WIDTH;
```

```
for (int iRow = iStartRow; iRow < ROWS; ++iRow)
{
  int yPos = iRow * ROW_HEIGHT;
  yPos += HEADER_HEIGHT - yScrollPos;

  CString stBuffer;
  stBuffer.Format(TEXT("%d"), iRow + 1);

  CRect rcHeader(0, yPos, HEADER_WIDTH, yPos + ROW_HEIGHT);
  pDC->Rectangle(&rcHeader);
  pDC->DrawText(stBuffer, &rcHeader, DT_SINGLELINE |
              DT_CENTER |DT_VCENTER);
}
// The column header of the spreadsheet.
for (int iCol = iStartCol; iCol < COLS; ++iCol)
{
  int xPos = iCol * COL_WIDTH;
  xPos += HEADER_WIDTH - xScrollPos;

  CString stBuffer;
  stBuffer.Format(TEXT("%c"), (TCHAR) (TEXT('A') + iCol));

  CRect rcHeader(xPos, 0, xPos + COL_WIDTH, HEADER_HEIGHT);
  pDC->Rectangle(&rcHeader);
  pDC->DrawText(stBuffer, &rcHeader, DT_SINGLELINE |
              DT_CENTER |DT_VCENTER);
}
pDC->SelectObject(pOldPen);
pDC->SelectObject(pOldBrush);

CPoint ptScroll(xScrollPos, yScrollPos);
CSize szHeader(HEADER_WIDTH, HEADER_HEIGHT);
pDC->SetWindowOrg(ptScroll - szHeader);

int iCellStatus = m_pCalcDoc->GetCalcStatus();
CellMatrix* pCellMatrix = m_pCalcDoc->GetCellMatrix();

Reference rfEdit = m_pCalcDoc->GetEdit();
Reference rfFirstMark = m_pCalcDoc->GetFirstMark();
Reference rfLastMark = m_pCalcDoc->GetLastMark();

// The cell space.
int iMinRow = min(rfFirstMark.GetRow(),
              rfLastMark.GetRow());
int iMaxRow = max(rfFirstMark.GetRow(),
              rfLastMark.GetRow());
int iMinCol = min(rfFirstMark.GetCol(),
              rfLastMark.GetCol());
int iMaxCol = max(rfFirstMark.GetCol(),
              rfLastMark.GetCol());
```

The variables `bEdit` and `bMark` are initalized to avoid compiler warnings. The cell is in the edit state if the application is in the edit state and this particular cell is being edited. The cell is in the mark state if the application is in the mark state and the cell is inside the marked block. Finally, the cell is drawn relative the top left corner of the cell.

```
for (int iRow = iStartRow; iRow < ROWS; ++iRow)
{
  for (int iCol = iStartCol; iCol < COLS; ++iCol)
  {
    BOOL bEdit = FALSE, bMark = FALSE;

    switch (iCellStatus)
    {
      case CS_EDIT:
        bEdit = (iRow == rfEdit.GetRow()) &&
                (iCol == rfEdit.GetCol());
        bMark = FALSE;
        break;
      case CS_MARK:
        bEdit = FALSE;
        bMark = (iRow >= iMinRow) && (iRow <= iMaxRow) &&
                (iCol >= iMinCol) && (iCol <= iMaxCol);
        break;
    }

    CPoint ptTopLeft(iCol * COL_WIDTH, iRow * ROW_HEIGHT);
    Cell* pCell = pCellMatrix->Get(iRow, iCol);
    pCell->Draw(ptTopLeft, bEdit, bMark, pDC);
  }
}
```

Summary

- We generated the code with the Application Wizard.

- The `Reference` class keeps track of references in the spreadsheet.

- The `Scanner` class group characters together into tokens, the least significant parts of the formula. The `Token` class represents the tokens.

- The `Parser` class parses the tokens given by the scanner and generates a syntax tree (an object of the `SyntaxTree` class).

- The `Cell` class handles a single class in the spreadsheet. A cell can hold a test, a value, or a formula. The `CellMatrix` and `TSetMatrix` methods handle the cells and the target sets of the spreadsheet.

- `CCalcDoc` manages the internal logic of the application. The application is always in the edit or mark state. In the edit state, a caret is visible. In the mark state, one or more cells are marked.

- `CCalcView` handles the input and display of the application. In this case, the view class handles the marking of cells by itself.

The Word Application

The Word application is a word processor program. It is capable of handling text on the character level. That is, unlike the Draw and Calc applications, single characters can have their own font, size, and style. The application also supports paragraph management with left, center, right, and justified alignment, cut and paste, load and save as well as print preview. The following screenshot depicts a classic example of the Word Application:

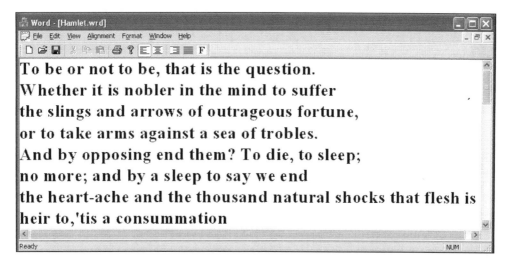

- In this application we have five classes to work with. Line is a small class that keeps track of the first and last characters as well as the height of a line in a paragraph.

- Position is also a small class, it handles a position in a document. It has two fields to keep track of the paragraph and character positions.

- A Word document consists of one or more *paragraphs*. A paragraph may span one or more lines. The Paragraph class handles one paragraph. It has methods for splitting and merging paragraphs.

- Page is another small class, it keeps track of the first and last paragraphs on a page. A paragraph is never split into two pages. If a paragraph does not fit on the rest of the page, it is moved in full to the next page.

- The CWordDoc class handles the internal logic of the application. It manages the paragraphs of the document. A document always has at least one paragraph. It also keeps track of the pages of the document.

- The CWordView class accepts input from the mouse and keyboard. It also displays text in the window client area.

We use the Application Wizard to generate the classes CWordApp, CMainFrame, CChildFrame, CWordDoc, CWordView, and CAboutDlg. We follow the default settings with the exception of the **File extension** and **File type long name**, let us set it to **Wrd** and **A Word Document**.

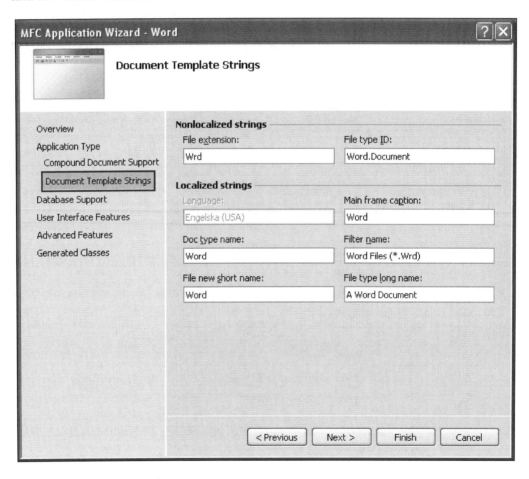

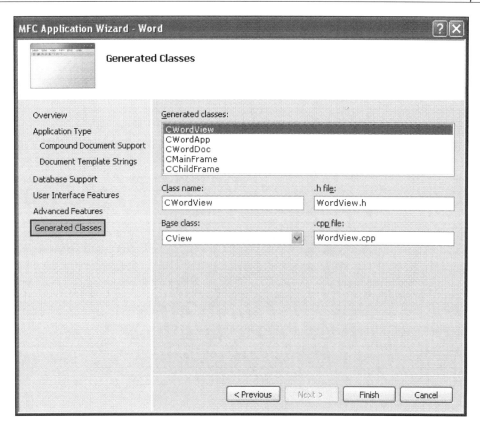

We will modify `CWordDoc` and `CWordView` as we develop the application. Similar to the earlier applications, we need to add some include lines to `Word.cpp`. Otherwise, we will not alter the classes.

Word.cpp

```
#include "stdafx.h"
#include "Word.h"
#include "MainFrm.h"
#include "ChildFrm.h"
#include "..\\Set.h"
#include "..\\Font.h"
#include "..\\Caret.h"
#include "Line.h"
#include "Position.h"
#include "Paragraph.h"
#include "Page.h"
#include "WordView.h"
#include "WordDoc.h"
```

The Resource

Here follows a summary of the added menus, accelerators, toolbar buttons, and strings.

Id	Menu Item	Toolbar Accelerator	String Table
ID_EDIT_CUT	Edit\Cut	Ctrl-X	Cut the selection and put it on the Clipboard\nCut
ID_EDIT_COPY	Edit\Copy	Ctrl-C	Copy the selection and put it on the Clipboard\nCopy
ID_EDIT_PASTE	Edit\Paste	Ctrl-V	Insert Clipboard contents\nPaste
ID_ALIGN_LEFT	Alignment\Left		Horizontal Alignment Left\n Left Alignment
ID_ALIGN_CENTER	Alignment\Center		Horizontal Alignment Center\n Center Alignment
ID_ALIGN_RIGHT	Alignment\Right		Horizontal Alignment Right\n Right Alignment
ID_ALIGN_JUSTIFIED	Alignment\Justified		Horizontal Alignment Justified \nJustified Alignment
ID_FORMAT_FONT	Format\Center		Choose a Font\nFont

The Line

As a paragraph can be split over several lines, the Line class keeps track of the first and last character index of the line as well as the height (in logical devices) of a line.

Line.h

```
class Line
{
  public:
    Line();
    Line(int iFirstChar, int iLastChar, int iHeight);
    int GetFirstChar() const {return m_iFirstChar;}
    int GetLastChar() const {return m_iLastChar;}
    int GetHeight() const {return m_iHeight;}
    void Serialize(CArchive& archive);
  private:
    int m_iFirstChar, m_iLastChar, m_iHeight;
};
```

`Line` needs a default constructor because its objects are stored in a `m_lineArray` — the paragraph class.

Line.cpp

```
Line::Line()
 :m_iFirstChar(0),
  m_iLastChar(0),
  m_iHeight(0)
{
  // Empty.
}
Line::Line(int iFirstChar, int iLastChar, int iHeight)
 :m_iFirstChar(iFirstChar),
  m_iLastChar(iLastChar),
  m_iHeight(iHeight)
{
  // Empty.
}
void Line::Serialize(CArchive& archive)
{
  if (archive.IsStoring())
  {
    archive >> m_iFirstChar >> m_iLastChar >> m_iHeight;
  }
  if (archive.IsLoading())
  {
    archive >> m_iFirstChar >> m_iLastChar >> m_iHeight;
  }
}
```

The Position

`Position` is a rather simple class that handles the position of a character in a paragraph. The fields `m_iParagraph` and `m_iChar` store the paragraph and character number of the position.

Position.h

```
class Position
{
  public:
    Position(int iParagraph, int iCharacter);
    Position(const Position& position);
    Position& operator=(const Position& position);

    BOOL operator==(const Position& position) const;
    BOOL operator!=(const Position& position) const;
    BOOL operator<(const Position& position) const;
```

```
    BOOL operator>(const Position& position) const;
    int Paragraph() const {return m_iParagraph;}
    int& Paragraph() {return m_iParagraph;}
    int Character() const {return m_iCharacter;}
    int& Character() {return m_iCharacter;}
  private:
    int m_iParagraph, m_iCharacter;
};
```

In the class definition, the methods `Paragraph` and `Character` are overloaded. The constant version returns the value itself. This implies that the fields of the class (`m_iParagraph` or `m_iCharacter`) cannot be changed and the methods are allowed to be constant. The second version returns a reference to the field. This implies that the value of the field can be changed by assigning the result of a call to the method. The following statement is correct if `pos` is not a constant object. In that case, the method referring a reference is called.

```
    pos.Character() = 0;
```

Assignment of function calls are only allowed when the function returns a reference. If `pos` is a constant object, the second method is called. As it returns a regular integer, the previous statement is not allowed. However, the following statement is allowed.

```
    int ichar = pos.Character();
```

Two positions are equal if they have the same paragraph and character. In order to test whether two positions are equal or not, we can call the equality operator. This position is less than the given one if the paragraph is less than the given one, or if the paragraphs are equal and the character is less the given one.

Position.cpp

```
BOOL Position::operator==(const Position& position) const
{
  return (m_iParagraph == position.m_iParagraph) &&
         (m_iCharacter == position.m_iCharacter);
}
BOOL Position::operator!=(const Position& position) const
{
  return !(*this == position);
}
```

```
BOOL Position::operator<(const Position& position) const
{
  return (m_iParagraph < position.m_iParagraph) ||
         ((m_iParagraph == position.m_iParagraph) &&
          (m_iCharacter < position.m_iCharacter));
}
```

The Paragraph

`Paragraph` is the class that handles one paragraph of the document. It has methods for adding characters, for cutting and pasting a block of text, as well as merging and splitting paragraphs.

The classes `IntArray`, `SizeArray`, `RectArray`, `FontArray`, `LineArray`, and `RectSet` are implemented with the template MFC class `CArray`, the utility classes `Font` and `Set` from Chapter 5 *Utility Classes* and `Line` from this chapter. `ParagraphPtrArray` holds an array of pointers to paragraphs. It is used by the document class.

A paragraph can be left, right, centered, and justified aligned, `m_eAlignment` holds the current setting. It has the enumeration type `Alignment`.

```
enum Alignment {ALIGN_LEFT, ALIGN_RIGHT, ALIGN_CENTER,
                ALIGN_JUSTIFIED};
```

Justified alignment means that the text is spread over the width of the page. In this cases the spaces of the line are increased in order to allow the text to fit the page. A paragraph cannot be vertical aligned.

The field `m_stText` holds the actual text of the paragraph. `m_fontArray` holds the font for every character in `m_stText`. The two arrays have the same size. When a new character is entered in the paragraph, it normally gets the font of the preceding character. However, if it is inserted at the beginning of the paragraph, it receives the font of the first character unless the paragraph is empty. If it is empty, `m_emptyFont` is used. See the method `AddChar` that follows this section.

The field `m_rectArray` is an array of rectangles, representing the graphical areas (in logical units) of the characters in the paragraph relative the upper left corner of the paragraph. The size of the array is one more than the size of `m_stText` and `m_fontArray` because the user may put the caret one step beyond the last character in the paragraph.

A paragraph can be divided into several lines. The field `m_lineArray` is an array of `Line` objects holding indexes of the first and last characters of the line as well as the height (in logical units) of the line. The method `Recalculate` is called every time the paragraph is modified. It generates the values of `m_lineArray` and `m_rectArray`.

The field m_yStartPos is the position (in logical units) of the paragraph's upper border relative to the beginning of the document; m_iHeight is the height of the paragraph (in logical units). If the paragraph is empty and marked, m_iEmptyAverageWidth is used to decide the size of the marked area.

The methods GetAlignment and SetAlignment return and set the alignment of the paragraph, respectively. GetLength returns the number of characters in the paragraph and GetHeight returns the paragraph's height in logical units. Note that we do not need a method returning the width of the paragraph because all paragraphs have the same width, given by the constant PAGE_WIDTH in the document class.

The document method UpdateParagraphAndPageArray traverses and re-calculates the start position of all paragraphs. It compares the new positions with the old ones by calling GetStartPos. If they differ, SetStartPos is called and the paragraph is repainted.

Paragraph.h

```cpp
typedef CArray<int> IntArray;
typedef CArray<CSize> SizeArray;
typedef CArray<CRect> RectArray;
typedef CArray<Font> FontArray;
typedef CArray<Line> LineArray;
typedef Set<CRect> RectSet;

enum Alignment {ALIGN_LEFT, ALIGN_RIGHT, ALIGN_CENTER,
                ALIGN_JUSTIFIED};
enum KeyboardState {KM_INSERT, KM_OVERWRITE};

class CWordDoc;

class Paragraph
{
  public:
    Paragraph();
    Paragraph(Font emptyFont, Alignment eAlignment);
    Paragraph(const Paragraph& paragraph);
    void Serialize(CArchive& archive);

    void Draw(CDC* pDC, int iFirstMarkedChar,
              int iLastMarkedChar) const;
    int GetLength() const {return m_stText.GetLength();}
    int GetHeight() const {return m_iHeight;}

    void SetStartPos(int yPos) {m_yStartPos = yPos;}
    int GetStartPos() const {return m_yStartPos;}

    void AddChar(int iChar, UINT cChar, Font* pNextFont,
                 KeyboardState eKeyboardState);
```

```
    void DeleteText(int iFirstIndex = 0, int iLastIndex = -1);
  Alignment GetAlignment() const {return m_eAlignment;}
  void SetAlignment(Alignment eAlignment)
                    {m_eAlignment = eAlignment;}
  Font GetFont(int iChar) const;
  void SetFont(Font font, int iFirstIndex = 0,
            int iLastindex = -1);
  void GetRepaintSet(RectSet& repaintSet,
                    int iFirstIndex = 0, int iLastIndex=-1);
  BOOL GetWord(int iEditChar, int& iFirstChar,
            int& iLastChar);
  int GetHomeChar(int iChar) const;
  int GetEndChar(int iChar) const;
  Paragraph* ExtractText(int iFirstIndex = 0,
                        int iLastIndex = -1) const;
  void Insert(int iChar, Paragraph* pInsertParagraph);
  void Append(Paragraph* pSecondParagraph);
  Paragraph* Split(int iChar);
  int PointToChar(CPoint ptMouse);
  CRect CharToRect(int iChar);
  CRect GetCaretRect(int iChar);
  CRect CharToLineRect(int iChar);
  void Recalculate(CDC* pDC, RectSet*
                    pRepaintSet = NULL);
  void ClearRectArray();
private:
  void GenerateSizeArray(SizeArray& sizeArray, CDC* pDC);
  void GenerateAscentArray(IntArray& ascentArray, CDC* pDC);
  void GenerateLineArray(SizeArray& sizeArray);
  void GenerateRectArray(SizeArray& sizeArray,
                        IntArray& ascentArray);
  void GenerateRepaintSet(RectArray& oldRectArray,
                        RectSet* pRepaintSet);
private:
  CString m_stText;
  Font m_emptyFont;
  int m_yStartPos, m_iEmptyAverageWidth, m_iHeight;
  Alignment m_eAlignment;
  FontArray m_fontArray;
  LineArray m_lineArray;
  RectArray m_rectArray;
};

typedef CArray<Paragraph*> ParagraphPtrArray;
```

`Paragraph` needs a default constructor because it is serialized. When the user hits the return key a new paragraph object is created. It is given the alignment of the preceding paragraph. It is given the font of the last character of the preceding paragraph or, if it is empty, its empty font. One or more new paragraphs can also be created by the paste command. In that case, they are given the same empty font and alignment as the copied paragraphs. The height (`m_iHeight`) of the paragraph is determined by `Recalculate`, which also determines `m_lineArray` and `m_rectArray`. The start position (`m_yStartPos`) is determined by `UpdatePageAndParagraphArray` in the document class.

Paragraph.cpp

A new paragraph has left alignment. Before it is displayed, a call to `Recalculate` will initialize its start position and height. The copy constructor initializes the fields of the class. It is called when a paragraph is copied or pasted. Note that the assignment operator is not defined on the MFC class `CArray`, which means `Copy` must be called instead.

```
Paragraph::Paragraph(const Paragraph &paragraph)
 :m_stText(paragraph.m_stText),
  m_yStartPos(paragraph.m_yStartPos),
  m_iHeight(paragraph.m_iHeight),
  m_eAlignment(paragraph.m_eAlignment),
  m_emptyFont(paragraph.m_emptyFont),
  m_iEmptyAverageWidth(paragraph.m_iEmptyAverageWidth)
{
  m_fontArray.Copy(paragraph.m_fontArray);
  m_lineArray.Copy(paragraph.m_lineArray);
  m_rectArray.Copy(paragraph.m_rectArray);
}
```

`Draw` is called by the view class every time it needs to be re-drawn, partly or completely. Some part of the document may be marked. If a particular paragraph is marked, the parameters `iFirstMarkedChar` and `iLastMarkedChar` hold the first and last position of the marked area of the paragraph. Note that it only applies to that paragraph; other paragraphs may also be marked. If the paragraph is completely unmarked, the `view` class calls this method with the values 0 and -1, respectively. `Draw` also needs a pointer to a device context in order to write the characters. If the character is located inside the marked area, we inverse the text and background colors.

```
void Paragraph::Draw(CDC* pDC, int iFirstMarkedChar,
                     int iLastMarkedChar)const
{
  CSize szUpperLeft(0, m_yStartPos);
  int iSize = m_stText.GetLength();
```

```
if (!m_stText.IsEmpty())
{
  for (int iChar = 0; iChar < iSize; ++iChar)
  {
    if ((iChar >= iFirstMarkedChar) &&
        (iChar < iLastMarkedChar))
    {
        pDC->SetTextColor(WHITE);
        pDC->SetBkColor(BLACK);
    }
    else
    {
        pDC->SetTextColor(BLACK);
        pDC->SetBkColor(WHITE);
    }
```

We select the font of the character. Every character of the paragraph has its own
font. We have to translate the size of the font from typographical points to logical
units (hundredths of millimeters). The characters are written relative to their top
left corner.

```
      CFont cFont;
      Font font = m_fontArray[iChar];
      cFont.CreateFontIndirect(font.PointsToMeters());
      CFont* pPrevFont = pDC->SelectObject(&cFont);
      CString stChar = m_stText.Mid(iChar, 1);
      pDC->DrawText(stChar, m_rectArray[iChar] + szUpperLeft,
                    TA_LEFT|TA_TOP);
      pDC->SelectObject(pPrevFont);
    }
}
```

If the text is empty and the paragraph is marked, we paint a black rectangle of
average width and height. If the paragraph is empty and unmarked, we do nothing.

```
else if ((iFirstMarkedChar != 0) && (iLastMarkedChar != 0))
{
  CPen pen(PS_SOLID, 0, BLACK);
  CBrush brush(BLACK);
  CPen* pOldPen = pDC->SelectObject(&pen);
  CBrush* pOldBrush = pDC->SelectObject(&brush);
  CRect rcChar = CRect(0, 0, m_iEmptyAverageWidth,
                       m_iHeight) + szUpperLeft;
  pDC->Rectangle(rcChar);
```

```
        pDC->SelectObject(pOldPen);
        pDC->SelectObject(pOldBrush);
    }
}
```

AddChar is called every time the user adds a character to this particular paragraph. Its first task is to decide the font of the new character. The document class has a field m_pNextFont, which is set to a new font when the user chooses a new font. If the user moves the caret or pastes a text block, m_pNextFont is set to null. The value of the document class field m_pNextFont is passed on to the parameter pNextFont.

If the pointer is not null, we simply set the font of the new character to that value. Otherwise, we have to examine the text. If the paragraph lacks text (m_stText. IsEmpty() returns true) we use the empty font (m_emptyFont). If it has a text, but the new character is to be inserted at the beginning of the paragraph (iIndex == 0), we use the font of the first character. Finally, if the paragraph has text and the new character is not to be inserted at the beginning of the paragraph we use the font of the preceding character.

In the document class, there is the field m_eKeyboardState. It holds the state of the keyboard, which can be either insert or overwrite. Its value is passed as the parameter eKeyboardState. The character and its font are inserted if the keyboard is in the insert state. If it is in the overwrite state, they are overwritten unless the add position is at the end of the text.

```
    void Paragraph::AddChar(int iIndex, UINT uNewChar,
                    Font* pNextFont, KeyboardState eKeyboardState)
{
    Font newFont;
    if (pNextFont != NULL)
    {
        newFont = *pNextFont;
    }
    else if (m_stText.IsEmpty())
    {
        newFont = m_emptyFont;
    }
    else if (iIndex == 0)
    {
        newFont = m_fontArray[0];
    }
    else
    {
        newFont = m_fontArray[iIndex - 1];
    }
    CRect emptyRect(0, 0, 0, 0);
```

If the keyboard is in the insert state, we insert the character at the given index. The `InsertAt` method works even if the input index is one step to the right of the text. In the overwrite state, we overwrite the character at the input index with `SetAt` if it is not at the end of the text. In that case, we use `AppendChar` and `Add` instead.

```
switch (eKeyboardState)
{
  case KM_INSERT:
    m_stText.Insert(iIndex, (TCHAR) uNewChar);
    m_fontArray.InsertAt(iIndex, newFont);
    m_rectArray.InsertAt(iIndex, emptyRect);
    break;
  case KM_OVERWRITE:
    if (iIndex < m_stText.GetLength())
    {
      m_stText.SetAt(iIndex, (TCHAR) uNewChar);
      m_fontArray.SetAt(iIndex, newFont);
      m_rectArray.SetAt(iIndex, emptyRect);
    }
    else
    {
      m_stText.AppendChar((TCHAR) uNewChar);
      m_fontArray.Add(newFont);
      m_rectArray.Add(emptyRect);
    }
    break;
  }
}
```

`GetRepaintSet` is called when a part of the text is to be marked or unmarked. It adds to `repaintSet` the rectangles (from `m_rectArray`) of the characters in question. The index parameters have default values 0 and -1. If the last index is -1, the rest of the paragraph's rectangles shall be included in the set. In that case, it is set to the length of the text.

```
void Paragraph::GetRepaintSet(RectSet& repaintSet, int
              iFirstIndex /*= 0*/, int iLastIndex /*= -1*/)
{
  if (iLastIndex == -1)
  {
    iLastIndex = m_stText.GetLength();
  }
  CSize szUpperLeft(0, m_yStartPos);
  for (int iIndex = iFirstIndex; iIndex < iLastIndex;
```

```
        ++iIndex)
    {
      CRect rcChar = m_rectArray[iIndex];
      repaintSet.Add(rcChar + szUpperLeft);
    }
  }
```

`DeleteText` is called when the one or more (possibly all) characters of the paragraph are to be deleted. The index parameters indicate the first and last index of the part of the text. They can be omitted in the call because they are default parameters. If the last parameter is omitted, the rest of the text will be deleted and the parameter is set to the length of the text.

If the whole of the text is to be deleted, we set the empty font (`m_emptyFont`) to the one in the first character. Note that this method is not called if the paragraph is empty. Also, note the difference between deleting the whole text of the paragraph and deleting the paragraph itself. In the first case, the paragraph is a part of the document. In the second case, the paragraph object is de-allocated and removed from the paragraph array (`m_paragraphArray`) of the document class and this method is not called.

```
void Paragraph::DeleteText(int iFirstIndex /* = 0 */,
                           int iLastIndex /* = -1 */)
{
  int iLength = m_stText.GetLength();
  if (iLastIndex == -1)
  {
    iLastIndex = iLength;
  }
  if ((iFirstIndex == 0) && (iLastIndex == iLength))
  {
    m_emptyFont = m_fontArray[0];
  }
  m_stText.Delete(iFirstIndex, iLastIndex - iFirstIndex);
  m_fontArray.RemoveAt(iFirstIndex, iLastIndex - iFirstIndex);
  m_rectArray.RemoveAt(iFirstIndex, iLastIndex - iFirstIndex);
}
```

`GetFont` is called by the document class in order to set the default font in the font dialog that appears when the user wants to set the font. If the text is empty, we return the empty font. If the `iCaretIndex` is zero, we return the font of the first character. Otherwise, we return the font of the position preceding that of the caret.

```
Font Paragraph::GetFont(int iCaretIndex) const
{
  if (m_stText.IsEmpty())
```

```
  {
    return m_emptyFont;
  }
  else if (iCaretIndex == 0)
  {
    return m_fontArray[0];
  }
  else
  {
    return m_fontArray[iCaretIndex - 1];
  }
}
```

SetFont is called when one or more characters of the paragraph are given a new font. Unlike GetFont above, SetFont may affect more than one character if the user has marked a portion of the text and then changed the font. Like GetRepaintSet above, the two index parameters are default parameters. If the second of them is omitted in the call, the rest of the text is updated with the new font.

```
void Paragraph::SetFont(Font newFont, int iFirstIndex/* =0 */,
                        int iLastIndex /* = -1 */)
{
  if (iLastIndex == -1)
  {
    iLastIndex = m_stText.GetLength();
  }
  for (int iIndex = iFirstIndex; iIndex < iLastIndex;
       ++iIndex)
  {
    m_fontArray[iIndex] = newFont;
  }
}
```

GetWord is called when the user double-clicks on a word. It starts at the character that is edited (iEditChar) and traverses to the left and to the right until it finds a space character or the beginning or end of the paragraph. The parameters iFirstChar and iLastChar are reference parameters, which implies that their values can be obtained by the calling method. Finally, the method returns true if it finds a word to be marked. That is, if the index of the first character is less than the index of the last one.

```
BOOL Paragraph::GetWord(int iEditChar, int& iFirstChar,
                        int& iLastChar)
{
  int iChar;
  for (iChar = iEditChar; (iChar >= 0) &&
       isalnum(m_stText[iChar]); --iChar)
  {
```

```
    // Empty.
  }
  iFirstChar = (iChar + 1);
  int iLength = m_stText.GetLength();
  for (iChar = iEditChar; (iChar < iLength) &&
       isalnum(m_stText[iChar]); ++iChar)
  {
    // Empty.
  }
  iLastChar = iChar;
  return (iFirstChar < iLastChar);
}
```

GetHomeChar is called when the user presses the *Home* key. First we find out which line the current index holds. Then it returns the index of the first key on that line. GetEndChar is defined in a similar manner.

```
int Paragraph::GetHomeChar(int iChar) const
{
  int iLines = (int) m_lineArray.GetSize();
  for (int iIndex = 0; iIndex < iLines; ++iIndex)
  {
    Line line = m_lineArray[iIndex];
    int iFirstChar = line.GetFirstChar();
    int iLastChar = line.GetLastChar();

    if (iChar <= (iLastChar + 1))
    {
      return iFirstChar;
    }
  }
```

As the loop above always will find the correct index (every character belongs to a line of the paragraph), this point of the code will never be reached. The check is for debugging purposes only.

```
  check(FALSE);
  return 0;
}
```

ExtractText is called when the user marks one portion of the document's text and then copies it. It creates a new paragraph and fills it with the text and fonts of the marked area. Like GetRepaintSet and SetFont above, its two indexes are default parameters. If the last index is -1, the rest of the text will be extracted. The text is easy to extract with CString's Mid method. Unfortunately, there is no similar method for arrays. So, we must traverse the font array and add fonts one by one to the new paragraph. We also need to set the empty font of the paragraph. If the first index of the extracted text is less than the length of the text, we set the font of the first marked character. Otherwise, we use the font of the character preceding the first one. If the text is empty, we just copy the empty font.

```
Paragraph* Paragraph::ExtractText(int iFirstIndex /* = 0 */,
                                  int iLastIndex /* = -1 */) const
{
  Paragraph* pNewParagraph;
  check_memory(pNewParagraph = new Paragraph(*this));
  if (!m_stText.IsEmpty())
  {
    int iLength = m_stText.GetLength();
    if (iLastIndex == -1)
    {
      iLastIndex = iLength;
    }
    pNewParagraph->m_stText =
        m_stText.Mid(iFirstIndex, iLastIndex - iFirstIndex);
    CRect rcEmpty(0, 0, 0, 0);
    for (int iChar = iFirstIndex; iChar < iLastIndex; ++iChar)
    {
      pNewParagraph->m_fontArray.Add(m_fontArray[iChar]);
      pNewParagraph->m_rectArray.Add(rcEmpty);
    }
```

The empty font is set to the one of the first index, unless the first index is at the end of the text; in that case, it is set to the font of the last character. If the text is empty, we just copy the empty font. A succeeding call to Recalculate will initialize the rest of the fields.

```
    if (iFirstIndex < iLength)
    {
      pNewParagraph->m_emptyFont = m_fontArray[iFirstIndex];
    }
    else
    {
      pNewParagraph->m_emptyFont = m_fontArray[iFirstIndex-1];
    }
  }
  else
  {
    pNewParagraph->m_emptyFont = m_emptyFont;
  }
  return pNewParagraph;
}
```

`Insert` inserts a character in the paragraph. Unless the paragraph to insert is empty, we just insert its text and font array. If it is empty, we do nothing. `Append` adds a paragraph to the end of the paragraph simply by calling `Insert`.

```
void Paragraph::Insert(int iChar, Paragraph* pInsertParagraph)
{
   int iInsertLength = pInsertParagraph->GetLength();

   if (iInsertLength > 0)
   {
     m_stText.Insert(iChar, pInsertParagraph->m_stText);
     m_fontArray.InsertAt(iChar,
                        &pInsertParagraph->m_fontArray);

     CRect rcEmpty(0, 0, 0, 0);
     m_rectArray.InsertAt(iChar, rcEmpty, iInsertLength);
   }
}

void Paragraph::Append(Paragraph* pAppendParagraph)
{
   Insert(GetLength(), pAppendParagraph);
}
```

When the user presses the return key inside a paragraph, it is split into two parts. `Split` returns a new paragraph containing the second half of the split paragraph and deletes it from the paragraph.

```
Paragraph* Paragraph::Split(int iChar)
{
   Paragraph* pNewParagraph;
   check_memory(pNewParagraph = new Paragraph());

   pNewParagraph->m_stText = m_stText.Mid(iChar);
   m_stText = m_stText.Left(iChar);

   pNewParagraph->m_fontArray.Copy(m_fontArray);
   pNewParagraph->m_fontArray.RemoveAt(0, iChar);
   m_fontArray.SetSize(iChar);
   pNewParagraph->m_eAlignment = m_eAlignment;
   pNewParagraph->m_emptyFont = GetFont(iChar);
   return pNewParagraph;
}
```

When the user clicks the mouse, we have to decide which paragraph and character they clicked at. The mouse position in device units is caught by the view classes, converted to logical units, and sent to the document class. The document class first finds the paragraph in question and then finally calls `PointToChar` in order to find the position in the paragraph.

If the text is empty, we just return index 0. Otherwise, we traverse the lines of the paragraph one by one in order to find the correct line. Then we traverse the line in order to find the correct character. To start with, we subtract the start position of the paragraph from the mouse position, which origionally is relative to the beginning of the document.

```
int Paragraph::PointToChar(CPoint ptMouse)
{
  if (m_stText.IsEmpty())
  {
    return 0;
  }

  ptMouse.y -= m_yStartPos;
```

If the document is large enough, it will be divided into several pages. In that case, there will be a check that each page begins with a whole paragraph. This might give the result that the user clicks at the end of a page (or at the end of the whole document) where there is no paragraph. If that happens, the correct character will be the one above the mouse click. That is why we have to make sure that the position of the mouse does not exceed the height of the paragraph.

```
ptMouse.y = min(ptMouse.y, m_iHeight - 1);
int iLines = (int) m_lineArray.GetSize();
int iParagraphHeight = 0;
for (int iLine = 0; iLine < iLines; ++iLine)
{
  Line line = m_lineArray[iLine];
  int iLineHeight = line.GetHeight();
  iParagraphHeight += iLineHeight;
```

When we find the right line, the search continues for the right character. We cannot fail in finding the right line. Therefore, there is a check watch at the end of the method. When we look for the correct character, we first check if the mouse position is to the left of the first character of the line. In that case, we return the first index of the first character of the line. If instead it is to the right of the last character of the line, we return the index of the character to the right of the last character.

```
if (ptMouse.y < iParagraphHeight)
{
  int iFirstChar = line.GetFirstChar();
  int iLastChar = line.GetLastChar();
  CRect rcFirstChar = m_rectArray[iFirstChar];
  CRect rcLastChar = m_rectArray[iLastChar];
  if (ptMouse.x <= rcFirstChar.left)
  {
    return iFirstChar;
  }
```

```
      else if (ptMouse.x >= rcLastChar.right)
      {
        return (iLastChar + 1);
      }
```

If none of the above cases applied, we traverse through the line until we find the correct character. Then we have to decide whether the mouse cursor hits the left or right part of the character. If the cursor hits the left part we return the index of the character. If it hits the right part, we return the index of the next character. This will work even if the character is the last one in the paragraph since there is an extra rectangle in m_rectArray for this case, that the user places the carat to the right of the last character in the paragraph.

We cannot fail in finding the correct character once we have found the correct line. Therefore, we have a check watch at the end of the character search for debugging purposes only.

```
        else
        {
          for (int iChar = iFirstChar; iChar <= iLastChar;
               ++iChar)
          {
            CRect rcChar = m_rectArray[iChar];
            if (ptMouse.x < rcChar.right)
            {
              int cxLeft = ptMouse.x - rcChar.left;
              int cxRight = rcChar.right - ptMouse.x;
              if (cxLeft < cxRight)
              {
                return iChar;
              }
              else
              {
                return iChar + 1;
              }
            }
          }
          check(FALSE);
          return 0;
        }
      }
    }
  check(FALSE);
  return 0;
}
```

`CharToRect` returns the rectangle of the character at the given index in the paragraph. We have two special cases. First, the paragraph may be empty. In that case, we use the average size of the paragraph's empty font.

```
CRect Paragraph::CharToRect(int iChar)
{
   CSize szUpperLeft(0, m_yStartPos);
   if (m_stText.IsEmpty())
   {
      return szUpperLeft + CRect(0, 0, m_iEmptyAverageWidth,
                                 m_iHeight);
   }
```

Second, the given index may be outside the text. That is one step to the right of the last character. In that case, we return a rectangle holding the dimensions of the characters beyond the text using the size of the last character. Otherwise, we just return the rectangle of the given character.

```
   else if (iChar == m_stText.GetLength())
   {
      CRect rcChar = m_rectArray[iChar - 1];
      CRect rcCaret(rcChar.right, rcChar.top, rcChar.right +
                    rcChar.Width(), rcChar.bottom);
      return szUpperLeft + rcCaret;
   }
   else
   {
      return szUpperLeft + m_rectArray[iChar];
   }
}
```

The method `GetCaretRect` returns the rectangle of the given character. If the text is empty, we return a caret rectangle based on the empty font. If the text is non-empty but the given character is at index zero, we return the caret rectangle of the first character. If the character is a "home character"; that is, if it is the first on its line, then we return its rectangle. Otherwise, we find the preceding character and return a caret rectangle based on its size.

```
CRect Paragraph::GetCaretRect(int iChar)
{
   CSize szUpperLeft(0, m_yStartPos);
   int iSize = m_stText.GetLength();
   if (iSize == 0)
   {
      return szUpperLeft + CRect(0, 0, m_iEmptyAverageWidth,
                                 m_iHeight);
   }
```

```
     else if (iChar == 0)
     {
       return szUpperLeft + m_rectArray[0];
     }
     else if (isHomeChar(iChar))
     {
       CRect rcChar = m_rectArray[iChar];
       CRect rcCaret(rcChar.left, rcChar.top,
                     rcChar.right, rcChar.bottom);
       return szUpperLeft + rcCaret;
     }
     else
     {
       CRect rcChar = m_rectArray[iChar - 1];
       CRect rcCaret(rcChar.right, rcChar.top, rcChar.right +
                     rcChar.Width(), rcChar.bottom);
       return szUpperLeft + rcCaret;
     }
   }
```

When the user scrolls up and down through the document with the up and down arrows, we need to know the size of the current line. The method `CharToLineRect` returns a rectangle holding the dimensions of the line. Like `CharToRect` above, we cannot fail in finding the correct line, so we have a check watch at the end of the method.

```
CRect Paragraph::CharToLineRect(int iChar)
{
  int iParagraphHeight = 0;
  int iLines = (int) m_lineArray.GetSize();
  for (int iIndex = 0; iIndex < iLines; ++iIndex)
  {
    Line line = m_lineArray[iIndex];
    int iLastChar = line.GetLastChar();
    int iLineHeight = line.GetHeight();
    if (iChar <= (iLastChar + 1))
    {
      return CRect(0, m_yStartPos + iParagraphHeight,
                   PAGE_WIDTH, m_yStartPos + iParagraphHeight
                   + iLineHeight);
    }
    iParagraphHeight += iLineHeight;
  }
  check(FALSE);
  return CRect();
}
```

The `Recalculate` method is called in order to recalculate the rectangle
(`m_rectArray`) and line (`m_lineArray`) arrays every time one or more characters
have be added or removed, or when the font or alignment have been changed.
The `Recalculate` method can be regarded as a more complicated version of the
`GenerateCaretIndex` method of the Draw and Calc applications. It is rather
complex, and its functionality is divied into the rest of the methods of this class.

```
void Paragraph::Recalculate(CDC* pDC, RectSet* pRepaintSet
                                /* = NULL */)
{
  RectArray oldRectArray;
  if (pRepaintSet != NULL)
  {
    oldRectArray.Copy(m_rectArray);
  }
  m_iHeight = 0;
  m_lineArray.RemoveAll();
  m_rectArray.RemoveAll();
```

If the paragraph is empty, we find the height and average width of a character of the
empty font.

```
  if (m_stText.IsEmpty())
  {
    CFont cFont;
    cFont.CreateFontIndirect(m_emptyFont.PointsToMeters());
    CFont* pPrevFont = pDC->SelectObject(&cFont);
    TEXTMETRIC textMetric;
    pDC->GetTextMetrics(&textMetric);
    pDC->SelectObject(pPrevFont);
    m_iHeight = textMetric.tmHeight;
    m_iEmptyAverageWidth = textMetric.tmAveCharWidth;
    Line line(0, 0, 0);
    m_lineArray.Add(line);
  }
```

If the paragraph is not empty, we generate arrays of size and ascent lines for every
character as well as the line and rectangle array by calling `GenerateSizeArray`,
`GenerateAscentArray`, `GenerateLineArray`, and `GenerateRectArray`.

```
  else
  {
    SizeArray sizeArray;
    GenerateSizeArray(sizeArray, pDC);
    IntArray ascentArray;
    GenerateAscentArray(ascentArray, pDC);
    GenerateLineArray(sizeArray);
    GenerateRectArray(sizeArray, ascentArray);
  }
```

Finally, if the pointer to the re-paint set is not null, we also call
`GenerateRepaintSet`.

```
if (pRepaintSet != NULL)
{
  GenerateRepaintSet(oldRectArray, pRepaintSet);
}
}
```

The `ClearRectArray` method sets each rectangle of the rectangle array of the
empty rectangle.

```
void Paragraph::ClearRectArray()
{
  CRect emptyRect(0, 0, 0, 0);
  int iSize = (int) m_rectArray.GetSize();

  for (int iIndex = 0; iIndex < iSize; ++iIndex)
  {
    m_rectArray[iIndex] = emptyRect;
  }
}
```

The `GenerateSizeArray` method fills the given array with the size (width and
height) of each character in the paragraph (in logical units). For each character, we
load the device context with the font. Note that we need to translate the font from
typographical points at hundredths of millimeters by calling `PointToMeters`.

```
void Paragraph::GenerateSizeArray(SizeArray& sizeArray,
                                  CDC* pDC)
{
  int iLength = m_stText.GetLength();
  for (int iChar = 0; iChar < iLength; ++iChar)
  {
    CFont cFont;
    Font font = m_fontArray[iChar];
    cFont.CreateFontIndirect(font.PointsToMeters());
    CFont* pPrevFont = pDC->SelectObject(&cFont);

    CString stChar = m_stText.Mid(iChar, 1);
    CSize szChar = pDC->GetTextExtent(stChar);
```

Experience has shown that characters written in italic style tend to request slightly more space than `GetTextExtent` returns, so we increase the size by 20 percent. Plain text also tends to need a little bit more space, thats why we increase the size by 10 percent.

```
        szChar.cx = (int) ((font.IsItalic() ? 1.2 : 1.1) *
                          szChar.cx);
        szChar.cy = (int) ((font.IsItalic() ? 1.2 : 1.1) *
                          szChar.cy);
        sizeArray.Add(szChar);
        pDC->SelectObject(pPrevFont);
    }
}
```

The ascent line is separating the upper and lower part of the versals.

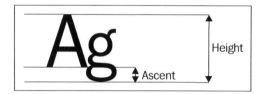

The `GenerateAscentArray` method fills the given array with the ascent line (the distance between the ascent line and the bottom of the character) of every character in the paragraph (in logical units). For every character, we load the device context with the font. Note that we have to translate the font from typographical points at hundredths of millimeters by calling `PointToMeters`.

```
    void Paragraph::GenerateAscentArray(IntArray& ascentArray,
                                        CDC* pDC)
    {
      int iSize = (int) m_fontArray.GetSize();
      for (int iIndex = 0; iIndex < iSize; ++iIndex)
      {
        CFont cFont;
        Font font = m_fontArray[iIndex];
        cFont.CreateFontIndirect(font.PointsToMeters());
        CFont* pPrevFont = pDC->SelectObject(&cFont);

        TEXTMETRIC textMetric;
        pDC->GetTextMetrics(&textMetric);
        pDC->SelectObject(pPrevFont);

        ascentArray.Add(textMetric.tmAscent);
      }
    }
```

The `GenerateLineArray` method generates the line array. That is, for each line we find the indexes of its first and last characters as well as the height of the line (in logical units). We have to decide how many words each line can hold. We traverse through the text, calculate the size of each word. When the next word does not fit on the line, we start a new line and save the index of the first and last character on the line as well as the height of the line which is the height of its highest character.

```
void Paragraph::GenerateLineArray(SizeArray& sizeArray)
{
  BOOL bSpace = FALSE;
  int iSpaceIndex = 0, iStartIndex = 0, iLineWidth = 0,
      iLineHeight = 0, iSpaceLineHeight = 0;
  int iSize = m_stText.GetLength(), iIndex = 0;
  while (iIndex < iSize)
  {
    CSize szChar = sizeArray[iIndex];
    iLineHeight = max(iLineHeight, szChar.cy);
```

As we try to avoid splitting words over lines, but rather to break the line after the last full word, we save the position of the last space. We will need it when we reach the end of the line.

The latest space is a suitable point to put a line break. We save the index to use it when we reach the end of the line.

```
    if (m_stText[iIndex] == TEXT(' '))
    {
      bSpace = TRUE;
      iSpaceIndex = iIndex;
      iSpaceLineHeight = iLineHeight;
    }
    iLineWidth += szChar.cx;
```

When there is no more room for the next characters, we insert a line break and look up the latest space. If there is one, we add the start index (`iStartIndex`) of the index before the latest space together with the line height of the line array (`m_lineArray`). We then set the new start index to the index after the latest space. Note that the index of the space—breaking the line—is not part of any line in `m_lineArray`. Each line starts and ends with the indexes of the first and last non-blank character.

```
    if (iLineWidth > PAGE_WIDTH)
    {
      if (bSpace)
      {
        Line line(iStartIndex, iSpaceIndex - 1, ilineHeight);
```

```
                        iSpaceLineHeight);
        m_lineArray.Add(line);

        iStartIndex = iSpaceIndex + 1;
        iLineWidth = 0;
        iLineHeight = 0;

        bSpace = FALSE;
        iIndex = iStartIndex;
    }
```

If there is no latest space, the word is wider than the page. In that case, we check that the word holds at least one character. If so, we just split the word, so the next line starts with the first character that does not fit on the line.

```
    else if (iStartIndex < iIndex)
    {
        Line line(iStartIndex, iIndex - 1, iLineHeight);
                    iSpaceLineHeight);
        m_lineArray.Add(line);

        iStartIndex = iIndex;
        iLineWidth = 0;
        iLineHeight = 0;
    }
```

In the rare event that there is a character wider than the page, we add it to the line and set the next start index to the next index.

```
    else
    {
        Line line(iStartIndex, iIndex,
                    iSpaceLineHeight);
        m_lineArray.Add(line);

        ++iIndex;
        iStartIndex = iIndex;
        iLineWidth = 0;
        iLineHeight = 0;
    }
    }
    else
    {
        ++iIndex;
    }
}
if (iStartIndex < iSize)
{
```

```
        Line line(iStartIndex, iSize - 1, iLineHeight);
        m_lineArray.Add(line);
    }
}
```

The method `GenerateRectArray` generates the rectangle array. With the size, ascent, and line arrays, we calculate the rectangle of each character. First, we traverse the lines of the paragraph, one by one.

```
void Paragraph::GenerateRectArray(SizeArray& sizeArray,
                                    IntArray& ascentArray)
{
    int iLines = (int) m_lineArray.GetSize();
    Line line = m_lineArray[0];
    int iFirstChar = line.GetFirstChar();
    int iLastChar = line.GetLastChar();

    for (int iLineIndex = 0; iLineIndex < iLines; ++iLineIndex)
    {
```

For each line, we look up its first and last character. Then we need to find the height, ascent line, and width of the line.

```
    int iLineWidth = 0, iLineHeight = 0, iLineAscent = 0;
    for (int iIndex = iFirstChar; iIndex <= iLastChar;
         ++iIndex)
    {
        TCHAR cChar = m_stText[iIndex];
        CSize szChar = sizeArray[iIndex];
```

The width of the line is the sum of the width of all characters. If the character is a space and the paragraph has justified alignment, we do not include its width into the total width because later on we need the width of the line without the spaces.

```
        if (!((cChar==TEXT(' ')) &&
              (m_eAlignment==ALIGN_JUSTIFIED)))
        {
            iLineWidth += szChar.cx;
        }
```

The height of the line is the height of its highest character. The accent line of the line is the ascent line of the character with the highest ascent.

```
        iLineHeight = max(iLineHeight, szChar.cy);
        iLineAscent = max(iLineAscent, ascentArray[iIndex]);
    }
```

We find the start position of the line by considering the alignment of the paragraph and the width of the line.

```
int xStartPos = 0, iSpaceWidth = 0;
switch (m_eAlignment)
{
```

In left alignment, the line starts at the left side. In center and right alignment, we compute the start position by comparing the width of the line with the width of the page.

```
case ALIGN_LEFT:
  xStartPos = 0;
  break;
case ALIGN_CENTER:
  xStartPos = (PAGE_WIDTH - iLineWidth) / 2;
  break;
case ALIGN_RIGHT:
  xStartPos = PAGE_WIDTH - iLineWidth;
  break;
```

In justified alignment, we need to find the number of spaces on the line and calculate the width of each space in order for the line to completely fill the width of the page. If there are no spaces in the line, the effect will be equivalent to left alignment because the start x position is at the left side of the page and the only word of the line will be written to the left.

```
case ALIGN_JUSTIFIED:
  xStartPos = 0;
  CString stTemp = m_stText.Mid(iFirstChar, iLastChar -
                                iFirstChar + 1);
  int iSpaces = stTemp.Remove(TEXT(' '));
  if (iSpaces > 0)
  {
      iSpaceWidth = (PAGE_WIDTH - iLineWidth) / iSpaces;
  }
  break;
}
```

Finally, we calculate the rectangle for each character. We traverse the line and with the sizes of the characters and the height and ascent line of the line we find each rectangle. We begin by the start position we found above and increase the position for each character on the line.

```
int xLeftPos = xStartPos,iWidth = 0,yTopPos = 0,iHeight=0;
for (int iIndex = iFirstChar; iIndex <= iLastChar;
```

```
        ++iIndex)
   {
     CSize szChar = sizeArray[iIndex];
     int iAscent = ascentArray[iIndex];
```

If the paragraph has justified alignment and the character is a space, we use the space width calculated as above.

```
     if ((m_stText[iIndex] == TEXT(' ')) &&
         (m_eAlignment == ALIGN_JUSTIFIED))
     {
       iWidth = iSpaceWidth;
     }
     else
     {
       iWidth = szChar.cx;
     }
     yTopPos = m_iHeight + iLineAscent - iAscent;
     iHeight = szChar.cy;
     CRect rcChar(xLeftPos, yTopPos, xLeftPos + iWidth,
                 yTopPos + iHeight);
     m_rectArray.Add(rcChar);
     xLeftPos += iWidth;
   }
```

If we are not on the last line of the paragraph, we add a rectangle for the space thus dividing the line with the next one, if there is one.

```
     if (iLineIndex < (iLines - 1))
     {
       Line line = m_lineArray[iLineIndex + 1];
       iFirstChar = line.GetFirstChar();
       if (iFirstChar > (iLastChar + 1))
       {
         CSize szChar = sizeArray[iLastChar + 1];
         CRect rcChar(xLeftPos, yTopPos, xLeftPos + szChar.cx,
                     yTopPos + iHeight);
         m_rectArray.Add(rcChar);
       }
       iLastChar = line.GetLastChar();
     }
```

Finally, the height of the paragraph is increased with the height of the line.

```
     m_iHeight += iLineHeight;
   }
 }
```

When a paragraph has been altered, we have to repaint the altered area of the client area. However, we do not want to repaint the whole paragraph, just the characters that have been altered. The GenerateRepaintSet method compares the original rectangle array with the newly generated one and fills the re-paint set with every rectangle that differs (both the old and new rectangle are added).

Remember that the position of each character is relative to its own paragraph, so we start by defining the top left corner of the paragraph relative to the document. Then we traverse the characters and add those that have been given new dimensions.

```
void Paragraph::GenerateRepaintSet(RectArray& oldRectArray,
                                   RectSet* pRepaintSet)
{
  CSize szUpperLeft(0, m_yStartPos);
  int iSize = (int) m_rectArray.GetSize();
  for (int iIndex = 0; iIndex < iSize; ++iIndex)
  {
    CRect rcOldChar = oldRectArray[iIndex];
    CRect rcNewChar = m_rectArray[iIndex];
    if (rcOldChar != rcNewChar)
    {
      if (!rcOldChar.IsRectEmpty())
      {
        pRepaintSet->Add(rcOldChar + szUpperLeft);
      }
      if (!rcNewChar.IsRectEmpty())
      {
        pRepaintSet->Add(rcNewChar + szUpperLeft);
      }
    }
  }
}
```

If the paragraph is non-empty, we add, for each line, the area to the left and to the right of the line.

```
if (!m_stText.IsEmpty())
{
  int iTotalHeight = 0;
  int iLines = (int) m_lineArray.GetSize();
```

We traverse the lines and for each line find the old and new area. We need the height and the position of the first character of the line. So we create and add the left area shown as follows:

```
for (int iLineIndex = 0; iLineIndex < iLines;
     ++iLineIndex)
{
  Line line = m_lineArray[iLineIndex];
  int iFirstChar = line.GetFirstChar();
```

```
                int iHeight = line.GetHeight();
                CRect rcFirstChar = m_rectArray[iFirstChar];
                CRect rcLeftBlock(0, iTotalHeight, rcFirstChar.left,
                               iTotalHeight + iHeight);
                if (!rcLeftBlock.IsRectEmpty())
                {
                  pRepaintSet->Add(rcLeftBlock + szUpperLeft);
                }
```

Finally, we look up at the position of the first character of the line. Then we create and add the right area.

```
                int iLastChar = line.GetLastChar();
                CRect rcLastChar = m_rectArray[iLastChar];
                CRect rcRightBlock(rcLastChar.right, iTotalHeight,
                               PAGE_WIDTH, iTotalHeight + iHeight);
                if (!rcRightBlock.IsRectEmpty())
                {
                  pRepaintSet->Add(rcRightBlock + szUpperLeft);
                }
                iTotalHeight += iHeight;
            }
        }
```

If the paragraph is empty, we just create and add an area holding the whole paragraph. Remember that even though the paragraph is empty, it still holds a height.

```
        else
        {
          CRect rcTotalBlock(0, 0, PAGE_WIDTH, m_iHeight);
          pRepaintSet->Add(rcTotalBlock + szUpperLeft);
        }
    }
```

The Page

A document can be divided into several pages. A paragraph is never split over two pages. If there is not enough room for it in the rest of the page, it is moved in full to the next page. Page is a small class. Its task is to keep track of the first and last paragraph of a page.

Page.h

```
    class Page
    {
      public:
        Page();
        Page(int iFirstParagraph, int iLastParagraph);
```

```
    int GetFirstParagraph() const {return m_iFirstParagraph;}
    int GetLastParagraph() const {return m_iLastParagraph;}

    void Serialize(CArchive& archive);
  private:
    int m_iFirstParagraph, m_iLastParagraph;
};
```

Page needs a default constructor beacuse its objects are stored in m_pageArray in the document class.

Page.cpp

```
Page::Page()
 :m_iFirstParagraph(0),
  m_iLastParagraph(0)
{
  // Empty.
}
Page::Page(int iFirstParagraph, int iLastParagraph)
 :m_iFirstParagraph(iFirstParagraph),
  m_iLastParagraph(iLastParagraph)
{
  // Empty.
}
void Page::Serialize(CArchive& archive)
{
  if (archive.IsStoring())
  {
    archive >> m_iFirstParagraph >> m_iLastParagraph;
  }

  if (archive.IsLoading())
  {
    archive >> m_iFirstParagraph >> m_iLastParagraph;
  }
}
```

The Document Class

The document class CWordDoc handles the pages and paragraphs of the document. It receives input from the view class CWordView, to which it also sends notification of repainting.

The unit of choice in this application is hundredths of millimeters (MM_HIMETRIC). As a letter 216 times 297 millimeter, its total width and height are 21,600 and 27,900 logical units. The paper has, however, a margin of 25 millimeters, or 2,500 logical units, which implies that the actual width and height are the dimensions of the pages subtracted from the margins. The constants PAGE_WIDTH and PAGE_HEIGHT hold those values.

The application can be in *edit* or the *mark* state and the keyboard can be in the *insert* or *overwrite* state. The fields m_eWordState and m_eKeyboardState keep track of the states. They have the enumeration types WordState and KeyboardState. As KeyboardState is used by the paragraph class, it is defined in Paragraph.h

```
enum WordState {WS_EDIT, WS_MARK};
enum KeyboardState {KM_INSERT, KM_OVERWRITE};
```

The field m_caret is an object of the Caret class from the *Utility Classes* chapter. It handles the caret of this application. The field m_pView is a pointer to the view object in focus. OnSetFocus and OnKillFocus handle the pointer. They also notify the caret object (m_caret) about a change of view.

There are two paragraph arrays. m_paragraphArray holds all the paragraphs of the document, and m_copyArray holds the copied paragraphs. When the application is in the edit state (m_eWordState == WS_EDIT), m_psEdit keeps track of the caret. When it is in the mark state (m_eWordState == WS_MARK), m_psFirstMark and m_iLastMark keep track of the first and last positions of the marked area. The position may refer to the same or different paragraphs. However, they cannot refer to the same character in the same paragraph. In that case, the word status will be set to edit, and m_psEdit will be set to the first position.

The field m_pageArray is an array of Page objects holding the index of the first and last paragraph of each page. It has the type PageArray, which is an implementation of the MFC class CArray with Page objects.

The user may choose to change the font with a font dialog. In that case, the new font is saved in m_pNextFont.

Several messages from the menu bar are routed to this class: the alignment messages, the cut, copy, and paste messages and the font message.

WordDoc.h

```
static const int PAGE_TOTALWIDTH = 21600;
static const int PAGE_TOTALHEIGHT = 27900;
static const int PAGE_MARGIN = 2500;

static const int PAGE_WIDTH = (PAGE_TOTALWIDTH-2*PAGE_MARGIN);
static const int PAGE_HEIGHT=(PAGE_TOTALHEIGHT-2*PAGE_MARGIN);
```

```
enum WordState {WS_EDIT, WS_MARK};
typedef CArray<Page> PageArray;
class CWordDoc : public CDocument
{
  private:
    DECLARE_DYNCREATE(CWordDoc)
    DECLARE_MESSAGE_MAP()
    CWordDoc();
  public:
    virtual ~CWordDoc();

  public:
    void Serialize(CArchive& archive);
    virtual BOOL OnNewDocument();
    ParagraphPtrArray* GetParagraphArray()
                      {return &m_paragraphArray;}
    void KeyDown(UINT uChar, CDC* pDC);
    void ShiftKeyDown(UINT uChar, CDC* pDC);
  private:
    void EnsureEditStatus();
    void EnsureMarkStatus();

    void LeftArrowKey();
    void ShiftLeftArrowKey();

    void RightArrowKey();
    void ShiftRightArrowKey();

    void UpArrowKey();
    void ShiftUpArrowKey();

    void DownArrowKey();
    void ShiftDownArrowKey();

    void PageUpKey(CDC* pDC);
    void ShiftPageUpKey(CDC* pDC);
    void PageDownKey(CDC* pDC);
    void ShiftPageDownKey(CDC* pDC);

    void HomeKey();
    void ShiftHomeKey();

    void EndKey();
    void ShiftEndKey();

    void DeleteKey(CDC* pDC);
    void BackspaceKey(CDC* pDC);
    void ReturnKey(CDC* pDC);
    void InsertKey();
  public:
```

```
      void CharDown(UINT uChar, CDC* pDC);
      int GetPageNum() const
                      {return (int) m_pageArray.GetSize();}
   private:
      int PointToParagraph(const CPoint& ptMouse) const;
   public:
      Position PointToChar(const CPoint& ptMouse) const;

      void MouseDown(const CPoint& ptMouse);
      void MouseDrag(const CPoint& ptMouse);
      void MouseUp();
      void DoubleClick();

      void MakeVisible();
      void UpdateCaret();

      void GetRepaintSet(RectSet& repaintSet, Position
                      psFirst, Position psLast);
      void DeleteText(RectSet& repaintSet, CDC* pDC, Position
                  psFirst, Position psLast);

      void UpdateParagraphAndPageArray();

      afx_msg void OnUpdateAlignLeft(CCmdUI *pCmdUI);
      afx_msg void OnAlignLeft();

      afx_msg void OnUpdateAlignCenter(CCmdUI *pCmdUI);
      afx_msg void OnAlignRight();

      afx_msg void OnUpdateAlignRight(CCmdUI *pCmdUI);
      afx_msg void OnAlignCenter();

      afx_msg void OnUpdateAlignJustifed(CCmdUI *pCmdUI);
      afx_msg void OnAlignJustified();

      BOOL IsAlignment(Alignment eAlignment) const;
      void SetAlignment(Alignment eAlignment);

      afx_msg void OnUpdateCopy(CCmdUI *pCmdUI);
      void ClearCopyArray();
      afx_msg void OnCopy();

      afx_msg void OnUpdateCut(CCmdUI *pCmdUI);
      afx_msg void OnCut();

      afx_msg void OnUpdatePaste(CCmdUI *pCmdUI);
      afx_msg void OnPaste();

      Font GetFont() const;
      afx_msg void OnFont();

      void OnSetFocus(CWordView* pView)
          {m_pView = pView; m_caret.OnSetFocus(pView);}
```

```
    void OnKillFocus()
        {m_pView = NULL; m_caret.OnKillFocus();}
    WordState GetWordStatus() {return m_eWordState;}
    Position GetFirstMarked() {return m_psFirstMark;}
    Position GetLastMarked() {return m_psLastMark;}
  private:
    WordState m_eWordState;
    KeyboardState m_eKeyboardState;
    CWordView* m_pView;
    Caret m_caret;
    ParagraphPtrArray m_paragraphArray, m_copyArray;
    PageArray m_pageArray;
    Position m_psEdit, m_psFirstMark, m_psLastMark;
    Font *m_pNextFont;
};
```

CWordDoc must have a default constructor because it will be created dynamically by
the Application Framework.

CWordDoc.cpp

```
CWordDoc::CWordDoc()
 :m_eKeyboardState(KM_INSERT),
  m_eWordState(WS_EDIT),
  m_psEdit(0, 0),
  m_psFirstMark(0, 0),
  m_psLastMark(0, 0),
  m_pNextFont(NULL)
{
  // Empty.
}
```

The destructor deallocates the memory associated with the paragraph and copy
arrays. It also deallocates the memory associated with the next font. This operation is
safe even if the pointer points to null, because the delete operator does nothing in
that case.

```
CWordDoc::~CWordDoc()
{
  int iParagraphs = (int) m_paragraphArray.GetSize();
  for (int iParagraph = 0; iParagraph < iParagraphs;
      ++iParagraph)
  {
    delete m_paragraphArray[iParagraph];
  }
  ClearCopyArray();
  delete m_pNextFont;
}
```

The method `OnNewDocument` does the work of a constructor. It creates and initializes the first paragraph with the standard system font and left alignment. The paragraph is recalculated and added to the paragraph array. The first page is also defined. It holds the new paragraph as its first and last paragraph (index 0). Note that this method is only called when the users create a new document, not when they open an existing document.

```
BOOL CWordDoc::OnNewDocument()
{
  Font defaultFont;
  Paragraph* pNewParagraph;
  check_memory(pNewParagraph =
              new Paragraph(defaultFont, ALIGN_LEFT));

  CClientDC dc(m_pView);
  m_pView->OnPrepareDC(&dc);

  pNewParagraph->Recalculate(&dc);
  m_paragraphArray.Add(pNewParagraph);
  Page page(0, 0);
  m_pageArray.Add(page);
  return CDocument::OnNewDocument();
}
```

The `Serialize` method reads from and writes to the file connected to the parameter `archive` of the paragraph array. As this method is called by the Application Framework every time the user loads or saves a document, we first have to call `Serialize` in the MFC base class `CDocument`.

We cannot serialize the paragraph array itself, as it holds pointers to paragraph objects, not the object themselves. Instead, we first read or write the size of the array, and then we serialize the paragraphs one-by-one. When we read from the archive, we have to create the paragraph first (that is why the paragraph needs a default constructor), and then serialize it. Finally, we add it to the array.

```
void CWordDoc::Serialize(CArchive& archive)
{
  CDocument::Serialize(archive);
  if (archive.IsStoring())
  {
    int iSize = (int) m_paragraphArray.GetSize();
    archive << iSize;
    for (int iIndex = 0; iIndex < iSize; ++iIndex)
    {
      m_paragraphArray[iIndex]->Serialize(archive);
    }
```

```
  }
  if (archive.IsLoading())
  {
    int iSize;
    archive >> iSize;

    for (int iCount = 0; iCount < iSize; ++iCount)
    {
      Paragraph* pParagraph;
      check_memory(pParagraph = new Paragraph());

      pParagraph->Serialize(archive);
      m_paragraphArray.Add(pParagraph);
    }
  }
}
m_pageArray.Serialize(archive);}
```

The methods KeyDown and ShiftKeyDown are called by the view class when the user presses any of the special keys. They call the appropriate method to handle the key.

```
void CWordDoc::KeyDown(UINT uChar, CDC* pDC)
{
  switch (uChar)
  {
    case VK_LEFT:
      LeftArrowKey();
      break;
    case VK_RIGHT:
      RightArrowKey();
      break;
    // ...
  }
```

If the next font points at an object, we deallocate it. If m_pNextFont points at null, the delete operator does nothing. We make the edit position of the first marked position visible and update the caret.

```
  delete m_pNextFont;
  m_pNextFont = NULL;
  MakeVisible();
  UpdateCaret();
}
void CWordDoc::ShiftKeyDown(UINT uChar, CDC* pDC)
{
  switch (uChar)
```

```
    {
      case VK_LEFT:
        ShiftLeftArrowKey();
        break;
      case VK_RIGHT:
        ShiftRightArrowKey();
        break;
      // ...
      }
    delete m_pNextFont;
    m_pNextFont = NULL;
    MakeVisible();
    UpdateCaret();
}
```

When the user presses one of the arrow keys as well as the *Page Up* or *Page Down* key without pressing the *Shift* key, we must make sure the application is in the edit state. The method `EnsureEditStatus` takes care of that. If the user, on the other hand, presses one of those keys together with the *Shift* key we must make sure the application is in the mark state. The method `EnsureMarkMode` deals with that.

```
void CWordDoc::EnsureEditStatus()
{
  if (m_eWordState == WS_MARK)
  {
    RectSet repaintSet;
    GetRepaintSet(repaintSet, m_psFirstMark,
                  m_psLastMark);
    m_eWordState = WS_EDIT;
    m_psEdit = m_psLastMark;
    UpdateAllViews(NULL, 0, (CObject*) &repaintSet);
  }
}
void CWordDoc::EnsureMarkStatus()
{
  if (m_eWordState == WS_EDIT)
  {
    m_eWordState = WS_MARK;
    m_psFirstMark = m_psEdit;
    m_psLastMark = m_psEdit;
  }
}
```

The method `LeftArrowKey` is called when the user presses the left arrow key. If the caret position in not at the beginning of the paragraph, we just move it one step to the left. If it is at the beginning, we move the caret to the end of the preceding paragraph. If there is no preceding paragraph, nothing happens.

```
void CWordDoc::LeftArrowKey()
{
  EnsureEditStatus();
  if (m_psEdit.Character() > 0)
  {
    --m_psEdit.Character();
  }
  else if (m_psEdit.Paragraph() > 0)
  {
    Paragraph* pPreviousParagraph =
              m_paragraphArray[--m_psEdit.Paragraph()];
    m_psEdit.Character() = pPreviousParagraph->GetLength();
  }
}
```

The method `ShiftLeftArrowKey` is a bit more complicated than `LeftArrowKey` above. First, we make sure the application is in the mark state and we get the set of marked characters. Then we move the position of the last marked character one step to the left unless it already is at the beginning of the paragraph. If it is, we set the position to the last character of the preceding paragraph, if there is one. In both cases, we need to update the marked area, and we call *SymmetricDifference* in order to pick out only the characters that actually have been marked or unmarked. We do not want to update the characters that were marked before and after the operation. Finally, if this operation sets the first and last marked character equal, we change to the edit state.

The methods `RightArrowKey`, `ShiftRightArrowKey`, `UpArrowKey`, `ShiftUpArrowKey`, `DownArrowKey`, `ShiftDownArrowKey`, `PageUpKey`, `ShiftPageUpKey`, `PageDownKey`, `ShiftPageDownKey`, `HomeKey`, `ShiftHomeKey`, `EndKey`, and `ShiftEndKey` work in similar manners.

```
void CWordDoc::ShiftLeftArrowKey()
{
  EnsureMarkStatus();
  RectSet unmarkRepaintSet;
  GetRepaintSet(unmarkRepaintSet, m_psFirstMark,
                m_psLastMark);
  if (m_psLastMark.Character() > 0)
  {
    --m_psLastMark.Character();
```

```
  }
  else if (m_psLastMark.Paragraph() > 0)
  {
    Paragraph* pPreviousParagraph =
    m_paragraphArray[--m_psLastMark.Paragraph()];

    m_psLastMark.Character() =pPreviousParagraph->GetLength();
  }
  RectSet markRepaintSet;
  GetRepaintSet(markRepaintSet, m_psFirstMark,
                m_psLastMark);

  RectSet resultRepaintSet =
      RectSet::SymmetricDifference(unmarkRepaintSet,
                                   markRepaintSet);
  UpdateAllViews(NULL, 0, (CObject*) &resultRepaintSet);

  if (m_psFirstMark == m_psLastMark)
  {
    m_eWordState = WS_EDIT;
    m_psEdit = m_psFirstMark;
  }
}
```

The method `ReturnKey` is called when the user presses the return key. If the application is in the mark state, we first have to remove the marked area and put the application in the edit state. Then we split the paragraph and insert the new paragraph into the paragraph array. Finally, we call `UpdateParagraphAndPageArray` that updates the page and paragraph arrays. We do this because the operation may affect the following paragraph and might move one or more paragraphs to another page.

```
void CWordDoc::ReturnKey(CDC* pDC)
{
  if (m_eWordState == WS_MARK)
  {
    m_eWordState = WS_EDIT;
    m_psEdit = min(m_psFirstMark, m_psLastMark);
    RectSet repaintSet;
    DeleteText(repaintSet, pDC, m_psFirstMark,
               m_psLastMark);
    UpdateAllViews(NULL, 0, (CObject*) &repaintSet);
  }
  Paragraph* pParagraph = m_paragraphArray
                              [m_psEdit.Paragraph()];
  Paragraph* pNewParagraph =
              pParagraph->Split(m_psEdit.Character());
  pParagraph->Recalculate(pDC);
  pNewParagraph->Recalculate(pDC);
```

```
      m_paragraphArray.InsertAt(++m_psEdit.Paragraph(),
                                 pNewParagraph);
      m_psEdit.Character() = 0;
      UpdateParagraphAndPageArray();
   }
```

In the edit state, `DeleteKey` deletes the key of the current position if it is not at the end of the paragraph. In that case, it instead merges the current paragraph with the next one, if there is one. In the mark state, it deletes the marked text, which may cover several paragraphs.

```
   void CWordDoc::DeleteKey(CDC* pDC)
   {
     switch (m_eWordState)
     {
       case WS_EDIT:
         {
           Paragraph* pParagraph = m_paragraphArray
                                    [m_psEdit.Paragraph()];

           if (m_psEdit.Character() < pParagraph->GetLength())
           {
             pParagraph->DeleteText(m_psEdit.Character(),
                                    m_psEdit.Character() + 1);
             RectSet repaintSet;
             pParagraph->Recalculate(pDC, &repaintSet);
             UpdateAllViews(NULL, 0, (CObject*) &repaintSet);
             SetModifiedFlag();
           }
           else if (m_psEdit.Paragraph() <
                    (m_paragraphArray.GetSize() - 1))
           {
             Paragraph* pNextParagraph = m_paragraphArray
                                        [m_psEdit.Paragraph() + 1];
             pParagraph->Append(pNextParagraph);

             RectSet repaintSet;
             pParagraph->Recalculate(pDC, &repaintSet);
             UpdateAllViews(NULL, 0, (CObject*) &repaintSet);
             m_paragraphArray.RemoveAt(m_psEdit.Paragraph()+1);
             delete pNextParagraph;
             SetModifiedFlag();
           }
         }
         break;

       case WS_MARK:
         m_eWordState = WS_EDIT;
```

```
        m_psEdit = min(m_psFirstMark, m_psLastMark);
        RectSet repaintSet;
        DeleteText(repaintSet, pDC, m_psFirstMark,
                   m_psLastMark);
        UpdateAllViews(NULL, 0, (CObject*) &repaintSet);
        break;
    }

    UpdateParagraphAndPageArray();
}
```

The method `CharDown` is called every time the user presses a regular character. If the character is not printable, nothing happens. Otherwise, if the text is marked, that text is first removed. Thereafter, the character is added to the current paragraph, the paragraph array is updated, and the next font is set to null.

```
void CWordDoc::CharDown(UINT uChar, CDC* pDC)
{
  if (isprint(uChar))
  {
    RectSet repaintSet;
    if (m_eWordState == WS_MARK)
    {
      DeleteText(repaintSet, pDC, m_psFirstMark,
                 m_psLastMark);
      m_eWordState = WS_EDIT;
      m_psEdit = min(m_psFirstMark, m_psLastMark);
    }

    Paragraph* pParagraph = m_paragraphArray
                                [m_psEdit.Paragraph()];
    pParagraph->AddChar(m_psEdit.Character(), uChar,
                        m_pNextFont, m_eKeyboardState);
    pParagraph->Recalculate(pDC, &repaintSet);

    ++m_psEdit.Character();

    delete m_pNextFont;
    m_pNextFont = NULL;

    SetModifiedFlag();
    UpdateAllViews(NULL, 0, (CObject*) &repaintSet);

    UpdateParagraphAndPageArray();
    MakeVisible();
    UpdateCaret();
  }
}
```

When the user clicks with the mouse, we first have to decide which paragraph they hit. The method `PointToParagraph` traverses the paragraph array to find the correct paragraph. If the user clicks beyond the last paragraph, the last one is returned. Likewise, if the user clicks at the end of a page, beyond the last paragraph of the page, the last paragraph of that page is returned.

```
int CWordDoc::PointToParagraph(const CPoint& ptMouse) const
{
  int iParagraphs = (int) m_paragraphArray.GetSize();
  for (int iParagraph = 0; iParagraph < iParagraphs;
      ++iParagraph)
  {
    Paragraph* pParagraph = m_paragraphArray[iParagraph];
    if (ptMouse.y < pParagraph->GetStartPos())
    {
      return iParagraph - 1;
    }
  }
  return iParagraphs - 1;
}
```

The method `PointToChar` returns the position of the clicked paragraph and character index by calling `PointToParagraph`.

```
Position CWordDoc::PointToChar(const CPoint& ptMouse) const
{
  int iParagraph = PointToParagraph(ptMouse);
  Paragraph* pParagraph = m_paragraphArray[iParagraph];
  int iChar = pParagraph->PointToChar(ptMouse);
  return Position(iParagraph, iChar);
}
```

When the user presses the left button of the mouse, `MouseDown` is called. First, we have to unmark any marked portion of the text. Then we set the application to the mark state.

```
void CWordDoc::MouseDown(const CPoint& ptMouse)
{
  if (m_eWordState == WS_MARK)
  {
    m_eWordState = WS_EDIT;
    m_psEdit = m_psFirstMark;
    RectSet repaintSet;
    GetRepaintSet(repaintSet, m_psFirstMark, m_psLastMark);
    UpdateAllViews(NULL, 0, (CObject*) &repaintSet);
  }
  m_eWordState = WS_MARK;
  m_psFirstMark = PointToChar(ptMouse);
  m_psLastMark = m_psFirstMark;
```

```
      delete m_pNextFont;
      m_pNextFont = NULL;
      MakeVisible();
      UpdateCaret();
  }
```

When the user moves the mouse with the left button pressed, `MouseDrag` is called. We find the position of the mouse and if it differs from the last one, we update the marked area.

```
  void CWordDoc::MouseDrag(const CPoint& ptMouse)
  {
    Position psNewLastMark = PointToChar(ptMouse);
    if (m_psLastMark != psNewLastMark)
    {
      RectSet unmarkRepaintSet;
      GetRepaintSet(unmarkRepaintSet, m_psFirstMark,
                    m_psLastMark);
      m_psLastMark = psNewLastMark;
      RectSet markRepaintSet;
      GetRepaintSet(markRepaintSet, m_psFirstMark,
                    m_psLastMark);
      RectSet resultRepaintSet =
          RectSet::SymmetricDifference(unmarkRepaintSet,
                                       markRepaintSet);
      UpdateAllViews(NULL, 0, (CObject*) &resultRepaintSet);
      MakeVisible();
    }
  }
```

When the user releases the left button of the mouse, we just have to check the last position. If it is the same as the first one (the user presses and releases the mouse button on the same character), we change `m_eWordState` to the edit state.

```
  void CWordDoc::MouseUp()
  {
    if (m_psFirstMark == m_psLastMark)
    {
      m_eWordState = WS_EDIT;
      m_psEdit = m_psLastMark;
    }
    else
    {
      m_eWordState = WS_MARK;
    }

    MakeVisible();
    UpdateCaret();
  }
```

When the user double-clicks the mouse, the word hit by the mouse is marked.
We know the application is in the edit state and the correct character is noted
because a double-click is always preceded by calls to MouseDown and MouseUp. If the
mouse is on a word, we mark it and update its client area.

```
void CWordDoc::DoubleClick()
{
  RectSet repaintSet;
  Paragraph* pParagraph = m_paragraphArray
                           [m_psEdit.Paragraph()];
  int iFirstChar, iLastChar;
  if (pParagraph->GetWord(m_psEdit.Character(), iFirstChar,
                          iLastChar))
  {
    m_eWordState = WS_MARK;
    m_psFirstMark.Paragraph() = m_psEdit.Paragraph();
    m_psFirstMark.Character() = iFirstChar;

    m_psLastMark.Paragraph() = m_psEdit.Paragraph();
    m_psLastMark.Character() = iLastChar;

    RectSet repaintSet;
    GetRepaintSet(repaintSet, m_psFirstMark,
                  m_psLastMark);
    UpdateAllViews(NULL, 0, (CObject*) &repaintSet);
    MakeVisible();
  }
  UpdateCaret();
}
```

The method MakeVisible makes sure the caret (in the edit state) or the last marked
position (in the mark state) is visible in the view window by calling MakeVisible.

```
void CWordDoc::MakeVisible()
{
  switch (m_eWordState)
  {
    case WS_EDIT:
      {
        Paragraph* pParagraph = m_paragraphArray
                                 [m_psEdit.Paragraph()];
        CRect rcChar=pParagraph->CharToRect
                                 (m_psEdit.Character());
        m_pView->MakeVisible(rcChar);
      }
      break;
    case WS_MARK:
```

```
      Paragraph* pParagraph = m_paragraphArray
                              [m_psLastMark.Paragraph()];
      CRect rcChar = pParagraph->CharToRect
                              (m_psLastMark.Character());
      m_pView->MakeVisible(rcChar);
      break;
    }
  }
}
```

The method `UpdateCaret` updates the visibility and position of the caret. In the edit state, we extract the caret block from the current paragraph. If the keyboard is in the insert state, the caret is set to a vertical bar with the size of one logical unit. It is later set to the width of at least one pixel by `OnUpdate` in the view class. In the mark state, we just hide the caret.

```
void CWordDoc::UpdateCaret()
{
  switch (m_eWordState)
  {
    case WS_EDIT:
      {
        Paragraph* pParagraph = m_paragraphArray
                                [m_psEdit.Paragraph()];
        CRect rcCaret = pParagraph->GetCaretRect
                        (m_psEdit.Character());
        m_pView->MakeVisible(rcCaret);
        if (m_eKeyboardState == KM_INSERT)
        {
          rcCaret.right = rcCaret.left + 1;
        }
        if (rcCaret.right >= PAGE_WIDTH)
        {
          rcCaret.left -= (rcCaret.right - PAGE_WIDTH);
          rcCaret.right = PAGE_WIDTH;
        }
        m_pView->MakeVisible(rcCaret);

        m_caret.SetAndShowCaret(rcCaret);
      }
      break;
    case WS_MARK:
      m_caret.HideCaret();
  }
}
```

When a portion of the area becomes marked or unmarked, we need the areas of the characters in question in order to repaint them. The method `GetRepaintSet` collects the rectangles needed to be repainted. Remember that `psFirst` and `psLast` refers to the chronological order they were set, not necessarily their order in the document. Instead, `psMin` and `psMax` refer to their positions in the document.

```
void CWordDoc::GetRepaintSet(RectSet& repaintSet,
                             Position psFirst, Position psLast)
{
  Position psMin = min(psFirst, psLast);
  Position psMax = max(psFirst, psLast);
  if (psMin.Paragraph() == psMax.Paragraph())
  {
    Paragraph* pParagraph = m_paragraphArray
                            [psMin.Paragraph()];
    pParagraph->GetRepaintSet(repaintSet, psMin.Character(),
                              psMax.Character());
  }
  else
  {
    Paragraph* pMinParagraph = m_paragraphArray
                               [psMin.Paragraph()];
    pMinParagraph->GetRepaintSet(repaintSet,
                                 psMin.Character());
    for (int iParagraph = psMin.Paragraph() + 1;
         iParagraph < psMax.Paragraph(); ++iParagraph)
    {
      Paragraph* pParagraph = m_paragraphArray[iParagraph];
      pParagraph->GetRepaintSet(repaintSet);
    }
    Paragraph* pMaxParagraph = m_paragraphArray
                               [psMax.Paragraph()];
    pMaxParagraph->GetRepaintSet(repaintSet, 0,
                                 psMax.Character());
  }
}
```

The method `DeleteText` removes the text between the two positions. It is quite complicated as we have several different special cases. Remember that `psFirst` and `psLast` refers to the chronological order they were set, not necessarily their order in the document. Instead, `psMin` and `psMax` refer to their positions in the document.

```
void CWordDoc::DeleteText(RectSet& repaintSet, CDC* pDC,
                          Position psFirst, Position psLast)
{
  Position psMin = min(psFirst, psLast);
  Position psMax = max(psFirst, psLast);
```

If both the character positions are at the beginning of their paragraphs (the positions still refer to *different* paragraphs), we simply remove the paragraphs in between.

```
if ((psMin.Character() == 0) && (psMax.Character() == 0))
{
  for (int iParagraph = psMin.Paragraph();
       iParagraph < psMin.Paragraph(); ++iParagraph)
  {
    delete m_paragraphArray[iParagraph];
  }
  m_paragraphArray.RemoveAt(psMin.Paragraph(),
                 psMax.Paragraph() - psMin.Paragraph());
}
```

If the last character position of the last paragraph is zero, and the last paragraph is the next one, we remove the first up until the last position in the next paragraph.

```
else if (psMax.Character() == 0)
{
  if ((psMin.Paragraph() + 1) == psMax.Paragraph())
  {
    Paragraph* pMinParagraph = m_paragraphArray
                            [psMin.Paragraph()];
    pMinParagraph->DeleteText(psMin.Character());
    Paragraph* pMaxParagraph = m_paragraphArray
                            [psMax.Paragraph()];
    pMinParagraph->Append(pMaxParagraph);
    m_paragraphArray.RemoveAt(psMax.Paragraph());
    pMinParagraph->Recalculate(pDC, &repaintSet);
  }
```

If the last character position of the last paragraph is zero, and the last paragraph is not the next one, we remove from the first position in the first paragraph and up to the last position in the last paragraph as well as the whole paragraphs in between.

```
else
{
  Paragraph* pMinParagraph = m_paragraphArray
                          [psMin.Paragraph()];
  pMinParagraph->DeleteText(psMax.Character());
  pMinParagraph->Recalculate(pDC, &repaintSet);
  for (int iParagraph = psMin.Paragraph() + 1;
       iParagraph <= psMin.Paragraph(); ++iParagraph)
  {
    delete m_paragraphArray[iParagraph];
```

```
      }
   m_paragraphArray.RemoveAt(psMin.Paragraph() + 1,
            psMax.Paragraph() - psMin.Paragraph() + 1);
   }
   UpdateAllViews(NULL, 0, (CObject*) &repaintSet);
}
```

If the marked area does not start at the beginning of the paragraph, and the marked area is restricted to the same paragraph, we just delete the marked text in that paragraph.

```
else
{
   if (psMin.Paragraph() == psMax.Paragraph())
   {
      Paragraph* pParagraph = m_paragraphArray
                           [psMin.Paragraph()];
      pParagraph->DeleteText(psMin.Character(),
                           psMax.Character());
      pParagraph->Recalculate(pDC, &repaintSet);
   }
```

If the marked area does not start at the beginning of the paragraph, and the marked area is not restricted to the same paragraph, we delete the text in the first and last paragraph as well as the paragraphs in between.

```
   else
   {
      Paragraph* pMinParagraph = m_paragraphArray
                           [psMin.Paragraph()];
      Paragraph* pMaxParagraph = m_paragraphArray
                           [psMax.Paragraph()];
      pMinParagraph->DeleteText(psMin.Character());
      if (psMax.Character() == pMaxParagraph->GetLength())
      {
         pMaxParagraph->DeleteText(0, psMax.Character());
      }
      else
      {
         pMaxParagraph->DeleteText(0, psMax.Character() - 1);
      }
      pMaxParagraph->ClearRectArray();
      pMinParagraph->Append(pMaxParagraph);
      pMinParagraph->Recalculate(pDC, &repaintSet);
```

```
        for (int iParagraph = psMin.Paragraph() + 1;
             iParagraph < psMin.Paragraph(); ++iParagraph)
        {
          delete m_paragraphArray[iParagraph];
        }
        m_paragraphArray.RemoveAt(psMin.Paragraph() + 1,
                          psMax.Paragraph() - psMin.Paragraph());
      }
      UpdateAllViews(NULL, 0, (CObject*) &repaintSet);
    }
  }
```

When a paragraph has been altered in some way, we need to recalculate and repaint the altered part of the paragraph. However, we need also check the rest of the paragraphs and repaint the ones that have been shifted on the page. Moreover, we need to examine the pages and update the first and last paragraph on each page.

```
void CWordDoc::UpdateParagraphAndPageArray()
{
  int iOldPages = (int) m_pageArray.GetSize();
  m_pageArray.RemoveAll();
  int iPageHeight = 0, iStartParagraph = 0;
  int iParagraphes = (int) m_paragraphArray.GetSize();
```

We traverse the paragraphs and divide them into pages of the document to examine their height.

```
  for (int iParagraph = 0; iParagraph < iParagraphes;
       ++iParagraph)
  {
    Paragraph* pParagraph = m_paragraphArray[iParagraph];
    int iHeight = pParagraph->GetHeight();
    if ((iPageHeight + iHeight) <= PAGE_HEIGHT)
    {
      iPageHeight += iHeight;
    }
```

When the current height exceeds the height of the page, we start a new page. If this page holds at least one paragraph, we add them to the page.

```
    else if (iStartParagraph < iParagraph)
    {
      Page page(iStartParagraph, iParagraph - 1);
      m_pageArray.Add(page);
      iStartParagraph = iParagraph;
      iPageHeight = iHeight;
    }
```

If a single paragraph is higher than the page, we include it on the page and start the new page with the next paragraph.

```
    else
    {
      Page page(iStartParagraph, iStartParagraph);
      m_pageArray.Add(page);
      iStartParagraph = iParagraph + 1;
      iPageHeight = iHeight;
    }
  }
  Page page(iStartParagraph, iParagraphes - 1);
  m_pageArray.Add(page);
```

The repaint set is used to collect the parts of the documents area that need to be repainted. For each page, we traverse the paragraphs and set their start position.

```
  RectSet repaintSet;
  int iNewPages = (int) m_pageArray.GetSize();
  for (int iPage = 0; iPage < iNewPages; ++iPage)
  {
    int iPageHeight = iPage * PAGE_HEIGHT;
    Page page = m_pageArray[iPage];
    int iFirstParagraph = page.GetFirstParagraph();
    int iLastParagraph = page.GetLastParagraph();
    for (int iParagraph = iFirstParagraph;
         iParagraph <= iLastParagraph; ++iParagraph)
    {
      Paragraph* pParagraph = m_paragraphArray[iParagraph];
      int iHeight = pParagraph->GetHeight();
      int yPos = pParagraph->GetStartPos();
```

If the previous start position of the paragraphs is being updated, we set the new start position and add the paragraphs' area to the repaint set.

```
      if (iPageHeight != yPos)
      {
        CRect rcOldParagraph(0, yPos, PAGE_WIDTH,
                             yPos + iHeight);
        repaintSet.Add(rcOldParagraph);
        CRect rcNewParagraph(0, iPageHeight, PAGE_WIDTH,
                             iPageHeight + iHeight);
        repaintSet.Add(rcNewParagraph);
        pParagraph->SetStartPos(iPageHeight);
      }
      iPageHeight += iHeight;
    }
```

For each page, we add the rest of the page to the re-paint set.

```
        CRect rcPageRest(0, iPageHeight, PAGE_WIDTH,
                         (iPage + 1) * PAGE_HEIGHT);
        repaintSet.Add(rcPageRest);
    }
```

If the number of pages has decreased, we need to repaint the rest of the document.

```
    if (iNewPages < iOldPages)
    {
        CRect rcRestDocument(0, iNewPages * PAGE_HEIGHT,
                             PAGE_WIDTH, iOldPages * PAGE_HEIGHT);
        repaintSet.Add(rcRestDocument);
    }
```

If the number of pages has been changed, we need to notify `OnUpdate` in the `view` class to reset the vertical scroll bars. In that case, the whole document will be repainted.

```
    if (iNewPages != iOldPages)
    {
        UpdateAllViews(NULL, (LPARAM) iNewPages);
    }
```

If the number of pages are unchanged, we only update the areas of the repaint set.

```
    else if (!repaintSet.IsEmpty())
    {
        UpdateAllViews(NULL, 0, &repaintSet);
    }
}
```

The method `OnUpdateAlignLeft` sets a radio button on the current alignment menu item. The methods `OnUpdateAlignCenter`, `OnUpdateAlignRight`, and `OnUpdateAlignJustifed` work in the same way. They simply call `IsAlignment` to check the current alignment.

```
    void CWordDoc::OnUpdateAlignLeft(CCmdUI *pCmdUI)
    {
        pCmdUI->SetRadio(IsAlignment(ALIGN_LEFT));
    }
```

In the edit state, `IsAlignment` checks whether the current paragraph has the given alignment. In the mark state, it checks that all partly or completely marked paragraphs have the given alignment. This implies that if several paragraphs are marked and not all of them have the same alignment, no menu item is checked.

```
BOOL CWordDoc::IsAlignment(Alignment eAlignment) const
{
  switch (m_eWordState)
  {
    case WS_EDIT:
      {
        Paragraph* pParagraph =
                    m_paragraphArray[m_psEdit.Paragraph()];
        return (pParagraph->GetAlignment() == eAlignment);
      }
    case WS_MARK:
      for (int iParagraph = m_psFirstMark.Paragraph();
           iParagraph <= m_psLastMark.Paragraph();
           ++iParagraph)
      {
        Paragraph* pParagraph = m_paragraphArray[iParagraph];
        if (pParagraph->GetAlignment() != eAlignment)
        {
          return FALSE;
        }
      }
      return TRUE;
  }
  return TRUE;
}
```

The method `OnAlignLeft` is called when the user choses an alignment. The methods
`OnAlignCenter`, `OnAlignRight`, and `OnAlignJustified` work in the same way.
They all call `SetAlignment`.

```
void CWordDoc::OnAlignLeft()
{
  SetAlignment(ALIGN_LEFT);
}
```

In the edit state, `SetAlignment` sets the given alignment to the current paragraph.
In the mark state, it traverses through the paragraphs and gives them the given
alignment one by one.

```
void CWordDoc::SetAlignment(Alignment eAlignment)
{
  CClientDC dc(m_pView);
  m_pView->OnPrepareDC(&dc);
  switch (m_eWordState)
  {
```

In the edit state, we just set the alignment of the current paragraph. Remember that this method can only be called when the paragraph has another alignment due to a previous call to one of the update methods above.

```
case WS_EDIT:
  {
    Paragraph* pParagraph = m_paragraphArray
                              [m_psEdit.Paragraph()];
    pParagraph->SetAlignment(eAlignment);
    pParagraph->Recalculate(&dc);
    int iHeight = pParagraph->GetHeight();
    int yPos = pParagraph->GetStartPos();
    CRect rcParagraph(0, yPos, PAGE_WIDTH,
                      yPos + iHeight);
    RectSet repaintSet;
    repaintSet.Add(rcParagraph);
    UpdateAllViews(NULL, 0, (CObject*) &repaintSet);
    MakeVisible();
    UpdateCaret();
  }
  break;
```

In the mark state, we traverse the marked paragraphs and set the alignment for those who have not already been set to the alignment in question. Remember that this method can only be called if at least one paragraph is not already set to the alignment in question.

```
case WS_MARK:
  RectSet repaintSet;

  for (int iParagraph = m_psFirstMark.Paragraph();
       iParagraph <= m_psLastMark.Paragraph();
       ++iParagraph)
  {
    Paragraph* pParagraph = m_paragraphArray[iParagraph];
    if (pParagraph->GetAlignment() != eAlignment)
    {
      pParagraph->SetAlignment(eAlignment);
      pParagraph->Recalculate(&dc);
      int iHeight = pParagraph->GetHeight();
      int yPos = pParagraph->GetStartPos();
      CRect rcParagraph(0, yPos, PAGE_WIDTH,
                        yPos + iHeight);
      repaintSet.Add(rcParagraph);
    }
  }
```

```
        UpdateAllViews(NULL, 0, (CObject*) &repaintSet);
        UpdateCaret();
        break;
    }
    SetModifiedFlag();
}
```

The cut menu item will be enabled when the application is in the edit state; that is, when the user has marked a portion of the text. The method OnCut is quite simple, it just copies the marked area into the copy buffer and then deletes it. Note that we do not have to check whether the application is in the edit or mark state. The cut menu item can only be chosen when it is enabled, and the condition is that the application is in the mark state.

```
    void CWordDoc::OnUpdateCut(CCmdUI *pCmdUI)
    {
        pCmdUI->Enable(m_eWordState == WS_MARK);
    }
    void CWordDoc::OnCut()
    {
        OnCopy();
        CClientDC dc(m_pView);
        m_pView->OnPrepareDC(&dc);
        DeleteKey(&dc);
    }
```

The method OnUpdateCopy works in the same way as OnUpdateCut, it enables the copy menu item when the application is in the mark state. The method ClearCopyArray deallocates the paragraphs in the copy buffer and clears the copy array.

```
    void CWordDoc::OnUpdateCopy(CCmdUI *pCmdUI)
    {
        pCmdUI->Enable(m_eWordState == WS_MARK);
    }
    void CWordDoc::ClearCopyArray()
    {
        int iParagraphs = (int) m_copyArray.GetSize();
        for (int iParagraph = 0; iParagraph < iParagraphs;
             ++iParagraph)
        {
            delete m_copyArray[iParagraph];
        }
        m_copyArray.RemoveAll();
    }
```

Similar to `OnCut`, `OnCopy` is called only when the application is in the mark state. First, we clear the copy buffer array and determine the minimum and maximum of the first and last marked character. Remember that `psFirst` and `psLast` refers to the chronological order they were set, and not necessarily their order in the document. Instead, `psMin` and `psMax` refer to their positions in the document.

Then we have two cases to consider. With only one paragraph marked, we simply extract the marked text from that paragraph and add it to the copy buffer array. If at least two paragraphs are marked, we extract the marked text from the first and last one. The paragraphs in between (if any) are to be completely marked, so we just copy them into the copy buffer array.

```
void CWordDoc::OnCopy()
{
  ClearCopyArray();
  Position psMin = min(m_psFirstMark, m_psLastMark);
  Position psMax = max(m_psFirstMark, m_psLastMark);

  CClientDC dc(m_pView);
  m_pView->OnPrepareDC(&dc);

  if (psMin.Paragraph() == psMax.Paragraph())
  {
    Paragraph* pParagraph = m_paragraphArray
                        [psMin.Paragraph()];
    Paragraph* pCopyParagraph = pParagraph->ExtractText
                    (psMin.Character(), psMax.Character());
    m_copyArray.Add(pCopyParagraph);
  }
  else
  {
    Paragraph* pMinParagraph = m_paragraphArray
                            [psMin.Paragraph()];
    Paragraph* pCopyMinParagraph =
            pMinParagraph->ExtractText(psMin.Character());
    m_copyArray.Add(pCopyMinParagraph);
    for (int iParagraph = psMin.Paragraph() + 1;
        iParagraph < psMax.Paragraph(); ++iParagraph)
    {
      Paragraph* pParagraph = m_paragraphArray[iParagraph];
      Paragraph* pCopyParagraph;
      check_memory(pCopyParagraph =
                  new Paragraph(*pParagraph));
      m_copyArray.Add(pCopyParagraph);
    }
```

```
      Paragraph* pMaxParagraph =
                  m_paragraphArray[psMax.Paragraph()];
      Paragraph* pCopyMaxParagraph = pMaxParagraph->ExtractText
                                      (0,psMax.Character());
      m_copyArray.Add(pCopyMaxParagraph);
    }
  }
```

Unlike the cut and copy menu item, the paste menu item can be called when the application is in the edit as well as the mark state. The only condition is that the copy buffer array is non-empty.

```
  void CWordDoc::OnUpdatePaste(CCmdUI *pCmdUI)
  {
    pCmdUI->Enable(!m_copyArray.IsEmpty());
  }
```

Just as when we copied the text, we have two cases to consider when we paste it. If the copy buffer array consists of only one paragraph, we just insert it and update the current caret position. Otherwise, we split the current paragraph into two halves and insert the copied paragraphs between the halves, merging the first part of the split paragraph with the first paragraph in the copy list (m_copyArray). In the same way, we merge the last paragraph in the copy list to the second half of the split paragraph.

```
  void CWordDoc::OnPaste()
  {
    CClientDC dc(m_pView);
    m_pView->OnPrepareDC(&dc);
    RectSet repaintSet;
```

If the application is in the mark state, we delete the marked text and put the application in the edit state.

```
      if (m_eWordState == WS_MARK)
      {
        DeleteText(repaintSet, &dc, m_psFirstMark,
                   m_psLastMark);
        m_eWordState = WS_EDIT;
        m_psEdit = min(m_psFirstMark, m_psFirstMark);
      }
      Paragraph* pEditParagraph =
                 m_paragraphArray[m_psEdit.Paragraph()];
      int iSize = (int) m_copyArray.GetSize();
```

If the copy buffer holds only one paragraph, we insert it at the current edit position.

```
if (iSize == 1)
{
  Paragraph* pCopyParagraph = m_copyArray[0];
  pEditParagraph->Insert(m_psEdit.Character(),
                         pCopyParagraph);
  pEditParagraph->Recalculate(&dc, &repaintSet);
  m_psEdit.Character() += pCopyParagraph->GetLength();
}
```

If the copy buffer holds more than one paragraph, we split the current paragraph into two halves and insert the copy list between them.

```
else
{
  Paragraph* pLastParagraph =
              pEditParagraph->Split(m_psEdit.Character());
  Paragraph* pCopyParagraph = m_copyArray[0];
  pEditParagraph->Append(pCopyParagraph);
  pEditParagraph->Recalculate(&dc, &repaintSet);
  for (int iParagraph = iSize - 2; iParagraph > 0;
       --iParagraph)
  {
    Paragraph* pCopyParagraph = m_copyArray[iParagraph];
    Paragraph* pInsertParagraph;
    check_memory(pInsertParagraph =
                new Paragraph(*pCopyParagraph));
    m_paragraphArray.InsertAt(m_psEdit.Paragraph() + 1,
                              pInsertParagraph);
  }
  pCopyParagraph = m_copyArray[iSize - 1];
  Paragraph* pInsertParagraph;
  check_memory(pInsertParagraph =
                new Paragraph(*pCopyParagraph));
  m_psEdit.Character() = pInsertParagraph->GetLength();
  pInsertParagraph->Append(pLastParagraph);
  pInsertParagraph->Recalculate(&dc);
  delete pLastParagraph;
  m_psEdit.Paragraph() += iSize - 1;
  m_paragraphArray.InsertAt(m_psEdit.Paragraph(),
                            pInsertParagraph);
}
```

Finally, we update the affected characters and the paragraph array. We also make the current position visible and update the caret.

```
UpdateAllViews(NULL, 0, (CObject*) &repaintSet);
UpdateParagraphAndPageArray();
MakeVisible();
UpdateCaret();
}
```

The method `OnFont` has no update method because the user can change the font. We initialize the font dialog with a default font. In the edit state, we initialize the dialog with `m_nextFont`. In the mark state, we choose the font of the first marked character.

```
void CWordDoc::OnFont()
{
  switch (m_eWordState)
  {
    case WS_EDIT:
      {
        Font defaultFont;
        if (m_pNextFont != NULL)
        {
          defaultFont = *m_pNextFont;
        }
        else
        {
          Paragraph* pParagraph =
                   m_paragraphArray[m_psEdit.Paragraph()];
          defaultFont = pParagraph->GetFont
                               (m_psEdit.Character());
        }
        LOGFONT oldLogFont = (LOGFONT) defaultFont;
        CFontDialog fontDialog(&oldLogFont);
        if (fontDialog.DoModal() == IDOK)
        {
          LOGFONT newLogFont;
          fontDialog.GetCurrentFont(&newLogFont);
          delete m_pNextFont;
          Font newFont = (Font) newLogFont;
          check_memory(m_pNextFont = new Font(newFont));
        }
      }
      break;
    case WS_MARK:
```

```
Paragraph* pParagraph =
          m_paragraphArray[m_psFirstMark.Paragraph()];
Font defaultFont =
    pParagraph->GetFont(m_psFirstMark.Character());
LOGFONT oldLogFont = (LOGFONT) defaultFont;
CFontDialog fontDialog(&oldLogFont);

if (fontDialog.DoModal() == IDOK)
{
  LOGFONT newLogFont;
  fontDialog.GetCurrentFont(&newLogFont);
  Font newFont = (Font) newLogFont;
  Position psMin = min(m_psFirstMark, m_psLastMark);
  Position psMax = max(m_psFirstMark, m_psLastMark);

  CClientDC dc(m_pView);
  m_pView->OnPrepareDC(&dc);

  RectSet repaintSet;
```

If only one paragraph is marked, we set the new font on its marked part.

```
  if (psMin.Paragraph() == psMax.Paragraph())
  {
    Paragraph* pParagraph =
              m_paragraphArray[psMin.Paragraph()];
    pParagraph->SetFont(newFont, psMin.Character(),
                      psMax.Character());
    pParagraph->Recalculate(&dc, &repaintSet);
  }
```

If at least two paragraphs are marked, we set the new font on the marked part of the first and last paragraphs and on the whole paragraphs in between (if any).

```
  else
  {
    Paragraph* pFirstParagraph =
              m_paragraphArray[psMin.Paragraph()];
    pFirstParagraph->SetFont(newFont,
                          psMin.Character());
    pFirstParagraph->Recalculate(&dc, &repaintSet);
    for (int iParagraph = psMin.Paragraph() + 1;
         iParagraph < psMax.Paragraph() - 1;
         ++iParagraph)
    {
      Paragraph* pParagraph =
                m_paragraphArray[iParagraph];
      pParagraph->SetFont(newFont);
```

```
                pParagraph->Recalculate(&dc, &repaintSet);
            }
            Paragraph* pLastParagraph =
                        m_paragraphArray[psMin.Paragraph()];
            pLastParagraph->SetFont(newFont, 0,
                                    psMax.Character());
            pLastParagraph->Recalculate(&dc, &repaintSet);
        }
        UpdateAllViews(NULL, 0, (CObject*) &repaintSet);
        UpdateParagraphAndPageArray();
        MakeVisible();
        UpdateCaret();
    }
    break;
    }
}
```

The View Class

The view class CWordView has only two fields. The field m_pWordDoc is a pointer to the document class object. Similar to the Calc application, we need to keep track of double-clicks. The field m_bDoubleclick is first set to false when the user clicks the mouse key, and then set to true if is followed by a double-click. When the user drags the mouse, we note the first and last position. However, in the case of a double-click, a word will be marked, and we should not finish the marking process by calling MouseUp in the document class.

WordView.h

```
const int LINE_WIDTH = 500;
const int LINE_HEIGHT = 500;
class CWordView : public CView
{
  private:
    DECLARE_DYNCREATE(CWordView)
    DECLARE_MESSAGE_MAP()
    CWordView();
  public:
    afx_msg int OnCreate(LPCREATESTRUCT lpCreateStruct);
    virtual void OnInitialUpdate();
    virtual void OnPrepareDC(CDC* pDC,
                             CPrintInfo* pInfo = NULL);
    afx_msg void OnSize(UINT uType, int cxClient,
```

```
                           int cyClient);
     afx_msg void OnSetFocus(CWnd* pOldWnd);
     afx_msg void OnKillFocus(CWnd* pNewWnd);
     afx_msg void OnVScroll(UINT nSBCode, UINT nPos,
                            CScrollBar* pScrollBar);
     afx_msg void OnHScroll(UINT nSBCode, UINT nPos,
                            CScrollBar* pScrollBar);
     afx_msg void OnLButtonDown(UINT uFlags, CPoint ptMouse);
     afx_msg void OnMouseMove(UINT uFlags, CPoint ptMouse);
     afx_msg void OnLButtonUp(UINT uFlags, CPoint ptMouse);
     afx_msg void OnLButtonDblClk(UINT nFlags, CPoint ptMouse);
     void MakeVisible(CRect rcArea);
     afx_msg void OnKeyDown(UINT nChar, UINT nRepCnt,
                            UINT nFlags);
     afx_msg void OnChar(UINT nChar, UINT nRepCnt,
                         UINT nFlags);
     virtual BOOL OnPreparePrinting(CPrintInfo* pInfo);
     virtual void OnUpdate(CView* pSender, LPARAM lHint,
                           CObject* pHint);
     afx_msg void OnPaint();
     virtual void OnPrint(CDC* pDC, CPrintInfo* pInfo);
     virtual void OnDraw(CDC* pDC);
  private:
     CWordDoc* m_pWordDoc;
     BOOL m_bDoubleClick;
};
```

The method OnCreate is called after the view has been created but before it has been shown. The pointer to the document class object is set and tested. Remember that an application can have several views, but only one document.

CWordView.cpp

```
int CWordView::OnCreate(LPCREATESTRUCT lpCreateStruct)
{
  if (CView::OnCreate(lpCreateStruct) == -1)
  {
    return -1;
  }
  m_pWordDoc = (CWordDoc*) m_pDocument;
  check(m_pWordDoc != NULL);
  ASSERT_VALID(m_pWordDoc);
  m_pWordDoc->OnSetFocus(this);
  return 0;
}
```

The method `OnInitialUpdate` is called once after the view has been created and shown. Its task is to initialize the scroll bars. The method `GetPageNum` in the document class returns the number of pages of this document. A document always has at least one page.

```
void CWordView::OnInitialUpdate()
{
  SCROLLINFO scrollInfo;
  scrollInfo.fMask = SIF_RANGE | SIF_POS;
  scrollInfo.nPos = 0;
  scrollInfo.nMin = 0;
  scrollInfo.nMax = PAGE_WIDTH;
  SetScrollInfo(SB_HORZ, &scrollInfo);

  scrollInfo.fMask = SIF_RANGE | SIF_POS;
  scrollInfo.nPos = 0;
  scrollInfo.nMin = 0;
  scrollInfo.nMax = (m_pWordDoc->GetPageNum()*PAGE_HEIGHT)-1;
  SetScrollInfo(SB_VERT, &scrollInfo);

  m_pWordDoc->UpdateCaret();
  CView::OnInitialUpdate();
}
```

The method `OnPrepareDC` is called directly after a device context object has been created. Its task is to set the relation between the logical and device coordinates. We choose the isotropic mode. This implies that the units are equal in the horizontal and vertical directions (otherwise, circles would not be round). We call `GetDeviceCaps` to get the size of the screen in millimeters (`HORZSIZE` and `VERTSIZE`) and in pixels (`HORZRES` and `VERTRES`).

We then set the screen in hundredths of millimeters to correspond to the screen in pixels. This gives that one logical unit is one hundredth millimeters. We also set the origin of the client area to be at the bottom left corner by looking up the current positions of the scroll bars.

```
void CWordView::OnPrepareDC(CDC* pDC, CPrintInfo* /* pInfo */)
{
  pDC->SetMapMode(MM_ISOTROPIC);
  CSize szWindow(100 * pDC->GetDeviceCaps(HORZSIZE),
                 100 * pDC->GetDeviceCaps(VERTSIZE));
  CSize szViewport(pDC->GetDeviceCaps(HORZRES),
                   pDC->GetDeviceCaps(VERTRES));

  pDC->SetWindowExt(szWindow);
  pDC->SetViewportExt(szViewport);

  SCROLLINFO scrollInfo;
```

```
      GetScrollInfo(SB_HORZ, &scrollInfo, SIF_POS);
      int xOrg = scrollInfo.nPos;
      GetScrollInfo(SB_VERT, &scrollInfo, SIF_POS);
      int yOrg = scrollInfo.nPos;
      pDC->SetWindowOrg(xOrg, yOrg);
}
```

The method `OnSize` is called every time the user changes the size of the window. We look up the size of the client area and set the size of the horizontal and vertical scroll bars to reflect the size of the visible client area compared to the size of the whole document. First, we translate the size of the client area from device to logical units. Then we set the size of a page at the scroll bars.

```
void CWordView::OnSize(UINT /* uType */, int cxClient,
                       int cyClient)
{
  CClientDC dc(this);
  OnPrepareDC(&dc);
  CSize szClient(cxClient, cyClient);
  dc.DPtoLP(&szClient);
  SCROLLINFO scrollInfo;
  scrollInfo.fMask = SIF_PAGE;
  scrollInfo.nPage = szClient.cx;
  SetScrollInfo(SB_HORZ, &scrollInfo);
  scrollInfo.fMask = SIF_PAGE;
  scrollInfo.nPage = szClient.cy;
  SetScrollInfo(SB_VERT, &scrollInfo);
}
```

The method `OnVScroll` is called every time the user scrolls the vertical bar. It is also called when the user presses some special key, see `OnKeyDown` below. The scroll bar and the client area are updated due to the changes. In order to update the area fast, we call the MFC method `ScrollWindow`. It moves a part of the window and repaints the area. The method `OnHScroll` works in a similar manner.

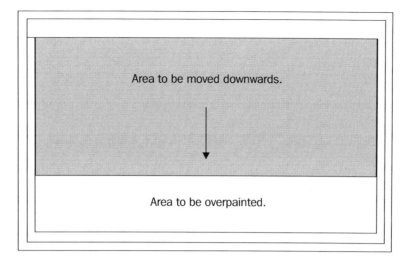

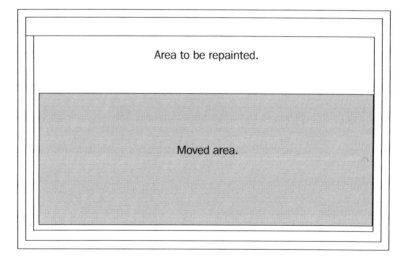

```
void CWordView::OnVScroll(UINT uSBCode, UINT /* yThumbPos */,
                          CScrollBar* /* pScrollBar */)
{
  SCROLLINFO scrollInfo;
  GetScrollInfo(SB_VERT, &scrollInfo);
  int yScrollPos = scrollInfo.nPos;
  switch (uSBCode)
  {
```

The top scroll position is always zero. The bottom position, however, is decided by the size of the client area (`scrollInfo.nPage`) because the scroll position is the top position of the visible part of the document.

```
case SB_TOP:
  yScrollPos = 0;
  break;
case SB_BOTTOM:
  yScrollPos = scrollInfo.nMax - scrollInfo.nPage + 1;
  break;
case SB_LINEUP:
  yScrollPos -= LINE_HEIGHT;
  break;
case SB_LINEDOWN:
  yScrollPos += LINE_HEIGHT;
  break;
```

Note the difference between scrolling a line and a page, the line is of constant height (`LINE_HEIGHT`) while the page height depends on the size of the client area (`scrollInfo.nPage`).

```
case SB_PAGEUP:
    yScrollPos -= scrollInfo.nPage;
    break;
case SB_PAGEDOWN:
  yScrollPos += scrollInfo.nPage;
  break;
```

When the user grabs and moves the scroll thumb, we can track the new position with `scrollInfo.nTrackPos`.

```
case SB_THUMBPOSITION:
    yScrollPos = scrollInfo.nTrackPos;
    break;
}
```

We have to check that the new position does not exceed the limits of the scroll thumb.

```
yScrollPos = max(yScrollPos, 0);
yScrollPos = min(yScrollPos, scrollInfo.nMax -
                            (int) scrollInfo.nPage + 1);
```

If the scroll position has been altered, we scroll the window the altered distance.

```
if (yScrollPos != scrollInfo.nPos)
{
  CSize szDistance(0, scrollInfo.nPos - yScrollPos);
  scrollInfo.fMask = SIF_POS;
  scrollInfo.nPos = yScrollPos;
  SetScrollInfo(SB_VERT, &scrollInfo);
```

We need to translate the distance into device coordinates before we scroll the window.

```
  CClientDC dc(this);
  OnPrepareDC(&dc);
  dc.LPtoDP(&szDistance);
  ScrollWindow(0, szDistance.cy);
  UpdateWindow();
}
}
```

The method `OnLButtonDown` is called every time the user presses the left button of the mouse. The position of the mouse is given in device units that have to be translated into logical units. For that, we need a device context. It is prepared and then used to translate the device units into logical units. Finally, the document object is notified.

```
void CWordView::OnLButtonDown(UINT /* uFlags */,
                              CPoint ptMouse)
{
  m_bDoubleClick = FALSE;
  CClientDC dc(this);
  OnPrepareDC(&dc);
  dc.DPtoLP(&ptMouse);
  m_pWordDoc->MouseDown(ptMouse);
}
```

The method `OnMouseMove` first checks whether the user moves the mouse at the same time as they press the left button. It is called mouse dragging and that is the only movement that interests us. We must also check that the user has not double-clicked. In that case, there is a possibility that a word is marked by now, and if we allow the document to deal with this movement, the word will be partly unmarked.

```
void CWordView::OnMouseMove(UINT uFlags, CPoint ptMouse)
{
  BOOL bLeftButtonDown = (uFlags & MK_LBUTTON);
```

```
    if (bLeftButtonDown && !m_bDoubleClick)
    {
      CClientDC dc(this);
      OnPrepareDC(&dc);
      dc.DPtoLP(&ptMouse);

      m_pWordDoc->MouseDrag(ptMouse);
    }
  }
}
```

The method OnLButtonUp is called when the user releases the mouse button, and it calls MouseUp in the document class.

```
void CWordView::OnLButtonUp(UINT /* uFlags */,
                            CPoint /* ptMouse */)

{
  m_pWordDoc->MouseUp();
}
```

The method OnLButtonDblClk is called when the user double-clicks. It sets the double-click field and calls DoubleClick in the document class.

```
void CWordView::OnLButtonDblClk(UINT /* nFlags */,
                                CPoint /* ptMouse */)

{
  m_bDoubleClick = TRUE;
  m_pWordDoc->DoubleClick();
}
```

The method MakeVisible makes sure the given area is visible in the window. If necessary, it moves the scroll bar positions.

```
void CWordView::MakeVisible(CRect rcArea)
{
  CClientDC dc(this);
  OnPrepareDC(&dc);
```

We find the size of the document in device units. If necessary, we will update the area of the document, not the whole client area, in order to avoid the gray area to the right of the document being updated.

```
  int iPageNum = m_pWordDoc->GetPageNum();
  CRect rcDocument(0, 0, PAGE_WIDTH, iPageNum * PAGE_HEIGHT);
  dc.LPtoDP(rcDocument);
```

We find the first and last position of the visible part of the document in the x direction. If the given area is to the left of the visible part of the client area, we simply change the scroll position.

```
      SCROLLINFO scrollInfo;
      GetScrollInfo(SB_HORZ, &scrollInfo);
      int xFirst = scrollInfo.nPos;
      int xPage = scrollInfo.nPage;
      int xLast = xFirst + xPage;

      if (rcArea.left < xFirst)
      {
        SetScrollPos(SB_HORZ, rcArea.left);
        InvalidateRect(rcDocument);
        UpdateWindow();
      }
```

If the given area is to the right of the visible part of the client area, we also change the scroll position. We need to add a distance to the scroll bar position. In order to make that distance as small as possible, we take the difference between the right corner of the given area and the client area.

```
      if (rcArea.right > xLast)
      {
        SetScrollPos(SB_HORZ, xFirst + (rcArea.right - xLast));
        InvalidateRect(rcDocument);
        UpdateWindow();
      }
```

The vertical scroll bar is changed in a way similar to the horizontal bar above.

```
      GetScrollInfo(SB_VERT, &scrollInfo);
      int yFirst = scrollInfo.nPos;
      int yPage = scrollInfo.nPage;
      int yLast = yFirst + yPage;

      if (rcArea.top < yFirst)
      {
        SetScrollPos(SB_VERT, rcArea.top);
        InvalidateRect(rcDocument);
        UpdateWindow();
      }

      if (rcArea.bottom > yLast)
      {
        SetScrollPos(SB_VERT, yFirst + (rcArea.bottom - yLast));
        InvalidateRect(rcDocument);
        UpdateWindow();
      }
    }
```

The method `OnKeyDown` is called every time the user presses a key. The application behaves differently if the shift or control key is pressed at the same time, so first we have to decide whether they are pressed by calling the Win32 API function `GetKeyState`. It returns a value less than zero if the given key is pressed.

When the control key is pressed, the view is being scrolled by calling `OnVScroll` or `OnHScroll` without notifying the document object. Otherwise, one of the document class methods `KeyDown` and `ShiftKeyDown` are called, depending on whether the *Shift* key was pressed.

```cpp
void CWordView::OnKeyDown(UINT uChar, UINT /* uRepCnt */,
                          UINT /* uFlags */)
{
  CClientDC dc(this);
  OnPrepareDC(&dc);
  BOOL bShiftKeyDown = (::GetKeyState(VK_SHIFT) < 0);
  BOOL bControlKeyDown = (::GetKeyState(VK_CONTROL) < 0);
  if (bControlKeyDown)
  {
    switch (uChar)
    {
      case VK_PRIOR:
        OnVScroll(SB_PAGEUP, 0, NULL);
        break;
      case VK_NEXT:
        OnVScroll(SB_PAGEDOWN, 0, NULL);
        break;
      case VK_UP:
        OnVScroll(SB_LINEUP, 0, NULL);
        break;
      case VK_DOWN:
        OnVScroll(SB_LINEDOWN, 0, NULL);
        break;
      case VK_LEFT:
        OnHScroll(SB_LINELEFT, 0, NULL);
        break;
      case VK_RIGHT:
        OnHScroll(SB_LINERIGHT, 0, NULL);
        break;
```

When the *Home* key is pressed, if the visible part of the document is not already located at the top left position, we set the scroll position and update the window.

```
case VK_HOME:
  if ((GetScrollPos(SB_HORZ) > 0) ||
      (GetScrollPos(SB_VERT) > 0))
  {
    SetScrollPos(SB_HORZ, 0);
    SetScrollPos(SB_VERT, 0);

    Invalidate();
    UpdateWindow();
  }
  break;
```

When the Bottom key is pressed, if the visible part of the document is not already located at the right bottom position, we set the scroll position and update the window.

```
case VK_END:
  {
    SCROLLINFO scrollInfo;
    GetScrollInfo(SB_HORZ, &scrollInfo,
                  SIF_PAGE | SIF_RANGE);
    int xNewPos = scrollInfo.nMax - scrollInfo.nPage;
    GetScrollInfo(SB_VERT, &scrollInfo,
                  SIF_PAGE | SIF_RANGE);
    int yNewPos = scrollInfo.nMax - scrollInfo.nPage;
    if ((GetScrollPos(SB_HORZ) != xNewPos) ||
        (GetScrollPos(SB_VERT) != yNewPos))
    {
      SetScrollPos(SB_HORZ, xNewPos);
      SetScrollPos(SB_VERT, yNewPos);

      Invalidate();
      UpdateWindow();
    }
  }
  break;
```

The rest of the characters are sent to the document object.

```
    default:
      m_pWordDoc->KeyDown(uChar, &dc);
      break;
  }
}
```

If the *Ctrl* key is not pressed, we send the key to the document object.

```
  else if (bShiftKeyDown)
  {
    m_pWordDoc->ShiftKeyDown(uChar, &dc);
  }

  else
  {
    m_pWordDoc->KeyDown(uChar, &dc);
  }

}
```

The method `OnUpdate` is called indirectly by the document class when it calls `UpdateAllViews`. It takes two parameters, `lHint` and `pHint`, that are used to update the vertical scroll bar (`lHint`) when the number of pages has been changed and to partly repaint the view (`pHint`) when the document text has been changed.

If `lHint` is not zero, the number of pages has been changed and we change the range of the vertical scroll bar. Note that the limits of the horizontal scroll bar never change as the width of the document is constant (stored in PAGE_WIDTH).

```
void CWordView::OnUpdate(CView* /* pSender */, LPARAM lHint,
                         CObject* pHint)
{
  if (lHint != 0)
  {
    int iPages = (int) lHint;
    SetScrollRange(SB_VERT, 0, iPages * PAGE_HEIGHT);

    CClientDC dc(this);
    OnPrepareDC(&dc);

    CRect rcDocument(0, 0, PAGE_WIDTH, iPages * PAGE_HEIGHT);
    dc.LPtoDP(rcDocument);

    InvalidateRect(rcDocument);
    UpdateWindow();
  }
```

If `pHint` is not null, the document needs to be repainted. `pHint` is a pointer to the set of rectangles to be re-painted. We translate them into device units and repaint them. Finally, we update the window.

```
  else if (pHint != NULL)
  {
    RectSet* pRepaintSet = (RectSet*) pHint;
    if (!pRepaintSet->IsEmpty())
```

```
    {
      CClientDC dc(this);
      OnPrepareDC(&dc);
      for (POSITION position = pRepaintSet->
          GetHeadPosition(); position != NULL;
          pRepaintSet->GetNext(position))
      {
        CRect rcRepaint = pRepaintSet->GetAt(position);
        dc.LPtoDP(&rcRepaint);
        InvalidateRect(rcRepaint);
      }

      UpdateWindow();
    }
  }
```

If `lHint` is zero and `pHint` is null, the window has just been created. `OnUpdate` is indirectly called by `OnInitialUpdate`. In that case, we just repaint the whole client area.

```
    else
    {
      Invalidate();
      UpdateWindow();
    }
  }
```

The method `OnPaint` is called by the system every time the client area of the window needs to be (partly or completely) repainted or when the client area is re-painted and `UpdateWindow` is called. In the applications in the earlier chapters of this book, `OnDraw` was called instead. In those cases, `OnPaint` in `CView` was called, which in turns call `OnDraw`. In this application, there is a difference between whether the text shall be written in a window on the screen or sent to a printer (or print preview). In the case of printing, see `OnPrint` below.

The method `OnPaint` has two tasks before it finally calls `OnDraw`. First, we need to fill the area to the right of the document, if any (`rcClient.right > PAGE_WIDTH`). We do that by loading a brush with a light gray color and drawing a rectangle at the right of the document. Note that we do not need to fill any space below the document as the vertical scroll bar is set to match the height of the document.

Second, we insert pages breaks in case the document consists of more than one page (`iPageNum > 1`). As a document always has one page with at least one paragraph, it is never completely empty. We pick a black pen and set the text output to be centered on the x position. The x position is in the middle of the document or in the middle of the client area, whichever is smaller. The y position is the page height for each page.

```
void CWordView::OnPaint()
{
  CPaintDC dc(this);
  OnPrepareDC(&dc);
  CRect rcClient;
  GetClientRect(&rcClient);
  dc.DPtoLP(&rcClient);
  if (rcClient.right > PAGE_WIDTH)
  {
    CBrush brush(LIGHT_GRAY);
    CBrush *pOldBrush = dc.SelectObject(&brush);
    dc.Rectangle(PAGE_WIDTH, 0, rcClient.right,
                 rcClient.bottom);
    dc.SelectObject(pOldBrush);
  }
  int iPageNum = m_pWordDoc->GetPageNum();
  if (rcClient.bottom > (iPageNum * PAGE_HEIGHT))
  {
    CBrush brush(LIGHT_GRAY);
    CBrush *pOldBrush = dc.SelectObject(&brush);
    dc.Rectangle(iPageNum * PAGE_HEIGHT, 0, rcClient.right,
                 rcClient.bottom);
    dc.SelectObject(pOldBrush);
  }
  if (iPageNum > 1)
  {
    dc.SetTextColor(BLACK);
    dc.SetTextAlign(TA_CENTER | TA_BASELINE);
    int xPos = min(PAGE_WIDTH / 2,
                   (rcClient.left + rcClient.right) / 2);
    for (int iPage = 1; iPage < iPageNum; ++iPage)
    {
      int yPos = iPage * PAGE_HEIGHT;
      dc.TextOut(xPos, yPos, TEXT("-- Page Break --"));
    }
    dc.SetTextAlign(TA_LEFT | TA_TOP);
  }
```

In order to not write character outside the page, we clip the writing area to match the document before we call OnDraw to do the actual writing.

```
dc.IntersectClipRect(0, 0, PAGE_WIDTH,
                     max(1, iPageNum) * PAGE_HEIGHT);  OnDraw(&dc);
}
```

The method OnPreparePrinting is used to set the range of pages to print. The paragraphs of the document are partitioned into a number of pages. GetPageNum in the document class returns the number of pages.

```
BOOL CWordView::OnPreparePrinting(CPrintInfo* pInfo)
{
  pInfo->SetMinPage(1);
  pInfo->SetMaxPage(m_pWordDoc->GetPageNum());
  return DoPreparePrinting(pInfo);
}
```

The method OnPrint is called by the Application Framework when the user chooses the file print menu item. First, OnPreparePrinting is called to decide the number of pages to be printed and then OnPrint is called once for each page to be printed. The task for OnPrint is to write the file name of the document at the top of the page and the page number on the bottom of the page as well as drawing a rectangle around the text. Finally, OnDraw is called to write the actual text. Note that both OnPaint and OnPrint call OnDraw to draw the actual text of the document.

First, we draw the surrounding rectangle. Second, we write the header with the path name of the document and the footer with the page number and the total number of pages. Moreover, we need to set the offset so that this page is printed as the first page, no matter which page it actually is. Finally, we need to exclude the merging from the draw area in order for the page not to write outside its area.

```
void CWordView::OnPrint(CDC* pDC, CPrintInfo* pInfo)
{
```

The initial problem with OnPrint is that pDC has already been set with OnPrepareDC. We have to start by undoing that operation.

```
int xScrollPos = GetScrollPos(SB_HORZ);
int yScrollPos = GetScrollPos(SB_VERT);
pDC->OffsetWindowOrg(-xScrollPos, -yScrollPos);
```

Next, we draw a rectangle around the text of each document. We define the border of that rectangle and select a black pen and draw the surrounding rectangle.

```
int xLeft = PAGE_MARGIN / 2;
int xRight = PAGE_TOTALWIDTH - PAGE_MARGIN / 2;
int yTop = PAGE_MARGIN / 2;
int yBottom = PAGE_TOTALHEIGHT - PAGE_MARGIN / 2;
CPen pen(PS_SOLID, 0, BLACK);
CPen* pOldPen = pDC->SelectObject(&pen);
pDC->Rectangle(xLeft, yTop, xRight, yBottom);
pDC->SelectObject(pOldPen);
```

In order to write the header and footer of the document, we need to select a font. If we create a font object with the default constructor, the system font will be the result. It is often the Arial font of size 10 points.

```
CFont cFont;
Font defaultFont;
cFont.CreateFontIndirect(defaultFont.PointsToMeters());
CFont* pPrevFont = pDC->SelectObject(&cFont);
```

We write the path name of the document at the top of the page. The method GetPathName returns the saved pathname. It returns an empty string if the document has not yet been saved.

```
CString stPath = m_pWordDoc->GetPathName();
CRect rcHeader(xLeft, 0, xRight, 2 * yTop);
pDC->DrawText(stPath, rcHeader, DT_SINGLELINE | DT_CENTER |
              DT_VCENTER);
```

Then we write the page numbers together with the total number of pages at the bottom of the page.

```
CString stPage;
int iPageNum = pInfo->m_nCurPage - 1;
stPage.Format("Page %d of %d", iPageNum + 1,
              m_pWordDoc->GetPageNum());
CRect rcFooter(xLeft, PAGE_TOTALHEIGHT -
               2 * (PAGE_TOTALHEIGHT - yBottom),
               xRight, PAGE_TOTALHEIGHT);
pDC->DrawText(stPage, rcFooter, DT_SINGLELINE | DT_CENTER |
              DT_VCENTER);
pDC->SelectObject(pPrevFont);
```

Before we call `OnDraw` to write the paragraphs, we have to re-do the setting of the window origin at the beginning of this method.

```
int yPagePos = (iPageNum * PAGE_HEIGHT);
pDC->OffsetWindowOrg(-PAGE_MARGIN, yPagePos - PAGE_MARGIN);
```

As `OnDraw` tries to write all paragraphs (not only those on the current page) we have to exclude the area of the document not on the current page.

```
CRect rcPage(0, iPageNum * PAGE_HEIGHT, PAGE_WIDTH,
             (iPageNum + 1) * PAGE_HEIGHT);
pDC->IntersectClipRect(&rcPage);
```

Finally, we call `OnDraw` to do the actual writing of the paragraphs.

```
OnDraw(pDC);
}
```

The method `OnDraw` is called by both `OnPaint` and `OnPrint` to do the actual writing by calling the `Draw` of each paragraph. One thing that complicates matters is that some portion of the text to be written could be marked. If the application is in the edit state, we just call `Draw` for each paragraph. If it is in the mark state, we have four possible cases for the current paragraph. The paragraph may be the only marked one, it may the first of at least two marked paragraphs, it may be the last of at least two marked paragraphs, or it may be not marked at all.

```
void CWordView::OnDraw(CDC* pDC)
{
  int eWordStatus = m_pWordDoc->GetWordStatus();
  ParagraphPtrArray* pParagraphArray =
                    m_pWordDoc->GetParagraphArray();
  Position psFirstMarked = m_pWordDoc->GetFirstMarked();
  Position psLastMarked = m_pWordDoc->GetLastMarked();
  Position psMinMarked = min(psFirstMarked, psLastMarked);
  Position psMaxMarked = max(psFirstMarked, psLastMarked);
  int iParagraphs = (int) pParagraphArray->GetSize();
  for (int iParagraph = 0; iParagraph < iParagraphs;
       ++iParagraph)
  {
    Paragraph* pParagraph =
               pParagraphArray->GetAt(iParagraph);
    switch (eWordStatus)
    {
```

If the application is in the edit state, we just write the paragraph.

```
case WS_EDIT:
    pParagraph->Draw(pDC, 0, -1);
    break;
```

If the application is in the mark state, we have to check if the paragraph is marked, partly or completely.

```
case WS_MARK:
    int iLength = pParagraph->GetLength();
```

If this paragraph is the only one marked in the document, we write it and dispatch the beginning and end of the marked area.

```
if ((iParagraph == psMinMarked.Paragraph()) &&
    (iParagraph == psMaxMarked.Paragraph()))
{
    pParagraph->Draw(pDC, psMinMarked.Character(),
                    psMaxMarked.Character());
}
```

If the paragraph is at the beginning of the marked area, we write it and dispatch the beginning and end of the marked area. The end of the marked area for this paragraph is the end of the paragraph.

```
else if (iParagraph == psMinMarked.Paragraph())
{
    pParagraph->Draw(pDC, psMinMarked.Character(),
                    iLength);
}
```

If the paragraph is completely inside the marked area, we write it and dispatch the beginning and end of the paragraph as the limits of the marked area.

```
else if ((iParagraph > psMinMarked.Paragraph()) &&
        (iParagraph < psMaxMarked.Paragraph()))
{
    pParagraph->Draw(pDC, 0, iLength);
}
```

If the paragraph is the end of the marked area, we write it and dispatch the beginning and end of the marked area. The beginning of the marked area for this paragraph is the beginning of the paragraph.

```
else if (iParagraph == psMaxMarked.Paragraph())
{
    pParagraph->Draw(pDC, 0, psMaxMarked.Character());
}
```

If the paragraph is not marked at all, we just write it.

```
else
{
   pParagraph->Draw(pDC, 0, -1);
}
break;
         }
      }
   }
```

Summary

- Line and Page are two small classes of this application. Line holds the indexes of the first and last characters of a line in a paragraph together with the height of the line. Page holds the indexes of the first and last paragraph of a page in the document.

- Position is also a small class; it handles a position in a document. It has two fields for keeping track of the paragraph and character positions.

- CWordDoc handles the paragraphs of a class. It accepts input from the view class and updates the list of paragraphs in response.

- Paragraph handles one paragraph. It has methods for splitting and merging paragraphs.

- CWordView accepts input from the mouse and keyboard. It also displays text in the window client area.

References

If you want to learn more about C++ programming, I recommend *Deitel and Deitel* (2007). They discuss in depth the theory as well as practice of object-oriented programming in C++, with many clear and comprehensive examples. In Chapter 5, we constructed a list and a set. If you want to learn more about data structures, you may read *Weiss* (2007). He describes data structures such as stacks, queues, trees, and graphs.

As MFC is built upon the Win32 API, you may want to learn more about it. The classic book in the field is *Petzold* (1999). He describes in detail how to develop Windows application with the Win32 API. The parallel book on MFC is *Prosise* (1999). He has a similar disposition as *Petzold*'s book and describes in matching detail the features of MFC. *Feuer* (1997) is a shorter version of *Prosise*'s book and concentrates on the advanced parts of MFC. *Shepherd* and *Wingo* (1996) describe the inside of MFC, how the classes and macros are defined and how they interact with the underlying Win32 API.

If the scanner and parser of Chapter 8 have made you want to know more about compilers, *Aho el at* (2007) is the book for you. It is the second edition of the classic *Dragon Book*. They explain the theory and practice of compilers from scanning and parsing to advanced optimization. If the concept of graphs has gained an interest in you, I recommend *West* (2000). He reasons about graphs from a mathematical point of view.

Aho, A. V. el at. *Compilers: Principles, Techniques, and Tools*. Second Edition. Boston: Addison Wesley Publishing Company, 2007, 1009 pages.

Deitel, H. M. and Deitel, P. J. *C++ how to Program*. Sixth Edition. Indianapolis: Prentice Hall, 2007, 1429 pages.

Feuer, A. R. *MFC Programming*. Reading: Addison Wesley Developers Press, 1997, 452 pages.

Petzold, C. *Windows Programming: The Definitive Guide to the Win32 API*. Fifth Edition. Redmond: Microsoft Press, 1999, 1497 pages.

Prosise, J. *Programming Windows with MFC: The Premier Resource for Object-Oriented Programming on 32-bit Windows Platforms*. Second Edition. Redmond: Microsoft Press, 1999, 1337 pages.

Shepherd, G. and Wingo, S. *MFC Internals: The Inside the Microsoft Foundation Class Architecture*. Reading: Addison-Wesley Professional, 1996, 736 pages.

Weiss, M. A. *Data Structures and Algorithm Analysis in C++*. Third Edition. Reading: Addison Wesley, 2007, 586 pages.

West, D. B. *Introduction to Graph Theory*. Indianapolis: Prentice Hall, 2000, 470 pages.

Index

Figure.h 162, 163
FigureFileManager class, draw application
FigureFileManager.cpp 215
FigureFileManager.h 214
figure information, tetris application
about 167
blue figure 171
brown figure 168
FigureInfo.cpp 168
green figure 169
purple figure 171, 172
red figure 168
turquoise figure 169
yellow figure 170, 171
file processing 83, 84
font class, MFC class
about 130-133
LOGFONT 131
for statement 30
formula interpretation, calc application
about 243, 244
bottom-up parser 254
parser 251-257
parser, types 254
parser.cpp 259-261
parser.h 258
reference.cpp 247
reference.h 247
reference class 246
scanner.cpp 248-250
scanner.h 248
SyntaxTree.cpp 263-268
SyntaxTree.h 262
SyntaxTree class 262
Token.h 246
tokens class 244
top-down parser 254
function
about 32, 33
call-by-reference 36-39
call-by-value 36-39
declaration 42, 43
default parameters 39, 40
definition 42
global variable 34-36
higher order function 43, 44

local varable 34-36
main() function 44
overloading 40
recursion 41, 42
static variables 40, 41
void function 34

G

goto statement 32

H

higher order function 43, 44

I

if-statement 27
if-else statement 27
inheritance 51
about 58
example 58
inspector 52
integral types
signed type 10
unsigned type 10

J

jump statement 32

K

keyboard
catching 116
RingView.cpp 116, 117

L

linker 8
LineFigure class, draw application
LineFigure.cpp 189-192
LineFigure.h 188
LineFigure class, MFC application
line.cpp 333
line.h 333
list class, MFC class 136

M

macros 46
menus
  adding 117
  RingDoc.cpp 118
  RingDoc.h 117
message map 90
message system 90-93
methods 50
metric system 93
MFC 88, 89
MFC application wizard
  about 104-109
  calc application 240, 241
  color dialog 123
  colors 109
  coordinate system, setting 113
  dialog 105
  keyboard, catching 116
  menus, adding 117
  mouse, catching 110
  mouse button, clicking 110
  registry 123
  rings, drawing 112, 113
  scroll bar, setting 114
  serialization 124, 125
  toolbar, adding 104
  word application 329, 331
MFC class 127
Microsoft Foundation Classes. *See* **MFC**
modifier 52
model
  document/view model 89
mouse
  catching 110
  RingDoc.h 112
  RingView.cpp 111
multiple inheritance 51

N

namespaces 80, 81, 82

O

object-oriented model
  about 50, 51

operator overloading
  about 70, 71
  example 71-76
operators
  about 21
  arithmetic operator 21
  assignment operator 25
  associativity operator 26
  bitwise operator 24
  condition operator 25
  decrement operator 23
  increment operator 23
  logical operator 23, 24
  pointer arithmetic 22
  precedence operator 26
  relational operator 23

P

page class, MFC application
  page.cpp 361
  page.h 361
paragraph class, MFC application
  about 335
  paragraph.cpp 338-360
  paragraph.h 336, 337
parameter
  default parameter 39
pointers 13, 14
pointers and linked lists
  about 65
  stack and linked lists 66-70
point class, MFC class
  CPoint class 128
position class, MFC application
  position.cpp 334, 335
  position.h 333, 334
preprocessor tool 45-47
private 50
protected 50
public 50
pure virtual method 51

R

RectangleFigure class, draw application
  RectangleFigure.cpp 198-200
  RectangleFigure.h 197

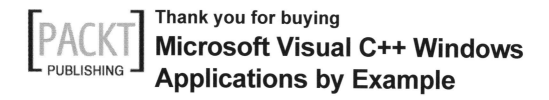

Thank you for buying
Microsoft Visual C++ Windows Applications by Example

About Packt Publishing

Packt, pronounced 'packed', published its first book "*Mastering phpMyAdmin for Effective MySQL Management*" in April 2004 and subsequently continued to specialize in publishing highly focused books on specific technologies and solutions.

Our books and publications share the experiences of your fellow IT professionals in adapting and customizing today's systems, applications, and frameworks. Our solution based books give you the knowledge and power to customize the software and technologies you're using to get the job done. Packt books are more specific and less general than the IT books you have seen in the past. Our unique business model allows us to bring you more focused information, giving you more of what you need to know, and less of what you don't.

Packt is a modern, yet unique publishing company, which focuses on producing quality, cutting-edge books for communities of developers, administrators, and newbies alike. For more information, please visit our website: www.packtpub.com.

Writing for Packt

We welcome all inquiries from people who are interested in authoring. Book proposals should be sent to authors@packtpub.com. If your book idea is still at an early stage and you would like to discuss it first before writing a formal book proposal, contact us; one of our commissioning editors will get in touch with you.

We're not just looking for published authors; if you have strong technical skills but no writing experience, our experienced editors can help you develop a writing career, or simply get some additional reward for your expertise.

GDI+ Application Custom Controls with Visual C# 2005

ISBN: 1-904811-60-4   Paperback: 272 pages

A fast-paced example-driven tutorial to building custom controls using Visual C# 2005 Express Edition and .NET 2.0

1. Learn about custom controls and the GDI+

2. Walks through great examples like PieChart control

3. Customize and develop your own controls

Programming Windows Workflow Foundation: Practical WF Techniques and Examples using XAML and C

ISBN: 1-904811-21-3   Paperback: 300 pages

A C# developer's guide to the features and programming interfaces of Windows Workflow Foundation

1. Add event-driven workflow capabilities to your .NET applications.

2. Highlights the libraries, services and internals programmers need to know

3. Builds a practical "bug reporting" workflow solution example app

Please check **www.PacktPub.com** for information on our titles

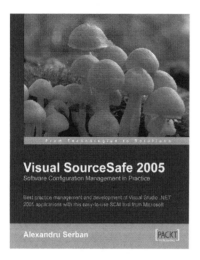

16985094R00234

Made in the USA
Lexington, KY
20 August 2012